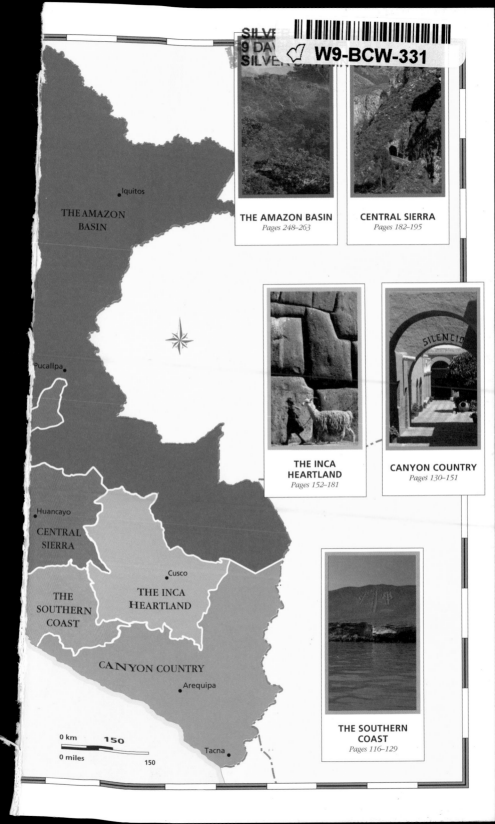

W9-BCW-331

Iquitos

THE AMAZON
BASIN

Pucallpa

THE AMAZON BASIN
Pages 248–263

CENTRAL SIERRA
Pages 182–195

**THE INCA
HEARTLAND**
Pages 152–181

CANYON COUNTRY
Pages 130–151

Huancayo

CENTRAL
SIERRA

THE INCA
HEARTLAND

Cusco

THE
SOUTHERN
COAST

CANYON COUNTRY

Arequipa

**THE SOUTHERN
COAST**
Pages 116–129

0 km   150

0 miles   150

Tacna

EYEWITNESS TRAVEL

PERU

EYEWITNESS TRAVEL

PERU

MAIN CONTRIBUTOR: MARYANNE BLACKER

DK

LONDON, NEW YORK,
MELBOURNE, MUNICH AND DELHI
www.dk.com

MANAGING EDITOR Aruna Ghose
DESIGN MANAGER Priyanka Thakur
PROJECT EDITOR Shikha Kulkarni
PROJECT DESIGNER Shruti Singhi
EDITOR Jyoti Kumari
DESIGNERS Pooja Badola, Anchal Kaushal
SENIOR CARTOGRAPHIC MANAGER Uma Bhattacharya
CARTOGRAPHER Mohammad Hassan
SENIOR DTP DESIGNER Vinod Harish
SENIOR PICTURE RESEARCHER Taiyaba Khatoon
PICTURE RESEARCHER Sumita Khatwani
ASSISTANT PICTURE RESEARCHER Shweta Andrews

CONTRIBUTORS
Maryanne Blacker, Jorge Riveros Cayo,
Dominic Hamilton, Rob Rachowiecki,
Joby Williams

PHOTOGRAPHERS
Demetrio Carrasco, Nigel Hicks, Linda Whitwam

ILLUSTRATORS
Chapel Design & Marketing Ltd., Chinglemba Chingbham,
Surat Kumar Mantoo, Arun Pottirayil,
T. Gautam Trivedi, Mark Arjun Warner

Printed and bound in China by L.Rex Printing Co. Ltd

First American Edition, 2008
12 13 14 15 10 9 8 7 6 5 4 3 2 1

Published in the United States by:
Dorling Kindersley Limited, 80 Strand, London WC2R 0RL, UK

Copyright © 2008, 2012 Dorling Kindersley Limited, London
A Penguin Company

Reprinted with revisions 2010, 2012

A CATALOG RECORD FOR THIS BOOK IS
AVAILABLE FROM THE LIBRARY OF CONGRESS.

ISSN 1542-1554
ISBN: 978-0-75668-561-4

Front cover main image: Machu Picchu

**The information in this
DK Eyewitness Travel Guide is checked regularly.**
Every effort has been made to ensure that this book is as up-to-date
as possible at the time of going to press. Some details, however,
such as telephone numbers, opening hours, prices, gallery hanging
arrangements and travel information are liable to change. The
publishers cannot accept responsibility for any consequences arising
from the use of this book, nor for any material on third party websites,
and cannot guarantee that any website address in this book will be
a suitable source of travel information. We value the views and
suggestions of our readers very highly. Please write to: Publisher,
DK Eyewitness Travel Guides, Dorling Kindersley, 80 Strand,
London, WC2R 0RL, UK or email: travelguides@dk.com.

◁ The Inca Inti Raymi festival celebrated at Sacsayhuamán

Inhabitants of Islas Uros, Lake Titicaca

CONTENTS

INTRODUCING
PERU

DISCOVERING
PERU **8**

PUTTING PERU ON
THE MAP **10**

A PORTRAIT OF
PERU **12**

PERU THROUGH
THE YEAR **34**

THE HISTORY
OF PERU **40**

LIMA AREA BY
AREA

LIMA AT A GLANCE **56**

CENTRAL LIMA **58**

MIRAFLORES &
SAN ISIDRO **74**

**Nazca ceramic bottle with
stylized patterns**

PERU REGION BY REGION

PERU AT A GLANCE 114

THE SOUTHERN COAST 116

CANYON COUNTRY 130

THE INCA HEARTLAND 152

CENTRAL SIERRA 182

CORDILLERA BLANCA 196

THE NORTHERN DESERT 214

THE NORTHERN HIGHLANDS 234

THE AMAZON BASIN 248

TRAVELERS' NEEDS

WHERE TO STAY 266

WHERE TO EAT 282

SHOPPING IN PERU 302

Brightly painted plates at a local market, Chinchero

OUTDOOR ACTIVITIES 306

SPECIALIZED HOLIDAYS 312

SURVIVAL GUIDE

PRACTICAL INFORMATION 316

TRAVEL INFORMATION 326

GENERAL INDEX 334

ACKNOWLEDGMENTS 346

PHRASE BOOK 350

BARRANCO 84

FARTHER AFIELD 92

SHOPPING IN LIMA 100

ENTERTAINMENT IN LIMA 102

LIMA STREET FINDER 104

Strikingly carved blue balconies, Cusco

Golden pectoral of the Lord of Sipán

San Francisco Church and Convent, Lima

INTRODUCING PERU

DISCOVERING PERU 8–9

PUTTING PERU ON THE MAP 10–11

A PORTRAIT OF PERU 12–33

PERU THROUGH THE YEAR 34–37

THE HISTORY OF PERU 40–53

DISCOVERING PERU

Peru neatly divides into nine regions, each with its own distinct character and landscape. The capital, Lima, lies on the parched coast, hemmed in by the Andes. The other regions include high peaks and glaciers in the Andes, desert landscape in the south, marvelous beaches in the north, and

Colorful ceramic artifact

unparalleled biodiversity in the Amazon Basin. The country's architecture stands testament to the great Inca builders and their Spanish conquerors, while numerous monumental ruins reveal how Peru was one of the cradles of civilization in the ancient world. Below is an overview of the highlights of each region.

Shop stocked with an array of Peruvian handicrafts, Lima

LIMA

- Top-notch museums
- San Francisco
- Gastronomic capital
- Handicraft markets

The bustling coastal capital is Peru's main entry point. The impressive **Plaza de Armas** (see pp60–61) is home to church and state. Explore the **Cathedral** (see p62), **San Pedro** (see p67), and the religious complex of **San Francisco** (see pp64–6). The country's leading museums are here, displaying collections of pre-Columbian artifacts, Colonial and contemporary paintings, as well as folkloric works.

Miraflores (see pp76–7) and **San Isidro** and the coastal enclaves of **Barranco** (see pp86–7) are full of bars, restaurants, and art galleries. Miraflores is also home to the ancient adobe pyramid, **Huaca Pucllana** (see pp80–81).

THE SOUTHERN COAST

- Nazca Lines
- Abundant marine life
- Afro-Peruvian culture
- Sand-boarding adventures

Birds and marine life found on the beaches and rocky outcrops of the **Islas Ballestas** (see p121) are a magnet for nature-lovers, while the **Nazca Lines** (see pp126–7) and the **Cahuachi** pyramids (see p128) draw those in search of history. Dunes at **Huacachina** (see p121) are very popular with sand-boarders. **Chincha Alta** (see p120) and **El Carmen** (see p121) are centers of Afro-Peruvian music and culture.

CANYON COUNTRY

- Santa Catalina Monastery
- White-water rafting
- Lake Titicaca
- Andean condors in flight

The presence of deep gorges and volcanoes makes the region a haven for adventure

lovers. The Ríos **Cotahuasi** and **Colca** (see pp142–4) are among the world's best canoeing circuits. The white city of **Arequipa** (see pp134–7) is home to **Santa Catalina** (see pp138–9), the city's grand Colonial mansions, and **Juanita**, the ice mummy (see p137). The islands in the serene **Lake Titicaca** (see pp146–51) are a must-see, along with the **Sillustani Burial Towers** (see p151).

THE INCA HEARTLAND

- Machu Picchu
- Hiking on the Inca Trail
- Cusco School artworks
- Handicrafts at Chinchero

No trip to Peru is complete without visiting the mesmerizing ruins of **Machu Picchu** (see pp176–81). **Cusco** (see pp156–163) is home to Baroque buildings, Cusco School artworks, and Inca walls. More remarkable architecture of the Incas can be found at **Pisac** (see p169), **Sacsayhuamán** (see p164), **Ollantaytambo** (see p168),

A view of Lake Titicaca, Canyon Country

◁ Detail of a vividly-colored embroidered textile from Ollantaytambo

Stone terraces of Machu Picchu, the Inca Heartland

The Moche pyramid, **Huaca del Sol** (see p223), is the highest pre-Columbian adobe structure in the Americas. **Museo Tumbas Reales de Sipán** (see pp228–31) displays the treasures of the Lord of Sipán. Peru's northernmost tip is a beacon for surfers, with some of the most outstanding beaches. There is also a wildlife corridor hailed as one of the most diverse in the Equatorial Dry Forest (see p18).

THE NORTHERN HIGHLANDS

- **The stone citadel of Kuélap**
- **Cumbemayo stone canals**
- **Mysterious cloud forests**
- **Cajamarca carnival**

The Spanish influence is evident in the Colonial cathedral, churches, and mansions but pre-Hispanic remnants survive in the lush countryside beyond the city – in **Ventanillas de Otuzco**, in **Cumbemayo**, at **Los Baños del Inca** (see p242), and in the **Kuélap** fortress (see pp244–6), hailed as the Machu Picchu of the north. In February–March **Cajamarca** (see pp238–9) is crowded with locals taking part in parades.

THE AMAZON BASIN

- **Watching wildlife**
- **Voyaging on a riverboat**
- **Climbing onto the canopy**
- **Iquitos**

The Amazon offers superb opportunities for jungle-trekking, fishing, and rafting on the **Río Tambopata** (see pp262–3). **Reserva Nacional Allpahuayo-Mishana** (see p254) and **Reserva Nacional Pacaya-Samiria** (see p255) are home to sea cows, anacondas, and elusive pink dolphins. **Iquitos** (see p252) harkens back to the 19th-century rubber fever. **Parque Nacional Manu** (see p261) is Peru's largest protected area.

Figure at Museo de Sipán

and the ruins of **Sayacmarka** and **Wiñay Wayna** (see p173), which are accessible only via the pathway known as the **Inca Trail** (see pp170–173). The **Sacred Valley** (see pp164–9) boasts lush green crop terraces, snowcapped mountains, and Class III rapids on the Urubamba.

CENTRAL SIERRA

- **Train ride from Lima to Huancayo**
- **Mantaro Valley villages**
- **Barrio Santa Ana**
- **Ayacucho's Semana Santa processions**

One of the world's greatest train journeys runs from **Lima to Huancayo** (see p187). Splendid **Ayacucho** (see pp192–3) is known for its Colonial churches and lively workshops, especially along the ancient cobblestone streets of **Barrio Santa Ana**. During **Semana Santa** (see p194), huge numbers of people visit the streets carpeted with flowers. Processions, music, folk dancing, and intense partying are integral to the Easter celebrations in the area. The **Mantaro Valley** (see p188) is a must for lovers of handicrafts and history. Entire villages specialize in one type of craft, from weaving to silverwork.

CORDILLERA BLANCA

- **Lagunas Llanganuco**
- **The Santa Cruz Trek**
- **Scaling Peru's highest peaks**
- **Ruins at Chavín de Huántar**

With the second highest mountain range in the world, this region has great appeal for climbers, hikers, and adventure lovers. It has a collection of glaciers, ice caves, jagged summits, and the glowing cerulean **Lagunas Llanganuco** (see p204), the starting point for the famed **Santa Cruz Trek** (see p204). There are isolated villages, rare Andean flora and fauna, and pre-Inca ruins, including **Chavín de Huántar** (see pp208–9).

THE NORTHERN DESERT

- **Trujillo's historic downtown**
- **Huaca del Sol**
- **Museo Tumbas Reales de Sipán**
- **Incredible surfing**

The area is packed with archaeological sites, beaches, and wildlife. Beautifully preserved **Trujillo** (see pp218–21) boasts Colonial homes, churches, and museums.

Putting Peru on the Map

With the Pacific Ocean lapping its 1,500-mile (2,400-km) coast, Peru shares borders with Ecuador and Colombia to the north, Brazil and Bolivia to the east, and Chile to the south. The third largest country in Latin America, its 500,000 sq miles (1,300,000 sq km) encompasses soaring mountains, vast canyons, coastal desert, and lush jungle, with dozens of microclimates in between. Peru has a population of 29 million, more than half of whom live in coastal areas. Lima, the capital, is home to 8 million people, while a million live in Arequipa, the second largest city. Other major cities include Trujillo, Piura, Iquitos, Cusco, Cajamarca, Puno, and Ayacucho.

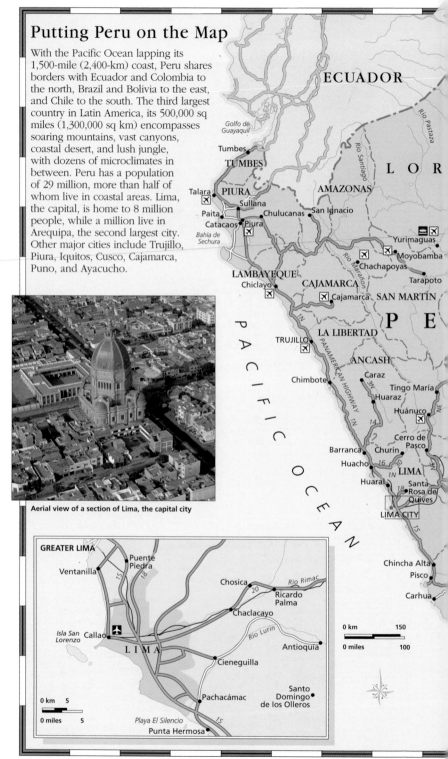

Aerial view of a section of Lima, the capital city

ECUADOR

Golfo de Guayaquil

Tumbes
TUMBES
Talara   PIURA
Paita   Sullana
Catacaos Piura
Bahía de
Sechura

AMAZONAS
San Ignacio
Chulucanas

Río Pastaza
Río Santiago

L O R

Río Marañón

Yurimaguas
Moyobamba
Chachapoyas
Tarapoto
SAN MARTÍN

LAMBAYEQUE
Chiclayo   CAJAMARCA
Cajamarca

P   E

LA LIBERTAD
TRUJILLO

ANCASH
Chimbote   Caraz
Tingo María
Huaraz
14
Huánuco

PANAMERICAN HIGHWAY   1N

Cerro de
Pasco
Barranca Churín
Huacho   16
1N   LIMA
Huaral   18
Santa
Rosa de
Quives

LIMA CITY

GREATER LIMA

Ventanilla   Puente
Piedra
15   18

Chosica   20
Ricardo
Palma
Chaclacayo
Río Rimac

Isla San
Lorenzo   Callao
L I M A
Río Lurín
Cieneguilla
Antioquia

Pachacámac   Santo
Domingo
de los Olleros

Playa El Silencio   1S
Punta Hermosa

Chincha Alta
Pisco
Carhua

0 km   5
0 miles   5

0 km   150
0 miles   100

A PORTRAIT OF PERU

Peru conjures up images of the Inca citadel of Machu Picchu, but there's much more to see. Besides archaeological sites, there are several natural treasures, including the world's deepest canyons and the highest navigable lake. Peru is also a racial melting pot, a mix of indigenous peoples, mestizos, and African, Chinese, and Japanese migrants, whose profound cultural influence is everywhere.

Even before the Spanish arrived in the 1500s, Peru was a collage of cultures determined by its geography. Anthropologists and analysts have likened it to an archipelago, with population pockets scattered across the diverse and isolated regions. The soaring Andes exert the greatest influence on climate, topography, flora and fauna, and best illustrate the division in society: the mountains remain a refuge for impoverished indigenous peoples, who practise subsistence farming.

Dozens of rivers flow from the Andes down to the narrow ribbon of desert coastline but only about a third of them contain water year-round,

Andean Cock of the Rock, Peru's national bird

thus emphasizing the importance of seasonal rains. The coast is wealthier, has better infrastructure, and is more industrialized and urbanized. This glimmer of opportunity has led to an influx of rural poor from the highlands, generating *pueblos jovenes,* or young towns, around Lima which usually lack water, electricity, and other basic services.

The Amazon accounts for more than half of Peru's territory, and one-quarter of the world's jungle. Towns are few and rivers are the thoroughfares. An estimated 5 percent of the population lives in the jungle, with 55 ethno-linguistic groups.

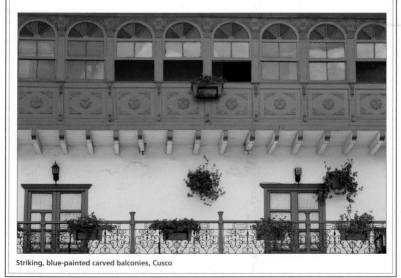

Striking, blue-painted carved balconies, Cusco

◁ Traditionally dressed villagers prepare for a fiesta in the Inca Heartland

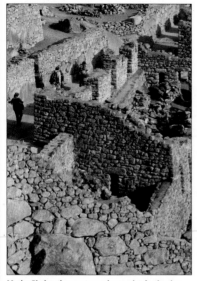

Machu Picchu, the most popular tourist destination of Peru

after China, and the leading fishmeal producer. Thirty-three percent of the population is employed in agriculture. Tourism is booming with some 1.5 million tourists visiting Peru each year. Machu Picchu remains the main attraction, PromPeru, the tourism and marketing board, is promoting other destinations too. Today, nature tourism draws ever increasing numbers. Peru is home to 84 of the earth's 114 life zones, while almost 10 percent of the world's mammals and 20 percent of birds are found here. The country has 25,000 species of plants, 30 percent of which are found only in Peru.

THE ECONOMY

To a large extent the economy reflects Peru's geography – mineral-rich mountains and coastal waters brimming with sea-life. Mining and fishing, as well as agriculture and tourism, dominate and account for most of the employment and investment. Mining supplies almost half of export earnings. Antamina in Ancash is one of the world's biggest copper-zinc mine and Peru is the world's fifth largest gold producer. It is the world's second largest fishing nation

POLITICS

The president, who is head of both the state and the government, is elected for a five-year term and cannot be re-elected for a second consecutive term. The government is divided into three branches: the Executive, comprising a Council of Ministers appointed by the president, the Congress, which consists of 120 representatives, and the Judiciary. Peru is divided into 24 departments (*departamentos*), sometimes referred to as regions, and one constitutional province (*provincia constitucional*), Lima-Callao. Regional authorities, including prefects and governors, and the administrative system, come directly under the

Agriculture provides major employment opportunities in Peru

President Alan Garcia with his supporters in 2006

shoeshine-boy-turned Stanford-educated economist, became the first democratically elected president of Quechua descent. Both Toledo and Fujimori owed their election to their position as outsiders, untainted by the political system.

Executive. Political parties form around individuals and rarely last longer than the person's political career. The one exception is the left-leaning Alianza Popular Revolucionaria Americana (APRA), Peru's oldest and best-established political party founded in 1924.

With President Belaunde Terry's election in 1980, Peru returned to democratic leadership after years of military rule. In 1985, the 36-year-old Alan Garcia became the region's youngest leader and was dubbed the "Latino Kennedy," because of his charisma. He inherited a country in deep economic crisis and in the grip of a guerrilla war waged by the Maoist Shining Path. By the time Garcia left office in 1990, inflation was rampant at 7,500 percent, the insurgents' campaign had intensified, and poverty had soared.

Alberto Fujimori's presidency ushered in a decade that saw a dramatic upturn in the economy and significant curbing of guerrilla activity. However, his increasingly authoritarian stance, an economic slump in the late 1990s, and allegations of corruption led to his ousting. In 2001, Alejandro Toledo, the

Traditionally dressed indigenous man

THE PEOPLE

Peru has a clear-cut class structure with indigenous peoples at the bottom, and the descendants of the Spanish at the top. The rich are very rich, and the poor very poor. A middle class is only just beginning to evolve. Political and economic power has been in the hands of a small white and Mestizo (of mixed European and indigenous descent) elite for centuries.

Almost half the population is indigenous and poor. The majority speak Quechua, although Aymara is spoken near Lake Titicaca. There are different languages in the Amazon. Sixty-four percent of rural residents live in the sierra, which has 10 of Peru's 12 poorest provinces.

In the central regions of Huancavelica, Ayacucho, and Apurímac 44 percent live in extreme poverty. The indigenous communities

Women selling vegetables at a local market

were hardest hit by the armed conflict that plagued Peru for almost two decades. From 1980 to 1990, an estimated 200,000 people were driven from their homes, and an estimated 70,000 were killed, many in the department of Ayacucho.

Visitors enjoying breakfast in one of the many hotels in Peru

By and large, the people are friendly and enormously patriotic. Participants in an annual poll conducted around Independence Day unfailingly rejected the idea of having another nationality, with 90 percent declaring themselves happy to be Peruvian. Corruption tops the list of what they are most ashamed of, with poverty coming fourth or fifth.

Peruvians will hustle for any advantage and they are persistent. At the same time, they are reserved and polite. Family is sacred, often united economically and socially. Grandparents, married daughters, sons, and their children often share the same house. A nanny or servant is the norm in middle and upper class households. Despite its complex multicultural mix or perhaps because of it, discrimination is not uncommon. Upscale bars in Lima and some country clubs have been known to refuse admission to non-whites or members of a particular race or religion. Nicknames, such as negro (black), gringo (white skinned), chino (Asian), and cholo (Indian) exist, and can be used affectionately or as put-downs. In addition, there are local identities, such as a Limeño from Lima, a Cuzqueño from Cusco, and a Huaracino from Huaraz.

Although Roman Catholicism is the official religion, the constitution permits the practice of any religion. Nine out of ten people regard themselves as Catholic. No village, no matter how remote or tiny, is without a church. Peruvian Catholicism, however, does incorporate Andean elements. When conversions first began, churches were often built on ancient foundations and many Christian holidays were made to coincide with existing festivals.

Large statues of saints are carried through Cusco's streets during the Corpus Christi procession

EDUCATION

There is widespread belief among the young that worthwhile education can only be obtained overseas. As a result, more than 400,000 Peruvians leave the country each year, most between the ages of 15 and 29. Primary education is free and compulsory, but in many rural areas textbooks and desks are scarce and parents struggle to provide their children with pen or notepad. Private schools are out of reach for most due to the high fees.

Most urban youth are likely to finish secondary education, but the vast rural majority does not. By law each provincial capital must have a public secondary school, yet the best are concentrated in the major cities, particularly Lima. Not surprisingly, a relatively high percentage of urban youth attend post-secondary school.

Shipibo artisan working on pottery design

ARTS AND SPORTS

Peruvians have a rich tradition of expression. Ancient cultures transmitted their stories orally, often through song. Since the 19th century, however, writers have felt compelled to put pen to paper and scrutinize society. These include Ricardo Palma *(see p78)* and Clorinda Matto de Turner (1852–1909), whose controversial *Aves sin nido (Birds without a Nest)* focused on the love affair between a white man and an indigenous

Native musicians playing traditional instruments

woman. Many regard Cesar Vallejo as Peru's finest poet and Mario Vargas Llosa as its best novelist, but there are others, such as Jose Maria Arguedas, Manuel Scorza, Jaime Bayly, and Diego Trelles Paz.

Formal works of art by Cusco School painters and modern artists such as Fernando de Szyszlo, Joaquin Roca Rey, and Victor Delfín constitute only a part of Peru's artistic traditions. Just as vibrant are expressions of folk art that testify to the peoples' creativity and ability to make the most of natural elements.

The easily recognizable and restful Andean flute music (the famous "El Condor Pasa") has drawn fans from across the globe. Also popular is the up-tempo Afro-Peruvian music of Susana Baca and Eva Ayllon, which has its roots in the communities of black slaves brought to coastal Peru in the 1500s.

Like their Latino neighbors, soccer is a national obsession, even though the team hasn't qualified for the World Cup since 1982. Several Peruvians play in the European League including Claudio Pizarro and Nolberto Solano. As popular is women's volleyball, and Peru is today ranked number 12 in the world, and second in South America.

Bullfighting has gripped the imagination since it was introduced in 1542. More than 500 festivals are held every October all over Peru, with Lima's Lord of Miracles being the largest and most important. No patron saint's day is complete without *la corrida de toros.*

Claudio Pizarro, a popular soccer player

Peru's Landscape & Wildlife

Peru is located in the heart of the richest and most diverse region of the world, the Tropical Andes, which contains about a sixth of all plant life in less than one percent of the world's land area. Very few countries can rival the immense diversity of flora and fauna that lies within its borders, spread out between 11 ecoregions with a unique combination of climate, geographic conditions, and wildlife. The country is home to 84 of the world's 114 Holdridge life zones. Peru has two ecoregions that are almost exclusively located in its territory and are difficult to find elsewhere – the Peruvian Cold Ocean Current and the Coastal Pacific Desert. The Equatorial Dry Forest, unique to Africa and South America, is also found here.

Huascarán, *part of the western Andes, is the highest peak in Peru and the fourth highest in South America.*

PERUVIAN COLD OCEAN CURRENT

The Humboldt Current extends 621 miles (1,000 km) off the coast of Peru, bringing cold, nutrient-rich water up to the surface of the sea, creating one of the most productive marine systems in the world.

Guano birds, *producers of guano fertilizer, are the Peruvian pelican (right), Peruvian booby, and guanay cormorant.*

Seals, *such as the Juan Fernandez fur seal and South American fur seal, and sea lions are common.*

The Humboldt penguin *is an endangered species that breeds in coastal Peru. It nests on the islands and rocky coasts by burrowing holes in guano.*

PUNA OR HIGH ANDEAN PLAIN

Located at over 12,500 ft (3,800 m), the plains are classified into three types – wet puna, located mainly in nothern Peru and along the eastern Andes, moist puna, found in most of Peru, and dry puna in south Peru.

Vicuña *have been protected since Inca times. They produce small amounts of very fine wool which is highly sought-after.*

Queñual *are the highest growing trees in the world. Their copper-colored bark continually peels off.*

Andean condors *are the largest flying land birds in the Western Hemisphere with a wingspan of more than 10 ft (3 m).*

COASTAL PACIFIC DESERT

One of the driest spots on the planet, this strip of desert is brought to life by moisture carried in fog and low-lying clouds each winter. It has a highly seasonal ecosystem that adapts to severe dry conditions during summer and humidity in winter.

Peruvian thick-knee, *commonly known as* huerequeque, *is a large, unmistakable nocturnal bird.*

Sechura fox, *also called Peruvian desert fox, is the smallest of the South American* zorros.

Reserva de Lomas de Lachay Nacional *was established in 1977 and is the only protected area in the coastal hills of Peru. It is home to 74 plant and 55 bird species, some on the verge of extinction.*

MONTANE CLOUD FOREST

This tropical ecoregion lies on the eastern side of the Andes between 11,500 ft (3,500 m) and 1,900 ft (600 m). Cloud and mist frequently come in contact with vegetation, allowing mosses, ferns, and orchids to flourish.

AMAZON RAINFOREST

Peru's Amazon jungle encompasses almost 60 percent of its territory. With an average temperature of 65–97° F (18–36° C), and wet climatic and geographical conditions, the forest has incomparable biodiversity.

Cock of the Rock, *locally known as* tunky, *are found close to rocky areas, where they build their nests. The males have orange or reddish colors.*

Paiche *is the world's largest freshwater fish reaching lengths of more than 10 ft (3 m). It weighs up to 441 lb (200 kg) and is a prize catch.*

Hummingbirds *are tiny, nectar-drinking birds. Peru has 127 species that range from sea level to 15,000 ft (4,500 m).*

Macaws and parrots *in Peru make up 49 species of the world's 354 Psittacidae bird family members, including the beautiful blue-and-yellow macaw.*

The Andean spectacled bear *is South America's only bear species. Locally known as* ucumari, *this endangered animal normally lives in the mountain forest.*

The red uakari monkey *is an arboreal creature that lives mainly in the primary forests. It has been spotted on the border of Peru and Brazil.*

The Biodiversity of Peru

KEY

- Amazon Rainforest
- Cloud Forest
- Equatorial Dry Forest
- Highlands and Puna
- Coastal Desert

Butterfiles, Tambopata

A paradise for nature-lovers, Peru's biodiversity is guarded through the 71 national parks, reserves, sanctuaries, and other categories of natural protected areas that have been created throughout the country. Peru holds world records in highest diversity for birds (1,816 species), butterflies (3,532 species), and orchids (3,500 species). The country also has a huge number of mammals (462 species), and amphibians (379 species). There are at least 6,288 endemic species of plants and animals.

Santuario Nacional Manglares de Tumbes, on the Ecuadorian border, covers the coastal mangrove area. It is the only place in Peru where American crocodiles are found.

Río Pastaza

Río Maraño

Reserva de Biósfera del Noroeste *covers four protected areas: Santuario Nacional Manglares de Tumbes, Reserva Nacional de Tumbes, Parque Nacional Cerros de Amotape, and Coto de Caza El Angolo (see p233), which protects the biggest Equatorial Dry Forest in the world.*

Parque Nacio Tingo Marí

Reserva Nacio Junin

Parque Nacional Huascarán (see pp202–3) *protects the Cordillera Blanca, the highest tropical mountain range in the world. Peru's highest mountain, the Huascarán (22,200 ft/6,768 m) is also located here. Created in 1975, the park protects 50 snowcapped peaks, 663 glaciers, 296 lakes, and 41 rivers.*

Reserva Nacional de Paracas (see p123), *created in 1975, is the country's only protected area that encompasses both terrestrial and marine ecosystems. It features unique flora and fauna such as 216 bird, 19 mammal, 52 fish, and 6 reptile species. It is a haven for a variety of migratory birds and is recognized by the Ramsar Convention as a wetland of international importance.*

Reserva Nacional Pacaya-Samiria (see p255) *is the largest conservation area in Peru. It can be reached from Iquitos by boat. Among the protected wildlife here are 449 bird, 102 mammal, and 256 fish species.*

UNSURPASSED DELIGHTS

Peru, with its world records in orchid, bird, and butterfly species is perfect for ecotourism. New species are continually being discovered every year in the cloud forests, Amazon jungles, and the Andes. The protected areas provide opportunities for visitors to observe them.

Orchids *are found all over Peru but mainly in the Montane Cloud Forest ecoregion. They grow at altitudes of 328 ft (100 m) to 16,000 ft (4,800 m).* Phragmipedium peruvianum, *discovered here, is considered the greatest orchid find in the last 100 years.*

Butterflies *in Peru make 20 percent of the world's species. Pakitza in Parque Nacional Manu, with 1,300 species, is the world's richest butterfly community.*

World records *for the maximum number of birds in one place (650) and the greatest number seen in a single day (361), were recorded in Reserva Nacional de Tambopata (see pp262–3) and Parque Nacional Manu respectively.*

Parque Nacional Cordillera Azul has the highest number of habitats with around 6,000 species of plants and animals.

Rio Curaray

Rio Amazonas

Rio Ucayali

Rio Alto Purús

Rio Urubamba

Rio Madre de Dios

Parque Nacional Manu

Parque Nacional Bahuaja-Sonene

Reserva Nacional Titicaca

Reserva Nacional de Tambopata is a lowland reserve with diverse plants and animals.

Santuario Histórico de Machu Picchu (see pp176–7) *is not just famous for its Inca sites. It also has 10 percent of Peru's total biodiversity, including 9 Holdridge life zones and 200 orchids, and an average of 90 tree species per hectare.*

0 km 300

0 miles 200

Indigenous Peoples of Peru

Peru has the largest indigenous population of South America, with almost half its nearly 29 million people being of native descent. Living in the Amazonian Basin or in remote mountain villages, they still dress in their traditional style, observe ancient customs, and continue to speak Quechua, Aymara, or other languages. The Ashaninka, Aguaruna, and Shipibo-Conibo, who developed elaborate shamanistic traditions, are the main ethnic groups of the Amazon. The Quechua, Q'eros, and Aymara, who were great builders, live in the Andean region.

Shipibo woman *sewing patterns on to a cloth. The graphic designs are said to be inspired by impressions induced by ayahuasca, a hallucinogenic drug used by shamans. They work with cotton muslin usually in black, white, and beige.*

Musicians with flutes and drums accompany the dancers.

THE SHIPIBO PEOPLE

The Shipibo have been living in the Amazon for over a 1,000 years. Their universe is a highly patterned one. The intricate geometric designs, which appear in their textiles, pottery, homes, tools, and even body-art, are believed to be spiritual in origin and a manifestation of shamanic visions.

Handpainted skirts, with a distinct vine pattern, are worn by the women.

The Aymara Nation *is the second largest Andean ethnic group. About 2.3 million live in the south-eastern region of Peru in the Altiplano and around Lake Titicaca, Bolivia, northern Chile, and northeastern Argentina. The Aymaras are presumed to descend from the Tiahuanaco, a technologically-advanced culture that flourished during the Middle Horizon period (AD 600–1000).*

Ashaninka *is the biggest indigenous nation in the Amazon, with 65,000 people living in the central jungle region of Peru. They have a long history of struggle against colonization, slavery, and the Shining Path Maoist group.*

Pachamama *(Mother Earth), wife of Pachacamac (Earth-Maker), being worshiped with varied offerings. She has been the supreme deity of the Andean indigenous communities since Inca times and is also worshiped in Bolivia, Ecuador, northern Chile, and northwestern Argentina.*

Q'eros *inhabit the northeast of Cusco at a height of almost 16,000 ft (5,000 m). Living in isolation, they have preserved the Inca traditions for almost 1,000 years.*

Quechua *is the largest indigenous group, about 13 million, living in the Andean region. It is also the name of Peru's second official language spoken by no less than 3 million. Its origins trace back to the Inca period.*

Lamas *is situated 13 miles (20 km) northwest of Tarapoto. This small settlement in the high jungle is home to the descendants of the Chanca tribe that escaped from the Andes in the 15th century after having been defeated by the Incas. Also called Quechua-Lamistas, they have a distinct lifestyle, a mix of jungle and Andean culture.*

Fight sequences are an integral part of all Shipibo dances.

IMPORTANCE OF PLANTS

Various plants have been used in Peru over the centuries in religious ceremonies as offerings to gods, as medicines, as well as in shamanistic rituals. The Andean people have traditionally used the sacred coca leaves, also known for making cocaine, as a natural energizer and for its curative qualities. Brews made with ayahuasca contain hallucinogenic and purgative properties.

Mapacho (black jungle tobacco) smoke is said to be the food of the plant spirits. The shaman heals by blowing smoke over a patient.

Ayahuasca (the rope of the dead) is a giant vine used by shamans for medicinal and religious purposes.

Coca leaves have been used since pre-Columbian times as offerings to different deities, and to cure diverse ailments such as altitude sickness.

The Culture of the Incas

At its height in the 15th and 16th centuries, the Inca Empire encompassed thousands of square miles, stretching almost the entire length of the Andes. The Incas were audacious engineers, building spectacular mountain-top citadels. They developed elaborate farming terraces, sustaining their crops by canal and drainage systems. Their social structure was extremely rigid with the emperor enjoying absolute power, and revered as a living god. The Incas worshiped the sun, moon, earth, and mountains. Animals, such as the condor and puma, were also considered sacred.

The Incas' sun and moon calendar provided timings for agriculture

CULT OF THE SUN

The Incas revered Inti, the Sun God, who nourished the earth and controlled the harvests. The emperor, believed to be the son of the Sun God, made offerings to the sun during religious ceremonies.

The red macaw, a commonly depicted figure.

Inti Raymi (Festival of the Sun) *was celebrated annually on June 21, the winter solstice in the Southern Hemisphere. Mummies of nobles were brought into Cusco's main plaza to witness the event. It is still held on June 24 at Sacsayhuamán.*

Ancestors *were worshipped with offerings of food and drink. Inca mummies were lavishly dressed.*

Sacrifice *of animals was practised daily by the Incas. Human sacrifice was reserved for special occasions and only the most beautiful children from the most powerful families were chosen to be sacrificed.*

The lower band shows mainly harvesting or floral motifs.

Infusions of ayahuasca and coca leaves were integral to all ceremonies.

Divination *played a large part in religious life. Everything, from treating illness to determining the correct sacrifices, was performed by the high priest consulting the oracles, observing the path of a spider in a dish, the position of scattered coca leaves, or by drinking ayahuasca (see p23).*

Canal systems *were used to divert water from rivers, sometimes many miles away, to the fields. Channels along the terraces directed the rainwater.*

FARMING

The Incas carved up mountains into vast terraced farmlands. The banks of the terraces were held up by stone walls. In 1500 there was more land in cultivation in the Andes than there is today. They cultivated corn and potatoes, and raised llama and alpaca for food and as pack animals.

The crop terraces *at Moray are like an agricultural laboratory in which the Incas experimented with different varieties of plants to help improve their production.*

The top section usually depicts a narrative scene which could also be a representation of a real historical event.

The central band comprises a of series of geometric patterns.

The food technology *of the Incas was innovative. They developed the earliest type of freeze-drying: potatoes were left out at night to freeze in the frost and when the water evaporated during the day a dry potato pulp remained, called* chuño.

KEROS (INCA CUPS)

These drinking vessels were made of ceramic or wood and were used during ceremonies to drink *chicha* (corn beer). Their decoration is usually in three distinct bands, each with its own iconography, and with a limited palette of black, red, white, yellow, and orange.

RECORD KEEPING

It is believed the Incas had no formal writing tradition. No documents, letters, books, or evidence of libraries have been uncovered. However, anthropologists have found many *quipus,* strings which were used as a record-keeping device through a complicated system of knots. Made of wool or cotton strings fastened at one end to a cross cord, each *quipu* was different from the other in size or color. The simple or compound knots and their size and colors represented details of crop measures, thefts and debts, and possibly events. This device was perhaps inherited from the Wari.

Keeping records with the help of the *quipus*

Traditional *quipu*

Architecture in Peru

Peru's greatest architectural heritage can be seen in its Inca ruins, most famously at Machu Picchu, but there are many other distinctive historical styles. Pre-Inca civilizations have also left their architectural legacy, visible in many archaeological sites around the country. With the arrival of the Spanish came European architectural influences and the building of ornate Colonial churches and mansions that continue to dominate many of the country's urban centers. Lima's cityscape has changed significantly due to the growth of contemporary architecture in its financial and port districts.

The ruins at Sacsayhuamán show the stone blocks used by the Incas

The Post-Classical period *saw the Chimú (AD 1000–1470) create northern Peru's architectural marvel: Chan Chan's enormous adobe compound* (see p223).

PRE-INCA

Monumental ceremonial mounds dating from as far back as 2500 BC have been found at various sites on the coast, and also at Kotosh *(see p186)*, in the Northern Highlands, where terracing and temple structures were discovered.

Spiral access leading down to the underground aqueducts.

Stone and flat rock have been used to build this complicated subterranean system.

The Nazca Civilization *built many aqueducts for irrigation purposes and some are still in use. The Cantalloc Aqueduct is the most famous.*

Huaca de la Luna's *Moche pyramid (see p223) has some wonderful examples of intricate polychrome murals and reliefs.*

INCA

The Incas set themselves apart with their superior architectural stonework, city building, and landscaping. The undecorated and precise style is characterized by immense stone foundations and mortarless walls.

Trapezoidal window directs the sun's light.

Walls made of stone blocks snugly fitted together.

The many-sided stone blocks fit together like a jigsaw without use of mortar

The Temple of the Sun, *Machu Picchu (see p180) is tapered so that on the winter solstice, the sun's rays illuminate the central stone through a window.*

COLONIAL

Once the Spanish conquistadores had established their military might, they ordered the construction of churches in praise of God instead of the Inca pagan figures, thus creating places of worship for their new converts. Concurrent with these religious imperatives was the establishment of grand mansions, with cloistered courtyards and high ceilings, for the wealthy European settlers. Many of these architectural styles can be seen in Lima, Cusco, Arequipa, and Trujillo among other cities.

Iron House, *designed by Gustave Eiffel, was built out of steel in Paris before being shipped to Iquitos in 1890.*

Ox eyes – the octagonal cupola – is typical of the Cusco style.

The Belfry is joined to the façade by a cornice.

The Baroque façade is spectacularly carved.

Balcony with projecting corbels.

Iglesia de la Compañia (see p157) *shows the influence of the Cusco School, a 17th-century movement that blended European and indigenous elements to create a new decorative style.*

Monasterio de Santa Catalina (see pp138–41) *is a beautiful example of Jesuit religious architecture, which displays a notably Spanish Mudéjar influence in its shady courtyards and cupolas.*

CONTEMPORARY

Although most emphasis, as well as finance, is placed on the restoration of older buildings in Peru, some new designs are springing up, particularly in Lima's financial district of San Isidro and the port area of Miraflores.

Blue glass is used on the façade.

The 25-story hotel has great ocean views.

Larcomar (see p79) *in Lima is a large and modern shopping mall with terraces carved out of the side of the Miraflores cliffs.*

Lima Marriott (see p271) *is the city's tallest building. With its glass façade it is, along with other buildings, helping to transform the skyline of this urban coastal area.*

Music and Dance

Music and dance are an essential feature of life in Peru; local and national festivals are celebrated with the lilting, infectious beat of the *huayno* or the teasing and coquettish national dance, the *marinera*. The style of music and dance, as well as the instruments used, varies regionally and reflects the landscape and way of life. Generally speaking, an aural distinction can be made between the melancholy, wind-based music of the sierras and the lively, drum-based rhythms of the coast. But, within these geographical areas there are many more localized variations.

Música Criolla has a mix of African and Spanish elements

The marinera *mimics the mating ritual of birds. A female dancer marks the beat with a white handkerchief held above her head, and shakes the folds of her skirt, while a suitor struts around her.*

Costumes, colorful and traditional, include skirts for girls and caps for boys.

HUAYNO

Though the *huayno* developed in the rural Altiplano, it has now spread nationwide. The lively rhythms encourage couples to dance through the streets and can be very raucous when accompanied by alcohol.

Couples perform movements such as the *zapateo*, a rhythmic footwork to mark time.

MUSICAL INSTRUMENTS

Many Peruvian instruments have pre-Columbian roots – evidence of pipes, thought to date back thousands of years, has been found in coastal areas. Before the conquest there were only wind and percussion instruments; with the Spanish, came stringed instruments such as the guitar.

Zampona *in Spanish or* sicu *in Quechua, is the Andean panpipe. Comprising any number of reed tubes, each with a different octave, it is bound together by a knotted string or a strap. The two rows of pipes are open at one end and closed at the other.*

Ocarina *is an oval whistle flute made of clay, stone, wood, and large seeds. It produces a haunting sound and can imitate bird calls.*

Charango *is a small mandolin created by the indigenous population of Peru and Bolivia in the early Colonial days of the 1500s. It is still very popular throughout the southern Andes, including Argentina and Chile.*

Son de los Diablos, *or the Devil's Dance, is a popular Afro-Peruano dance performed with much gusto during the Carnaval in Lima and the surrounding areas. It symbolizes cultural resistance. The accompanying orchestra plays the guitar,* cajón, *and the* quijada *or donkey's jaw.*

Susana Baca, *whose song on a 1995 compilation album,* The Soul of Black Peru *produced by David Byrne of Talking Heads, caused an international sensation.*

Costumes comprise smocks, trousers, masks with feathers, tails, cord shoes, cloak, and numerous bells.

Eva Ayllon, *one of the foremost Afro-Peruvian musicians, began singing in school competitions and later on radio and television. Today, she is a composer and singer of international acclaim. She has over 25 albums to her credit.*

MUSICA AFRO-PERUANO

The country's black population largely resides in the central coastal region and produces some of the most captivating music. It has become an essential part of Peruvian culture, thanks to its lively rhythms and strong percussion.

Cajón, *crafted from a wooden box with a sound hole at the back, provides another percussion element to the music of the coast. The musician sits on top and beats on the front surface with the palms.*

Andean harp *is a 36-stringed instrument with a large boat-shaped and half-conical sound box. It creates a uniquely rich and powerful bass. It is an essential part of most bands in the highlands.*

Quena, *a delicate, reed-like, notched flute, is a versatile instrument. Once made from llama or condor bone, today it is often made from wood or bamboo. It produces a distinctive melancholic tone.*

Art and Literature

Little evidence of pre-Columbian literature or fine arts remains, thanks to the dominance of the oral tradition in Inca society and to the obliteration of Inca culture by the Spanish. However, native Peruvians gradually began to appropriate European artistic and literary styles in order to resist their Colonial oppressors. After independence, these art forms were increasingly used to analyze issues of race and identity. Peruvian art and literature is a combination of its diverse culture, and today, a rich and varied body of work reflects the changing sentiments with regard to national identity, politics, and issues related to ethnicity and gender.

Cusco School painting of Saint Joseph with the young Christ

ART

When the Spanish arrived in Peru in the 16th century, they brought with them a number of European artists who were commissioned to undertake religious works to adorn the interiors of churches and monasteries throughout the country. A number of examples of these works of art can still be seen, particularly in cities such as Lima, Cusco, and Arequipa.

As demand increased, the colonizers began to teach their techniques to local indigenous artists and there began a new pictorial interpretation of Peruvian life, dominated by Catholic and regal imagery. In the 17th century, a group of largely anonymous native artists, which later became popularly known as the Cusco School *(see p167)*, began to blend this religious iconography with indigenous motifs to create a new and popular art form. Initially, under the tutelage of the Spaniards, these artists painted devotional scenes, using classical Spanish and Flemish techniques, and incorporated Andean flora and fauna, customs, and traditions. The Cusco School went on to dominate the Peruvian artistic tradition for the next 200 years.

The early 20th century saw artists such as Francisco Fierro (1807–79) and José Sabogal (1888–1956) contribute to a new Indigenista movement, which recognized the importance of Andean culture and sought to portray typical events and customs of contemporary Peru. Later in the century artists returning from Europe began to combine national themes with more international styles as is evident from the works of Fernando de Szyszlo (b.1925), who combined abstract expressionism with pre-Columbian motifs and iconography – thereby pushing the Peruvian world of art towards modernism.

The country's current economy has allowed the arts to flourish and several Peruvian painters have achieved international acclaim. They include Gerardo Chávez, Fernando de Szyszlo, and Ramiro Llona, as well as the sculptor Victor Delfín, whose gigantic sculpture, *El Beso*, is a highlight of the Parque de Amor *(see p79)* in Lima.

El Beso, the giant kissing statue by Victor Delfin in Lima.

USKO AYAR SCHOOL OF ART

Painting titled *Arcoiris* by Pablo Amaringo

Established in 1984, by Pablo Amaringo, a self-taught artist from the Amazon region, the Usko Ayar has been recognized as a Not-for-Profit Cultural Organization (with some financial help from the Finnish government). Under his own roof, Amaringo – a former shaman – has given free instruction to more than 700 students who create unusual, vibrant and visionary paintings depicting the landscapes, myths, as well as the diverse flora and fauna of the jungle in colorful and meticulous detail.

Peruvian author and Nobel Prize winner, Mario Vargas Llosa

LITERATURE

The tradition of Colonial literature in Peru began with the arrival of Garcilaso de la Vega from Spain. He chronicled his impressions of the New World and Inca Empire in *Royal Commentaries of the Incas* (1609). Later that century, a different perspective was presented in *Nueva Cronica y Buen Gobierno*, an account of Spanish abuses on the continent, written to King Philip III of Spain by Guaman Poma de Ayala, a native descendant of the Incas from the Huamanga region in the southern Peruvian Andes. The persuasive 1,200-page tract, with full pages of intricate illustrations, sought to convince the Spanish to rethink their devastating methods of colonization.

The late 19th and early 20th century saw many educated Peruvian writers, often urban and socially privileged, taking up the cause of the indigenous population, whose oppression was the focus of the works of Ciro Alegría (1909–67). Alegría's novel *El Mundo es Ancho y Ajeno*, written in 1941, analyzed the humiliations suffered by the Latin American indigenous population. Clorinda Matto de Turner (1852–1909), who embraced indigenous culture, spoke out on behalf of women. Her 1889 novel *Aves sin Nido* (*Birds Without a Nest*) dealt with a love affair between a white man and an indigenous woman, and was considered to be extremely controversial. The short stories and poems of José Maria Arguedas – who was brought up in an indigenous community – explore the conflict between the Hispanic community and traditional native cultures.

The 1960s saw open social exploration and criticism of national cultural identity. Alfredo Bryce Echenique expressed the sensibilities of a culturally conflicted generation of educated and liberal minded young Peruvians in the 1970s with *Mundo Para Julius*, which exposed the social differences between classes in Peruvian society.

The most famous Peruvian author, Mario Vargas Llosa (b.1936), awarded the Nobel Prize in Literature in 2010, is considered one of the frontrunners of Latin America's literary boom (which also includes writers such as Carlos Fuentes and Gabriel García Márquez from Mexico and Colombia respectively). His novels present a social critique of racial and social hierarchies in the country. His most famous works include *La Ciudad y Los Perros*. Written in 1963, this novel is an account of life in a military academy. The 1969 book *Conversación en la Catedral* deals with life in Peru under the dictatorship of Manuel Odría during the 1950s. Llosa also ran for the country's presidency in 1990 and was defeated by Alberto Fujimori. Another popular contemporary novelist, Beto Ortiz (b.1968), lived in the US for many years after openly criticizing the Fujimori government. His novel, *Maldita Ternura*, written in 2004, gives an inside view of the media world.

Writer Alfredo Bryce Echenique

POPULAR TITLES

La Ciudad y Los Perros *by Mario Vargas Llosa was made into a movie of the same name in 1985.*

Aves sin Nido, *a two-part novel, is the first of three novels written by Clorinda Matto de Turner.*

Maldita Ternura, *a novel by Beto Ortiz, portrays the area around Parque Kennedy of the 1980s.*

Craft and Textiles

Peruvian craft and textiles reflect the diverse identities that evolved from the country's complex cultural and historical formation. Pre-Inca cultures, such as the Chavín, Moche, Nazca, and Chimú, displayed a high quality of craftsmanship in their pottery, sculpture, and textiles. The Incas further developed these skills when they came to dominate the continent. Cultural stories were expressed through artistic means, in ceramic design and weaving, in the absence of the written word. Pre-Columbian traditions survived the conquest and have been appropriated by contemporary artists, thus preserving the indigenous culture. These crafts and textiles add to the mystical nature of the area.

Alpaca *and Andean llama wool is woven using trad- itional pre-Columbian looms, although European spinning wheels are now used commercially.*

Chimú textiles *were adorned by geometric and zoomorphic designs similar to the wall relief found in Chan Chan (see p223).*

Unku or tunic, *worn by Inca men, was usually in bright colors and decorated with geometrical motifs.*

Traditionally woven rugs are popular souvenirs.

TEXTILES

Both practical and illustrative, textiles and clothes can communicate status as well as identity. Beautifully woven and using natural dyes, ponchos and belts can indicate a woman's marital status or the standing of a man's family within the community.

JEWELRY

Indigenous peoples manipulated the abundant precious metals with great skill, and the Spanish brought with them new techniques.

Metalworking, *to create jewelry and other artifacts, dates back to pre-Columbian Peru.*

Threads, beads, *shells, bones, and seeds, were some of the natural materials used to make jewelry amongst pre- Columbian cultures.*

Silver filigree *was introduced with the arrival of the Spanish and is still popular.*

CERAMICS

Peru has produced some of the finest pottery in the world. The excellent pre-Columbian Art Museum in Cusco shows how their aesthetics still pleases the eye.

Traditional Nazca pottery *is polychromatic and characterized by birds and animals with mainly feline features.*

Miniature clay churches, *painted with corn and flowers, are a famous craft of Ayacucho (see pp192–3).*

Moche ceramics *are delicately painted with extraordinary detail. Some "portrait vessels" have different male faces that are amazingly realistic.*

Clay bulls, *made in Pucara, are often flasks too and were used during ritual ceremonies conducted by priests.*

ARTIFACTS

Regionally distinctive artifacts, such as engraved gourds, gilt-edged mirrors, woven baskets, and hats can be found throughout the country.

Engraved gourds, *dating back over 4,000 years, have been found on the southern coast. They were used in ritualistic ceremonies by the Incas.*

Peruvian dolls *are bright, colorful, and mostly dressed in traditional clothes.*

WOODWORK

Carved wooden objects are ubiquitous, varying from drums to masks to magical sticks and the intricate *tablas*.

Wooden masks, *both humorous and sinister, are painted in bright colors and used during festivals and carnivals.*

Tablas, *or colorful painted boards showing every-day life and rural activities, are mainly made in Ayacucho.*

Wooden plate *with intricate Nazca symbols painted in bright natural dyes.*

PERU THROUGH THE YEAR

It appears that every day is cause for celebration in Peru, with its estimated 3,000 festivals each year. Although most derive from the Christian calendar introduced by the Spanish, indigenous Andean beliefs are also woven into the fabric of worship. Celebrations honoring patron saints sit side-by-side with fertility and harvest rituals. *Marinera,*

Woman dancing the *marinera*

the national dance, along with the Paso horse, the sun, spring, and all manner of saints are celebrated. The religious festivals include processions with masks and colorful costumes. Peru has two distinct seasons. The dry season is more popular with visitors. Although festivals are common to the country during the wet season, the sierra and the jungle see fewer visitors.

WET SEASON

December to April are the wettest months though early rains begin in November. Roads and trails in the Andes become impassable. By contrast, the coast is hot and dry, making city dwellers head for the beach. Beaches near Ecuador are warm enough to swim year-round. Day and night temperatures are mild in the mountains. Most mornings are dry with downpours in the afternoons. Frequent showers swell waterways and the Amazon River can rise up to 50 ft (15 m) in the rains. The jungle gets more rain in the dry season than the mountains in the wet season.

Orchid bloom

NOVEMBER

All Saints' Day and Day of the Dead *(Nov 1)*, Cajamarca. Families bring paper flower crowns to cemeteries, clean

their relatives' gravestones, and share food and drink with the departed. In Piura, families illuminate the graveyard with candles and hold a wake until dawn. Parents who have lost a child go to the main plaza and give sweets to children. Across the country, *guaguas* (bread shaped like dolls and horses) are baked for children.

Founding of Puno *(1st week)*. Students organize dances and street parades. On November 5, people act out the Inca Empire's creation, when Manco Capac and Mama Ocllo emerged from the lake.

Festival de la Orquídea *(1st week)*, Moyobamba. The festival showcases the orchids of Moyobamba, which has 10 percent of the 3,500 catalogued species.

DECEMBER

Homenaje a la Liberdad Americana *(Dec 2–9)*, Huamanga Province. Athletes

Enacting the creation of the Inca Empire, Founding of Puno

from South America descend for games to celebrate the defeat of the Spanish in the 1824 Battle of Ayacucho.

Yawar Fiesta *(1st week)*, Apurímac region. As part of the Blood Fiesta, a condor representing Andean defiance is tied to a bull's back for a fight unto death.

Feast of the Immaculate Conception *(Dec 7–10)*, Chivay. After the procession celebrating Jesus' conception, men in women's clothing perform a dance in which they abduct the women.

Santurantikuy *(Dec 24)*, Cusco. Meaning "saints for sale," this is one of Peru's largest arts-and-crafts fairs. Artisans gather to sell nativity scenes, religious carvings, and pottery in the main plaza.

Festival of the Negritos *(Dec 24–Jan 19)*, Huánuco. The Brotherhood of the Slaves of Huánuco dance through the streets and wait at the

Families offering flowers to their loved ones on All Saints' Day

nativity for the arrival of baby Jesus, commemorating the day in 1648 when a Spanish noble freed his black slaves.

JANUARY

Founding of Iquitos *(Jan 5)*. Day of civic parades and parties that everyone can attend.
Marinera Festival *(Jan/Feb)*, Trujillo. Couples of all ages compete to be named Peru's best *marinera* dancers.

FEBRUARY

Virgen de la Candelaria *(Feb 2–20)*, Puno. This is the most important religious celebration. Masses, dance contests, banquets, and a procession featuring remarkable masks and costumes are spread over 18 days. The festival is also linked to the pre-Hispanic agricultural cycles of sowing and harvesting, as well as mining activities.
Carnaval *(Feb)*. Across Peru costumed revelers dance and feast throwing water buckets and balloons in the lead up to Lent. In most highland towns, people dance around a *yunza*, an artificially planted tree trunk filled with gifts, trying to chop it. The couple that fells the tree gets to be next year's organizer.

MARCH

Festival de la Vendimia *(2nd week)*, Ica. The Harvest Queen and her handmaidens

Candles and white roses used as decorations for Semana Santa

stomp grapes in a vat and throw grapes to the crowd. There are floats, music, and Afro-Peruvian dancing.
Fiesta de la Cruz *(Mar/Apr)*. Processions of crosses, along with music and dancers, are held across Peru commemorating ancient agro-astronomical rituals. In Porcón (near Cajamarca), 100 reed and palm crosses decorated with mirrors – the souls of the dead – are paraded. On Palm Sunday the crosses are led into the church, along with a female donkey signifying Jesus' entry into Jerusalem.

APRIL

Semana Santa *(Easter week)*. Ayacucho stages Peru's most elaborate Easter procession. Cross processions occur many times a day and differ each day. On Good Friday the figure of Señor del Santo Sepulcro (Lord of the Holy

Sepulcher), is borne on a litter adorned with white roses and thousands of candles from the Santa Clara Monastery. It is followed by an image of the grieving Mary (Virgen Dolorosa) and lines of people with candles. The main plaza's lights are turned off and candles illuminate it. There is dancing as well as fireworks on Saturday night. On Sunday the resurrected Christ is brought from the cathedral, mounted on a huge structure and paraded around the square.

In Tarma and Ica, streets are carpeted with flowers and decked with blooming arches for the processions.
Peruvian Paso Horse National Show *(mid- to late Apr)*, Lima. Distinguished by its unique gait, the Peruvian Paso horse is recognized as a "cultural patrimony" of Peru. It is hailed as one of the world's most elegant steeds.

Colorful procession at the Virgen de la Candelaria Festival

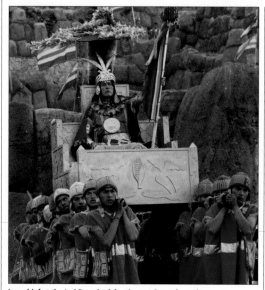
Inca chief at the Inti Raymi celebrations at Sacsayhuamán

DRY SEASON

May to October is cooler, drier, and ideal for visiting most of Peru. It is the time for outdoor activities such as climbing, hiking, and mountain biking. In the highlands, days are clear and sunny from June to September, although temperatures can plummet at night. Hikers planning on doing the Inca Trail should aim for these months. This is also a good time to visit the jungle as both mosquito and river levels are down. Lima is blanketed in a grey haze during this period, with high humidity making the days and nights chilly. The waters of the Pacific are too cold for swimming.

MAY

Corpus Christi (*end May/early Jun*), Cusco. This is the most impressive Corpus Christi procession. Statues of 16 saints are carried to the cathedral to greet "the body of Christ", a consecrated wafer held in a 57-lb (26-kg) gold tabernacle. The Andean and Spanish worlds merge here as the Incas too carried their sovereigns' mummified remains in processions at the same time of year. At night, typical dishes including guinea pig with hot peppers, *chicha*, and corn bread are served. At sunrise the parade moves around the main plaza and enters the cathedral.

JUNE

Qoyllur Rit'i (*1st week*), Cusco region. More than 10,000 people gather at Sinakara at the foot of Mount Ausangate (20,870 ft/6,362 m) at a shrine bearing a painting of Jesus as a child. According to popular belief the infant Christ appeared to a native boy here. A group of Q'eros, hailed as Peru's purest Quechua community, ascend to the summit searching for the buried Qoyllur Rit'i (Star of the Snow). They haul massive blocks of ice on their shoulders back to their communities for the symbolic watering of their lands with holy water from Ausangate.

Inti Raymi (*Jun 24*), Sacsayhuamán. The Festival of the Sun celebrates the winter solstice and honors the Sun God worshipped by the Incas. An Inca chief presides over the ceremony, a llama is sacrificed to the sun, and at dusk the ceremony finishes and the music and dancing begins.

Day of Saint John the Baptist (*Jun 24*). Religious services, dancing and musical celebrations, and craft fairs take place across Peru to mark the feast day of this saint. In the Amazon the event takes on special significance due to the connection with water.

Chaccu Ceremony (*end Jun*), Lucanas (Pampa Galeras National Reserve, Ayacucho). The communal herding and shearing of the vicuña, whose ultra fine wool was worn by Inca royalty, was revived in 1992 to revitalize local cultural practices. People from across the region gather as a human chain is formed around the wild vicuñas to herd them into a pen. An Inca king blesses the ceremony, recites a prayer in Quechua and the shearing begins.

People gather at Sinakara, Cusco, during Qoyllur Rit'i celebrations

JULY

Virgen del Carmen *(Jul 15–16)*, Paucartambo (near Cusco). Musicians play, choirs sing in Quechua and groups act out events in history as a tribute to Virgin del Carmen, patroness of the mestizo people. Elaborately dressed dancers accompany the procession with the Virgin blessing the faithful. As a finale, a war is waged and the virtuous triumph over the demons.

Eco-tourism and Coffee Festival *(Jul 25–30)*, Oxapampa. An opportunity to explore ecotourism circuits and coffee plantations run by indigenous people.

Fiestas Patrias *(Jul 28–29)*. The whole country celebrates July 28, the day Peru gained its independence from Spain in 1821. All buildings are required to fly the Peruvian flag at this time.

Apurímac Tourist Week *(Jul 31–Aug 3)*, Andahuaylas, Apurímac, and Abancay Provinces. Festivities include paragliding, white-water rafting, mountain biking contests, a cockfighting championship, and a hiking competition at Ampay Sanctuary.

AUGUST

Pachamama Raymi *(Aug 1)*, Cusco. The ritual offering of *pagapus* (gifts) to Pachamama (Mother Earth) is an age-old Andes tradition. Offerings, such as *chicha*, coca leaves, *huayruro* (mystical jungle seeds), and wine, are made to her for good harvests and fortune. It marks the beginning of the Andean New Year.

Yaku Raymi *(Aug 20–26)*, Ayacucho. An ancient ceremony cleanses the water in the canals and offerings are made to Pachamama. There is a competition of dances such as Danzantes de Tijera (Scissors Dance)

Santa Rosa de Lima *(Aug 30)*, Lima. Believers flock to the sanctuary of America's first saint, asking for miracles in letters dropped into the well in which she reportedly threw her chastity belt's key.

Dancers with masks at the Virgen del Carmen festival

SEPTEMBER

Ruraltur *(1st weekend)*, Huayllay National Sanctuary, Pasco Province. Festivities include Andean gymkhana, offerings to Pachamama, llama load-carrying contests, wool spinning competitions, pottery demonstrations, rock-climbing contests, and hiking.

Spring Festival *(Sep/Oct)*, Trujillo. Spring is celebrated all over Peru but Trujillo's festivities are the most impressive, with flower-decked houses, floats, and a procession with a beauty queen flanked by drum majorettes from the world over. Horses perform the *marinera* at the Peruvian Paso Horse Contest.

PUBLIC HOLIDAYS

New Year (Jan 1)

Easter Thursday and Good Friday (Mar/Apr)

Labor Day (May 1)

Fiestas Patrias/ Independence Day (Jul 28, 29)

Battle of Angamos (Oct 8)

All Saints' Day (Nov 1)

Feast of the Immaculate Conception (Dec 8)

Christmas Day (Dec 25)

OCTOBER

El Señor de los Milagros *(Oct 18–28)*, Lima. Tens of thousands of penitents in purple robes solemnly follow an image of the Lord of Miracles on a two-ton (2,000 kg) litter carried on the shoulders of believers on a 24-hour journey from the church of Las Nazarenas to La Merced. Some women wear purple garments for a month.

Bullfighting Season *(mid-Oct–end Nov)*, Lima. International matadors come to Lima to compete in the Lord of Miracles bullfights.

Día de la Canción Criolla *(Oct 31)*. A day for celebrating Peruvian Creole music, with street musicians, and concerts in bars, restaurants, and *peñas*.

Procession of El Senor de los Milagros, Lima

The Climate of Peru

There are two main seasons in Peru – wet and dry. Arid deserts line the coast courtesy of the icy Humboldt Current, which causes clouds to release moisture before they reach land. While it rarely rains here, mist and *garúa* (light drizzle) are common in winter (May–Oct), except in the far north, where it is sunny year round. Lima, by contrast, is blanketed in grey gauze for seven months. Inland, temperatures get colder as the altitude increases – in the Andes it can drop from 20°C (68°F) to 2°C (36°F) in one day. In the tropical jungle, summer (Dec–Sep) means hot, sunny days. River levels swell in the rainy season causing flooding.

CAJAMARCA

°C/F				
	21/70	**21**/70	**22**/72	**22**/72
	8/46	**5**/41	**8**/46	**9**/48
☀	NA	NA	NA	NA
☂	81 mm	5 mm	82 mm	84 mm
month	Apr	Jul	Oct	Jan

TRUJILLO

°C/F				
	23/73	**20**/68	**20**/68	**24**/75
	19/66	**17**/63	**16**/61	**19**/66
☀	NA	NA	NA	NA
☂	0 mm	0 mm	0.2 mm	1.4 mm
month	Apr	Jul	Oct	Jan

Average daily maximum temperature

Average daily minimum temperature

Average daily hours of sunshine

Average monthly rainfall

NA: Data not available

KEY

▨	Semi-arid areas: sunny all year round with low rainfall
▢	Desert regions: dry and mild with cool, cloudy winters
▨	Grasslands: dry and temperate climate with cold nights
▨	Highlands: colder conditions with higher rainfall in winters
▢	Tropical: humid with distinct dry and wet seasons

HUARAZ

°C/F				
	22/71	**23**/73	**23**/73	**22**/72
	7/45	**3**/37	**6**/43	**6**/43
☀	NA	NA	NA	NA
☂	49 mm	1 mm	48 mm	106 mm
month	Apr	Jul	Oct	Jan

 Cajamarca

Trujillo

Huaraz

Lima

Snow-capped peaks of Huascarán, Cordillera Blanca

LIMA

°C/F				
	27/81		**22**/72	**28**/84
	17/63	**19**/66 **14**/57	**14**/57	**19**/66
☀	7 hrs	1 hrs	3 hrs	6 hrs
☂	0 mm	3 mm	1 mm	1 mm
month	Apr	Jul	Oct	Jan

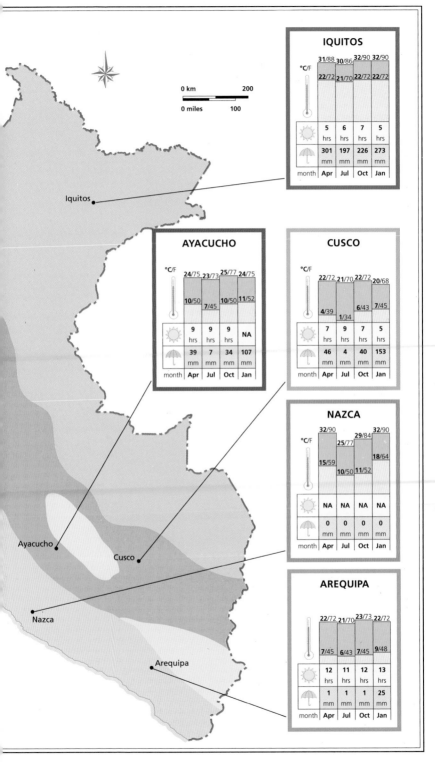

IQUITOS

°C/F	31/88	30/86	32/90	32/90
	22/72	21/70	22/72	22/72
☀ hrs	5 hrs	6 hrs	7 hrs	5 hrs
☂ mm	301 mm	197 mm	226 mm	273 mm
month	Apr	Jul	Oct	Jan

AYACUCHO

°C/F	24/75	23/73	25/77	24/75
	10/50	7/45	10/50	11/52
☀ hrs	9 hrs	9 hrs	9 hrs	NA
☂ mm	39 mm	7 mm	34 mm	107 mm
month	Apr	Jul	Oct	Jan

CUSCO

°C/F	22/72	21/70	22/72	20/68
	4/39	1/34	6/43	7/45
☀ hrs	7 hrs	9 hrs	7 hrs	5 hrs
☂ mm	46 mm	4 mm	40 mm	153 mm
month	Apr	Jul	Oct	Jan

NAZCA

°C/F	32/90	25/77	29/84	32/90
	15/59	10/50	11/52	18/64
☀	NA	NA	NA	NA
☂	0 mm	0 mm	0 mm	0 mm
month	Apr	Jul	Oct	Jan

AREQUIPA

°C/F	22/72	21/70	23/73	22/72
	7/45	6/43	7/45	9/48
☀ hrs	12 hrs	11 hrs	12 hrs	13 hrs
☂ mm	1 mm	1 mm	1 mm	25 mm
month	Apr	Jul	Oct	Jan

0 km 200
0 miles 100

Iquitos

Ayacucho

Cusco

Nazca

Arequipa

THE HISTORY OF PERU

T he origins of civilization in Peru can be traced back 20,000 years before the Incas, making the country one of the cradles of ancient cultures along with Mesopotamia, Egypt, India, and China. Today, Peru stands as the result of a collision between the Western and the Andean world, a process that began with the arrival of the Spanish in 1532. After independence, Peru set about forging its own identity, a complex process that continues even today.

Peru's earliest settlers are thought to have arrived via the Bering Strait, crossing from Asia (present day Russia) to North America during the last Ice Age between 20,000 and 40,000 years ago. Another theory, based on Thor Heyerdahl's raft expeditions in the last century, suggests that early migration may also have been possible from the Pacific and the Atlantic Oceans.

Depiction of nomadic people

The first evidence of human civilization dates back probably to 20,000 BC, to Pikimachay Cave near Ayacucho where remnants of the first nomads, including human and animal skeletons and stone tools, have been found. Stone blades, hunting knives, human remains, and cave paintings have also been uncovered in Paiján, La Libertad; Guitarrero, Ancash; Lauricocha, Huánuco; and Telarmachay, Junín.

These cultures probably began domesticating Andean camelids (llama, alpaca) and cuys (guinea pigs) as early as 7000 BC, moving on to establish small hunter-gatherer villages around 6000 BC. The nomadic tribes followed animal migration patterns, swapping mountain winters for the milder coast. Towards 2900 BC, they began to plant crops such as manioc, corn, quinua, lima beans, and cotton, thus establishing Peru's long-standing agricultural tradition. Scientists believe the potato, Peru's staple, was first cultivated around 8,000 years ago by farmers living near Lake Titicaca.

Fishing, agriculture, and trade formed the economic base of the Preceramic Period (2700–1800 BC). Cotton was used to weave fishing nets and to make ceremonial paraphernalia. Small amounts of obsidian, a glassy volcanic rock used to fashion stone tools that occurs naturally over 13,000 ft (4,000 m), has been found on the coast, indicating an active exchange of goods between the coast and highland communities. These people worked collectively, with a sense of communal ownership. This, and the control of critical resources, resulted in the development of the first cities along the coast and the highlands.

TIMELINE

20,000 BC Nomadic tribes cross the Bering Strait from Asia to the Americas, gradually spreading south

Stone tools used for hunting

8000 The Paiján Man, a consummate hunter with highly developed tool craftsmanship, lived in the Northern Desert coast

20,000 BC	16,000 BC	12,000 BC	8000 BC	4000 BC

11,000 First nomadic tribes roam the Peruvian highlands hunting giant animals such as the megatherium, an elephant-sized ground sloth

7000 Domestication of animals and agricultural cultivation begins

Megatherium, giant sloth

◁ A tile design in Cajamarca showing the 13th Inca, Atahualpa

View of the temple and amphitheater excavated at the sacred city of Caral

CARAL: THE MOTHER CITY

The biggest and most impressive example of monumental architecture during the Formative Period (2700–1000 BC) is Caral, dubbed the oldest city in the New World. The discovery of 5,000 year-old Caral provides indisputable evidence that a complex urban center formed in the Central Andes at the same time as those in the Old World of Egypt, Mesopotamia, India, and China were developing – 1,500 years earlier than previously believed. Radiocarbon dating of plant fibers indicate that Caral, which is just one of 18 sites attributed to the Caral-Supe culture, was built in 2627 BC, 1,000 years before the Olmecs established settlements in Mesoamerica.

Discovered in 1905, the site was overlooked for almost a century because it failed to yield any gold or ceramics. However, dogged research by Peruvian archaeologist, Ruth Shady, since 1994, has unearthed 20 stone-built structures featuring six pyramids and many artifacts including woven religious offerings known as *ojos de Dios* (God's eyes).

Recreated model of Caral man

The huge structures at Caral were built in a short period of time, indicating complex planning, centralized decision-making, and the mobilization of a large labor force. Society was hierarchical; religion was used as a means to ensure social cohesion and control. According to estimates, about 3,000 people lived here at its height and the varying sizes of the homes indicate clear class distinctions within the society. This sacred mother city served as a model for other religion-inspired urban centers in Peru.

While it is true that other villages in Peru were occupied before 2600 BC, some of which had small scale platforms or ceremonial structures, they are dwarfed by the size of Caral and its monuments. Caral appears to have been abandoned after some 500 years of permanent occupation, with scientists speculating that a drought may have led to the people's departure.

The concentration of urban settlements along the valley with such monumental architecture is unparalleled anywhere in the world at that time.

TIMELINE

2627 Caral, the oldest city of the New World, is built in the Supe valley

Flutes made from pelican and animal bones, engraved with the figures of birds, found at Caral

3000 BC	2500 BC	2000 BC

2500 First fragments of cotton textiles found at Huaca Prieta in Chicama Valley

Cotton cultivated by 2900

2000–1500 Temple of Kotosh constucted near the Andean town of Huánuco

THE RISE AND FALL OF CHAVÍN

The best known of the early Peruvian civilizations, the Chavín culture is considered the South American counterpart of China's Shang or Mesopotamia's Sumerian civilizations. Chavín flourished around 900 BC in what is known as the First or Early Horizon (1000 BC–AD 200) era, emerging after the societies responsible for building the monumental complexes on the coast began to collapse.

The Chavín culture managed to unite coastal, highland, and eastern lowland societies with its powerful religious ideology. They constructed an ornate stone temple at Chavín de Huántar, in the Northern Highlands of Peru, filling it with finely carved stone sculptures and elaborate iconography. The iconography of the Raimondi Stone and Lanzón monolith depicts their worship of a supreme feline deity in the shape of a stylized jaguar head, as well as other natural spirits.

Some archaeologists have suggested that Chavín de Huántar was an Andean oracle controlled by a powerful high-priest elite that relied on San Pedro cactus and other hallucinogens to interact with supernatural forces. Rivaling other sanctuaries such as Kunturwasi in Cajamarca or Sechín in the Casma Valley, it presumably attracted travelers and

Stone carvings on a wall at Sechín

Stylized jaguar carving, a feature of the Chavín

pilgrims from Ecuador in the north as well as the southern Andes. The discovery of strombus shell trumpets and spindle shells found only in tropical waters off the coast of Ecuador add weight to this hypothesis.

The Chavín were also innovative metallurgists, potters, and weavers.

Sometime around 300 BC Chavín's influence began to wane but its adroitness in unifying communities through religion resonates even today.

The Chavín de Huántar ruins at the base of the Cordillera Blanca

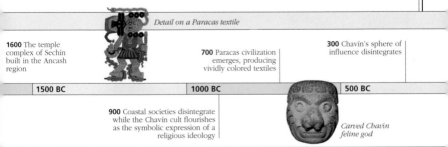

Detail on a Paracas textile

1600 The temple complex of Sechín built in the Ancash region

700 Paracas civilization emerges, producing vividly colored textiles

300 Chavín's sphere of influence disintegrates

1500 BC

1000 BC

500 BC

900 Coastal societies disintegrate while the Chavín cult flourishes as the symbolic expression of a religious ideology

Carved Chavín feline god

Depiction of a Moche pyramid under construction

REGIONAL DEVELOPMENT

With the demise of Chavín, numerous regional cultures began to emerge generating an epoch known as the Regional Development Period or the Classical Era (200 BC–AD 900). During this time, cultures including the Moche (northern coast), Recuay and Cajamarca (northern highlands), Lima (central coast), Nazca (southern coast), Wari and Tiahuanaco (southern highlands) established strong regional states each with unique features.

The Moche (220 BC–AD 600) was a militaristic society that expanded along Peru's northern coast. They were skillful engineers building large scale adobe pyramids such as the Huaca de la Luna and the Huaca del Sol as well as an impressive network of desert irrigation canals. They are also famed for their finely crafted metallurgy and ceramics, the best examples of which are the Lord of Sipán's tomb, and the tomb of a tattooed female mummy at the Huaca

Cao Viejo at El Brujo. Both provided archaeologists with unprecedented evidence that the Moche was one of the most sophisticated civilizations in pre-Columbian Peru. It is believed that drought was a factor in their demise.

Around the same time, the Nazca (100 BC–AD 700) were displaying remarkable inventiveness in their textiles and ceramics. The Nazca are thought to be the perpetrators of the desert drawings known as the Nazca Lines, and they also constructed Cahuachi, a temple and burial complex that became the main pilgrimage center for the region around AD 100.

Farther inland, near Lake Titicaca, the Tiahuanaco culture (AD 200–1000) built Tiahuanaco, an urban and ceremonial center that flourished for close to a millennium and was home to an estimated 40,000 people. The Tiahuanaco developed a specialized system of farming, which meant they could grow crops despite the icy temperatures of the altiplano.

The Wari (AD 600–1100) built a city near Ayacucho that thrived for some 300 years and was thought to have a population of 70,000. By AD 650 both the Wari and Tiahuanaco Empires had expanded sufficiently so as to share common boundaries. Archaeological evidence indicates there was

Nazca textiles with stylized motifs

TIMELINE

220 Moche culture flourishes

Moche head sculpted in gold

450 The Lady of Cao, presumably a female warrior or high-priestess, dies at 25 and is buried in El Brujo complex

650 Beginning of the Wari-Tiahuanaco period

200 BC	AD 1	200 AD	400 AD	600 A

100 AD Cahuachi, the pilgrimage center of the Nazca, becomes the most important site in the region

200 Tiahuanaco city is built on the southeastern shore of Lake Titicaca.

Moche earrings

600 Decline of the Moche Empire begins

interchange between the two cultures – both shared intriguing similarities in their iconography on stone sculptures and motifs in ceramics and textiles. While the Wari-Tiahuanaco Empire grew to encompass almost all of Peru, its inability to contain emerging tribal warfare along the coast resulted in its downfall.

Inca construction blends architecture with terrain, Machu Picchu

CONQUERING KINGDOMS

Around AD 900 the Andean region underwent radical political reorganization. During this period, known as the Conquering Kingdoms (AD 900–1532), two powers emerged on the northern coast: the Sicán in La Leche Valley, and the Chimú (or Chimor) in the Moche Valley. The Sicán, who were descendants of the Moche, constructed adobe pyramids at Bátan Grande while the Chimú built Chan Chan, the largest adobe city in the world. At its zenith around AD 1400 the Chimú kingdom extended from the northern Tumbes area to southern Chancay.

Other important cultural centers sprang up on the coast, including Chancay to the north of Lima, and Ychma at Pachacamac, to the south. Pachacamac had previously been a Wari religious and political center, uniting the Rímac and Lurín Valleys. Farther south lay the Chincha (Ica culture) domain.

Golden Chimú funerary mask

Between 1200 and 1400 many small kingdoms emerged in the highlands but only two obtained the same level of political complexity and territorial control as the coastal empires. The Chachapoyas built huge fortresses and cities in the northern jungles in San Martín, with Kúelap being the most famous. The second was an assemblage of forceful groups based in the Cusco Valley, birthplace of the Incas.

THE INCAS

The Incas (1197–1532), who created Peru's first multicultural society, descended from the families based around Cusco, the heart of a confederation of tribes in 1197. Around the 13th century, they began a slow expansion but it wasn't until the 15th century that they exerted their full dominance, subjugating surrounding territories under the leadership of emperor Pachacútec. The empire, Tahuantinsuyu (Land of the Four Quarters), at one time covered more than a third of South America.

Manco Cápac, the legendary founder of the Inca Empire

1200 Mythical foundation of Cusco by Manco Cápac

1400 Maximum expansion of the Chimú kingdom

1438 The 9th Inca, Pachacutec's 33-year reign begins

800 AD	1000	1200	1400

900 Twenty pyramids are built at Batán Grande by the Sicán people

Chimú ceremonial gold knife

1375 Chimú occupy Túcume

1450 Incas conquer the Chimú kingdom and occupy Chan Chan and Túcume

The Inca Empire

In a relatively short space of time – barely a century – the Incas built not only the largest empire in pre-Columbian America but also one of the largest in history. Their vast domain encompassed dramatic contrasts, from icy peaks to coastal desert and the Amazonian jungle, with the high-altitude city of Cusco at its center. Prior to the arrival of the Incas in the central Andes, which some estimates put as early as AD 1000, the area was home to a host of diverse, and often hostile, cultures. The conquering Incas united the region under one social system and language, but did adopt aspects of the cultures they absorbed.

INCA EXPANSION

■ *Under Pachacútec, 1438–71*

▨ *Under Tupac Inca, 1471–93*

■ *Under Huayna Cápac, 1493–1527*

THE INCA RULERS

Inca history divides into two stages: the Legendary and Historical Periods. The Incas' oral history lists 13 emperors (Incas) with the first six from Manco Cápac to Viracocha being mythical. Events from Pachacútec to Atahualpa's reign are more precisely recorded.

Bridges were made from plaited grass and roads were paved with stones.

Manco Cápac, *the first Inca, is said to have emerged from Lake Titicaca or a cave at Pacariqtambo and led his ayllu (clan) to found the city of Cusco. He married one of his sisters, Mama Ocllo, to establish the royal Inca bloodline.*

Pachacútec Inca Yupanqui (1438–71), *the ninth Inca who many consider to be the first true Inca. He was also their greatest ruler. He transformed Cusco into an empire, implementing a comprehensive code of laws to reign over his far-flung domain.*

Atahualpa (1502–33), *the 13th and last emperor, was the illegitimate son of Huayna Cápac. When the old emperor died, the kingdom was divided between Atahualpa, who ruled from Quito, and Huáscar, the legitimate heir, who ruled from Cusco. Atahualpa defeated his half-brother in a ruinous civil war over control of the kingdom.*

Conquest and assimilation *was achieved due to the Incas' highly developed social and economic system. They expanded through political alliances and conquest.*

LURE OF GOLD

Gold was the "sweat of the sun" for the Incas and by law it belonged only to the emperor. It was the legend of this gold and silver that brought the Spanish conquistadores to the Inca land. They collected 11 tons in gold artifacts alone as ransom for the release of Atahualpa.

Gold pieces from a belt

Decorated headpiece

A pair of llamas

The Incas created walls without mortar, and they have withstood centuries of earthquakes.

POWER CENTER

Power was centered in Cusco and a strict social structure was imposed. To ensure complete control, entire populations were moved so as to destroy any local power base. The empire, a theocracy, was ruled by the Inca, who was considered divine.

THE CÁPAC ÑAN (ROYAL ROAD)

Roads were crucial to Pachacútec's program of unification. Under his reign alone, the Incas constructed some 2,500 miles (4,000 km) of tightly packed stone roads, some scaling heights of more than 16,500 ft (5,000 m). This impressive Cápac Ñan network of roads, about 3 ft (1 m) wide, connected all four regions of the empire, running from Quito in Ecuador, past Santiago in Chile and La Paz in Bolivia to Tucuman in Argentina.

Message to the king delivered on a quipu

The Conchucos-Jauja section of the road is considered the most well-preserved stretch along the Cápac Ñan.

The fish trail enabled fresh fish to reach Cusco in less than two days.

The Spanish arrival was viewed by Atahualpa as a curiosity rather than a threat. Pizarro's men ambushed Atahualpa, held him for ransom and finally executed him in 1533. His enemies aligned with the Spanish to avenge their former oppressors.

EXPLORATION AND CONQUEST

In 1524, the conquistador Francisco Pizarro, along with the soldier Diego de Almagro, and the priest Hernando de Luque, set out to explore and conquer "Birú", a legendary kingdom rich in gold and silver situated south of present-day Colombia and Ecuador.

Although the first expeditions resulted in high casualties, Pizarro returned to Spain with impressive stories and booty to prove

Pizarro asking Charles I for the authority to conquer Peru

the existence of the fabulous yet undiscovered "El Dorado". In 1529, Charles I authorized him to conquer Peru and appointed him Governor and Captain-General. When Pizarro landed in Tumbes in 1532, the Inca Atahualpa was involved in a war with his brother Huáscar over succession, a situation Pizarro felt he could exploit.

The Spanish invasion was one of the first and bloodiest clashes between the Old and the New Worlds. Pizarro easily entered Cajamarca and captured and later executed Atahualpa, in an act of great treachery. With the Inca's death, Pizarro was able to conquer the leaderless empire with the support of the regional kingdoms of Chimú, Huanca, and Chanca. Huáscar's younger brother, Túpac Huallpa, was crowned to legitimize Pizarro's plans to seize and sack Cusco. When he was poisoned, another brother, Manco Inca, became the puppet emperor.

Humiliated after the fall of Cusco, Manco Inca led a revolt in 1536 that almost annihilated the Spaniards defending the city. Manco later took advantage of the rivalry between Pizarro and Almagro to establish a parallel court in the inaccessible mountains of Vilcabamba. After his death in 1544, the rebel Inca state passed on to his sons.

THE COLONIAL WORLD

Political turmoil and rivalry did not stop with the execution of Almagro in 1538, which led to the assassination of Pizarro in 1541 by Almagro loyalists, including his son Diego, who was proclaimed the new governor. However, within a year an emissary from the court of King Charles I, Cristóbal Vaca de Castro, aided by a pro-Pizarro army, crushed the Almagrists at Chupas in 1542.

The Spanish conquest and colonization (1532–1821), driven by the lure of gold and evangelical zeal, tore apart the society and created a divide

Inca Atahualpa captured by Spanish soldiers

TIMELINE

1525 Huayna Cápac dies and his son, Huáscar succeeds; war with Atahualpa

1533 Atahualpa tried and executed; Cusco sacked

1541 Almagro's son kills Pizarro

1572 After fierce fighting Túpac Amaru I is captured, tried, and executed

Potosí mines

1500   1550   1600   1650

1532 Pizarro lands in Tumbes with 168 men, meets Atahualpa and captures him

1535 Pizarro founds Lima on January 18

1600 Potosí mines reach population peak with 160,000 people

Francisco Pizarro

between the victorious colonizers and defeated natives. The conquistadores introduced the language and religion that most Peruvians still speak and adhere to, and the economic classes they established survive to this day.

The feudal *encomienda* system they introduced resulted in colossal abuses and produced immense inequalities. To curtail the abuses by the conquistadores the Spanish king issued new laws. From 1542 to 1548 the new colony was in the throes of a civil war between the conquistadores, who saw their livelihoods under threat, and the Viceroyalty. Viceroy Francisco de Toledo reintroduced the Inca *mit'a* tax in 1574, forcing Indians to work unpaid, to their death, in mines such as the Huancavelica mercury mine and Potosí silver mine. Mindful of an Indian rebellion, Toledo had Manco Cápac's son executed in 1571. Two hundred years later Túpac Amaru II, a descendant of the last Inca, Atahualpa, staged an uprising which spread throughout Peru. Though he was captured and executed in 1781, the Indians continued their fight against the Spanish until 1783.

José de San Martín
(1778–1850)

PERUVIAN INDEPENDENCE
With the abdication of Spain's King Charles IV in the early 1800s, thoughts of independence spread throughout South America. In 1821, José de San Martín, who liberated Argentina and Chile, defeated the royalist forces in Peru and proclaimed its independence on July 28, 1821. San Martín then met Venezuelan general Símon Bolivar,

liberator of Venezuela, Colombia, and Ecuador, and ceded control. Peru finally gained complete independence from Spain in 1824 after crucial battles in Junín and Ayacucho.

Cross border bickering put an end to Bolivar's vision of a union of states, though Peru and Bolivia did form a confederation from 1836–39. In the 40 years after independence, the presidency changed hands 35 times and 15 different constitutions were produced. Only four presidents were constitutionally chosen during the time. Despite the political mayhem, there was money to be made. Humble dried seabird droppings (guano) became big business. It was the main export to America and Europe and even sparked the Peruvian-Spanish War in 1866 when Spain occupied the guano-rich Chincha Islands. Peru was again at war in 1879, but this time with Chile, a conflict that saw parts of the country occupied and some territory lost.

Guano being loaded on boats at Chincha Islands

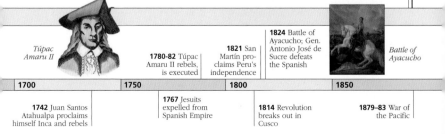

Túpac Amaru II	**1780-82** Túpac Amaru II rebels, is executed	**1821** San Martín proclaims Peru's independence	**1824** Battle of Ayacucho; Gen. Antonio José de Sucre defeats the Spanish	*Battle of Ayacucho*
1700	**1750**	**1800**		**1850**
1742 Juan Santos Atahualpa proclaims himself Inca and rebels	**1767** Jesuits expelled from Spanish Empire	**1814** Revolution breaks out in Cusco	**1879–83** War of the Pacific	

The War of the Pacific (1879–83)

The Guerra del Pacifico was sparked off by a dispute over control of the nitrate-rich beds of the northern Atacama Desert on the Pacific coast. It was fought between Chile and the joint forces of Bolivia and Peru, and it remains a thorny issue, dividing historians, politicians, and ordinary citizens even today. The price which Chile extracted from its defeated neighbors has perpetuated a bitter rivalry and dislike among the affected nations. Bolivia lost its sea access leaving it landlocked, while Peru ceded substantial territory and endured widespread pillaging by the conquering Chilean forces. The rivalry was most apparent with pisco, a brandy over which both countries claimed exclusive rights to produce till 2005 *(see p289)*.

Bust of Admiral Miguel Grau, the "Knight of the Seas"

The Battle of Iquique *(then in Peru, now in Chile) caused Peru to suffer a huge loss on May 21, 1879, when its warship, the* Independencia, *was sunk.*

CAPTURE OF LIMA

On January 17, 1881, when Chilean forces captured the capital, looting followed and much of Chorrillos and Miraflores was set on fire. Chilean soldiers took thousands of Peru's most valuable books from the National Library back to Chile where they remain even today.

THE HEROIC *HUÁSCAR*

Victory in the War of the Pacific was contingent on the command of the seas, and the Chilean fleet was considered superior to the Peruvian. With the loss of *Independencia* in the Battle of Iquique, the iron-clad warship *Huáscar* was all that stood between Peru and Chilean domination. Refusing to concede that Peru was facing naval defeat, the

The battle between the Peruvian battleship *Huáscar* and the Chilean forces

commander of the ship, Admiral Miguel Grau, launched a series of daring raids against the Chilean fleet. He broke through the Chilean block-ade of Callao three times, capturing transport ships and severely interrupting Chile's communi-cation lines. Chilean ships pursued the *Huáscar* and finally, on October 8 near Punta Angamos, the Chilean fleet surrounded the Peruvian ship, opened fire and destroyed the bridge, killing Grau. The Chileans prevented the surrendering officers from sinking the *Huáscar* and instead had the boat repaired and refitted, using it to attack the Peruvians at Arica in February 1880.

The Saltpetre War *was fought for control of nitrate fields, including sodium nitrate (salt-petre) and guano, operated by Chile in Peruvian and Bolivian territories. In the 1870s, with the rising demand for nitrates, a key ingredient in fertilizers and explosives, Bolivia tried to tax the Chilean companies operating in Bolivia. When Chile refused, Bolivia declared war in 1879 and asked Peru for aid.*

Fallen heroes *from the War of the Pacific are buried in the Panteón de los Próceres in Lima's Presbítero Maestro cemetery. Over its entrance are the words "La Nación a sus Defensores" (From the Nation to its Defenders).*

PERU

Lake Titicaca

BOLIVIA

Tacna

Arica

Lake Poopó

Iquique

CHILE

Calama

Paposo

ARGENTINA

DISPUTED TERRITORY

	Returned to Peru 1929
	Awarded to Chile 1929
	Awarded to Chile 1883
	Bolivia awards to Chile 1883
	Bolivia awards to Chile 1874
—	Present international boundary
---	Disputed area boundary

Tense relations *with Chile continue. In 1975, Peruvian president General Juan Velasco Alvarado was close to declaring war on Chile in order to regain the two lost Peruvian territories – Arica and Tarapacá. The two nations are currently embroiled in a dispute over fishing waters in the Pacific.*

Victor Raúl Haya de la Torre, founder of APRA

DEMOCRACY & DICTATORS

After the War of the Pacific, Peru oscillated between democracy and military dictatorship. In 1920, Augusto Leguía, who had assumed the presidency in a coup in 1919, introduced a new constitution which gave the state wide-ranging power and also allowed him to run unopposed for re-election. His crackdown on worker militancy coupled with the Russian and Mexican Revolutions spawned dissent, prompting exiled political leader Victor Raúl Haya de la Torre in 1924 to form the Alianza Popular Revolucionaria Americana (APRA), a workers' party which today still exerts tremendous influence on politics.

Alan Garcia with his party (APRA) flag

General Juan Velasco Alvarado seized power in 1968 and immediately suspended the constitution, nationalized mines, banks, factories, oil companies, and the media, and pushed for a more independent foreign policy. Intending to impose a "controlled revolution," he confiscated large privately-owned land holdings (haciendas), transferring them to worker co-ops as part of a wide-ranging *Reforma Agraria*. He also proclaimed Quechua as the official second language. This restructuring, however, wreaked havoc on the economy and led to his ousting in 1975.

In 1980, the first fully democratic election in Peru brought Fernando Belaúnde Terry to power for a second time. Intent on privatizing industry and boosting exports, Belaúnde's term was severely hampered by high inflation, rising drug trafficking, and the threat of guerrilla movements.

Accumulated inflation and corruption too plagued Alan Garcia's presidency (1985–1990). Accused of embezzlement, Garcia fled Peru in 1992 exiling himself to Colombia and then France.

GUERRILLA TACTICS

The growth of the Maoist terrorist movement Sendero Luminoso (Shining Path) and the Marxist Movimiento Revolucionario Túpac Amaru (MRTA) led to a bloodthirsty internal war between 1980 and 2000. According to the Truth and Reconciliation Commission, some 70,000 Peruvians were killed during this period by both the terrorists and the military forces fighting them. When two car bombs exploded in Lima's middle-class Miraflores in July 1992, the Fujimori government stepped up its anti-terror crackdown.

TIMELINE

1919–30 Leguía's 11-year civil dictatorship, marked by strong foreign investment and restriction of civil rights

Peruvian soldiers, led by Luis Sanchez Cerro, revolted against Leguía's reign in 1930

1955 Women get to vote for the first time

| 1900 | 1920 | 1940 | 1960 |

1914–18 World War I affects Peru's economy, brings in recession

1941 Peru enters a seven-week war over disputed border territories with Ecuador

Within two months, Abimael Guzmán, Sendero Luminoso's founder, was captured and tried by a military court behind closed doors. The sentence of life imprisonment he received was sanctioned by a civilian court in 2006.

On December 17, 1996, the MRTA seized the Japanese Embassy in Lima and took 452 guests hostage, including President Fujimori's brother and other officials. Over the months several hostages were released. Finally, on April 22, 1997, all but one of the 72 remaining hostages were rescued in a dramatic raid by Peruvian commandos. All 14 rebels, one hostage, and two soldiers were killed in the assault.

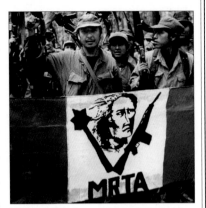

MRTA, behind the Japanese Embassy hostage crisis

THE RISE AND FALL OF FUJIMORI

Guzmán's capture and the successful release of the hostages increased the popularity of Alberto Fujimori, who had been sworn in as president on July 28, 1990. Under his stewardship inflation dropped to 20 percent, the currency stabilized, and a series of arrests decimated Sendero Luminoso. Fujimori took office for an unprecedented third time in 2000. However, when an explosive bribery scandal involving his former spy chief came to light, he fled and faxed through his resignation as president from Japan.

Alejandro Toledo, first president of native descent

In 2007, Fujimori was extradited to Peru to face charges of corruption and human rights abuses. He was tried and sentenced to 25 years in prison.

PERU TODAY

In 2001, Alejandro Toledo defeated Alan Garcia to become the first elected Peruvian president of Indian descent. Taking over a country mired in political scandal, the former shoe-shine boy turned World Bank economist steered Peru to strong economic growth (6.5 percent) and an export boom. Toledo's five-year term, however, was dogged by scandals.

When ex-president Alan Garcia returned to power in 2006, a period of strong economic growth made Peru one of the most successful economies in the region. Although poverty was reduced, it still remained high however, and social conflicts increased amid corruption scandals.

In 2011, nationalist Ollanta Humala, was elected president by a narrow margin on a platform of social reform, social inclusion, and a greater government role in development.

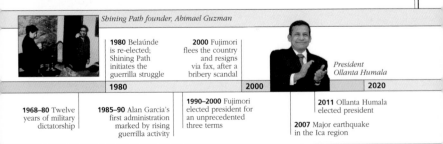

Shining Path founder, Abimael Guzman

1980 Belaúnde is re-elected; Shining Path initiates the guerrilla struggle

2000 Fujimori flees the country and resigns via fax, after a bribery scandal

President Ollanta Humala

| 1980 | | 2000 | | 2020 |

1968–80 Twelve years of military dictatorship

1985–90 Alan Garcia's first administration marked by rising guerrilla activity

1990–2000 Fujimori elected president for an unprecedented three terms

2007 Major earthquake in the Ica region

2011 Ollanta Humala elected president

LIMA AREA BY AREA

LIMA AT A GLANCE 56–57
CENTRAL LIMA 58–73
MIRAFLORES & SAN ISIDRO 74–83
BARRANCO 84–91
FARTHER AFIELD 92–99
SHOPPING IN LIMA 100–101
ENTERTAINMENT IN LIMA 102–103
STREET FINDER 104–111

Lima at a Glance

Intihuatana statue

Lima is a city of contrasts, culture, and commotion. Jugglers, fire-eaters, and street-sellers scamper through traffic that idles down streets flanked by Colonial mansions, pre-Inca ruins, historic churches, and museums full of treasures. Long maligned as nothing more than the gateway to Peru, Lima is a fascinating destination in itself. Central Lima is the city's pounding heart, Barranco is the bohemian *barrio*, Miraflores is a restaurant, hotel, and club haven, and San Isidro is the elegant business district complete with an ancient olive grove.

LOCATOR MAP

La Catedral (see p62), *considered a masterpiece of Colonial architecture, has been re-constructed several times since the 16th century due to earthquakes.*

CENTRAL LIMA
(see pp58–73)

FARTHER AFIELD, LIMA
(see pp92–99)

Museo Larco Harrera *(see p94)* has more than 40,000 ceramics, including erotic Moche creations.

0 km   10
0 miles   10

Museo de la Nación (see p95) *features re-creations of the magnificent Lord of Sipán tombs, as well as ceramics and textiles from different civilizations.*

San Francisco *church and convent* (see pp64–6) *was developed by the Spanish as a place for worship and education. The 17th-century structure houses famous paintings including a* Last Supper *with guinea pig and "Passion of Christ" series by Rubens. The main attraction is the catacombs where city residents were buried until the early 1800s.*

Huaca Pucllana (see pp80–81) *is the site of the remains of a pre-Inca adobe pyramid complex and includes a museum of Wari culture.*

Parque Kennedy (see p78) *is famous for the market set up by artists who come here to sell their wares. The park is also a favorite meeting place for locals at the weekend.*

MIRAFLORES & SAN ISIDRO *(see pp74–83)*

0 km   3

0 miles   3

BARRANCO *(see pp84–91)*

Parque Municipal (see p88) *is known for the striking Biblioteca Municipal, its beautiful marble statue of the Daughter of Venus, and a lively, bohemian nightlife of bars and discos.*

CENTRAL LIMA

Founded by Francisco Pizarro in 1535, Lima was the capital of the Spanish Empire in South America for almost two centuries. Dubbed the City of Kings, it was at the time the most important metropolis in the region, the center of power and wealth. Its coat of arms bears three crowns, representing the three kings of the nativity, and the motto proclaiming, "this is truly the sign of kings." Based on a Roman plan, the original 117 city blocks radiate out from

Statue at Casa de Aliaga

Plaza Mayor, where the imposing presence of both church and state accent its pivotal role. Centuries-old streets house buildings dating mainly from Colonial times as an earthquake in 1746 razed most original structures. Private homes have since morphed into museums or government offices. Fervent devotion to the Catholic doctrine, introduced by the Spanish, means there is a Baroque-, Renaissance-, or Rococo-inspired church or convent on almost every street corner.

SIGHTS AT A GLANCE

Historic Buildings
Casa de Aliaga ❸
Palacio de Gobierno ❷

Churches and Monasteries
La Catedral ❶
Convento de los Descalzos ❾
Las Nazarenas ❿
San Francisco pp64–6 ❹
San Pedro ❻
Santo Domingo ❼

Squares and Parks
Parque de la Muralla ❺
Plaza San Martín ⓫

Museums and Galleries
Museo Andrés del Castillo ⓬
Museo de Arte ⓮
Museo de Arte Italiano ⓭
Museo Nacional de la Cultura Peruana ⓯
Museo Taurino ❽

SEE ALSO
- **Where to Stay** p270
- **Where to Eat** p290

GETTING AROUND
Buses and *combis* run from Miraflores and Barranco to Central Lima. Use only council-sanctioned or registered yellow cabs (*see p333*).

KEY

	Street-by-street area pp60–61
🚉	Railroad station
ℹ	Visitor information
✝	Church
⊠	Post office

LOCATOR MAP

◁ **Wooden balconies of the Archbishop's Palace, Plaza Mayor**

Street-by-Street: Plaza Mayor

Formerly called the Plaza de Armas, it was here that Francisco Pizarro founded Lima. Major institutions such as La Catedral, the Palacio Arzobispal (Archbishop's Palace), the Municipalidad (Town Hall), and the Palacio de Gobierno (Government Palace) were established here and today they form the city's historic center. The plaza has witnessed

Detail of statue in bronze fountain

many significant historical events including the first bullfight, the execution of those condemned by the Spanish Inquisition, and the declaration of Peru's independence in 1821. The large bronze fountain in the center, erected in 1651, is the square's oldest feature.

Palacio de Gobierno
The president's residence was remodeled and inaugurated in 1938. ❷

Casa de Aliaga
This oldest piece of family-owned real estate on the continent was built on top of an Inca shrine in 1535. ❸

Municipalidad

★ **Casa Riva-Agüero**
Named after the original owner, writer Don José de la Riva Agüero, this 19th-century casa houses archives, a fine library, and the Museo de Arte Popular (Folk Art Museum). It is now run by Lima's Catholic University.

The bronze fountain was commissioned by the Count of Salvatierra, and Viceroy of Peru, in 1650.

STAR SIGHTS

- ★ Casa Riva-Agüero
- ★ La Catedral
- ★ Palacio Arzobispal

0 meters   50
0 yards   50

Jirón de la Unión links Plaza Mayor with Plaza San Martín via a busy pedestrian thoroughfare.

★ **Palacio Arzobispal**
Home to the Archbishop of Lima, the Archbishop's Palace was reconstructed in 1924. It is famed for the Moorish-style carved balconies that decorate its imposing and ornate façade.

The Museum of Religious Art and Treasures is in the Cathedral.

★ **La Catedral**
Ambitious building plans combined with earthquakes saw the rebuilding of Lima Cathedral several times, until it was finally reconstructed in 1758. The choir chairs are one of the greatest works of Peruvian art. ❶

Museo Del Banco Central de la Reserva
Specializing in pre-Columbian archaeology, the museum displays 19th- and 20th-century Peruvian art. There's also an exhibition of Peru's currency.

Iglesia de la Merced is where Lima's first Latin mass was held.

LAMPA

UCAYALI

MIRÓ QUESADA

Palacio Torre Tagle
Considered the best representation of 18th-century Lima architecture, it was built in 1735. It is famed for its carved wooden balcony and finely worked stone entrance.

KEY

– – – Suggested route

La Catedral dominates the east view, Plaza Mayor

La Catedral ❶

Plaza Mayor. **Map** 1 F1. **Tel** 01 427 9647. 🕐 9am–4:30pm Mon–Sat. 📷 🎫 🔊 📷 with flash. 📷 📷 Corpus Christi (9th Thu after Easter).

With its imposing twin towers, the Cathedral dominates the eastern side of Plaza Mayor. Conquistador and founder of Lima, Francisco Pizarro (1478–1541) carried the first log for the construction of the original adobe wall and the straw roof structure on this site in 1535.

Construction began on the current Baroque-Renaissance-style structure in 1564. However, work stalled due to lack of funds and the devastating earthquakes of 1687 and 1746. The reconstruction ended in 1758, but it had to be rebuilt after the destructive earthquake of 1940.

The Cathedral has five naves and 10 side chapels, with the smaller ones dedicated to religious figures. The chapel of John the Baptist has a carving of Jesus, said to be the most beautiful in the Americas. The remains of Francisco Pizarro lie in the mosaic-covered chapel to the right of the entrance. A headless body thought to be his languished in the crypt until tests in 1990 proved that wrong remains were on display.

The ornate choir stalls, carved by 17th-century Spanish sculptor, Pedro Noguera, are a highlight, along with the gold-leaf altars and religious museum with its collection of art.

Intricately carved wooden portable altar, La Catedral

Palacio de Gobierno ❷

Plaza Mayor. **Map** 1 F1. **Tel** 01 311 3900. 🛈 PR office, Jirón de la Unión. 🕐 visits are currently restricted; call ahead for opening times. Changing of the Guard 11:45am daily.

Known as the Casa de Pizarro, the Government Palace was built by Pizarro on the land once owned by Taulichusco, a pre-Hispanic chief of the Rimac Valley. It has been the seat of political power in Peru ever since, undergoing major reconstruction in the 1920s and 1930s following a fire.

Inaugurated in 1938, the palace is a grand example of Colonial affluence. Rooms are festooned with mahogany and cedar carvings, French glass, Carrera marble, and Czech crystal. A marble staircase dominates the Grand Hall, which is flanked by busts of key figures in Peru's history.

The gilded Salon Dorado (Golden Room) is modeled on Versailles Palace's Hall of Mirrors, while the dining hall takes its cue from local life.

Casa de Aliaga ❸

Jirón de la Unión, 224. **Map** 1 F1. **Tel** 01 427 7736. 🕐 9:30am–1pm, 2:30–5:45pm daily. 📷

The *quincha* (earthquake resistant material) mansion was built by Jerónimo de Aliaga, one of Pizarro's lieutenants. It is the oldest and best preserved home in the continent and is owned by the same family 17 generations later.

The ornate balcony offers the only clue to the lavish 66-room house. Marble stairs lead to the second floor patio and the main entrance. The part open to the public showcases Colonial art and decor from the 16th to 18th century such as Louis XIV mirrors and furniture, family portraits, and Cusco School paintings. One of the two Andalusian patios has a bronze fountain.

Paintings and Seville tiles adorn the interior of Casa de Aliaga

Colonial Architecture

Spanish and indigenous design often merges in Colonial architecture, resulting in a kind of Creole style. The Moorish influence, which crossed into Spain from North Africa and was then transplanted to the Americas, is discernible in the Mudéjar style (Arabic patterns that appear in decorative details). Two such impressive Colonial buildings are the Casa de Aliaga, built by Jerónimo de Aliaga, and the Santo Domingo church (see p67), built by friar Vicente de Valverde. These two friends of Pizarro were with him on his conquest of Peru and he bestowed on them the choicest plots of land near Plaza Mayor. The old quarter of the city originally mapped out by Pizarro – *el damero de Pizarro* (Pizarro's chessboard) – is now a UNESCO Mankind Heritage Site.

Chapel, Casa de Aliaga

CASA DE ALIAGA

Dating back from 1535, this mansion displays an outstanding array of Colonial art and decor.

Paintings from the Cusco School are interspersed with Aliaga family portraits.

Furniture, *paintings, and porcelain from Spain, Asia, and Peru add to the elegance of the mansion's decor.*

Arabesque-style tiles add color and detail to the second floor balcony.

Tiles were always used in the patios, modeled after Seville houses.

Courtyards commonly featured a second floor wooden balcony.

The Dining Room *has a coffered ceiling with intricately carved squares. It also showcases original period furniture and artwork.*

FEATURES OF COLONIAL ARCHITECTURE

Enclosed wooden balconies are very much a trait of Colonial Lima, along with ornamental doorways, painted façades, glazed Seville tiles, high ceilings, imposing stairways, and an inner courtyard.

Palacio de Torre Tagle, *built in 1730, features two intricately carved wooden balconies made of Nicaraguan cedar and a Panamanian stone entrance.*

Casa de Osambela Oquendo, *with its four levels, is Colonial Lima's tallest house. Built between 1803 and 1807, its elaborate street-front balconies reflect the Mudéjar style.*

Iglesia San Pedro *offers the best preserved example of early Colonial religious architecture.*

San Francisco

Plaster relief on column

The striking yellow and white Colonial complex of San Francisco comprises a church, a convent, the chapels of La Soledad and El Milagro, and eerie catacombs. The original mud and wood church constructed in 1557 was destroyed in the 1656 earthquake, and the rebuilt church was completed in 1672 by Portuguese architect Constantino de Vasconcellos. The façade is one of the best examples of 17th-century Baroque architecture in Peru. Original blue tiles from Seville decorate the convent cloisters and patio, and the library is home to centuries-old manuscripts and books.

Glazed Sevillan Tiles
Lima's largest collection of blue tiles from Seville, dating back to 1620, line the cloisters.

Convent Cloister and Garden
The tiled patio has a machimbrado ceiling (wooden pieces fitted together without nails) made from mahogany, and the walls are painted with frescoes.

The wooden dome was constructed in 1625.

Fountain

★ Baroque Church Façade
Two towers flank a stone altarpiece-portal, a lavish mass of sculptures, frontispieces, niches, windows, and pilasters dating from 1664.

★ Convent Library
This 17th-century library houses more than 20,000 books from the 15th–18th centuries including many first editions and parchments.

The High Altar
*Designed by the
renowned Spanish
architect, Presbítero
Matías Maestro, this
impressive structure,
entirely carved in a
Neo-Classical style, is
complemented by the
Mudéjar ceiling.*

The convent cloisters
feature a wall fresco
on the life of Saint
Francis of Assisi.

Earthquake-resistant *quincha*
– a mix of rushes, mud, and
plaster – was used to
construct the entire church.

The Church interior
features three 7-span
aisles, a transept, and
a presbytery.

Painting of the *Last Supper*
The 1656 painting of the Last Supper, *with the apostles
supping on guinea pig (see p66) and drinking from
golden* keros *(Inca cups), adorns the Dining Hall.*

★ Catacombs
*The church is built on
a network of inter-
connected underground
tunnels or catacombs
which were used as a
cemetery during the
Colonial period.*

STAR SIGHTS

★ Baroque Church
  Façade

★ Catacombs

★ Convent Library

Exploring San Francisco

Detail of carved convent ceiling

In 1535, Emperor Charles I ordered Francisco Pizarro to put aside two sites in Lima so that the Franciscans could build a church and convent. Located on the banks of the Río Rimac, the sites were approximately one eighth the area of the city, the largest in the New World. The best artists of the day, from silversmiths to sculptors to wood-carvers, were brought in to add decoration. A factory was organized to produce *azulejos* (painted tiles).

Interior of the church of San Francisco

Church and Convent

With the exception of the stone altarpiece-portal and the lateral portal, the church is made of the earthquake-resistant *quincha* (a mix of rushes, mud, and plaster). The architectural layout is simple, with three 7-span aisles, a transept, and a presbytery. Detailed decorative patterns can be seen on the altarpieces, façade, domes,

and towers. The carved saints and lectern in the friar's choir are superb examples of Baroque sculpture.

Being the preferred place of worship for the Spanish viceroy and his court, the church received generous donations, especially from the gold and silver mines of Peru that were under Spanish control. Thus, it amassed a valuable collection of treasures.

Unfortunately, some of these vanished during the wars of independence in the 19th century, though some remarkable works of art, architecture, and literature remain. The first dictionary published by the Real Spanish Academia is housed in the convent library. The beautiful courtyards with tiled walls, frescoes, paintings, and ornate woodwork are highlights of the convent.

Religious Museum

The Religious Museum has a series of the "Passion of Christ" paintings from the workshop of 17th-century Flemish painter, Peter-Paul Rubens, in Antwerp. Portraits of the apostles from the studio of Francisco Zurbarán, the famous Spanish painter, hang in the Zurbarán Room.

Though the Catholic church was vicious in its suppression of indigenous religious icons, insisting local artists copy European images, some distinctly Andean touches can be seen in the works of art.

The Catacombs

The bone-packed crypt, the site of an estimated 70,000 burials, features rows of bones, along with a circle of skulls and femurs deep in a well. Bodies were laid on top of each other, dusted with lime, and once decayed, the bones were sorted and stored.

Azulejos on a wall of the convent cloister, San Francisco

GUINEA PIG SUPPER

Guinea pigs are integral to Peruvian life and millions are eaten every year. No special occasion is complete without one and evidence shows that guinea pigs were domesticated in Peru as far back as 2500 BC. Guaman Poma de Ayala

Last Supper by Marcos Zapata (18th century)

(1550–1616) reported that the Incas sacrificed 1,000 guinea pigs and 100 llamas in Cusco's plaza each year for the safety of their fields. When Spanish priests ordered Geronimo de Loayza, Lima's first bishop (1545–75), to conduct an extermination of guinea pigs he refused, fearing a rebellion. Small wonder that San Francisco's *Last Supper*, painted by Marcos Zapata, shows Jesus and his 12 disciples sitting down to *cuy chactado* (roast guinea pig), with papaya and *chicha* (corn beer) in Inca cups.

For hotels and restaurants in this area see p270 and p290

Parque de la Muralla ❺

Jirón Amazonas and Av. Abancay.
Map 1 F1. **Tel** 01 427 4125.
◯ 9am–9pm daily. 🖼 ♿ ▣

Situated behind the Iglesia San Francisco, next to the river Rimac, this park exhibits the remains of a 17th-century wall that once protected the city from pirates and enemies of the Spanish crown. The park also contains a small exhibition of maps, prints, and artifacts, as well as a statue of Francisco Pizarro.

San Pedro ❻

Jirón Ucayali, 451. **Map** 1 F2.
Tel 01 428 3017. ◯ 9:30–11:45am,
5–6pm daily. ✝

The only church in Lima with three entrances (normally a feature of cathedrals), the small church of San Pedro is considered to be one of the finest examples of early Colonial architecture in the city. Built in 1636, it was conse-crated two years later. Inspired by the Jesuit's Church of Jesus in Rome, it has three naves.

The restrained exterior sits in stark contrast to the inte-rior, which is opulent. It is adorned with Churriguresque (Spanish Baroque) and gilded altars, along with gilded carv-ings of the founders of vari-ous religious orders, and Moorish balconies. The side chapels, with their superb glazed tiles, are awash with paintings from the Lima, Quito, and Cusco Schools.

The impressive golden main altar, designed by priest Matiás Maestro (1760–1835), features columns, balconies, and sculpted figures.

A painting of the coronation of the Virgin Mary by Bernardo Bitti (1548–1610), who wor-ked with Michelangelo in Italy and supervised the construc-tion of San Pedro, hangs in the beautifully tiled sacristy.

SANTA ROSA DE LIMA (1586–1617)

The Americas' first saint, Lima-born Isabel Flores de Oliva was nicknamed "Rose" due to her beauty. Isabel used pain to focus solely on God and rubbed hot peppers on her cheeks to make herself less attractive. She joined the Third Order of St Dominic and her penance became more persistent. She fasted constantly and reportedly slept on a bed of broken glass, wore a spiked metal crown covered by roses, and an iron chain around her waist. Working tirelessly for Lima's poor, she advocated rights for indigenous people. Sanctuario de Santa Rosa de Lima, built near the house she was born in, has a chapel, a lemon orchard, and the well where she threw the key of the chain she always wore. Thousands flock here on August 30 tossing letters into the well, asking for her help.

Statue of Santa Rosa de Lima

Santo Domingo ❼

Cnr of Conde de Superunda and Camaná. **Map** 1 E1. **Tel** 01 427 6793.
◯ 9am–12:30pm, 3–6pm Mon–Sat, 9am–1pm Sun & pub hols. 🖼 🎥 ✝

Glazed tiles, San Pedro

Construction of the Santo Domingo church began in 1540, a few years after Francisco Pizarro granted the land to Dominican friar Vicente de Valverde, who was with him during his conquest of Peru. Pizarro had sent Valverde to meet the Inca ruler Atahualpa *(see p46)* in Cajamarca as he wanted him to try and convert the Inca to Christianity or face a war with the Spanish. However, Valverde failed.

Work was not completed on the church until the late 16th century.

The church features superbly carved cedar choir stalls, an imposing dome, and the *Retablo de las Reliquias*, an altar with relics of three Dominican Peruvians who attained sainthood – Santa Rosa de Lima, San Martin de Porras (1579–1639), and San Juan Masias (1585–1645). The alabaster statue of Santa Rosa was presented by Pope Clement in 1669.

To the right of the church tower are the chapel and the convent cloisters, said to be the best preserved in Lima.

The **Universidad Nacional Mayor de San Marcos** (the San Marcos University), the first in South America, was founded here in 1551. It still has a campus in downtown Lima.

View of the convent's courtyard, Santo Domingo

Colonial painting of the Three Kings, Convento de los Descalzos

Museo Taurino ❽

Hualgayoc 332. *Tel* 01 482 3360.
◯ 8:30am–4:30pm Mon–Fri. 🎟

Lima's main bullring, the
Plaza de Acho, was founded
in 1768 by Viceroy Amat y
Juniet and is the oldest bullring in the Americas. Naturally
enough, the Museo Taurino,
located next to the plaza,
pays tribute to centuries of
clashes between man and
the horned beast.

There are brave bull's heads
mounted on walls, photo-
graphs of matadors flourishing
their capes perilously close to
the animals, a bloodstained
costume worn by a Spanish
matador who was gored to
death in the Lima ring, swords,
capes, matador suits, and
posters. Also of interest are

the numerous *toro*-centric
(bull) paintings and drawings,
which include works by
Goya as well as Picasso, a
bullfight fanatic.

Convento de los Descalzos ❾

Alameda de los Descalzos. *Tel* 01
481 0441. ◯ 10am–1pm, 3–6pm
Tue–Sat, 11:30am–6pm Sun. 🎟
🎟 for a tip.

The Convent of the Shoeless
Ones, named after the bare-
footed Franciscan monks
who originally lived here,
was founded in 1592 by the
Corsican priest, Andres Corso.
The Franciscans lived a
silent, spartan life in this
spiritual retreat relying on
donations to meet their

needs. Missionaries, who took
over the convent in 1852, said
it breathed "poverty, order-
liness and thrift, in contrast
to the ostentation of other
religious establishments."

Today, it is home to a priceless collection of religious and
Colonial paintings from the
17th and 18th centuries, which
includes a Murillo (1617–82)
of Saint Joseph with Jesus.

The chapel has a gold
leaf altar, kitchen with wine-
making equipment, a refectory,
an infirmary, and monks' cells.
Seville tiles adorn the patio
walls and Cusco School *(see
p167)* paintings hang in the
chapel dedicated to Nuestra
Señora de la Rosa Mística.

Take a taxi and make it wait
as this area is very poor and
assaults have been known.

Las Nazarenas ❿

Cnr of Jirón Huancavelica and Av.
Tacna. **Map** 1 E1. *Tel* 01 423 5718.
◯ 7am–noon, 4–8:30pm daily.
🎟 🎟 El Señor de los Milagros (Oct
18, 19, 28).

The Church of the Nazarene
was built in the 18th century
outside the city's walls in
Pachacamilla, a neighborhood
then inhabited by freed black
slaves from Angola and
Pachacámac Indians. It was
constructed around a local
slave's painting of Christ on
an adobe wall, El Señor de los
Milagros (Lord of Miracles),
which inexplicably survived
the massive 1655 earthquake
when every other wall crumbled. The major earthquakes of
1687 and 1746 also caused it
no harm. Sensing a miracle,
people began to flock to see
the painting, and the church
sprang up at the site.

Today, behind the altar, on
the still-standing adobe wall,
is an oil replica of *The Purple
Christ*, as it is also known.

A copy of the image is paraded through Lima streets on a
one-ton silver tray during the
El Señor de los Milagros procession in October *(see p37)*.

The procession, which
takes different routes on three
different days, draws thousands of devout believers, all
dressed in purple robes.

**Traditional Chinese celebration
in a Lima neighborhood**

CHINATOWN

Between 1849 and 1874,
about 100,000 Chinese immigrants arrived in Peru to
replace African slave labor on
coastal cotton and sugarcane
plantations. As their contracts
ended many moved to Lima
settling around Calle Capón,
which became known as
Barrio Chino, one of the
Western Hemisphere's earliest
Chinatowns. They fiercely
guarded their cultural identity
and traditions, opening small
businesses, including eateries
serving Cantonese food. Now,
Peru has more than 2,000
Chinese restaurants, called
chifas, meaning "eat rice" in
Mandarin. Their influence on
local cuisine is significant – the Peruvian classic *lomo saltado*, a beef stir-fry, is served with both rice and potatoes.

The Bullfighting Festival

Lima's first bullfight took place in the Plaza Mayor in 1538, organized by city founder Francisco Pizarro, who set in motion Limeños' passion for the spectacle. The South American circuit kicks off in Peru in late-October, and sweeps through Colombia and Ecuador, ending in Venezuela in February. In Lima, the Feria Taurina del Senor de los Milagros (Bullfighting Festival for the Lord of Miracles) follows the centuries-old Spanish tradition of combining a public display of bullfighting with a saint's feast day or a village fiesta. Peruvian writer Mario Vargas Llosa reportedly never misses a bullfight during the October fair.

Bullhead in Museo Taurino

BULLFIGHT SEASON
The Lima season starts in late October and runs until early December. Celebrated matadors from the Americas and Europe fly in to flaunt their skills in Spanish-style contests – meaning that the bull is killed as a finale.

Posters *such as this one dating back to 1918 can be seen at the Museo Taurino.*

The Lord of Miracles procession, *on October 18, coincides with the start of the bullfighting season in Lima. Both events are extremely popular and attract large and enthusiastic crowds.*

Plaza de Acho, *Lima's main bullring, has a perimeter of 804 ft (245 m), a diameter of 256 ft (78 m), and can seat 13,000 people.*

Picadores *goad the bull with steel pointed lances, testing its bravery. The lances weaken the animal's shoulder muscles.*

The Lima Municipalidad (Town Hall) in the flower-filled Plaza Mayor ▷

Plaza San Martín ⓫

Map 1 E2. ♿

Built to commemorate 100 years of independence, Plaza San Martín was opened in 1921. At its center is a statue of the Argentinian liberator of Peru, General José de San Martín *(see p49)*, crossing the Andes on horseback. A statue of Madre Patria, the symbolic mother of the country, stands beneath the nation's protector and sports a rather bizarre headdress. She should have been adorned with a crown of flames, known as *llama* in Spanish. Instead she has a little Peruvian llama – the animal – sitting on her head. The double meaning of the word was obviously lost on the artist who crafted the image in Spain.

The plaza has a distinct French architectural influence which can be seen in the exclusive men-only Club Nacional and the Gran Hotel Bolivar *(see p270)*, built in 1924 to accommodate the visiting heads of state and other dignitaries who came to Lima for the celebrations of the centenary of the Battle of Ayacucho.

The pedestrianized Jirón de la Unión, lined with shops and restaurants, connects Plaza San Martín with Plaza Mayor.

Statue of General José de San Martín in Plaza San Martín

Museo Andrés del Castillo ⓬

Jiron de la Unión 1030. **Map** 1 E2. **Tel** *01 433 2831.* ⏰ *9am–6pm Wed–Mon.* ♿📷🛍🏛 **www.**madc.com.pe

Located in Casa Belén, this beautifully restored 19th-century house is home to a private museum set up in memory of Andrés del Castillo, a young student of mining engineering who died tragically in 2006. The museum has three separate exhibitions, reflecting Andrés' studies and interests. A unique and vast collection of crystallized minerals from the Peruvian Andes incorporates cabinet specimens and beautiful, museum-quality pieces, while a display of exceptional Chancay ceramics dating from AD 900 to 1400 includes many sculptures and pots. In the fascinating collection of pre-Hispanic clothing and accessories, the robes, corsets, shoes, belts, hats, wigs, and jewelry demonstrate the use of plant fibers, animal hair, human hair, feathers, and natural dyes.

Museo de Arte Italiano ⓭

Paseo de la Republica 250. **Map** 1 E3. **Tel** *01 423 9932.* ⏰ *10am–5pm Mon–Fri.* 🖼📷🏛

Designed by the Milanese architect, Gaetano Moretti (1860–1938), the Italian Art Museum was gifted to Peru, in 1921, by the Italian community living in Lima to mark the centenary of the country's independence. Inaugurated two years later, the museum has a grand white Renaissance-style façade that features the coats of arms of major Italian cities and reliefs made of marble.

EARTHQUAKES IN LIMA

Peru is prone to earthquakes due to its location on a geological fault that spans the entire length of the country and Lima has endured its fair share of earth-quakes over the centuries. The worst one occurred on October 28, 1746, when a colossal tremor rattled the country. The ground shook for four minutes – more than 15,000 people died in the capital, many vanishing in the tsunami that swallowed Callao, sinking all the boats in the harbor and reportedly carrying one vessel as far as 1 mile (2 km) inland. Lima was in ruins, with each of its 74 churches, 12 monasteries, and all except 20 of the 3,000 private houses, severely damaged. In the aftermath of the quake, one account said of Lima's 40,000 survivors that "it was not life they were living but death they were enduring." The church sent out priests exhorting citizens to "take advantage of such terrible punishment to reconcile themselves with God through penitence," while the viceroy authorized the police to hang anyone found looting or robbing. However, Lima recovered and was quickly rebuilt and most of the Colonial buildings seen today date from after 1746. Lima's last major earthquake of May 1940, demolished 23 percent of its buildings.

San Francisco church and convent, rebuilt after the 1652 earthquake

There are two detailed mosaic panels on the façade which depict some of the illustrious figures from Italian history.

Inside, there are decorative details inspired by the great Italian masters such as Donatello, Michelangelo, and Botticelli. More than 300 works by about 100 Italian artists of the 20th century are also represented here. These include a broad selection of paintings, engravings, sculptures, and drawings, as well as ceramics.

Museo de Arte ⑭

Paseo Colón 125. **Map** 1 E3.
Tel 01 204 0000. ◯ 10am–5pm Thu–Tue. 🖼 🖋 🛒 🏛
www.mali.pe

Nestled in the Parque de la Exposición and surrounded by statues and gardens, the Neo-Renaissance Palacio de la Exposición (the Palace of the Exhibition) was built in 1872 for the big industrial expo held in the city. The palace, once at the heart of Lima's most important 19th-century urban projects, is home to the city's Art Museum. It has a collection of Peruvian art, ranging from ancient ceramics and textiles to jewelry, furniture, and paintings from the last 3,000 years.

Intricate detail on Colonial-style cupboard, Museo de Arte

The Colonial Art Gallery on the second floor has several fascinating exhibits. Some of the highlights include paintings by Juan de Santa Cruz Pumacallao, Diego Quispe Tito, and Juan Zapata Inca. These paintings of the Cusco School *(see p167)* combine Andean mythology with Catholic symbols and contrast marvelously with the conventional religious parables depicted by Bernardo Bitti (1548–1610). The collection includes painted Nazca ceramics, Inca cups, and flouncy Colonial dresses.

Amphitheater in Parque de la Exposición, home to free cultural events

Also on view are portraits of wealthy 19th-century families by José Gil Castro (1785–1841) and Carlos Baca Flor (1867–1941), renowned for his paintings of eminent people such as Pope Pius XII, US banker J.P. Morgan, and famous fashion designer, Worth. Challenging contemporary works by 1960s vanguardists, such as Jesus Ruiz Durand, are also on display in this popular museum.

Parque de la Exposición, also known as the Parque de la Cultura, provides a welcome respite from the noise and bustle of Lima's traffic. The park houses an amphitheater, a children's puppet theater, and other performance areas, to give citizens free access to various cultural events taking place. The grounds also have a peaceful Japanese garden and an artificial lake dotted with paddle-boats. Monuments, such as the Chinese fountain, Seismograph, the Bizantino (Byzantine) Pavilion, and the pretty Morisco (Moorish) Pavilion, all celebrate Peru's centenary of independence.

Exercise caution here as thieves have been known to frequent the park. Avoid visiting after dark.

Museo Nacional de la Cultura Peruana ⑮

Av. Alfonso Ugarte 650. **Map** 1 D1.
Tel 01 423 5892. ◯ 10am–5pm Tue–Fri, 10am–2pm Sat. 🖼 🖋
http://museodelacultura.peru cultural.org.pe

Founded in 1946, the National Museum of Peruvian Culture was set up to conserve Peru's ethnographic heritage. The building's design was inspired by the iconography of the Tiahuanaco culture, which flourished around Lake Titicaca in 300 BC.

Folkloric and ethnographic exhibits have been gathered from all over the country, and have been divided into four sections. The one on the Amazon includes objects from the 42 different groups that inhabit the Peruvian jungles, while the Andes section displays works from Ayacucho, Cusco, Cajamarca, and Puno. The other two sections are devoted to functional and traditional objects. Folk art lovers should not miss the miniature *retablo* depicting the *marinera*, Peru's national dance, by Joaquín López Antay (1897–1981). The engraved gourds, particularly the donkey pen by Alicia Bustamante, and the geometric designs on the ceramics of the Shipibo people, are also spectacular.

MIRAFLORES & SAN ISIDRO

Founded in 1857, Miraflores today is Lima's prosperous commercial hub, boasting shopping zones, theaters, art galleries, cinemas, and the city's highest concentration of cafés. Vestiges of the area's ancient past remain, however, in the form of the Huaca Huallamarca and the Huaca Pucllana, ancient adobe pyramids dating back to AD 200 and 500 respectively. Miraflores is also known for its flowery parks,

Gaudi-esque mosaic, Parque del Amor

which regularly host craft and food markets. Despite concerns about water cleanliness, the beaches that line Miraflores' Costa Verde or Green Coast draw hordes each summer, and wet-suited surfers all year round. San Isidro is the city's garden district and features an olive grove which was established in 1560. The area is the preferred address of Lima's upper echelons.

SIGHTS AT A GLANCE

Historic Buildings
Casa Ricardo Palma ②

Museums and Galleries
ICPNA ⑥
Museo Amano ⑦
Museo Enrico Poli ⑧

Parks and Other Areas
Bosque El Olivar ⑨
Larcomar ④

Miraflores Clifftops ③
Parque Kennedy ①

Archaeological Sites and Ruins
Huaca Huallamarca ⑩
Huaca Pucllana pp80–81 ⑤

SEE ALSO

• *Where to Stay* pp270–71

• *Where to Eat* pp290–92

LOCATOR MAP

KEY

▨ Street-by-street area
  pp76–7

🛈 Visitor information

✝ Church

⊠ Post office

GETTING AROUND

Buses and *combis* operate from Central Lima to Miraflores. Walking is the best way to get around Miraflores. Use taxis from registered companies or council-sanctioned yellow cabs (*see p333*). The road along the Costa Verde is considered unsafe to stroll along.

0 meters   750
0 yards   750

◁ Mosaic wall at Parque del Amor, Miraflores Clifftops

Street-by-Street: Miraflores

When feminist and grandmother to Paul Gauguin, Flora Tristán, visited Lima in the 1830s, she wrote that Miraflores was "the most beautiful village" she had visited in South America. Some of the village atmosphere still remains, particularly around Parque Central, a key gathering place for locals and visitors. Between the main shopping artery, Avenida Larco, and traffic-heavy Diagonal, the park offers space for quiet contemplation. Miraflores earned the tag Ciudad Heroica (Heroic City), which appears on vendor carts and signs, after the War of the Pacific fought against Chile in 1881 *(see pp50–51).*

Roadside stall selling flowers

Avenida Larco is the area's commercial hub, housing boutiques, cafés, cultural centers, galleries, and casinos.

Municipal Palace

Luis Miro Quesada Garland Art Gallery, which opened in 1984, exhibits interactive installations and contemporary paintings.

The amphitheater plays host to dancing couples on Sundays.

★ **Iglesia de la Virgin Milagrosa**
Built on the old San Miguel de Miraflores church, this Church of the Miraculous Virgin dates from 1939. It is the work of Polish architect Ricardo de Jaxa Malachowski.

This avenue is named after one of Peru's favorite sons, writer Ricardo Palma.

AVENIDA LARCO

AVENIDA RICARDO PALMA

OLAYA

AVENIDA JOSE PARDO

Paseo de los Pintores
Artists set up their easels on this pedestrianized street to show off completed works focusing on Peruvian landscapes and people. A sculptor is usually present and can be seen carving out images from wooden blocks.

Artisans from Cusco region selling their handicrafts in Parque Kennedy

0 meters   50

0 yards   50

KEY

– – – Suggested route

★ Parque Kennedy

With its shady benches, food vendors, craft market, and dancing couples, Parque Kennedy is the area's most popular park and attracts a large number of people. ❶

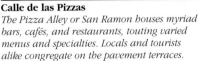

Calle de las Pizzas

The Pizza Alley or San Ramon houses myriad bars, cafés, and restaurants, touting varied menus and specialties. Locals and tourists alike congregate on the pavement terraces.

Municipal Palace

This building was opened in July 1944 and houses the town council. It was designed by architect Luis Miro Quesada Garland and has paintings and murals by famous artists.

STAR SIGHTS

★ Iglesia de la Virgin Milagrosa

★ Parque Kennedy

Paintings by local artists for sale at Parque Kennedy

Parque Kennedy ❶

Cnr of Av. Benavides & Calle Schell, Miraflores. **Map** 4 B1. ♿

The shady, tree-lined Parque Kennedy and the adjoining Parque 7 de Junio offer a welcome escape from Lima's jostling crowds and lurching traffic. Its modern playground with numerous swings and slides is a bonus for families traveling with children.

Local artists line the pedestrianized street in front of the Virgen Milagrosa church, proffering color-saturated canvases of Peru's landscapes and street scenes. Throughout the day food vendors and shoe-shiners can be seen plying their trade across the park.

The weekends are even more lively with all kinds of entertainment. A small but colorful craft market springs up in the center of the park in the Rotonda de los Artesanos. Innumerable stalls are set up to sell a wide variety of Peruvian crafts, including jewelry, antiques, as well as garments. Occasionally, artisans are brought in from various parts of rural Peru for week-long craft fairs.

The small amphitheater in the park is transformed into a dance arena on the weekends. Couples take to the floor sashaying to everything from robust salsa beats and Andean pipes, to brash Latino music.

Casa Ricardo Palma ❷

General Suarez 189, Miraflores. **Map** 4 B1. **Tel** 01 445 5836. ☐ 9am–12:45pm, 2:30–4:45pm Mon–Fri. ● pub hols. 📷 📷 in Spanish only. ♿ 📷

Peruvian writer Ricardo Palma's witty historical anecdotes or *tradiciós* have won him a prominent place in Latin American literature. His love for writing and books was reflected in his efforts to rebuild Lima's National Library. He was director of the library from 1884 until his retirement in 1912. It is said that he recovered several books dumped by Chilean soldiers from some street vendors he happened to pass one day.

Built at the beginning of the 20th century, the house where Palma spent his last years celebrates his life and works. Palma became such an institution in Lima that a pilgrimage to his home was deemed essential for connoisseurs of Latin-American literature. Even though Palma has been dead for over eight decades, his desk, favorite chair, manuscripts, letters, and photographs have been preserved for posterity.

Visitors can wander around the music room, study, and bedroom to get a glimpse of Ricardo's life and his possessions. His binoculars and books set aside for reading can be seen exactly where he left them.

RICARDO PALMA (1838–1919)

Ricardo Palma, one of Latin America's most popular writers, was also a naval officer, journalist, politician, and historian. He is renowed for rebuilding the National Library of Lima into one of the finest in Latin America, after it was destroyed during the War of the Pacific. Some of his historical sketches, called *Tradiciónes Peruanas*, have been translated into English as *The Knights of the Cape*, and have won him many accolades. These imaginative tales of pining monks, corrupt conquerors, lovers, magistrates, and all manner of foolish folk in Colonial Peru are part fiction and part reconstruction of history. Palma called himself a good tailor, artfully sewing together different stories. His funeral on October 6, 1919, was an elaborate affair with a procession of white robed priests and a military escort for his hearse.

Author and historian, Ricardo Palma

Miraflores Clifftops ❸

Malecon Cisneros & Malecon de la Reserva. **Map** 4 B2. ♿ 🖥 *in Parque del Amor.*

The clifftops, overlooking the Pacific Ocean, are one of Lima's most popular outdoor destinations. The weekends are particularly busy with strolling families, picnickers, skaters, paragliders, kissing couples, ice-cream vendors on bicycles, and rehearsing musicians and dancers. People eager for a bird's-eye view of Lima's coastline opt for paragliding from Raimondi Park, which is a focal point for visitors. These tandem or solo paragliders race the ocean-front bluffs, hovering just meters above the heads of the promenading public.

At the northern end, colorful flower beds in the shape of the Nazca Lines, the mysterious Peruvian "drawings" in the desert *(see pp126–7)*, dominate the view at the Parque Grau. On Sundays, during the summer, tango dancers gather on a paved area overlooking the sea to show off their skills.

Southward is the black-and-white striped La Marina lighthouse. It is located in Parque El Faro, or the Lighthouse Park, which commemorates 100 years of navigation. The lighthouse is a beacon for children, along with the adjacent playground.

The nearby skate park, with 1.6 miles (2.6 km) dedicated to ramps, tracks, and sandy hills, swarms with padded-up BMX bikers, boarders, and bladers on the weekends.

The pretty Parque del Amor, or Love Park, inaugurated on February 14, 1993, is devoted to the old Peruvian custom of courting in public gardens. In the center of the park is a colossal statue of a kissing couple, *El Beso*, or *The Kiss*, by sculptor Victor Delfín, which is perhaps a source of inspiration for the couples who come here. A serpentine mosaic bench, recalling Gaudí's *Parc Güell* in Barcelona, is embedded with names and notes of love.

View of the seaside from the terrace of Larcomar, Miraflores

Across the Puente Villena Rey bridge is the imposing *Intihuatana* statue by abstract artist Fernando Szyszlo, celebrating the Incas' sacred stone *(see p176)*. Intihuatana in Quechua translates as "hitching post of the sun," an apt premise for a coastline that is blanketed in gray and mist for more than half a year.

Love-themed mosaic bench at Parque del Amor

Larcomar ❹

Av. Malecón de la Reserva 610, Miraflores. **Map** 4 B2. *Tel* 01 620 6000. 🕐 24 hours. ♿ partial. 🍴 🖥 🛗 **www**.larcomar.com

Built in 2002, Larcomar, a shopping mall, comprises three terraces carved into the Miraflores cliffs. It has boutiques specializing in Peruvian handicrafts, a 12-screen cinema complex, cafés, bars, clubs, restaurants, a bowling alley, and gaming arcade. Limeños are in two minds about the mall. Some lament that it replaced a park, bringing traffic and noise into a once-tranquil area, while others consider it a great addition to the neighborhood.

Whatever they think of it, most locals find themselves here during the week. Some come to shop, others to admire the ocean views.

VICTOR DELFÍN (b.1927)

Victor Delfín studied painting and drawing at the School of Fine Arts in Lima and, on graduation, directed the Regional Schools of Art in Puno and Ayacucho. His monumental sculptures which adorn several public spaces – a dove in Piura, a condor in Quito, and *El Beso* in Lima – owe much to Peru's rich folk art traditions. Delfín believes that you have to "put your eyes in the earth to discover your roots." His imaginative sculptures are made from ceramics, concrete, tiles, and metal. His passion for Peruvian culture is visible in all his works. Delfín's vibrant tapestries often depict birds inspired by the traditional mantels of the Paracas culture and Incan symbols.

Victor Delfín at work

Huaca Pucllana ❺

Ceramic from the Wari culture

More than 10,000 years ago, nomadic fishermen and farmers built camps in the area now known as Miraflores. The villages expanded and an adobe-brick administrative and ceremonial center covering 15 acres (6 ha) was built. The complex was a meeting place where produce was exchanged and religious ceremonies held. Around AD 700 the center was abandoned, probably due to the influx of new religions and ideas, and the Wari took over, transforming the center into a cemetery for its elite. Over time it became a place for offerings and was worshiped as a *huaca* or shrine. Pucllana was the Quechua name given to the site in the 16th century.

Huaca Pucllana
Overlooking the Huaca, a restaurant with the same name offers great views.

Main Plaza is located at the tip of the pyramid. It features adobe walls up to 13 ft (4 m) high. Access is via a ramp on the side of the pyramid.

Mannequins with Ceramics
These recreate the ritual offering of ceramics to the gods. It was believed that breaking the jars and sacrificing children and women helped to maintain cohesion within the community.

★ Pyramid
Religious rites and ceremonies, including human sacrifices, were performed at the pyramid and plazas by the priests, who functioned as local governors.

★ Ceramics
The ceramics in the museum are mainly sea-dominated. The waves symbolize movement while the two-headed shark is considered the bringer of life and death.

★ Wari Mummy
The dead were buried in a sitting position, wrapped in elaborate bales of fabric and tied with rope made of vegetable fiber. The oldest mummy found in Lima is 1,300 years old.

Huaca Pucllana with the city in the backdrop, contrasting old and new

VISITORS' CHECKLIST

Calle General Borgoño, block 8.
Map 2 C4. **Tel** *01 617 7366
or 01 617 7138.* ◯ *9am–
4:30pm Wed–Mon.* ⬛ ♿
🚫 🍴

Detail of Sun-Dried Bricks
*Small handmade
adobe bricks were
arranged like books
in shelves to build
walls and platforms
for the main
pyramid and
adjacent plazas.*

Wari Textile
*The Wari fabrics were characterized by
geometric and animal shapes. Wari textiles
are among the most vibrant and finely
woven in the world. Intricately patterned
tunics were worn for ceremonial occasions.*

On-Going Excavation
*Work began on the site in
1967 and continues today
with the help of specialists.*

STAR SIGHTS

★ Ceramics

★ Pyramid

★ Wari Mummy

PLAN OF SITE

Administrative Sector had
a series of plazas and
enclosures that were
used for public meetings.

North Plaza has walls with
trapezoidal panels up to
33 ft (10 m) wide.

Museum

Pyramid

Fortified enclosures
believed to be where
food and construction
material was made.

| 0 meters | 150 |
| 0 yards | 150 |

KEY

▨ Area illustrated

Woven Chancay textile on display at Museo Amano, Miraflores

Instituto Cultural Peruano Norteamericano ❻

Av. Angamos Oeste 160, Miraflores. **Map** 3 D5. *Tel 01 706 7000.*
◯ 11am–8pm Tue–Sun.
▨ varies. ▣ www.icpna.edu.pe

The Peruvian–North American Cultural Institute (ICPNA) has a long tradition of promoting the arts in Lima. It was founded in 1938 by a group of Peruvian and North American writers, intellectuals, and scientists. The ICPNA organizes exhibitions ranging from photography, painting, and printing to sculpture, ceramics, and installations featuring local as well as international artists.

Every three years, the ICPNA holds the International Sculpture Encounter attracting sculptors from across the world. In a period of one week, each artist creates a piece which is later exhibited in the ICPNA galleries.

The Institute's widely-known engraving and water-color competitions have been in existence since 1965 and 1971 respectively.

Classical, acoustic, and Peruvian music concerts are also staged here, along with plays, ballet, and modern dance performances, all of which are usually held in the evenings, starting at 7pm. The Institute has five branches in different parts of the city.

Museo Amano ❼

Retiro 160, Miraflores. **Map** 2 B5.
Tel 01 441 2909. ◯ Mon–Fri by appointment. ▨ by donation. Ⓖ only in Spanish. Ⓟ

The house of Yoshirato Amano (1898–1982), and his collection of exhibits, was opened to the public in 1964 as the Museo Amano. It houses one of the most comprehensive private collections of pre-Hispanic textiles and handicrafts in Lima. The ceramics section has objects from the Kotosh, Moche, Chimú, Cupisnique, and Nazca cultures and charts the development of pottery in Peru through the ages.

The exhibits are organized chronologically, illustrating the differences and the advances made, between one culture and the next. It reveals how people in the north, such as the Moche, focused more on sculptural images, while those in the southern areas, the Nazca for example, used vibrant and vivid colors.

However, the section dedicated to pre-Hispanic textiles is what draws the crowds. On display, among others, are beautiful woven pieces by the Chancay people, some of which resemble fine lacework,

and an ancient Incan *quipu*, their unique system of recording events and keeping track of livestock with multicolored threads and knots.

Museo Enrico Poli ❽

Lord Cochrane 466, Miraflores.
Map 2 B5. *Tel 01 422 2437.*
◯ Mon–Fri by appointment only.
▨ Ⓖ only in Spanish. Ⓟ

Among the many private collections of pre-Columbian art in Peru, Enrico Poli's is considered the finest, hailed by *National Geographic* as one of the world's "25 great adventures." Of Italian descent, Poli moved to Peru in the 1950s, and amassed an astonishing number of treasures. The museum, inside his villa, is full of Cusco paintings, Colonial silver, and furniture dating to the 15th and 16th centuries. There is a spectacular display of pre-Columbian artifacts, comprising gold objects from the Moche royal tombs in Sipán, discovered in 1987 *(see pp228–9)*. There are also exquisite gold masks, jewels, textiles, sculptures, mummified heads of Inca nobility, and erotic figurines. Poli, associated with many archaeological expeditions in South America, acts as the tour guide.

Silver artifact in Museo Enrico Poli

Bosque El Olivar ❾

Av. La Republica, San Isidro.
Map 2 C3.

Spread over a large area in central San Isidro, the beautiful Bosque El Olivar (Olive Grove) was declared a national monument in 1959. Antonio de Rivera, a former mayor of Lima, introduced the olive tree to Peru in 1560. Of the numerous saplings he brought from Seville, only three survived the journey. He planted these in the middle of San Isidro.

By 1730, when Nicolas de Rivera, a descendant, decided to build his hacienda – Los Condes de San Isidro – among the olive trees, with a grinding mill and an olive press, the number of trees had swelled to over 2,000. In 1828, there were 2,831 trees in the garden.

Today, the garden contains over 1,500 olive trees, many of them centuries old. The grove is also home to around 15 species of birds. San Isidro Council organizes birding tours for school children to encourage awareness of habitat conservation.

Spending a lazy day under the sprawling branches is a favorite with picnickers and couples. The trees also provide an ideal backdrop for wedding photographs. The central pathway, spanning several blocks, is perfect for a leisurely evening stroll.

Rufous-collared sparrow

Huaca Huallamarca ❿

Nicolás de Rivera 201, San Isidro.
Map 2 B3. **Tel** 01 222 4124.
⬜ 9am–5pm Tue–Sun.
⬤ pub hols.

Also known as the Sugar Loaf or Pan de Azucar, the Huaca Huallamarca is a fully restored ancient adobe pyramid dating from AD 200 to 500. In the Quechua language, *marca* denotes "region or town" and consequently, *huallamarca* means the "place or residence of the Hualla people." Experts believe it to be a ceremonial center. The floors show little sign of wear, indicating that it was used only by the religious elite.

The tombs uncovered in the *huaca* (shrine) show the changes in funerary practices from AD 300 up to the 15th century, when the center was finally abandoned. During the Early Intermediate Period (AD 200–600), bodies were laid on their backs on reed mattresses. Later, the dead

Well-preserved mummy at Huaca Huallamarca, San Isidro

were put in a fetal position and wrapped in fine fabrics. During the Middle Horizon (AD 600–900), wrapped bodies had a mask of wood or painted fabric placed over the head.

Archaeologists have recovered farming tools, children's games, crockery, woven cotton, and sewing baskets from the tombs. The presence of the latter emphasizes the importance of women within these ancient communities.

Some of the mummies, as well as the artifacts found with them, are on display at the on-site museum. The ceremonial platform located on top of the *huaca* provides a vantage point for an excellent view of San Isidro.

Centuries-old olive trees line the pathway in Bosque El Olivar, San Isidro

BARRANCO

Just a stone's throw from Miraflores, Barranco is located on the cliffs at the southern tip of Lima Bay. It divides neatly into three parts: the bustling working-class neighborhood, the center sporting elegant 100-year-old villas, and the coast lined with modern apartment blocks. It was a quiet windmill-dappled hamlet until the 19th century, when Lima's elite moved in and began to build grand summer mansions, spurred on by the new fashion of bathing in the sea. Small colonies of Europeans, mainly English, French, and Italians, settled here, adding their own stylistic traits to local architecture. The Parque Municipal retains a hint of the refined airs of days gone by. Many of Barranco's cafés, restaurants, and bars are located around here, and in nearby Bajada de los Baños, which runs below the Puente de los Suspiros, or Bridge of Sighs, down towards the ocean.

Statue of Saint Gregorio, Las Pallas

SIGHTS AT A GLANCE

Bridge
Puente de los Suspiros ❸

Church
La Ermita ❹

Museums and Galleries
Museo de Arte
    Contemporáneo ❻
Museo de la Electricidad ❷
Museo Pedro de Osma ❺

Park
Parque Municipal ❶

SEE ALSO
• *Where to Stay* p270
• *Where to Eat* p290

GETTING AROUND
Regular buses and *combis* operate from Central Lima to Barranco. Only registered yellow cabs should be used. Walking is the best option.

KEY

	Street-by-street area *pp86–7*
i	Visitor information
✝	Church

LOCATOR MAP

◁ **An example of the many grand villas located in Barranco**

Street-by-Street: Barranco

It is easy to visualize Barranco's previous life as an aristocrat's playground, while wandering along the stately Avenida Sáenz Peña, past mansions that dot both sides, or are hidden away on nearby leafy streets. Some, however, are crumbling and Barranco has launched an "Adopt a Façade" program to promote private investment as a means of restoring the neighborhood's beauty. Colorfully painted façades along Calle Junín, Avenida Grau, and Bajada de los Baños merge the past with the present.

Avenida Sáenz Peña is lined by graceful old mansions with their sepia, rose, ochre, or lapis lazuli painted façades that recall the bygone era of pomp.

★ **Puente de los Suspiros**
This emblematic symbol of romantic Barranco was remodeled in 1921. Legend has it that anyone who crosses this bridge for the first time while holding their breath will be granted their wish. ❸

★ **Bajada de los Baños**
The present-day bajada (slope) corresponds with the path of a stream once followed by local fishermen down to the ocean. Over time it has morphed into a lane of elegant summer homes.

La Ermita
The devastating 1940 earthquake considerably damaged the church; the disintegrating roof is a reminder of the tremor's ferocity. ❹

STAR SIGHTS

★ Bajada de los Baños

★ Biblioteca Municipal

★ Puente de los Suspiros

0 meters 50

0 yards 50

KEY

--- Suggested route

426–428 Avenida Grau: Rancho Rosell

This lavish summer house, built in the early 1900s, was once the setting for opulent balls. After a period of neglect it has now been restored and is once again used for special private and public events.

Iglesia Santisima Cruz

Following the destruction of La Hermita in 1940, prominent local parishioners asked the Archbishop of Lima to authorize the building of a new parish church in the municipal plaza. The first stone was laid in 1944 and the Santisima Cruz church was finally consecrated in 1963.

★ Biblioteca Municipal

The Municipal Library, which opened in 1922, functioned as the Barranco Town Hall for many years. The columns at the entrance and along the façade are repeated on each side of the elongated windows.

To Sanchez Carrion

Sanchez Carrion

This pedestrainized street, famed for its bars and clubs, including multi-level, multi-faceted La Noche, is loved by night owls.

Puente de los Suspiros

Clock tower of the Biblioteca Municipal, Parque Municipal

Parque Municipal ❶

Av. Grau. **Map** 5 D5. ♿

Inaugurated in February 1898, Barranco's Parque Municipal, with its wooden benches, towering palms, and colorful flower beds, is a favorite stop for locals, especially after mass in the nearby Santisima Cruz church.

During the late afternoon, resident artists often display their canvases under the watchful gaze of the Cararra marble statue of *La Donaide*, or *Daughter of Venus*. She floats languidly over the clear waters of the central pool alongside two small angels or puttis. An exquisite original Etruscan vase – Barbenini's *Candelabro* – also in marble, sits nearby.

The striking crimson-colored **Biblioteca Municipal**, constructed between 1895 and 1899 and opened in 1922, dominates this popular park. The tower, that was added in 1911, displays the Barranco crest and a clock. Designated a "historic monument of exceptional worth" by Peru's Ministry of Culture, the

Biblioteca organizes regular lectures in Spanish, on diverse topics ranging from Peruvian identity and gastronomy to art and theater.

On weekends, a food market takes over the plaza opposite the park, with Peruvian cooks showing off their baking, roasting, frying, and selling skills.

Museo de la Electricidad ❷

Av. Pedro de Osma 105. **Map** 5 D5. **Tel** 01 477 6577. ◯ 9am–5pm daily. 📷 book ahead. **http://**museoelectri.perucultural.org.pe

Most people come to this museum not to learn about the history of electricty in Peru, or to gaze upon an old Wurlitzer jukebox or ancient television models, they come instead to ride the tram.

Lima's tram cars were built in the 1920s in Italy and operated in the center of the city, while larger carriages serviced Barranco. In 1997, some 30 years after the last tram stopped running in Lima, the museum rebuilt a car that it found abandoned in a city

scrapyard. It was placed back in service on a six-block section of track down Avenida Pedro de Osma in Barranco. It bears the number 97 in honor of the year it was restored. The tram runs on all days of the week from 10am to 5pm, except Mondays.

Today, this quaint tram car, using mechanical parts imported from France, gives its enthralled passengers a chance to enjoy a mode of transport once so common in Lima. Officially known as Vagón del Recuerdo, or the Car of Memories, this unusual tram is double-ended. It has doors, lights, and controls at both ends for the motor and brakes. The seats can be flipped around according to the direction the tram is heading. Perfectly customized to cope with Lima's extremely narrow streets, the trams were designed with doors on both sides, so that commuters could conveniently board or disembark on either side of the line.

Inside the museum there are some photographs of other trolleys that once plied the streets of Lima. Today, it may seem very hard to believe that Lima's public transport during those early days had such an advanced and efficient system of trolley-buses and trams.

Also on display are a wide array of electrical appliances and machines that have been used over the years by the people of the area.

The old tram rebuilt by the Museo de la Electricidad

For hotels and restaurants in this area see p270 and p290

Puente de los Suspiros ❸

Between Calles Ayacucho and La Ermita. **Map** 5 D5. ♿

Visitors crossing the Puente de los Suspiros

The 19th-century "Bridge of Sighs," which survived the earthquake of 1940, is steeped in legend. It derived its name from the thwarted love of a beautiful girl who lived on the Bajada de los Baños. She fell in love with a lowly street sweeper, but her father forbade her to see the boy and she spent the rest of her days gazing out of the window hoping for a glimpse of him. People crossing the bridge used to hear her sighing for her lost love.

The Bajado de los Baños, a pretty walkway which was built in 1870, slopes gently to the sea connecting the streets of Ayacucho and La Ermita. It is flanked on both sides by grand old homes that were once shaded by leafy olive and fig trees and framed by colorful French bougainvillea. Reflecting the times, the façades were brightly painted, moving away from the favored rich brown of the Colonial era. Today, most of them have been transformed into quality cafés, bars, and restaurants but their balconies and carved ceilings are a reminder of their former Colonial grandeur.

During the late 19th and early 20th centuries, Barranco was transformed into a fashionable summer address for upper-class Peruvian families. Many of them built fancy country homes here. Wooden baths were built in 1876, and rebuilt in 1906 following their destruction during the War of the Pacific (see pp50–51). Unfortunately, the baths were demolished in the 1960s to make way for a coastal road.

La Ermita ❹

Jirón Ermita. **Map** 5 D5.
🚫 not open to public.

The façade of the Church of the Hermitage is a famous Barranco landmark. According to legend, a group of fishermen, lost in a winter mist blanketing Lima's coast, prayed to be rescued. They rowed towards a glow that suddenly appeared in the distance and, once on land, they found only a wooden cross in the place from where the light had emanated. Believing divine intervention had spared them, the fishermen erected La Ermita on that same spot.

In front of La Ermita is a statue commemorating Peruvian singer Chabuca Granda, most famous for her tribute to Barranco's bridge known as the Puente de los Suspiros (see p89).

A pathway bordering the side of the church, built in 1988, leads past colorful houses and cafés to El Mirador Catalina Recavarren, a lookout point offering panoramic ocean views.

BARRANCO, THE SEASIDE RESORT

In 1876, President Ignacio Prado spent the majestic sum of 15,000 soles to build a path from the Barranco clifftop down to the beach. That same year, wooden baths were constructed for summer holidaymakers on what was then known as the Baño de Pescadores, or Fishermen's Bath. Five years later the baths were destroyed during the war with Chile. In 1906 they were rebuilt, this time with a large pier stretching into the sea, 400 changing rooms, and a huge restaurant with a dance floor that played host to the best orchestras of the day. Barranco, thus, was transformed from a simple seaside hideaway into the most popular summer address for aristocratic Peruvians and expatriates escaping Lima's heat. Postcards from 1915 show women in expansive hats and white dresses promenading on the pier, escorted by men in straw boaters and crisp, pressed suits. Windmills, used to draw water for the houses, dot the area. A funicular, inaugurated in 1895, ferried patrician families around.

Visitors on a Barranco beach during the mid-20th century

The beautiful French-influenced architecture of the Museo Pedro de Osma

Museo Pedro de Osma ❺

Av. Pedro de Osma 423. **Map** 5 D5.
Tel 01 467 0141. ◯ 10am–1:30pm,
2:30–6pm Tue–Sun. 🏛 🚻 🍴
📷 with flash. **www**.
museopedrodeosma.org

This sugar-white structure is one of Barranco's oldest mansions, erected in the early 20th century for the distinguished Osma family, who were natives of the region of La Osma Riojana in Spain.

The main building houses a fine collection of Colonial art and furniture, amassed from the top cultural centers of the time.

Paintings from the Cusco School, melding Spanish Baroque with Andean imagery, offer fascinating examples of subversion, such as the Virgin Mary portrayed with dark Andean hair. Outstanding religious sculptures, many from the Lima School, also line its walls. Of particular interest are the bleeding head of John the

Baptist and Adam and Eve reaching for the apple.

The second building, set amongst palm trees, geranium beds, and marble sculptures in the back garden, was originally the dining room. It now houses photographs and dinnerware of the Osma family. A third building is home to an impressive collection of silverware.

Museo de Arte Contemporáneo ❻

Av. Grau 1511. **Map** 4 C3. **Tel** 01 652 5100. ◯ 8am–9pm daily. 🏛
📷 with flash. **www**.mac-lima.org.pe

This modern, glass-walled museum set within a public park houses a permanent collection of more than 120 contemporary paintings, sculptures, and installations by some of today's leading Peruvian and Spanish-American artists, including Fernando de Szyszlo, Ramiro Llona, Oswaldo Guayasamin, Sonia Praga, Lika Mutal, and José Tola. The museum also hosts temporary exhibitions and events, and has a research library. Visitors also have access to the gardens, where sculptures are displayed. The popular "Art in the Park" program offers weekend art workshops for all ages.

BOHEMIAN BARRANCO

Barranco has long been a popular spot with artists and intellectuals. From 1913 through to the 1950s, it saw many days of memorable partying, especially during Carnaval which took over the streets for days with revelers in dazzling costumes and masks. One of Peru's most beloved singers, Chabuca Granda, lived here, singing its praises thus: "there is an age-old belief we Barranquinos have, that the founder of Barranco was none other than God." Today, it is Lima's evening haunt, with music spilling out of hole-in-the-wall bars, posh nightclubs, and a number of busy *peñas*. Gian Marco, local pop hero and popular Latin music composer, honed his skills here with bar gigs, and after a stint abroad returned to live in his favourite *barrio* (district). While writer Mario Vargas Llosa's seafront house has been replaced by an apartment block, other homes remain, such as that of renowned sculptor and artist Victor Delfín (*see p79*).

Statue of Chabuca Granda

Peñas, Peru's Music Clubs

Peñas originated in the *callejones* (tenements) of central Lima, traditional home to immigrants and the rural poor. They began as small, informal clubs for family and friends, united in their love of a particular kind of folk music. Like Peruvian cuisine, the music is a product of its Andean, African, and Spanish roots with the African slaves contributing

Traditional
charango

percussion instruments. Lima's *peñas* generally focus on folkloric or *criolla* (Creole) music, though some cross all borders. Fans may argue that today's *peñas,* with their all-singing, all-dancing performances, are more variety shows than traditional clubs, where participation and knowledge-sharing is the goal, but the bottom line is that they are very popular.

Spanish influences
from the 16th century introduced the harp and the guitar. Until then, pre-Hispanic Andean music mostly consisted of wind instruments and small drums.

Musica *criolla*
is a blend of African music with Spanish and Andean rhythms. It has a Creole version of Spanish guitar and cajon *drum.*

A LIVELY EVENING AT A POPULAR PEÑA

Far from the intimacy of a traditional *peña*, today's clubs provide energetic singing and dancing performances while encouraging participation from a willing audience. Modern *peñas,* such as La Candelaria, offer a taste of culture showcasing dances from several regions of the country.

Dances *that are performed in a* peña *range from the* marinera *from the north to Cusco's* huayno, *Puno's* tuntuna, *and* diablada.

Musicians *dressed in colorful costumes play traditional music, and the revelers, fueled by pisco sour, can't help but take to the dance floor.*

Retablo *detail depicts musicians playing various Andean instruments. South Andes is famous for the* huayno, *a mestizo chant of melancholic vocals, the harp, and* charango.

FARTHER AFIELD

Beyond the key areas of Central Lima, Miraflores, and Barranco, the sights of interest are somewhat dispersed. The village-like suburb of Pueblo Libre to the south of Central Lima, is home to a number of museums. Museo Nacional de Arqueologia, Antropologia e Historia del Peru, and the privately run Museo Arqueologico Rafael Larco Herrera are people-friendly spaces that chronicle Peru's intriguing past. Far away from the confines of museum walls is Pachacámac, a couple of adobe pyramids, which at one time hosted

Nazca pottery, Museo Arqueologia

both Wari as well as Inca cultures and was renowned as the site of a powerful oracle. Evidence of Peru's strategic importance in the region during the time of the Spanish colonization is displayed at the Fortaleza del Real Felipe, a fortress built in the 18th century on the port of Callao. The Museo Naval nearby also showcases and celebrates Peru's maritime prowess. Stately mansions in the nearby district of La Punta are a reminder of the area's popularity with Lima's aristocracy in the 19th century, and again, in the 1930s and 40s.

SIGHTS AT A GLANCE

Historic Buildings and Sights
Fortaleza del Real Felipe ❸
Pachacámac ❼

Museums and Galleries
Museo Arqueológico Rafael
  Larco Herrera ❷
Museo de la Nacion ❺
*Museo Nacional de
  Arqueologia pp96–7* ❶
Museo Naval del Peru ❹
Museo de Oro del Peru ❻

SEE ALSO

• *Where to Stay* pp270–71

• *Where to Eat* pp290–92

KEY

	Central districts
✈	Airport
🚉	Railroad station
═	Highway
═	Major road
═	Minor road

GETTING AROUND
Museums are widely scattered and a good way to visit them is to hire a registered taxi. Buses and *combis* operate from Miraflores to Pueblo Libre. They also connect Central Lima to Callao, and Pachacámac.

0 km	3
0 miles	3

◁ **Adobe bricks used in the construction of the pyramids at Pachacámac**

Bright blooms adorn the façade of Museo Arqueológico Rafael Larco Herrera

Museo Nacional de Arqueologia ❶

See pp96–7.

Museo Arqueológico Rafael Larco Herrera ❷

Bolivar 1515, Pueblo Libre. **Tel** 01 461 1312. ◯ 9am–6pm daily. ▨ ▣ ▧ ▨ www.museolarco.org

A grand 18th-century mansion built on a pyramid dating back to the 7th century provides more than a fitting home for 3,000 years of ancient history. The Larco Herrera Museum, founded in 1926, houses the biggest private collection of Peruvian pre-Columbian art – 45,000 pieces – amassed by sugar baron Rafael Larco Hoyle.

The Culture Hall, divided into North Coast, South, Center, and Highlands, is a good starting point as it gives a comprehensive view of the cultures that existed from 7000 BC to the 16th century.

In the Andean world, the beauty and durability of metals gave objects an almost divine value. They were designed to be offered to the gods. The Incas, as representatives of the gods, wore them or took them to their grave on their way to the other world.

The gold and silver collection, which is nothing short of heavenly, comprises head-dresses, beads the size of golf balls, and chest plates inlaid with precious stones. Enormous ear "plugs," nose ornaments, crowns with quartz and turquoise, funerary masks, and a shirt made of gold discs are also displayed.

There are ancient textiles, including a fragment from a Paracas weaving showing 389 threads to 1 inch (3 cm) – a world record. Other exhibits range from a Wari loom-woven wall-hanging made from parrot feathers, to an Inca *quipu*, the ancient way of recording facts and events with colored threads and knots *(see p25)*. The museum also showcases tools, kaolin, clay, molds, paints, as well as unbaked ceramics.

Separate from the main house is a gallery of erotic art, with myriad vessels depicting the sex lives of ancient Peruvians. They were made by Larco Hoyle in the 1960s, based on his research on Peruvian pre-Columbian art.

Golden neck-piece, Museo Larco Herrera

Fortaleza del Real Felipe ❸

Plazuela de la Independencia, Callao. **Tel** 01 465 8394/429 0532. ◯ 9am–4pm daily. ● pub hols. ▨ ▣ www.ejercito.mil.pe

The stone-walled Royal Felipe Fort is one of the largest forts built by the Spanish in the 18th century. Of interest to both the visitor and the historian, it was designed by Frenchman Luis Gaudin and inaugurated in 1774 by Viceroy Amat. The fort was named in honor of Felipe V, the first Bourbon king of Spain, who died in 1746.

The austere, pentagon-shaped fort was intended to defend against pirate attacks. During the 19th century, Callao *(see p98)*, where the fort stands, was considered to be the most powerfully protected port on the west coast of South America. Real Felipe had been "war-ready" since Colonial times, and had repelled many attacks. The fort had been besieged five times but never conquered. It also played a pivotal role in Peru's War of Independence *(see p49)*, acting as the first line of defense.

Covering more than 84,000 sq yards (70,000 sq m), the fort contains brass and iron cannons, military tanks, the Governor's House, Towers of the King and Queen, as well as the Museo del Ejército (Military Museum), with its impressive collection of weapons, documents, military uniforms, and relics dating back to 1730.

Environs

Two islands visible from the fort are **San Lorenzo** and **El Frontón**. San Lorenzo, Peru's largest island, was said to be a pirates' lair in Colonial times. Dutch pirate, Jacob the Hermit, who died in 1624, is buried here. The Spanish Armada also used the island as a refuge during the Battle of Angamos in 1879.

The history of El Fronton (Island of the Dead) is less romantic. It operated as a political prison during Colonial times but later became a jail for common criminals. The nearby **Cabinzas Islands** are a haunt of sea birds, while **Palomino Island** is home to sea lions, some weighing up to 660 lb (300 kg).

Boat tours for the islands depart from the Muelle de Guerra in Plaza Grau.

Museo Naval del Perú ❹

Av. Jorge Chavez 123, Callao.
Tel 01 613 6868. ◯ 9am–3pm
Mon–Fri. 🅰 🗗 www.museonaval.
com.pe

The Naval Museum, near the
Fortaleza del Real Felipe, is a
key site for seafaring history
buffs. Instigated by Capitán
de Navío Julio J. Elías
Murguía, a Peruvian naval
hero, the museum has an
important collection of
historical, naval documents,
oil paintings, uniforms, and
relics from the 1879–83 War
of the Pacific (see pp50–51).
Also included are many
personal objects of those
involved in the conflict,
photographs, weapons, and
navigational instruments.

Prized items are those that
belonged to one of Peru's
great military heroes,
Admiral Miguel Grau,
who died in the
Battle of Angamos.
Also known as the
Caballero de los
Mares (Gentleman
of the Seas), his
letters, navigational
charts, and medals, as
well as a sarcophagus
with a fragment of
his shinbone, his only
remains found after the
battle, are displayed here.

One room is devoted
entirely to model ships,
showcasing vessels from
different eras and countries.

**Nazca pottery,
Museo de la Nacion**

Museo de la Nacion ❺

Javier Prado Oeste 2465, San Borja.
Tel 01 476 9875. 🚍 ◯ 9am–5pm
Tue–Sun. ◐ Jan 1, Easter Thu & Sat,
May 1, Jul 28 & 29, Dec 25. 🅰 🗗
🗗 🖵 📱

Although this imposing
concrete building embodies
the architecture of Peru's
military government of the
1970s, the exhibits inside
celebrate Peru's rich archaeological past.

Opened as a museum in
1990, the collection highlights
Peru's history dating back to
its prehistoric cultures. It

Extensive display of ceramics at the Museo de la Nacion

includes extensive displays of
Chavín stone carvings, Wari
textiles, and Paracas and
Chancay weavings. Moche
ceramics, wooden idols, and
a sarcophagus from the
Amazon, are also on view.
The museum gives an
insightful overview of
Peru's past, which
will be of interest
to visitors about to
tour the country's
main sites. Entire
floors are given over
to ancient ceramics:
huge glass cases
showcase Nazca
pottery adorned with pumas
and condors, the distinctive
white, cream, and black
Chancay pottery, as well as

the yellow and white designs
favored by the people from
around Cajamarca.

Also displayed are good
models of Peru's most famous
ruins – Machu Picchu (see
pp176–81), the Nazca Lines
(see pp126–7), and the Lords
of Sipán tomb (see pp228–
31); the latter hailed as one
of the greatest discoveries
in Latin American history.

In a separate section of the
museum there are interesting
displays of traditional costumes from across Peru, as
well as a selection of popular
regional art.

The museum hosts various
temporary exhibitions and is
also a venue for dance and
theater performances.

RAFAEL LARCO HOYLE (1901–66)

Born on a sugar plantation in Trujillo, Rafael Larco Hoyle
rose to be one of Peru's most noted businessmen, with a
sharp eye for the country's ancient crafts. His passion saw
the family hacienda break sugar
production records when he
mechanized it after completing his
studies in the USA. In 1926, he
opened a museum on his plantation and dedicated it to north
Peruvian pre-Columbian pottery.
He continued to collect the rarest
and finest of the arts, at one point
commandeering the largest
swimming pool on the hacienda to
remove salt from a newly acquired
8,000-piece collection. Don Rafael
also began to explore and
excavate sites in northern Peru
collecting artifacts, pottery, and
vessels. He moved the entire
collection to Lima in 1958.

**Rafael Larco Hoyle studying
an artifact**

Museo Nacional de Arqueologia, Antropologia e Historia del Peru ❶

Ceramic musician

This comprehensive collection of Peruvian historical artifacts is displayed in Casa Huerta, a mansion used by Peru's liberators José de San Martín and Símon Bolivar. Thousands of objects chart the country's history, from pre-Hispanic to the Colonial and Republican times. It boasts the largest collection of ceramics, the most important collection of ancient human remains, including mummies, and *fardos funerarios* (wrapped bodies), as well as a series of Viceroy portraits from the 18th and 19th centuries.

Textile with geometric iconography typical of the Paracas culture

Moche Ceramics

Moche potters used a molding technique to produce bottles with spouts and handles as well as musical whistling bottles depicting men, women, animals, and deities in realistic activities such as hunting, fishing, or fighting.

Café

★ Mummies

The Paracas culture buried their dead in a sitting position, wrapped in layers of fabric. Their mummies are said to be the best preserved in the world due to the freeze-drying effect of the arid climate there.

★ Estela Raimondi

This enomorous stone obelisk was recovered from Chavín de Huántar ceremonial center. Carved with intricate images of snakes, condors, jaguars, and the Staff God, it is one of the most important pieces in the museum.

Principal entrance

Obelisko Tello, named after the archaeologist who discovered it at Chavín de Huantár, was used to mark the beginning and end of the agricultural year by projecting shadows in certain areas.

The Lithics Gallery
Comprising 18,250 stone artifacts (lithics) from all over Peru, some dating from 12,000 BC. The display includes knives, axes, hammers, grinding stones, sculptures, beads, and bowls.

The library

Grave of archaeologist Julio C. Tello

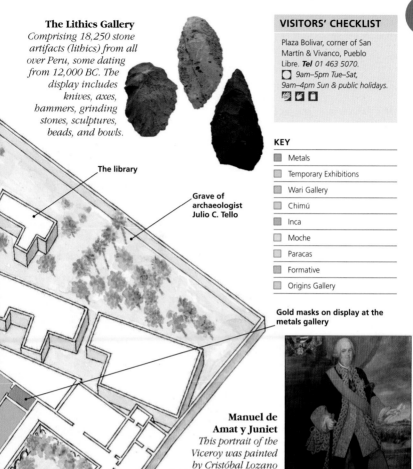

KEY

⬜	Metals
⬜	Temporary Exhibitions
⬜	Wari Gallery
⬜	Chimú
⬜	Inca
⬜	Moche
⬜	Paracas
⬜	Formative
⬜	Origins Gallery

Gold masks on display at the metals gallery

Manuel de Amat y Juniet
This portrait of the Viceroy was painted by Cristóbal Lozano (1609–67). Amat, Viceroy from 1761–1776, was responsible for building Fortaleza de Real Felipe.

GALLERY GUIDE
Beginning at the left of the main entrance, exhibits are displayed chronologically in a series of connecting rooms on one level, each devoted to a specific period. The main house, Casa Huerta, is accessed via the final gallery to the right of the entrance.

STAR EXHIBITS

★ Estela Raimondi

★ Mummies

★ Nazca Ceramics

★ Nazca Ceramics
Unlike the Moche, the Nazca did not use moulds for their pieces which feature meticulous designs, stylized naturalistic themes, and a greater variety of colors.

Museo de Oro del Peru ❻

Alonso de Molina 1100, Monterrico-Surco. **Tel** *01 345 1292/345 1271.*
🚗 *ask driver to wait.* ◯ *11:30am–7pm daily.* ● *Jan 1, May 1, Jul 28 & Dec 25.* 📷 💳 🚫 🔲 🛈 **www**.museooroperu.com.pe

One of Lima's top attractions, Miguel Mujica Gallo's massive private Gold Museum displays numerous ceremonial knives and vases studded with turquoise. Ornate funerary masks, crowns, helmets, figurines, earrings, necklaces, an impressive gold ceremonial bag, and a tunic appliquéd with gold are also on view.

In addition, there are ceremonial objects, a Nazca poncho woven with parrot feathers, "hats" made of human hair, a feathered head-dress, tapestries, ceramics, and mummies, some even with tiny babies. Labeling on

Windowed patio of the House of the Chosen Women, Pachacámac

Chimú mask, Museo de Oro del Peru

the exhibits is unfortunately poor, with inadequate explanation in Spanish, and almost none in English, making an audio guide essential.

The building's upper floor is set aside for Armas del Mundo (Arms of the World), a vast collection of ancient firearms and military paraphernalia. On view is an 1812 sword of Russian Tsar Alexander, and the pistol that belonged

to Chilean President Salvador Allende. In 2001, the museum was rocked by scandal with the National Institute of Culture and the Tourism Protection Bureau declaring that almost all its estimated 7,000 pieces were fake. However, the owners claim to have only genuine gold pieces on display.

Pachacámac ❼

Panamerican Highway South, KM31.5, Lurin. **Tel** *01 430 0168.*
🚗 *ask driver to wait.* ◯ *9am–5pm daily.* 📷 💳 ♿ 🚫 *in museum.* 🔲 🛈

Dating from AD 200, this complex of adobe pyramids rising out of the Lurin Valley was a key pilgrimage center

on Peru's central coast, and home to a much venerated oracle. It flourished through the centuries and pilgrims traveled great distances to pay homage to God Pachacámac (He who Enlivens the Universe and Everything).

Pachacámac was expanded by the Wari and their designs can be seen on the ceramics and textiles found here. However, most of the compounds and pyramids date from after their downfall.

When the last Inca king, Atahualpa, was imprisoned by Pizarro, he complained that the oracle had falsely predicted his victory. His account of gold at the site led soldiers there but they were disppointed by the "ugly" idol they found instead.

The Incas built five separate complexes, including the Templo del Sol (Temple of the Sun) and the Palacio de Las Mamaconas (House of the Chosen Women), with stonework on its entrance gate, a rarity on the coast.

The on-site museum houses a collection of pre-Hispanic relics, including Paracas textiles, ceramics, and a two-faced image of Pachacámac.

Environs
The **Pantanos de Villa**, a wetland area 11 miles (18 km) south of Lima, is one of the main coastal refuges for more than 150 bird species, including the majestic white heron. With its *totora* reed-lined pools, it is Lima's last remaining natural reserve. There are signposted trails and lookout towers for bird-lovers.

CALLAO'S BATTLES

As a leading commercial port, Callao was the site of many battles

Founded in 1537, Callao became the leading port for Spanish commerce in Latin America. Its colorful history saw attacks by pirates and buccaneers, including Sir Francis Drake, who seized all the valuables from the anchored Spanish ships and sank them in 1574. Later, the earthquake and tsunami of 1746 destroyed the entire port. Battles were waged here during the independence and the Pacific wars, and it was occupied by Chile for three years.

Lima's Beaches

With more than 1,156 miles (1,860 km) of shoreline, Peruvians have long worshipped the Pacific. Wave-riding is documented in friezes in the 2,000-year-old archaeological complexes on the coast. Beaches, headlands, and coves are plentiful, providing lots of opportunity for keen surfers and swimmers. Come December, when

Surfer with board

Lima's grey haze finally lifts, Limeños head south for week-ends. On Sundays, the Panamerican Highway back to Lima can become so clogged that it reverts to one-way, with outgoing traffic diverted to another road. By January, most city-dwellers move for the summer to one of the string of beaches stretching down the coast.

Playa San Pedro ①
This is just past the Pachacámac site (see p98) so it is possible to combine a visit to the pre-Inca ruins with an afternoon at the beach.

LIMA

Pachacámac

El Silencio ②
The sheltered bay, with its placid waves, is good for swimming, but upmarket residential complexes have drawn the crowds away.

ISLAS DE PACHACAMAC

① Playa San Pedro

② El Silencio

③ Punta Rocas

④ Punta Hermosa

⑤ Pico Alto

⑥ San Bartolo

⑦ Santa Maria del Mar

⑧ Pucusana

Pucusana ⑧
This traditional fishing village with a harbor is the pick of seaside towns for many. Boats can be hired to see the sea lions basking in the sun.

Santa Maria del Mar ⑦
With calm waters and sand dotted with rustic thatched umbrellas, this is a preferred family destination.

Punta Rocas ③
This beach is a fixture on the international surfing circuit, with the championship tour starting here in February.

San Bartolo ⑥
One of the most popular beaches close to Lima, clear water and gentle waves sustain its appeal.

Punta Hermosa ④
The beaches and bays near this bustling resort town have waves that vary in size, attracting surfers of all abilities.

0 km	10
0 miles	10

KEY

— Major road

--- Minor road

Pico Alto ⑤
A sandbank out at sea with waves reaching 40 ft (12 m), it is dubbed the "wave-making machine" and is a surfing hotspot.

For additional map symbols *see back flap*

SHOPPING IN LIMA

If you missed buying those blankets from the weavers near Lake Titicaca, the odds are that you will find the same in Lima. The shops here are stacked with handicrafts from different regions of Peru. Silver aficionados can sate their appetite on Avenida La Paz, which is lined with sparkling shops, while souvenir hunters are spoilt for choice at Lima's indigenous markets. Specialist shops

Face mask at a handicraft shop

and galleries stock myriad hand-made folk art objects and upmarket items. Although Lima is not a fashion capital, the city's largest mall, Jockey Plaza, does have some designer label boutiques, along with department stores stacked high with locally made jeans and outfits. Remember it is illegal to take historical artifacts out of Peru; visitors need to be extra careful while shopping.

POTTERY, CERAMICS, ART, AND CRAFTS

Mari Solari's shop-gallery, **Las Pallas**, is a Peruvian treasure trove. You can find anything from hand-painted masks to engraved gourds and from pottery to amulets – some masquerading as funky fridge magnets. *Retablos*, hinged wooden boxes containing painted figures crafted from dough, are also available. If you are in luck, Solari might even allow you a glimpse of her private collection of Inca *keros* (cups).

Housed in a mansion on Barranco's designer store strip, **Dédalo**'s maze of rooms brims with Peruvian home-wares, Spanish-language books, toys, furniture, clothes, handbags, ceramics, jewelry, and glassware crafted by local artisans. The back garden-café offers excellent espresso.

Colorful fabric with traditional pattern for sale

FABRICS

Kuskaya works with artisans across Peru to preserve handicraft traditions while modernizing them. Cotton table linen and pillows are produced by the Callua weavers in Cajamarca, feather-soft scarves woven from Suri alpaca by Puno artisans, and cotton handbags are embroidered in the jungle. In addition, alabaster-like napkin rings are sculpted in Ayacucho and decorative ceramics come from the northern Chulucanas. Kuskaya also tailor-makes pieces to match your existing decor.

For clothes, **Alpaca 111** has a reputation as the place to shop for alpaca, with downy baby alpaca jumpers, coats, capes, and vicuña scarves and shawls on sale. Vicuña, a tiny distant cousin of the llama, is said to produce the world's

finest wool, boasting a diameter of 11–13 microns, against 16 microns for cashmere, 17–19 microns for alpaca, and 30 microns for sheep wool. Prices are a little higher than normal but then so is the quality.

WOODWORK

Jorge Flores of the **Galería de Arte Popular y Artesanía** collects antique *artesanía* from across Peru and displays it in his shop-cum-gallery. Here, folkloric *retablos* from Ayacucho, dating from the mid-20th century, nestle beside elaborately carved 18th-century religious statues.

Wiñay's range includes elegant trays, screens, lamps, plates, and jewelry boxes. Alicia Barrantes, the owner, combines the old with the new. Passionate about Peruvian textiles, she sources intricately woven fabrics from Andean communities in Pitumarca, Parabamba, and Paucartambo, and teams them with mahogany from the Peruvian jungle. She also adds local stones and silver to create beautiful and unique pieces.

Wooden angel playing music

SILVER

Argentinian-born designer **Ester Ventura** combines objects and fragments from centuries-old pre-Columbian cultures with silver for her exclusive jewelry. Chunky silver bands or delicate mesh are entwined with Chavín

Ceramic churches from the owner's collection, Las Pallas

beads, and Paracas or Nazca textiles. Elongated shell beads, hand-carved monkey bone from the Peruvian jungle, mother-of-pearl, coral, turquoise, and ceramic shards are used to create exquisite one-off pieces.

Necklaces at **Ilaria** range from chic silver bands and sparsely threaded beads to elaborate amethyst, turquoise, and other stone-studded pendants. Silver tableware is a specialty and decorative pieces such as polished wooden angels with silver wings are also appealing.

Camusso is a bastion of traditional silverware. Founded in 1933 by an Italian immigrant Carlo Mario Camusso, it boasts some 3,600 pieces in its collection, ranging from cutlery to cocktail shakers. Tours of the factory can be arranged.

A host of silver shops proffering frames, vases, trays, plates, and jewelry are concentrated around Avenida La Paz in Miraflores. Prices don't differ that much, but most merchants are willing to reduce from the price tag.

MARKETS

Avenida Petit Thouars is lined with handicraft markets and the unassuming **Mercado Indio**, with its 100 or so stalls

Peruvian handicrafts shop, Larcomar Shopping Mall, Miraflores

offering items from all over Peru, is a good place to start. Although most items are mass produced, you can stumble on some unique pieces, including colorful hand-woven baskets and elaborate wooden candlesticks and mirrors in the Cusco style. You can haggle, but prices are pretty much standard.

The covered **Mercado Surquillo** is one of the most interesting places in Lima to shop for food. Stocked with fruit, vegetables, fish, cheese, and meat from all over Peru, the market is a favorite with Peruvian super-chef Gaston Acurio. However, you need to be beware of pickpockets.

MALLS AND DEPARTMENT STORES

Opened in 1997, **Jockey Plaza** in Monterrico is Lima's largest mall, housing big stores such as Ripley and Saga Falabella. It has a movie theater, food court, fashion stores including Hugo Boss, along with home decor specialist Casa y Ideas. The mall also has some books and CD shops, and there is a supermarket as well as a hardware store.

Larcomar *(see p79)* in Miraflores is a good one-stop shop for local handicrafts, quirky accessories, designer sunglasses, swim- and surfwear, cigars, and books.

DIRECTORY

POTTERY, CERAMICS, ART AND CRAFTS

Dédalo
Paseo Sáenz Peña 295,
Barranco.
Tel 01 477 0562.

Las Pallas
Calle Cajamarca 212,
Barranco.
Tel 01 477 4629.

FABRICS

Kuna (Alpaca 111)
Av. Larco 671,
Miraflores.
Map 4 B2.
Tel 01 447 1623.
www.kuna.com.pe

Kuskaya
Av. Conquistadores 556,
San Isidro.
Map 2 C4.
Tel 01 222 0625.
www.kuskayaperu.com

WOODWORK

Galería de Arte Popular y Artesanía
Calle Colón 534,
Miraflores.
Tel 01 447 2578.

Wiñay
Calle Alcanfores 699,
Miraflores.
Tel 01 372 5081.

SILVER

Camusso
Av. Oscar Benavides 679.
Map 4 B1.
Tel 01 425 0260.

Ester Ventura
Malecón Almirante Grau
1157, Chorrillos.
Tel 01 467 1180.

Ilaria
Av. Dos de Mayo 308,
San Isidro.
Map 2 B2.
Tel 01 512 3530.

MARKETS

Mercado Indio
Av. Petit Thouars 5245,
Miraflores.
Map 3 D5.

Mercado Surquillo
Paseo de la República,
Cnr of Angamos Este.
Map 3 D5.

MALLS AND DEPARTMENT STORES

Jockey Plaza
Javier Prado 4200,
Surco/Monterrico.
Tel 01 437 4100. www.
jockey-plaza.com.pe

Larcomar
Avenida Malecón de la
Reserva 610, Miraflores.
Map 4 B2.
Tel 01 620 6000.
www.larcomar.com

ENTERTAINMENT IN LIMA

Barman mixing cocktails

Peru has a rich tradition of dance and music reflected by Lima's *peñas (see p91)*, proudly flying the red and white flag, encouraging crowds of locals and tourists to try their hand and feet at local dances. Movies are another popular pastime and the city has more cinemas than the rest of Peru combined. There is also a small but active theater scene, although most productions are in Spanish, naturally. Bar-hoppers and live music fans flock to Barranco, while Miraflores also has its share of pubs and dance clubs. Come October, Limeños are out in droves for the annual bullfighting season, which features world-renowned matadors.

Enraptured viewers with a mural in the backdrop at La Candelaria, Barranco

PEÑAS AND SALSODROMOS

Peru has two main types of music – *folklórico* and *criollo*. Folkloric is from the Andean highlands while Creole is more coastal. Whatever the musical theme, a *peña (see p91)* is a recipe for a rowdy night aided by helpings of Peruvian food, pisco, and beer.

Creole **Peña Del Carajo** often features well known Creole performers such as Arturo "Zambo" Cavero and Pepe Vásquez, while **Las Brisas del Titicaca** showcases some of the 250-plus dances from Puno, including the famous devil dance. **La Candelaria** has a little bit of everything, offering dances from coast and mountain, as well as from the jungle.

As the name implies, *salsodromos* pulsate to the sound of salsa and Caribbean music. Weekends at **El Pizzotón** are dedicated to Puerto Rican and Cuban sounds; rhumba and Afro-Peruvian music feature on other nights. **Timbalero Latin Club** hosts some of the best salsa bands and the huge dance-floor is always teeming.

BARS, CLUBS, AND DISCOS

Barranco is the place for bars and clubs. Since everything is within walking distance, just a few steps can mean a change of pace from electronica at **La Noche** to seasoned Peruvian musicians playing boleros and cha-cha-cha tunes at **El Ekeko**. **Posada del Ángel** offers cold beer and Latino-style troubadors, while **El Dragon** is an underground jazz club with live music and cool decor. The classy **Ayahuasca Bar** offers a colorful selection of cocktails and snacks. Miraflores discotheque **Gótica** features international DJs and is always jam-packed. Pubs such as **O'Murphy's** draw Limeños and expats with its on-tap Guinness, wide choice of imported and local beers, and pool table.

CINEMA AND THEATER

Lima has a huge number of multiplex cinemas, mostly showing Hollywood blockbusters, often in English with subtitles. Children's films, however, are always dubbed. For those who prefer classic or independent films, there's the **Centro Cultural de España** and **El Cinematógrafo de Barranco**. Lima theaters host a number of productions during the year, with all offerings listed in *El Commercio* newspaper.

Teatro Marsano is known for light comedy. **Teatro Segura**, which hosted its first performance in 1615, presents classical and contemporary works including musicals and ballets. The **Teatro Británico** occasionally stages plays in English. Film festivals, concerts, and exhibitions as well as theater and dance events are held regularly in

Musicians performing at the Estacion del Barranco

A bullfight in full swing at the popular Plaza de Acho bullring

cultural centers such as **Instituto Cultural Peruano Norteamericano (ICPNA)**, **Central Cultural PUCP**, and **Alianza Francesa**. The Museo de la Nacion *(see p95)* is often used as a venue for a variety of events, from children's plays to international dance and circus performances.

CASINOS

Lima is awash with casinos but the most reputable ones are located in major hotels, such as the **Sheraton**, the **Marriott**, and **Los Delfines**. Slot machine fans be aware that Lima's one-arm bandits have a reputation for paying out very little, if anything.

SPECTATOR SPORTS

Fútbol (soccer), is the national sport and **Estadio Nacional** is the venue for most big matches. The bullfighting season, which runs from October to the end of November at the **Plaza de Acho** bullring, coincides with Lima's biggest festival, Feria Taurina del Señor de los Milagros *(see p69)*. Famous matadors from Spain and France take part, along with local luminaries, and tickets are sold well in advance. Prices for the seats in *la sombra*, or the shade, are the most expensive, while seats in *el sol*, the sun, are cheaper. The tickets are available from TeleTicket counters in the Wong and Metro supermarkets.

DIRECTORY

PEÑAS AND SALSODROMOS

El Pizzotón
Calle de las Pizzas 290.
Map 4 B1.
Tel 01 9330 0829.

La Candelaria
Av. Bolognesi 292.
Tel 01 247 1314/2941.

Las Brisas del Titicaca
Jirón Wakulski 168. **Map** 1 D3. *Tel* 01 332 1901.

Peña Del Carajo
Catalino Miranda 158.
Map 5 D3.
Tel 01 247 7023.

Timbalero Latin Club
Av. José Galvez. **Map** 1 E3. *Tel* 01 221 4283.

BARS, CLUBS, AND DISCOS

Ayahuasca Bar
Prolg. San Martín 130.
Map 5 D4.

El Dragon
Nicolas de Piérola 168.
Map 5 D4.
Tel 01 797 1033.

El Ekeko
Av. Grau 266.
Map 5 D5.
Tel 01 247 3148.

Gótica
Larcomar Commercial Centre, Level 5, Malecon de la Reserva 601.
Map 4 B2.
Tel 01 242 7869.

La Noche
Av. Bolognesi 307.
Map 5 D4.
Tel 01 477 5829.

O'Murphy's Irish Pub
Schell 627. **Map** 4 C1.
Tel 01 445 1444.

Posada del Ángel
San Martín 157.
Map 4 C4.
Tel 01 247 5544.

CINEMA AND THEATER

Alianza Francesa
Av. Arequipa 4595,
Miraflores. **Map** 3 D4.
Tel 01 610 8000.
www.alianzafrancesa
lima.edu.pe

Centro Cultural de España
Natalio Sanchez 181,
Santa Beatriz. **Map** 1 E4.
Tel 01 330 0412.

Central Cultural PUCP
Av Camino Real 1075,
San Isidro. **Map** 5 E5.
Tel 01 222 6899. www.
cultural.pucp.edu.pe

El Cinematógrafo de Barranco
Pérez Roca 196,
Barranco. **Map** 4 C4.
Tel 01 477 1961.

ICPNA
(see p82).

Teatro Británico
Bellavista 527,
Miraflores. **Map** 4 B1.
Tel 01 447 9760.

Teatro Marsano
General Suárez 409,
Miraflores. **Map** 3 F4.
Tel 01 422 5373.

Teatro Segura
Huancavelica 265. **Map** 1 E1. *Tel* 01 426 7189.

CASINOS

Sheraton Lima
(see p270).

JW Marriott
(see p271).

Los Delfines
(see p271).

SPECTATOR SPORTS

Estadio Nacional
Via Expressa.

Plaza de Acho
Hualgayoc 332, Rimac.
Tel 01 481 1467.

STREET FINDER

The map below shows the area covered by the maps on the following pages. All map references given with sights, entertainment venues, and shops described in the Lima section of the guide refer to the Street Finder maps in this section. Map references are also given for Lima hotels and restaurants as well as for useful addresses in the *Travelers' Needs* and the *Survival Guide* sections at the back of the book. The main sights in the Central Lima area can be found on page 107 and those in San Isidro on pages 108 and 109. The main attractions of Miraflores are on pages 108–111, while Barranco's are shown on the maps on pages 110 and 111.

A 3-wheeler mototaxi

KEY TO STREET FINDER

■ Major sight	ℹ Visitor information
■ Other sight	⊠ Post office
■ Other building	▣ Police station
▣ Railroad station	▭ Highway
✚ Church	═ Railroad

SCALE OF MAPS 1–5

0 meters   500

0 yards   500

0 km   2

0 miles   2

Street Finder Index

15 de Enero **4 C2**
2 de Mayo **4 A1**
28 de Julio **5 D5**
8 de Agosto **1 D5**
8 de Octubre **2 A5**

A

Acacias **4 C3**
Águilas **3 D3**
Alcanfores **4 C2**
Althaus **2 C1**
Alzamora **2 B3**
Amapolas **3 D1**
Amazonas **1 F1**
Anaya **5 D5**
Andahuaylas **1 F2**
Andalucía **2 C4**
Andes **2 B3**
Angaraes **1 D1**
Ángeles **2 C4**
Antequera **2 C2**
Apurimac **1 F2**
Arce de la Oliva **5 D1**
Arenales **2 C4**
Arica **2 C5**
Arica (Prol) **5 E4**
Arñas **3 E2**
Arona **3 D3**
Arrieta **1 F5**
Avenida 2 de Mayo **2 B2**
Avenida 28 de Julio **4 B2**
Avenida A. Ugarte **1 D2**
Avenida A.Benavides **5 D2**
Avenida A.Tirado **1 F5**
Avenida Abancay **1 F2**
Avenida Aldania **3 F1**
Avenida Angamos
  Oeste **2 C5**
Avenida Aramburu **3 D3**
Avenida Arequipa **2 C3**
Avenida Argentina **1 D1**
Avenida Arica **1 D3**
Avenida Armendáriz **4 C3**
Avenida Arriola **3 E1**
Avenida Aviación **4 A1**
Avenida Balta **5 D4**
Avenida Basadre **2 B3**
Avenida Bauzate y
  Meza **1 F3**
Avenida Benavides **4 B1**
Avenida Bolivia **1 D3**
Avenida Brasil **1 D4**
Avenida Cáceres **4 C1**
Avenida Camino
  Real **2 B4**
Avenida Campodonico **3 D1**
Avenida Canada **3 E1**
Avenida Canaval y
  Moreyra **3 D3**
Avenida Canevaro **2 B1**
Avenida Carriquirry **3 E2**
Avenida Castilla **5 E2**
Avenida Castillo **5 E4**
Avenida Chávez **5 E4**
Avenida Colonial **1 D1**
Avenida Cuba **1 D5**

Avenida Cusco **1 F2**
Avenida de La
  Peruanidad **1 D4**
Avenida del Parque
  Norte **3 F2**
Avenida del Parque Sur **3 F3**
Avenida Ejército **2 B5**
Avenida El Sol **5 D3**
Avenida El Sol Oeste **4 C3**
Avenida Emancipación **1 E1**
Avenida Escuela Militar **5 D4**
Avenida Espinar **4 A1**
Avenida Galvez **2 C1**
Avenida Gálvez
  Barrenechea **3 F2**
Avenida Garcilaso
  de la Vega **1 E2**
Avenida Garzón **1 D4**
Avenida Grau **5 D4**
Avenida Guardia Civil **3 F2**
Avenida Guzmán
  Blanco **1 D3**
Avenida H.Unanue **2 B2**
Avenida Husares
  De Junin **2 A1**
Avenida Iquitos **2 C1**
Avenida Javier Prado
  Oeste **2 B2**
Avenida José Pardo **4 B1**
Avenida La Merced **5 E2**
Avenida La Paz **4 C1**
Avenida Larco **4 B1**
Avenida Manco Capac **1 F3**
Avenida Mariategui **1 D5**
Avenida Marsano **3 F4**
Avenida Militar **2 C1**
Avenida Miraflores **5 D4**
Avenida Montagne **5 E1**
Avenida N. de Pierola **1 F2**
Avenida Núñez de
  Balboa **4 C2**
Avenida O.Benavides **4 B1**
Avenida Palma **4 C1**
Avenida Pardo **2 C1**
Avenida Pardo y Aliaga **2 B4**
Avenida Petit Thouars **2 C2**
Avenida Pierola **5 D4**
Avenida Presccott **2 A2**
Avenida Principal **3 F4**
Avenida Reducto **4 C2**
Avenida República **2 C3**
Avenida República de
  Panamá **5 D2**
Avenida Roca y Boloña **5 D1**
Avenida Roosevelt **5 D4**
Avenida Rrepública
  Panamá **3 E4**
Avenida Salaverry **2 A1**
Avenida San Felipe **2 A1**
Avenida San Martín **4 C4**
Avenida Pedro
  de Osma **5 D5**
Avenida San Eugenio **3 D1**
Avenida Santa Catalina **3 E1**
Avenida Santa Cruz **2 C4**
Avenida Tacna **1 E1**

Avenida Tallanes **5 F3**
Avenida Tejada **5 D2**
Avenida Tomás
  Marsano **5 F1**
Avenida Ulloa **5 D1**
Avenida Uruguay **1 D2**
Avenida Venezuela **1 D2**
Avenida Villaran **5 E1**
Avenida Zavala **1 F3**
Avenida Zárdenas **1 D2**
Avenida Zorritos **1 D2**
Ayacucho **1 F2**
Ayacucho **5 F4**
Azángaro **1 F2**

B

B.Santos **5 D5**
Bañon **2 C2**
Barcelona **2 A2**
Batta Isola **5 D5**
Beaudiez **2 A4**
Begonias **3 D2**
Belaunde **2 B3**
Bélgica **1 F5**
Bella Vista **4 B1**
Berlín **4 A1**
Bermudez **1 E5**
Bernal **2 B2**
Bernales **3 E1**
Bernini **3 F2**
Bolívar **4 B2**
Bolognesi **4 A1**
Bonilla **4 B1**
Borgoño **2 C4**
Bresciani **5 D5**
Burgos **2 A2**
Bussalleu **3 E1**

C

Cáceres **5 F4**
Cachay Diaz **3 F1**
Cadiz **2 A2**
Calderon **2 C4**
Callao **1 E1**
Calle F **5 F1**
Calle J **3 F5**
Calle 0 **5 E1**
Calle 1 **5 E3**
Calle 10 **3 F2**
Calle 10 **5 E1**
Calle 12 **3 F2**
Calle 14 **5 D3**
Calle 16 **5 E3**
Calle 17 **5 D3**
Calle 18 **3 E2**
Calle 21 **3 E2**
Calle 22 **3 F3**
Calle 24 **3 F4**
Calle 25 **3 F4**
Calle 27 **3 F4**
Calle 3 **3 E3**
Calle 32 **3 F4**
Calle 33 **3 F3**
Calle 41 **3 E3**
Calle 5 **5 E2**
Calle 54 **3 E3**
Calle 6 **5 D3**

Calle 9 **3 F2**
Calle L **5 E1**
Camino Real **5 E5**
Candamo **2 C1**
Cañete **1 E1**
Canterac **1 D4**
Cápac Yupanqui **2 B2**
Carabaya **1 E2**
Caraz **5 D4**
Cárcamo **3 E1**
Cárdenas **1 F5**
Carhuaz **1 D2**
Carranza **1 F5**
Carrillo **1 E5**
Carrión **2 A2**
Casanova **2 C2**
Castañeda **1 F5**
Castañitas **3 E2**
Castaños **2 A3**
Castillo **4 C2**
Cavenecia **2 B4**
Cavero **5 D4**
Cde. de Superunda **1 E1**
Centenario **1 D4**
Central **3 D3**
Cervantes **2 B4**
Chacas **1 D2**
Chancay **1 E1**
Chávez **1 D3**
Chavín **1 D2**
Chiclayo **2 C5**
Chincha **1 E3**
Chinchón **3 D2**
Choquehuanca **2 B3**
Cipriani **3 F1**
Circuito de Playas **4 B2**
Codornices **3 E4**
Colina **4 B1**
Conde **2 C2**
Conquistadores **2 C4**
Córdova **2 B1**
Cornejo **5 F4**
Corpancho **1 E4**
Cotabambas **1 F2**
Cueto **2 B1**

D

Dalias **4 B2**
Dansey **1 D1**
Dante **3 E5**
Dasso **5 D3**
De la Torre Ugarte **2 C2**
Del Pino **1 F5**
Delucchi **4 C3**
Deportes **5 D5**
Deustua **3 F5**
Diaz **1 E4**
Diez Canseco **4 B1**
Domeyer **5 D4**
Don Aurelio **5 E2**
Don Bosco **1 D3**
Doña Edelmira **5 F3**
Dos de Mayo **5 D5**

E

Edison **2 A2**
El Carmen **3E5**
Eléspuru **2A3**

Enrique Palacios	**4 A1**	
Espejo	**3 E1**	
Esperanza	**4 B1**	
Estrella de Italia	**3 F2**	
Eucaliptos	**2 A3**	

F

Fanning	**4 B2**
Faustor	**5 F4**
Fedelli	**5 D3**
Fernandez	**1 F5**
Fernandez Concha	**5 D2**
Ferré	**4 B2**
Flores	**2 B1**
Francia	**5 D5**
Fray Luis de León	**3 F2**
Fuentes	**3 D3**

G

Galeón	**5 F2**
Gálvez	**5 F4**
Gálvez Jose	**4 A1**
García Naranjo	**1 F3**
Garcilaso de la Vega	**2 B2**
Gardenias	**3 D2**
Garzas	**3 D3**
Gibson	**2 C2**
Gómez	**2 B1**
Gonzáles	**4 B2**
Gonzáles Prada	**3 E5**
Gral. Cordova	**2 B5**
Granda	**2 A3**
Grau	**4 A1**
Grojillas	**3 E2**
Guido	**2 C1**
Guisse	**2 B2**

H

Habana	**2 C3**
Habich	**2 C5**
Halcones	**3 E4**
Harris	**2 A4**
Heraud	**5 D3**
Herrera	**2 C1**
Huallaga	**1 F1**
Huancavelica	**1 D1**
Huancayo	**1 E3**
Huántar	**1 D2**
Huaraz	**1 D2**
Huarochiri	**1 D1**
Huáscar	**2 A1**

I

Ica	**1 E1**
Iglesias	**2 B1**
Inclán	**3 D5**
Independencia	**2 C5**
Iquique	**1 D2**
Irigoyen	**5 D2**
Isaacs	**3 F4**
Isabel la Catolica	**1 F4**
Italia	**4 A1**
Iturregui Jose M	**3 E4**

J

Jara y Ureta	**5 E2**
Jazmines	**3 D2**
Jilgueros	**3 E2**
Junin	**3 E4**

K

Kenko	**5 F2**

L

La Mar	**2B5**
Lampa	**1 F2**
Larco Herrera	**2 C5**
Laurel Rosa	**5 F1**
Laureles	**2 A3**
Lavalle	**4 B2**
Lazo	**2 C1**
León	**4 A1**
León García	**3 D1**
León Velarde	**2 B1**
Leoncio Prado	**3 E5**
Leticia	**1 F2**
Lilas	**3 D1**
Lima	**5 D4**
Llona	**3 D4**
Lloque Yupanqui	**1 D5**
Lopez de Ayala	**3 F2**
Luna	**5 E4**
Luna Pizarro	**1 F4**
Luzuriaga	**1 D5**

M

Madrid	**4 A1**
Magnolia	**5 F1**
Malecón de La Reserva	**4 B2**
Malecón Harris	**4 C3**
Malecón Junín	**4 C4**
Malecón Osma	**4 C5**
Malecón Pazos	**4 C4**
Malecón Souza	**4 C4**
Mama Ocllo	**2 A1**
Manco Cápac	**4 B2**
Manco Segundo	**2 A2**
Marconi	**2 A2**
Mariategui	**5 D4**
Márquez	**1 D4**
Martinez	**4 C4**
Maurtua	**2 B4**
Meiggs	**2 C5**
Mendiburu	**2 B5**
Merino	**2 C1**
Miranda	**5 D3**
Miró Quesada	**2 A3**
Montero	**3 E4**
Montero Rosas	**1 F5**
Morales	**2 C3**
Morán	**2 B2**
Morococha	**3 E4**

N

Naranjos	**2 B2**
Negocios	**3 E4**
Nicaragua	**2 A2**
Nogales	**2 B3**

O

Ocoña	**1 E2**
Olavegoya	**2 A1**
Olmedo	**1 D3**
Oroya	**1 D1**
Orúe	**3 E4**
Osores	**2 A3**

P

Palmeras	**2 B2**
Parasol	**5 F1**

Paseo de La República	**1 E3**
Paseo La Castellana	**5 F3**
Paseo Padre Bolívar	**2 C3**
Paseo Parque Alto	**5 E4**
Pazos	**5 E5**
Pereyra	**5 D3**
Petit Thouars	**3 D5**
Pezet	**2 A4**
Pisac	**5 F2**
Piura	**2 B5**
Plaza	**1 D5**
Pomabamba	**1 D2**
Porta	**4 B2**
Portocarrero	**3 E4**
Progreso	**5 D3**
Puno	**1 F2**

Q

Quilca	**1 E2**
Quiñones	**2 B5**

R

Raimondi	**1 F3**
Rebagliati	**2 B1**
Ribeyro	**1 D4**
Recavarren	**4 B1**
Recuay	**1 D2**
Rep. de Chile	**1 E4**
Rep. Dominicana	**1 D5**
Retiro	**2 B5**
Ribeyro	**5 D2**
Rio de La Plata	**2 C3**
Robles	**2 B3**
Roma	**2 A2**
Rosales	**3 D2**
Rosario	**2 B3**
Ruiseñores	**3 E2**

S

Saenz Pena	**4 C4**
Salaverry	**3 E4**
Salguero	**5 F2**
San Agustín	**3 E5**
San Alberto	**3 F5**
San Carlos	**3 E5**
San Diego	**4 C1**
San Felipe	**3 E4**
San Fernand	**4 C2**
San Fernando	**3 F5**
San Lorenzo	**3 E4**
San Martín	**4 B2**
San Pedrito	**5 E4**
San Pedro	**3 E5**
San Tadeo	**5 E2**
Sánchez Cerro	**2 A1**
Sánchez Pinillos	**1 D2**
Santa Carmela	**5 D2**
Santa Cruz	**1 D5**
Santa Ines	**3 E5**
Santa Luisa	**2 C3**
Santa Margarita	**2 A4**
Santa Rosa	**3 E5**
Santa Teresita	**2 A4**
Santo Toribio	**2 B3**
Sartre	**3 F4**
Sauces	**2 B2**
Schell	**4 B1**
Segura	**1 F5**
Seminario	**3 D2**
Sevilla	**3 D4**

Silva	**4 C1**
Sinchi Roca	**2 A1**
Solar	**4 C2**
Soledad	**2 C2**
Sor Mate	**5 E2**
Souza	**5 D3**
Sucre	**2 B5**

T

Tambo de Belen	**1 E2**
Tacna	**5 F3**
Tamayo	**2 C3**
Tarapaca	**2 C5**
Tarma	**1 E3**
Tayacaja	**1 D1**
Tello	**2 B1**
Tenaud	**3 D4**
Teruel	**2 C4**
Tiendas	**3 E3**
Tizon y Bueno	**2 A1**
Tordillas	**3 E2**
Torrico	**1 E2**
Triana	**2 B5**
Trípoli	**4 A2**
Tudela y Varela	**2 B4**
Tulipanes	**3 D1**
Tupac Amaru	**2 B2**

U

Ucayali	**1 F1**
Ugarriza	**5 D2**
Unanue	**1 F4**
Union	**1 E2**
Urteaga	**1 D4**

V

Valdivia	**3 D2**
Valega Sayan	**5 D5**
Vanderghen	**2 B4**
Varela	**1 D3**
Vargas	**2 C4**
Vargas Machuca	**4 C1**
Velarde	**1 E4**
Venecia	**4 A2**
Venegas	**5 E4**
Vesaglio	**3 F3**
Vidal	**1 D4**
Vidaurre	**5 D3**
Vigil	**5 D4**
Villar	**2 A5**
Villarán	**3 E1**
Villavicencio	**2 B2**

W

Washington	**1 E2**

Y

Yauyos	**1 E3**
Yerovi	**2 B4**

Z

Zela	**2 B2**
Zepita	**1 D2**

PERU REGION BY REGION

PERU AT A GLANCE 114–115
THE SOUTHERN COAST 116–129
CANYON COUNTRY 130–151
THE INCA HEARTLAND 152–181
CENTRAL SIERRA 182–195
CORDILLERA BLANCA 196–213
THE NORTHERN DESERT 214–233
THE NORTHERN HIGHLANDS 234–247
THE AMAZON BASIN 248–263

Peru at a Glance

The massive Andes mountain range divides the country down the middle, with dense jungle on one side covering 60 percent of Peru's landmass, and sandy desert edging the coast on the other side. Unique animal and plant life flourish across all regions, which are also dotted with magnificent examples of ancient civilizations including the Nazca Lines, Chan Chan, Chavín de Huántar, and Machu Picchu. The Colonial monasteries and churches evoke the Spanish conquest in myriad towns and isolated villages.

Kuélap (see pp244–6) *is an imposing pre-Inca walled city perched above Río Utcubamba.*

Museo Tumbas Reales de Sipán (see pp228–31) *showcases the amazing archaeological finds of the Royal Tombs of Sipán, dubbed "the richest tomb of the New World" for all the beautifully crafted artifacts unearthed.*

THE NORTHERN DESERT
(see pp214–233)

THE NORTHERN HIGHLANDS
(see pp234–247)

Chavín de Huántar (see pp208-9) *is one of the best preserved Chavín sites and provides an insight into their sophisticated construction and artistic skills.*

CORDILLERA BLANCA
(see pp196–213)

LIMA
(see pp54–111)

Reserva Nacional de Paracas (see p123) *is the country's largest area of protected coastline, teeming with wildlife. Towering cliffs fringe the beaches along some of the richest seas in the world.*

◁ Amazing color of the salt terraces highlighted by the sunlight, Moray

Reserva Nacional Pacaya-Samiria (see p255), *Peru's largest reserve, covers a huge swathe of original Amazon rain-forest. It is the ideal place for boat trips, wildlife-spotting, and treks through the jungle.*

Huancayo to Lima (see p187) *is among the most spectacular train journeys in the world, and was, until recently, the highest too. The route passes through some breath-taking Andean scenery.*

THE AMAZON BASIN
(see pp248–263)

Machu Picchu (see pp176–81), *the lost city of the Incas, is the most famous archaeological site in South America. The mist-cloaked citadel is a big draw with tourists owing to its grandeur and the immense sense of mystery surrounding it.*

CENTRAL SIERRA
(see pp182–195)

THE INCA HEARTLAND
(see pp152–181)

THE SOUTHERN COAST
(see pp116–129)

CANYON COUNTRY
(see pp130–151)

0 km   150

0 miles   150

Lake Titicaca (see pp146–50), *legendary birthplace of the first Inca, is a place of folklore and traditional ways of life. The world's highest navigable lake is dotted with islands, some of which are man-made from reeds.*

THE SOUTHERN COAST

Peru's southern coast is a strange mix of barren desert and teeming sea. It is a parched landscape left arid by the icy air of the Humboldt ocean current, a phenomenon which contrastingly endows the water with an opulent supply of marine life, much of which is protected in coastal wildlife reserves.

Boobies, penguins, and flamingos fluff feathers, while sea lions bounce off rocks to swim in the chilly waters. Even the Andean condor, lured by the promise of abundant food, makes an appearance.

Remains uncovered in this dry tract reveal a fascinating blend of cultures, dating back at least 5,000 years. The Paracas civilization fashioned textiles in 300 BC with an artistry that still resonates today.

The Nazca people created their mysterious giant drawings in the desert some 2,000 years ago, and the purpose of these enormous geoglyphs puzzles experts to this day. Aqueducts which they built remain in use, and the ceramics they produced are among the finest of the pre-Columbian era.

African slaves, brought to local plantations by the Spanish conquistadores in the 16th century, sowed the seeds within their close-knit communities for the Afro-Peruvian music now venerated across the country.

Despite the aridity of the land, agriculture thrives here thanks to the centuries-old systems of irrigation that use underground water supplies. The Spanish first introduced grape stocks in the 1550s and such was the success that the district around Ica is now Peru's wine basin and home to the national drink, pisco.

The region also played an instrumental trading role in the 19th century due to its island deposits of guano (bird droppings), then a sought-after fertilizer. Nowadays, the local economy is powered by grapes, cotton, olives, fruits, and nuts.

Even the desert has its own appeal. Dunes whipped into peaks by strong winds attract sand-boarders and dune buggy riders, and hidden in the sands are the remains of prehistoric pelicans and whale-eating sharks.

Pink-walled Colonial hacienda of Bodega Tacama, the oldest vineyard in Peru

◁ The mysterious El Candelabro geoglyph, best seen on a boat trip to the Islas Ballestas

Exploring the Southern Coast

Sand dunes, wineries, and the enigmatic Nazca Lines are the tourist magnets of this region. The city of Ica is the ideal departure point for a marine fossil hunt through the desert in four-wheel drives – two million years ago there was an ocean here – or a leisurely pisco tasting in one of more than 80 vineyards. Tambo Colorado displays the Incas' building prowess, while the pyramids at Cahuachi are a souvenir of the earlier Nazca culture. Chincha is famed as the center of Afro-Peruvian music and traditions, with the nearby Hacienda San José providing an insight into plantation life in the 17th century. The Paracas National Reserve and the Ballestas Islands are sanctuaries for bird and other wildlife; the islands have been dubbed the "Peruvian Galapagos".

Owl Man geoglyph, Nazca Lines

SEE ALSO

- **Where to Stay** p272

- **Where to Eat** pp292–3

La Caravedo organic winery, Ica

SIGHTS AT A GLANCE

Towns and Cities
Chincha Alta **1**
Ica **5**
Nazca **9**
Pisco **2**

Archaeological Sites and Ruins
Cahuachi **10**
Cementerio de Chauchilla **11**
Nazca Lines pp126–7 **8**
Tambo Colorado **3**

Areas of Natural Beauty
Islas Ballestas **4**
*Reserva Nacional de Paracas
 p123* **7**

Tour
Pisco Bodegas **6**

Cliffs and clay beach at Reserva Nacional de Paracas

GETTING AROUND

Ica and Nazca have domestic airports for charter flights from Lima. The Panamerican Highway South links Lima with Ica and Nazca and there are regular daily bus services, though crime has been reported on some budget routes. Minibuses and *colectivos* operate from Ica to Nazca and Pisco. Boats leave from Pisco or Paracas for tours to the Ballestas Islands. Taxis can be hired in Ica for visits to Lake Huacachina or winery tours.

Chiara
Casacancha
Vilcanchos
Cangallo
Paccha
Vilcashuamán
Sarhua
Huancapi
Carhuanca
Hualla
Huanca Sancos
Sacsamarca
Querobamba
Soras
Putaccasa
Santa Ana de Huaycahuacho
AYACUCHO
Andamarca
Chipao
oca
CAHUACHI Lucanas **10**
Tambo Quemado
Puquio
26A
Reserva Nacional Pampa Galeras
San Pedro
Saisa
Santa Lucía
Chaviña
Sancos
San Javier de Alpabamba
Río Acari
Chumpi
Pararca
Lampa
Huanca
Río Yauca
Púllo
Incuyo
Pausa
Bella Holanda
Laguna Parinacochas
Río Huanca
Río Capnaayo
Cordillera de Huanzo

KEY

— Main road

═══ Minor road

•═•═ Untarred main road

═•═• Untarred minor road

- - - Track

— Regional border

0 km	50
0 miles	50

Chincha Alta ❶

Road Map C5. 121 miles (194 km)
S of Lima. 👥 *58,250.* 🚂 *from Lima*
📅 *Verano Negro (last week Feb),
Fiestas Patrias (Jul 28 & 29), Virgin
del Carmen (Dec 27).*

Up to the 14th century when
the Incas arrived, Chincha had
been the domain of the small
Chincha Empire, the ruins of
Tambo de Mora attesting to
their presence. Nowadays,
home to one of the country's
largest black communities, it is
renowned across Peru as the
hub of Afro-Peruvian music,
along with nearby El Carmen.

Slaves were originally
brought to the area to work
on the large sugar and cotton
plantations congregated here;
a census of 1570 registered
more blacks than Spanish
living in coastal Peru.

The blacks guarded their
music and traditions as best
they could, passing them
down over the centuries but
also melding them with indigenous and Spanish elements.

In February, the Verano
Negro (Black Summer) festival showcases all aspects of
Afro-Peruvian culture including food, music, dance, and
storytelling, drawing large
local and international crowds.

Environs

Originally built by Jesuits and
currently being rebuilt after
extensive earthquake damage,
Hacienda San José began as a
sugar plantation in 1688. It
was at one time the richest
hacienda, with 1,000 slaves.
With its founders' portraits and
cell for runaway slaves, it gives
a glimpse of 17th-century life
on both sides of the fence.

Chapel façade at Hacienda San José prior to earthquake damage

Pisco ❷

Road Map C5. 144 miles (231 km)
S of Lima. 👥 *56,300.* 🚌 *from Ica*
🚤 *boat tours of Paracas Bay and
Islas Ballestas.* ℹ️ *Municipalidad
(Town Hall) on main plaza.*

Founded in 1640, Pisco, a
quiet city of farmers and
fishermen, was unable to
withstand the earthquake
that rocked the area
on August 15, 2007.
Three-quarters of
the town was lost
as historic buildings
around the plaza
crumbled, tens of
thousands of adobe
homes collapsed and
hundreds of people
died. The statue of
liberator, José de
San Martín in the
main plaza was
left to survey the
ruins including the
18th-century San
Clemente church, which caved
in during mass, killing a
number of worshippers. Boats
bound for the Ballestas Islands
still depart from the port.

Statue of José de San
Martín, Pisco

Tambo Colorado ❸

Road Map C5. Los Libertadores
Highway, opposite Panamerican
Highway South, KM229. 🚌 *from
Pisco, negotiate half-day rate.*
🕘 *9am–4pm daily.* 📷 ✔️ *take
a tour from an agency in Pisco.*

Once a significant Inca
administrative center, Tambo
Colorado sits at the base
of steep foothills in the
Pisco river valley. It was
a connecting point on
the Inca road joining
Ayacucho with the
coast, making it ideal
for overseeing the
flow of people and
produce. It is thought
that the ninth Inca,
Pachacútec, lived
here at one time.
Despite its lack of
roofing, it is one of
the best preserved
adobe ruins in
Peru. Niches in the
stucco outer walls bear traces
of the red and yellow pig-
ment used to decorate them,
and alcoves are adorned with
carvings of human figures.

The Inca ruins of Tambo Colorado with traces of red paint just visible

For hotels and restaurants in this region see p272 and pp292–3

Islas Ballestas ❹

Road Map C5. 150 miles (240 km) S of Lima. 🚌 *from Pisco or El Chaco port, Paracas.* ⬤ *8:30am–10:30pm daily.* 🎟️ 📷 *can only be visited as part of organized tour from agencies in Pisco, Paracas, and Paracas hotels.*

The Ballestas Islands are among the most popular draws on the Southern Coast. It is possible to take a boat tour around the islands, but visitors are not allowed to disembark.

A series of arches and caves provide shelter for more than 160 species of marine birds, including Humboldt penguins, boobies, and pelicans, as well as immense numbers of sea lions, incessantly barking, biting, basking, and throwing their hefty bodies into the sea. Dolphins and whales sometimes appear, too.

Old factory remains on the islands are a throwback to the 19th century when guano (mineral-rich bird droppings) was an important fertilizer and provided a vital source of revenue for the country.

General San Martín landed his army here in 1820 before disembarking on the nearby mainland to secure Peru's independence from Spain.

Look out for the startling Candelabra geoglyph *(see pp116 and 123)* visible on the way to and from the islands. Some say it was a navigational aid while others claim it is a pirate's sign. Do take warm clothing and sun protection as the boats are not covered.

The desert oasis of Huacachina, ringed by palm and *huarangos* trees

Ica ❺

Road Map C5. 200 miles (325 km) S of Lima. 👥 *122,376.* ✈️ *charter services from Lima.* 🚌 *from Lima* 🎊 *Vendimia (Grape Harvest, first 2 weeks Mar), El Señor de Luren (3rd Sun of Oct).* **www**.muniica.gob.pe

Founded by the Spanish in 1563 as Villa de Valverde, the village was relocated and renamed in 1640, and is now Peru's premier wine center with vineyards dating back to the 16th century.

The city was badly affected by the 2007 earthquake, Peru's worst since 1974. A chapel in the Neo-Classical Sanctuario del Señor del Luren collapsed during evening mass, killing several people and injuring dozens. The church, named for Our Lord of Luren, the city's patron saint, was among an estimated quarter of the buildings that were damaged. Over 2,800 pre-Hispanic artifacts in museums across the Ica region suffered irreparable damage during the earthquake.

Ica's **Museo Regional Adolfo Bermúdez Jenkins**, which houses an interesting collection of Paracas, Nazca, Ica, Chincha, and Inca artifacts including mummies and skulls showing evidence of ancient surgical techniques, escaped relatively unscathed.

Environs

A green lagoon amidst towering dunes, the oasis of **Huacachina** is just 3 miles (5 km) from Ica. Swimming is allowed but most come to sand-board or ride the dunes.

🏛 **Museo Regional Adolfo Bermúdez Jenkins**
Av. Ayabaca 8va. **Tel** *034 234 383.* ⬤ *8am–7pm Mon–Sat, 9am–1pm Sun and pub hols.* 🎟️ 📷 🚫 ♿ *charge for cameras and video recorders.*

EL CARMEN

From the 16th to 18th centuries, slaves from all over West Africa made their homes in El Carmen. With no common language or tribal leader, they developed a distinctive style of music to help them unite. Combining African, Andean, and Spanish elements, Afro-Peruvian music is known for its use of traditional instruments like the *cajón*, a wooden box drum, and *quijada de burro*, made from a donkey's jaw bone. The music moved mainstream in the 1970s, when the group Peru Negro and singers such as Chabuca Granda embraced it. Today, it is the pride of Peru. El Carmen is also famous for 24-hour partying come festival time, especially around Christmas.

Boys playing Afro-Peruvian music

A nesting colony of Peruvian boobies, Islas Ballestas

A Tour of Pisco Bodegas ❻

El Catador pisco

Peru's first vineyards were planted near Ica in the 1550s, using vines brought by the Spanish conquistadores. The industry flourished until the 17th century when Spain banned the exportation of Peruvian wine because it was damaging their own economy. Wine-makers then turned their full attention to making a clear grape brandy, which came to be known as pisco. Today, the major producers and small artisans are still based around Ica, Peru's pisco capital.

TIPS FOR VISITORS

Getting there: *If you don't have your own transport, some bodegas can be reached by combis, or you can hire a taxi.*
When to visit: *Most are open year round for tours. The harvest festival (Vendimia) is in March.*

KEY

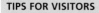

━━━ Tour route

═══ Other roads

| 0 km | | 3 |
| 0 miles | | 3 |

El Caravedo ⑥
Established in 1877, this bodega became Peru's first producer of organic pisco.

Bodega Tacama ③
Established in 1540, Tacama is the oldest vineyard in Peru. A bell tower, part of the watermelon-pink Colonial hacienda, overlooks 450 lush acres (180 ha) planted with 20 different grape varieties.

Bodega Lazo ⑤
Sipping pisco under arbors of bougainvillea, surrounded by 19th-century grape presses and barrels, is a local pastime at this tiny bodega.

Bodega Lovera ②
The Lovera family have been making pisco since 1867. Today, a sixth generation of producers combine their age-old artisanal methods with more advanced technology to create some award-winning pisco.

El Catador (Tres Esquinas) ④

Come harvest time, visitors to family-run El Catador are invited to join in treading grapes underfoot. Crushed grapes are still pressed in a vast adobe platform weighed down by a 19th-century tree trunk.

Vista Alegre ①
Founded by the Jesuits, it was taken over in 1857 by Italian Emmanuel Picasso and his brothers, and today remains in the hands of the same family. Peru's largest vineyard, it can distil up to 15,000 liters of pisco a day.

Reserva Nacional de Paracas **❼**

Pelican, Lagunillas

The desert meets the sea in dramatic fashion at the Paracas National Reserve, Peru's largest piece of protected coastline, with towering cliffs fringing beaches swarming with wildlife. The reserve is home to more than 1,800 species of plants and animals, and provides a habitat for both resident and migratory waterbirds, including flamingos, Humboldt penguins, pelicans, sanderlings, moorhens, boobies, cormorants, and terns. On occasions, condors can be seen circling overhead, along with ferocious-looking red-headed vultures.

SIGHTS AT A GLANCE

El Candelabro ④
La Catedral ②
Isla San Gallán ①
Lagunillas ⑤
Paracas Necropolis and Museo ③

KEY

🛥	Boat trips
═	Minor road
– –	Track
⋇	Viewpoint

VISITORS' CHECKLIST

Road Map C5. 150 miles (240 km) S of Lima. 🚌 🚗 from Pisco. 🚹 ⏰ 7am–6pm daily. 🖾 arrange agency tour in Pisco. 🏠 Lagunillas and Playa Atenas. 🏛 **Museo de Sitio Julio C. Tello** Bahía de Paracas. ⏰ 9am–5pm Tue–Sun. 🖾

The reserve has archaeological significance too. Behind the visitors' center is the **Paracas Necropolis**, burial ground of the Paracas people (700 BC), who buried their dead in elaborate funerary bundles of colorful embroidered textiles. They are considered the finest examples of pre-Columbian textiles in the country, though most are now housed in museums in Lima.

Museo de Sitio Julio C. Tello, named for the archaeologist who discovered the mummies, contains a small display of textiles, ceramics, and skulls.

The bay in front of the museum is home to flamingos. A trail leads down to a look-out with a great view of the scarlet-and-white birds that inspired the Peruvian flag. Liberator José de San Martín landed nearby and was supposedly impressed by them.

Beyond the museum, a trail off the road to Puerto San Martín leads to the three-pronged **El Candelabro**, a 490-ft- (150-m-) high geoglyph stamped into the desert hill-side. Some say it was a navigational aid, but more likely it's a Nazca ritual symbol.

Scuba diving, swimming, and kite- or windsurfing are possible off beaches but be warned there are stingrays and jellyfish. The tiny village of **Lagunillas** comprises pretty beaches and fish restaurants.

The **San Gallán** and **La Vieja Islands**, which lie just off the coast, are the only places for the endangered *potoyunco* (Peruvian diving petrel) to reproduce in Peru.

Marine mammals also abound including sea lions, seals, sea turtles, marine otters, dolphins, and the endangered *chinguno* (sea cat). **La Catedral**, a rock formation created by centuries of pounding from ocean winds and tides, was badly damaged in the 2007 earthquake but still provides one of the few homes to the *chinguno* in the area.

The cliff lookout of **Punta Arquillo** allows for views of a sea lion colony on the rocks below, which teems with the beasts during the December to March mating season. Unfortunately, several viewing areas were affected by the devastating earthquake.

The distinctive red-brown sands of a beach near Lagunillas

Ancient trapezoids and lines drawn in the desert near Nazca ▷

Nazca Lines ⑧

It never rains on the Peruvian coast which is why the remarkable Nazca Lines have survived so many centuries, preserving the secrets of an ancient culture. Dispersed over the high desert plateau between the towns of Nazca and Palpa, this collection of geoglyphs, comprising more than 70 human figures and stylized animals, and 10,000 lines, was first noticed from the air in 1927. Etched into the plains between 500 BC and AD 500, they were declared a UNESCO World Heritage Site in 1994. Debate continues about their original purpose – giant astronomical calendar, ceremonial center, or alien landing strip – ensuring they remain one of the world's great archaeological mysteries.

Flying the Lines
The graphic beauty and sheer complexity of the lines can best be seen from the air.

★ The Hummingbird
Measuring 315 by 217 ft (96 by 66 m), this is one of the best-known geoglyphs. The Nazca believed hummingbirds were messengers between the worlds of men and condors, which they considered to be gods.

Río Nasca

★ The Monkey
The monkey was regarded as a divine being. This image has only nine fingers and Maria Reiche suggested it may have been made to mark the equinoxes. The monkey also appears on Nazca ceramics.

Trapezoids
Researchers assumed the trapezoid figures in the desert were used for ceremonies, others have fancifully speculated they were runways for alien spaceships.

STAR SIGHTS

* ★ The Hummingbird
* ★ The Monkey
* ★ The Spider

★ The Spider
The spider is identified as being both a symbol of rain and fertility, and a representation of the soothsayers, who used the creatures to predict the future.

VISITORS' CHECKLIST

Road Map C5. 12 miles (20 km) N of Nazca, Panamerican Highway South, KM420.
🛈 *Nazca Municipalidad (Town Hall) 056 522 418, until 2pm.*
✈ *in Nazca for flights over lines.*
🚌 *to viewing platform only.*
🎧 *commentary from pilots.* ♿ *some planes may accommodate.*
Please note: map not to scale.

The Tree
The Tree is one of only a few figures visible from the viewing platform. The Nazca may have made the lines to worship Kon, a flying god of water, which explains why they were probably designed to be seen from above.

Viewing platform

VIEWING THE LINES
There's a free viewing platform at KM420 but the best way to see the lines is from one of the 3–9-seater planes flying out of Nazca airport. Prices of flights vary from company to company but range between US$30–51 for a 30- to 45-minute trip. Flights leave in the morning and early afternoon, weather permitting, with the best time usually between 8–10:30am, though it can be hazy in the early morning.

Nazca town

Panamerican Highway South

Airport

MARIA REICHE (1903–98)
German mathematician and astronomer, Maria Reiche, began studying the Nazca Lines in the 1940s and devoted her life to uncovering their mysteries. As the giant, perfectly proportionate geoglyphs seemed to be pointing to the stars, she believed they were sophisticated astral charts. Before her death in 1998, she concluded they were part of a huge astronomical calendar to commune with the gods, and thus secure water and blessings for crops. She believed the lines were created by tying a chord to an axis, just as a compass is used to draw a circle.

Maria Reiche

The Whale
The first geoglyph to be discovered, it probably depicts a killer whale or orca.

Adobe pyramid at Cahuachi, built by the Nazca culture

Nazca ⑨

Road Map C5. 273 miles (440 km) S of Lima. 🏚 26,000. ✈ from Lima and for Nazca Lines. 🚌 from Lima. 🚌 from Ica. 🛈 in Town Hall.

The discovery of the Nazca Lines put the sun-baked town of Nazca on the map, and that is the main reason most people visit the area.

The **Museo Antonini**, however, makes a worthwhile stop. It displays many of the finds from the Cahuachi site made by Italian archaeologist, Giuseppe Orefici. The collection gives an insight into all aspects of Nazca society, and includes mummies and distorted heads – the Nazca wrapped the heads of their newborns in leather or wood bands. It also has an important collection of ceramic *antaras* (pan flutes), and ceramics, portraying sea creatures and gods, and textiles, including one festooned with iconic birds gobbling serpents and four-legged animals.

The archaeological park behind the museum features a scale model of the Nazca Lines, a replica of a Nazca tomb, and the pre-Columbian Bisambra Aqueduct.

Nazca bowl, Museo Antonini

🏛 **Museo Antonini**
Av. de la Cultura 600. **Tel** 056 523 444. ◯ 9am–7pm daily. 🌐
http://digilander.libero.it/MD Antonini/English.htm

Cahuachi ⑩

Road Map C5. 11 miles (17 km) NW of Nazca. ◯ no set hours. 🌐 organized tour from Nazca.

Cahuachi, an enormous Nazca ceremonial center, reached its zenith more than 2,000 years ago. Extending across 370 acres (150 ha), it is dominated by a 100-ft (30-m) high central pyramid and plaza. Forty other pyramids were sculpted from the landscape with massive mud-brick adobe walls applied over them. Some 5,000 tombs have been identified but, sadly, Cahuachi has suffered from looting.

Archaeologist Giuseppe Orefici has been excavating the site for decades and has concluded it was home to priests who conducted public ceremonies and rituals to thank the gods for water. The site's numerous treasures can be seen at the Museo Antonini, and should help to unravel the secrets of the Nazca Line builders.

Cementerio de Chauchilla ⑪

Road Map C5. 19 miles (30 km) S of Nazca. 🚌 from Nazca, negotiate half-day rate. ◯ 8am–6pm daily. 🌐 best to visit on an organized tour.

Chauchilla Cemetery, naturally enough, is full of graves dating back to the Chincha period (AD 1000–1400). At one stage mummies were scattered across the site, courtesy of tomb-raiders who fleeced the bodies of valuables and discarded textile scraps, bones, and carcasses in the desert. From an archaeologist's point of view, they effectively robbed the bodies of their identities and in doing so hindered researchers' ability to piece together the history of the people found here.

There are thousands of graves but only 12 have been restored and they show carefully positioned, shrouded mummies in squatting positions with bleached skulls and long matted hair. There is also a children's-only grave.

Normally the mummies would have been well preserved because the arid sands are rich in salt and nitrates, but their exposure to the elements destroyed the mummified skin and faded the bones.

Squatting mummies in a restored tomb, Cementerio de Chauchilla

The Southern Beaches

The asphalt ribbon of the Panamerican Highway South carves through Peru's coastal desert, making beach-hopping an easy pursuit. The northern beaches might be more famous, but the southern coast has its own different attractions: archaeological ruins, rugged cliffs, rampant marine and bird life, along with the more

Sign for Inca ruins, Puerto Inca

traditional pleasures such as fishing and swimming. Most fishing villages have boats for rent, or locals who are happy to ferry visitors around for a small price. Secluded beaches dot the coast but be warned the water is cold and lifeguards rare. On remote or isolated beaches, campers should always camp in groups.

Punta San Fernando ①
The Humboldt Current flows close to the shore here, guaranteeing a rich supply of marine life which attracts the Andean condor.

Punta San Juan de Marcona ②
This protected zone provides refuge to almost 75 percent of Peru's Humboldt penguin population and 50 percent of its pure-bred sea lions.

Las Lomas ③
A small fishing village with a beach that is ideal for pelican watching. Good, too, for sole and sea bass fishing.

Puerto Inca ④
These pre-Columbian ruins are thought to be the starting point for one of the most important Inca trails (see p47). Fresh fish were dried and then transported to Cusco by a network of runners. The crescent-shaped beach is popular for swimming and fishing.

Chala ⑤
This tumbledown fishing village with a lighthouse is a favorite stop-off point for a bite of super-fresh seafood. Boat rental is also available if you want to go seal spotting.

Key to Symbols *see back flap*

CANYON COUNTRY

*N**owhere else in Peru is the air so clear and the sunlight so radiant as here in its folkloric heart. The Colonial city of Arequipa, with its stately mansions, churches, and cloisters, sits in stark contrast to its untamed surrounds, where high altitude deserts, active volcanoes, and yawning canyons – particularly Colca and Cotahuasi, reputed to be the deepest in the world – abound.*

This area embodies nature at its most spectacular. Majestic condors soar above the Colca and Cotahuasi Canyons and villages with thatched houses. Rock art found here is testimony to a civilization dating back more than 8,000 years, while lush 2,000-year-old agricultural terraces recall the ingenuity of the Collagua people.

In the 14th century, Inca leader Mayta Cápac sealed his victory over the Collagua by marrying the daughter of a local chief and building her a house made of copper. This same mineral wealth – gold, silver, lead, copper, quartz – drew the Spanish conquistadores in the 16th century. The Colonial heritage is on full display in the Baroque churches that dominate villages such as Chucuito.

The Colca River, which stretches from Peru's southern highlands through the western Andes and on to the Pacific Coast, courses through the Colca Canyon, providing adventurers with countless white-water rafting opportunities. Mount Ampato, near Arequipa, where the mummified body of Juanita, the Ice Maiden, was discovered, attracts climbers.

Farther east lies the sapphire expanse of Lake Titicaca, hailed in Inca mythology as the birthplace of their civilization. Legend has it that Manco Cápac, the son of the Sun, and Mama Ocllo, the daughter of the Moon, emerged from the lake to found the Inca Empire. The world's highest navigable lake is shared with Bolivia, as is the local language, Aymara.

Ancient settlements of weavers, fishermen, and farmers still ply their trade around the shore and on near and far islands, including the famous floating isles made entirely from reeds.

A group of local women and children in colorful traditional attire, Chivay

◁ The Silence Yard where nuns read the Bible in total silence, Monasterio de Santa Catalina, Arequipa

Exploring Canyon Country

The classic starting point for touring this area is Arequipa (7,546 ft/3,810 m), a Colonial jewel built on the slopes of a volcano and the commercial hub of southern Peru. Travelers often stop here en route to Lake Titicaca to get acclimatized to the altitude. The canyons of Colca and Cotahuasi, north of Arequipa, abound with hiking, rafting, and mountain biking opportunities. There is also ample scope to view diverse species of birds and herds of alpaca and vicuña. Near Lake Titicaca, the city of Lampa hosts a replica of Michelangelo's *La Pieta* while tiny Juli is replete with Colonial churches. In between lies Sillustani, with its burial towers, and Puno, the departure point for the islands dotting the lake. Along the lake, women in multi-colored, layered skirts can be seen knitting.

Fountain in the cloisters courtyard, La Compañia, Arequipa

SEE ALSO

• **Where to Stay** pp273–4

• **Where to Eat** pp293–4

0 km   50

0 miles   50

Mina Arcata

Puyca   Suycutambo

Ica

Mina Acari
Acari

Lomas

Yanamachay   Cahuacho

③ CAÑÓN DE COTAHUASI

Solimana
20,744 ft/
6,323m   Andagua

Chichas

Coropuma
21,696ft/
6,613m

Cordillera de Chillán

Rio

Tisco
18,362ft/
5,597m

Parcoy

Cerro
Rico

Caraveli

CAÑÓN DEL COLCA ②

Ampato
20,702ft/
6,310m

Chivay

Yanque

Yauca

Puerto Inca

Pampa Blanca
PANAMERICAN HIGHWAY

Aplao

Cordillera de Chillán

Huanca

Lluta

Viscach

Punta de Lobos

Pampa de Cortaderas

AREQUIPA

Yura   308

Chacl
19,93
6,075

Atico

Tambillo

AREQUIPA ①

Ocoña   15

El Alto

Río Camaná

Río Sibuas

Pi
Pi
18,27
5,57

San Gregorio

Río Vitor

Mina Chapi

Quilca

Punta Al Aire

Matarani

Huagri

Quelgu

La Curva   15A

Platanal

KEY

Fundición

▬▬	Main road
▬▬▬	Minor road
▬▪▬▪	Untarred main road
▪ ▪ ▪	Untarred minor road
- - -	Track
▬◆▬	Railroad
▬▬	International border
▬▬	Regional border
△	Peak

Ilo
Punta
Coles

Punta Hu
Li

A view of Río Colca meandering through the valley

SIGHTS AT A GLANCE

Towns and Cities
Arequipa pp134–41 ❶
Juli ❽
Lampa ❺
Puno ❹

Areas of Natural Beauty
Cañón del Colca pp142–3 ❷
Cañón de Cotahuasi ❸
Lake Titicaca pp146–51 ❻

Archaeological Site and Ruin
Sillustani Burial Towers ❼

Woman making handicrafts on the floating Isla Uros, Lake Titicaca

GETTING AROUND
Arequipa has a domestic airport with flights to and from Lima, Cusco, Juliaca, and Tacna. The airport servicing Puno is located in Juliaca, 23 miles (44 km) north, and has flights to Lima, Cusco, and Arequipa. *Combis (see p333)* are a cheap option between Juliaca and Puno. The roads between Arequipa and Puno are paved and efficient coach services operate between the two cities as well as on the Panamerican South highway to Lima. A train runs between Puno and Cusco. Boats from Puno leave regularly for various islands on Lake Titicaca. Bolivia is linked by bus only. Taxis can also be hired in Puno.

Street-by-Street: Arequipa ❶

Detail of wall pillar

Basking in the shadow of the snow-capped Misti, Chachani, and Pichu Pichu volcanoes, Arequipa is built almost entirely from *sillar*, a white volcanic rock, and thus its nickname – *la ciudad blanca*, or the white city. According to legend the city was founded when the fourth Inca, Mayta Cápac, camped here. After some of his soldiers asked permission to stay back, he responded in Quechua *"ari, quepay"* (yes, you may stay). In 1540, the Spanish re-founded the city and the Neo-Classical Cathedral, the Baroque churches, and the lordly mansions show their influence. Monasterio de Santa Catalina is the city's most amazing sight *(see pp138–41)*.

★ **Cathedral**
The Cathedral is one of the city's first 17th-century religious monuments. It has survived many earthquakes.

Casona Iriberry, an 18th-century mansion, is now a cultural center.

To Monasterio de Santa Catalina

MERCAD

LA MERCED

BOLIVAR

★ **Casa del Moral**
This 18th-century house is one of the oldest and best examples of Arequipa's Baroque style, with the façade featuring carvings of iconic pumas and serpents.

Iglesia San Agustín
Although the church was built in 1575, the mestizo façade dates back from the early 18th century. Made of sillar *stone, San Agustín contains a striking dome, Neo-Classical altars, and impressive gilded carvings.*

0 meters	750
0 yards	750

For hotels and restaurants in this region see pp273–4 and pp293–4

Casa Tristán del Pozo
Built in 1738, this mansion is a classic piece of Colonial architecture. The frieze above the door depicts medallions of Jesus, Joseph, and Mary.

VISITORS' CHECKLIST

Road Map D6. 627 miles (1,009 km) SE of Lima. 894,944. from Cusco. from Puno & Lima. iPeru, Plaza de Armas, 054 223 265, 9am–6pm daily. Semana Santa (week before Easter), Anniversary of Arequipa (Aug 15).

Museo Arte Textil is dedicated to textiles of the region.

★ La Compañia
Built to house the Jesuits as well as provide them with a spiritual center, this 17th-century church features carved wooden altars with gold leaf. The cloisters were added in the 18th century.

ALVAREZ THOMAS

GNESI

PALACIO VIEJO

Plaza de Armas
Tuturuto, *the statue that sits in the plaza's center, is a representation of a 16th-century soldier whose job it was to inform citizens of news and events.*

Casa Goyeneche houses sculptures from the 17th-century Granada School and works from the Cusco and Arequipa schools.

KEY

– – – Suggested route

STAR SIGHTS

★ Casa del Moral

★ Cathedral

★ La Compañia

Exploring Arequipa

Earthquakes have rocked Arequipa over the centuries due to a geological fault line known as *cadena del fuego* (chain of fire). However, most Colonial buildings have weathered the assaults, aided by Arequipeños' unwavering determination to retain their heritage. Today the city has been listed as a UNESCO World Heritage Site. It is Peru's second largest city and has a long history of commercial repute as a hub for sheep and alpaca wool exports, which still thrive today. Bordered by an impressive two-towered Cathedral and stately symmetrical colonnades, Arequipa's Plaza de Armas is one of Peru's finest.

Sculpture at the Cathedral

A view of the white *sillar* Cathedral from Plaza de Armas

🛡 Cathedral

Plaza de Armas. **Tel** *054 232 635.*
⏰ *7–11:30am & 5–7:30pm Mon–Sat, 7am–1:30pm & 5–7pm Sun.*
🎫 *for a tip.* 🚫 *during masses.*
✝ *7 & 8:30am, 5, 6 & 7pm daily; 4pm Thu (vigil).*

Originally constructed in 1621, the indomitable Cathedral was damaged during a series of earthquakes and fire. It was rebuilt by local architect Lucas Poblete in 1868.

The cathedral, which is made of *sillar* (white volcanic stone), is regarded as the most important Neo-Classical religious building in Peru. Flanked by two arches, it is the country's only cathedral that stretches the entire length of a plaza. The main altar is made of Carrara marble as are the 12 columns which represent the 12 apostles. The carved wooden pulpit held aloft by a devil with a serpent's tail was made in France, and the tower clock was made in England.

🏛 Casona Iriberry

Cnr of Santa Catalina & San Agustín. **Tel** *054 204 482.*
⏰ *9am–1pm, 4–8pm daily.*
♿ *downstairs only.* 💻 🎞

Built in 1793, the volcanic rock walls of the Casona Iriberry, also known as Casa Arróspide, are thought to be the thickest in Arequipa.

Formerly a private home, it is now the Cultural Centre Chavez de la Rosa, and part of the University of San Agustín. Rooms, where art and photography exhibitions are held, open on to a series of charming stone patios. There are messages and monograms carved out in Spanish above the doorways. The top terrace has great views of the beautiful Cathedral located nearby.

🏯 Casa del Moral

Calle Moral 318. **Tel** *054 210 084.*
⏰ *9am–5pm Mon–Sat.* 🌙 *1pm on pub hols.* 📷 🎫 ♿

The 18th-century Casa del Moral is named after an ancient *mora* (mulberry) tree that is still standing in its central patio.

Intricate carvings, in *sillar*, of puma heads with snakes emerging from their mouths adorn the stone gateway, along with a crown suspended above a coat of arms held up by two angels. Inside, there are displays of furniture from Colonial and Republican times, Cusco School *(see p167)* oil paintings and 16th-century maps. The view from the rooftop of this home looks out over the towering volcanoes that surround the city.

Intricately carved stone façade of Casa del Moral

🛡 Convento de la Recoleta

Jirón Recoleta 117. **Tel** *054 270 966.*
⏰ *9am–noon, 3–5pm Mon–Sat.* 📷
🎫 *for a tip.*

Situated in the Antiquilla neighborhood, a ten-minute walk from the main plaza, the Recoleta convent was founded by the Franciscans in 1648. Its enchanting four cloisters, featuring tranquil gardens and *sillar* columns, are a fine example of Arequipa's old Colonial style. Re-modeling campaigns have seen the addition of various architectural styles from Romantic and Neo-Gothic to 1940s modern.

Stone fountain in the cloister garden, Convento de la Recoleta

🏛 Museo Histórico Municipal

Plaza San Francisco. ⏰ *9am–5pm Mon–Fri.* 📷

The history of Arequipa is the focus here, with photographs of the old city, maps, historical documents, portraits of the city's nobles, and a number of archaeological pieces on show. Also highlighted are

Arequipa's heroes including painters, writers, and poets. A series of satirical caricatures and works by famous artist, Jorge Vinatea Reynoso (1900–31) are very insightful.

The naval museum displays objects relating to various conflicts, including items from the 1860s Arequipa Revolution and the historic Dos de Mayo combat with Chile. Arequipa was a bastion of nationalism during Peru's struggle for independence from Spain in the early 19th century, and during the War of the Pacific (*see pp50–51*) with Chile.

🔒 Iglesia San Francisco

Calle Zela. **Tel** *054 223 048.*
⬜ *7–9am, 5–8pm Mon–Sat, 7am–8pm Sun;* **Convent:** *9am–12:30pm, 3–5pm Mon–Sat.* 🎫 *for convent.* 📷 *for a tip.* 🚫 *in the church.* 🔔
Despite being battered by numerous earthquakes, the 16th-century San Francisco church is still standing, albeit with a few scars including a crack in the cupola. The church features an unusual brick entrance-way, a bas-relief Baroque pulpit and a main altar with a solid silver façade. The convent contains paintings from the Cusco School including one of The Last Supper.

🔒 Iglesia La Merced

Cnr of Calle Merced & Tristán. **Tel** *054 21 3233.*
⬜ *8am–1pm, 4–7pm Mon–Fri, 8am–noon Sat.* 🚫 *with flash.*
Construction began in 1551 and was completed in 1607. The side entrance of this *sillar* church features the image of the Virgin Mary with two "saints of mercy." A series of paintings portraying the Virgin de la Merced are on display. The convent has a library too.

🏛 Casa Tristán del Pozo

Calle San Francisco 108. **Tel** *054 212 209.* ⬜ *9:15am–12:45pm & 4–6pm Mon–Fri, 9:30am–12:30pm Sun.* ♿
This grand Colonial home takes its name from General Domingo Tristán del Pozo who commissioned the house in 1738. Built of white volcanic stone, its façade features intricately carved

Baroque detail above entrance and windows, Casa Tristán del Pozo

Baroque details above the windows and entrance. Inside, there are arched roofs and expansive patios. Today, the house is home to a bank, as well as a small museum and an art gallery.

🔒 Iglesia de la Compañía

Cnr of Calle General Morán & Álvarez Thomas. **Tel** *054 212 141.*
⬜ *9–11am, 3–6pm daily.* 🎫 *for chapel.* 🎫 🚫 *with flash.* 🔔 🔔
Built between 1595 and 1698, the Jesuit church of La Compañía is one of the city's oldest. Originally designed by Gaspar Baez in 1573, the first structure was flattened by an earthquake in 1584. Profuse mestizo ornamentation incorporating flowers, faces, spirals, and the completion date of the work, are engraved into the volcanic rock façade. Inside, the main altar is carved in the

Artifact from La Compañía

Churrigueresque style – Spanish Baroque with a Latin twist, involving gold leaf and cherubs with Inca faces.

La Compañía is also home to more than 60 canvases from the Cusco School, including works by Bernardo Bitti and Diego de la Puente. The cloisters now house shops.

🏛 Museo Santuarios Andinos de la Universidad Católica de Santa Maria

La Merced 110. **Tel** *054 21 5013.*
⬜ *9am–6pm Mon–Sat, 9am–3pm Sun.* 🎫 📷 *tips expected.* ♿ 🚫 *with flash.* 🔔 **www.ucsm.edu.pe/santury**
The museum's most famous exhibit is Juanita, la Dama de Ampato (the Lady of Ampato). Alongwith Juanita, there are other mummies that were discovered in Ampato. All children, they were found with textiles, gold and silver figurines, dolls, and ceramics in their mountain tombs.

JUANITA – THE ICE MAIDEN

A last-minute decision to photograph an erupting volcano gave anthropologist Johan Reinhard (b.1943) the find of his life – the Andes' first frozen female mummy. Reinhard and his assistant found "Juanita" bundled in alpaca wool lying near a 20,700-ft- (6,310-m-) high peak. The Ice Maiden is considered one of the world's best-preserved mummies. Sacrificed by Inca priests high on Mount Ampato, she was buried with wooden and gold figurines, and assorted items she would need in the afterlife. Carbon dating has shown that she died between 1440 and 1450. Her remarkable preservation has allowed researchers to gain amazing insights into Inca culture.

Juanita, one of the world's best preserved mummies

Arequipa: Monasterio de Santa Catalina

Taking up an entire block of the city, the Monastery of Santa Catalina was founded in 1580 by Doña María de Guzmán, a rich widow who became a nun. The first to join the Order of Saint Catherine of Siena were poor Creole women, daughters of *curacas* (local Indian chiefs), and women from upper-class families. The wealthy novices brought along home comforts including servants, living as they had previously, even hosting parties. The monastery underwent reform in the 1870s when Sister Josef Cadena, a Dominican nun, replaced the hedonistic lifestyle with religious austerity.

Stone relief above entrance

★ Pinacoteca
The portrait of St Jeronimo by Diego Quispe Tito is one of the highlights of the two-room Religious Art Gallery.

Claustro los Naranjos
The Orange Tree Cloister takes its name from the orange trees planted there. Three crosses are stationed in the middle of the cloister.

Architecture is a fusion of indigenous and Spanish, using *sillar* (local volcanic stone).

Calle Córdova

★ Iglesia de Santa Catalina
The white sillar dome of the church dominates the monastery. It has a long aisle and dates back to 1660.

STAR SIGHTS

★ Calle Sevilla

★ Iglesia de Santa Catalina

★ Pinacoteca

Fresco in Claustro Mayor
The Main Cloister is the largest in the monastery. It was built between 1715 and 1723 and is decorated with 32 frescoes, 26 of them depicting Mary's life and 9 showing the public life of Jesus.

★ **Calle Sevilla**
With its terra-cotta walls and bright flowers, Seville Street is one of the prettiest in the complex. Flying buttresses straddle the walkway and the old church of Santa Catalina, which was later converted into a kitchen, can be seen at the end of the street.

VISITORS' CHECKLIST

Calle Santa Catalina 301.
***Tel** 054 608 282.* ☐ *8am–8pm Tue–Thu, 9am–5pm Fri–Mon.*
🖼 🖊 *guides available for a tip.*
♿ ☐ 🖊 **www**.santacatalina.
org.pe

Nuns' cells were furnished frugally or lavishly according to their family circumstances.

Lavanderia
Water for the communal laundry, built in 1770, ran through a central channel into 20 earthenware jars which served as washing troughs.

Plaza Zocodovar is where the nuns met on Sundays to exchange items they had made.

Cocina
The kitchen was probably designed as a chapel, given its high roof. The walls are blackened with soot from the coal and wood burning stove. The original utensils now sit unused.

FLOORPLAN OF MONASTERIO DE SANTA CATALINA

Calle Córdova

Novices' Cloister

Closed to visitors

Orange Tree Cloister

Main Cloister

Iglesia de Santa Catalina

Street Entrance

KEY

☐ Area illustrated

Exploring Monasterio de Santa Catalina

Carved insignia of monastery

Resembling a small town, the monastery comprises 100 rooms, lined along six streets, three cloisters, a church, and a gallery full of superb Colonial paintings. In its heyday it housed 450 people, a third of them nuns and the rest servants. The servants were freed under the direction of Sister Josef Cadena in 1871 and many of them joined the order. The convent was opened to the public in August 1970, since tourism was thought to be the best option to raise the funds required to install electricity and running water. Today, more than 20 nuns live in the complex, in an area that is off-limits to visitors.

Statue of St Catherine at the entrance to the monastery

Three crosses standing in the colorful Claustro los Naranjos

Claustro los Naranjos
The three crosses stationed in the Orange Tree Cloister are used by nuns in the monastery to re-enact the Passion of Christ, or the final days of Jesus' life, on Good Friday every year. Unfortunately, the public cannot view this ancient tradition, since the monastery is closed on that day, recalling the days when the order was completely cloistered from the world.

Lavanderia
The communal laundry was built at a time when Arequipa's only water source was a series of small canals. The 20 huge earthenware jars, earlier used to hold grain or store wine, doubled up as wash basins.

The water for washing was channeled through a central canal, with offshoots leading into individual jars. At the bottom of each jar was a plug which was removed once the washing was finished. This helped in draining all

the dirty water down to an underground canal which was connected to the river.

The laundry is located at the end of a long boulevard called Calle Toledo.

Iglesia de Santa Catalina
Dating back to 1660, the Church of Santa Catalina has been reconstructed several times after a number of earthquakes in the region

caused serious damage to the structure. However, the original design of the chapel has been retained.

The long aisle leads to the main silver altar, which is heavily embossed with religious motifs. This altar is positioned under an impressive dome.

There is also an altar dedicated to Sister Ana of the Angels, a former Mother Superior. A grand European organ takes pride of place in the high choir.

Pinacoteca
When restoration began on the monastery before it was opened to the public in the 1970s, workers uncovered a cache of religious paintings dating back to the Peruvian Viceroyalty (see pp48–9). Experts restored the 400 artworks, many of which were hailed as the most important examples of religious art on the continent.

These works are displayed in the Religious Art Gallery which is housed in two large rooms in the shape of a

Painting of *Sor Ana de los Angeles* in the Religious Art Gallery (Pinacoteca)

The picturesque geranium-lined Córdova Street

cross with exposed block walls made of *sillar*. This space was once used as a shelter for homeless widows and single mothers. There are numerous paintings from the admired Cusco School (*see p167*) including the *Divine Shepherdess*, believed to be the work of Marcos Zapata (*see p66*). There is a depiction of St Michael, dressed in Spanish armor, complete with a feathery helmet, as well as a portrait of St Catherine, or Santa Catalina, with a description of the scene written on a panel that is held by an angel.

Bell on the steeple facing the street

Calle Córdova

Córdova Street, as the name implies, is inspired by the architecture of Andalusia. Terra-cotta pots filled with geraniums line the gleaming white walls, which trap the sun all year round.

The 18th-century wall on the right is made from volcanic stones from Arequipa. These *sillar* blocks each measure 18 in by 16 in (45 cm by 40 cm).

The 20th-century building on the left side of the street is out of bounds for visitors. The area forms part of the complex in which the nuns live today.

Torre del Campanario

Built in 1748, the steeple has four bells facing the streets around the monastery. The oldest bell is towards the south, facing Ugarte Street and bears the inscription "Santa Catalina Ora Pronobis 1749." The bell facing Bolivar Street on the west has "R.M. Maria de Villegas 1787," while other bells bear no inscriptions.

Claustro Mayor

The Main Cloister is bordered by five confessionals on the left side, ensuring the nuns a degree of privacy during their declarations.

Thirty-two beautiful frescoes decorate the cloister walls. The majority of them show biblical scenes depicting the life of Virgin Mary, while the remainder portray the life of Jesus.

Sor Ana de los Angeles Monteagudo

Santa Catalina was also home to Sor Ana de los Angeles Monteagudo (1595–1668), who was beatified by Pope John Paul II in 1985.

Sister Ana of the Angels was educated in the monastery until she was about 11 years old. She returned to join the order after having a vision of Santa Catalina in which she showed Sister Ana a Dominican nun's habit.

She was eventually elected Mother Superior but it was not a unanimous decision. According to reports, some of the nuns questioned the appropriateness of the choice given Sister Ana's inability to read and write and three attempts were made to poison her. She survived and went on to establish a reputation as a miracle-worker. It was said her "close relationship with the souls in Purgatory" enabled her to predict both death and disease.

She was also a healer, with nuns writing of cases where ailing patients miraculously recovered after touching her possessions. It is said that a stricken painter, who made the only known portrait of Sister Ana, was completely cured of all his ailments when he finished the painting.

Sister Ana was buried in the monastery. Her humble cell and the utensils she used more than 300 years ago are on display in her rooms.

Stairs leading to one of the five confessionals, Claustro Mayor

Cañón del Colca ②

Stones piled as offerings

Reaching a depth of 11,155 ft (3,400 m), the 62-mile (100-km) long Colca is one of the deepest canyons in the world, along with neighboring Cotahuasi Canyon *(see p144)*. The valley was home to the Cabana and Collagua people almost 2,000 years ago, who built a system of terraces that trap melting run-off water from nearby snow-capped volcanoes. The *colcas* (grain storehouses) are testament to their presence. When the Spanish arrived, they put the farmers to work in the mines and moved the scattered Collagua community into 14 villages, each with a main plaza and handsome Colonial church.

Sumbay cave paintings showing a group of camelids

★ La Cruz del Condor
Located on the canyon's highest point, it offers a vista of giant Andean condors wheeling over the valley. The lookout is jam packed with tourists and buses most mornings.

Collagua People
Originally inspired by the petticoats of Spanish women, the Collagua still embellish their clothing with colorful embroidery. The women wear two or three skirts, and beribboned or brightly stitched hats.

STAR FEATURES

★ Collagua Terraces

★ La Cruz del Condor

La Calera
Just outside Chivay are the sulphur and iron-rich waters of La Calera, said to help in the treatment of rheumatism and arthritis.

For hotels and restaurants in this region see pp273–4 and pp293–4

Reserva Nacional Salinas y Aguada Blanca
*Covering a huge area, the reserve shelters a variety of plants
and animals. Camelids such as llamas, alpacas, and vicuñas
are bred to help the sustainable development of villages.*

Yanque Town
*Iglesia de la Inmaculada Concepción has a
glorious mestizo façade covered in saints and
a 16th-century processional silver cross inside.*

★ Collagua Terraces
*Nearly 2,000 years ago, the Collagua and Cabana
people carved out a huge area of terracing in an
effort to control irrigation and erosion, and in
order to grow crops. Today, the communities living
in the valley still use the terraces for cultivation.*

CONDOR

The condor *(Vultur gryphus)* is the world's largest
flying bird, standing up to 4-ft (1.2-m) high with a
wingspan of 10 ft (3 m). Despite weighing up to
27 lbs (12 kg), the condor can fly for hours
without using its wings, simply gliding on thermal
currents. The condor feeds on carrion or newborn
animals which it can identify from the air thanks to
its heightened sense of smell and remarkable eye-
sight. The birds sleep on the canyon
walls at night. Considered a
sacred bird by the Incas, it
was once a common sight
in the Andes but is now
listed as "vulnerable" by
the World Conservation
Union due to centuries
of hunting, habitat loss,
and the rampant use of
pesticides by farmers.

**Condors perched atop a cliff
in the canyon**

Rafting on Río Colca
*The river is famous for its 300
rapids, with the best known rafting
route starting at Chivay and
running some 25 miles (40 km).*

Cañón de Cotahuasi ❸

Road Map D5. 124 miles (200 km) NW of Arequipa. 🏨 🍴 in Cotahuasi, Liucho, and Alca.

At 11,560 ft (3,535 m), Cotahuasi is reportedly the deepest canyon in the world and twice as deep as America's Grand Canyon. In Quechua *cota* means "union" and *huasi* is "house" thus Cotahuasi means "united house," or in this case "united community."

The impressive landscape of the canyon combines sheer shadowy cliffs rising out of riverbanks, towering snow-capped mountains, terraced citrus groves, fields of corn, stands of eucalyptus, adobe villages, and hot springs.

The canyon was an important route in the Inca times, connecting the Pacific Coast with Cusco. Remnants of these roads still link many of the traditional villages here.

There are ruins from the Wari culture and the unmistakable imprint of the Spanish conquistadores in the entire area. Every settlement has a chapel and belfry, and sometimes even a bullring.

Nearby villages have their own attractions. **Liucho** has soothing hot springs while **Sipia**'s charm is the 197-ft-(60-m-) high waterfall of Cataratas de Sipia.

Puno ❹

Road Map E6. 27 miles (44 km) SE of Juliaca. 🏙 129,000. ✈ in Juliaca. 🚌 from Cusco. 🚌 from Arequipa. 🛈 Plaza de Armas. 🎭 Fiesta de la Virgin de la Candelaria (Feb 2).

Viceroy Conde de Lemos founded the city in 1668, naming it San Carlos de Puno. The Spanish converted the indigenous people to Christianity and built several churches.

The Baroque-style **Catedral de Puno** on Plaza de Armas was designed by the 18th-century Peruvian architect Símon de Asto. The **Iglesia de San Juan Bautista** on Parque Pino is the sanctuary of Mamita Candelaria, Puno's patron saint, and is famous for its carvings.

Salmon colored houses of Lampa, the pink city

Parque Huajsapata, which is located on the hilltop, honors Puno's pre-Hispanic past with a statue of Manco Cápac, the first Inca. Legends claim there are tunnels in the hill that connect Puno with the Koricancha Temple in Cusco.

Museo Carlos Dreyer houses pre-Hispanic and Colonial artworks collected by the German artist Dreyer, including Moche ceramics, Inca silverwork, Paracas textiles, and religious objects. Striking gold pieces found at Lagarto *chulpa* in Sillustani are also displayed.

🏛 **Catedral de Puno**
Plaza de Armas.
🕐 7am–noon, 3–7pm daily. 🛈

🏛 **Iglesia de San Juan Bautista**
Parque Pino, Av. Independencia.
🕐 7am–noon, 3–7pm daily. 🛈

🏛 **Museo Carlos Dreyer**
Calle Conde de Lemon 289.
🕐 10am–10pm daily. 📷 📹 🚫
www.museodreyer.com

Details on the façade of Puno's cathedral

Lampa ❺

Road Map E5. 50 miles (80 km) N of Puno, 22 miles (35 km) N of Juliaca. 🏙 12,000. 🚌 from Juliaca. 🏨 🎭 La Fiesta de Santiago Apóstol (Jul 26). **http://**patronatolampa. perucultural.org.pe

Known as La Ciudad Rosada meaning "the pink city," the dusty salmon- and maroon-tinted roofs and walls of Lampa add a welcome splash of color to the surrounding golden grass plains.

The city's other main attraction is the **Iglesia de Santiago Apóstol**. The church is made from river stones and lime mortar and dates back to the 1650s.

Local luminary and mining engineer, Enrique Torres Belón, who was responsible for the restoration of the church in the 1950s, added a marble-covered chapel and crowned it with a replica of Michelangelo's statue *La Pietá*. The Vatican provided a plaster mold of the famous statue, which, instead of being destroyed after casting as agreed, is now on display in the Town Hall.

Torres Belón, who was also the president of Peru's Congress in 1957, was buried in the chapel along with his wife. Bones removed from the catacombs during restoration of the building hang on the walls around them.

The church also has a fine collection of beautiful Colonial paintings from the famous Quito and Cusco Schools *(see p167)* and an elaborate carved pulpit.

Puno: Peru's Folkloric Capital

Puno melds the two ancient Andean civilizations of the Aymara from the south and the Quechua from the north with Colonial influences. The result is a rich diversity of high-spirited folkloric festivals, often hailed as the best in all of Peru. More than 300 dances have been catalogued in the region. Some satirize the Spanish, some celebrate Andean beliefs, while others are pure religious revelry. The most important event in Puno is the festival of the Virgin of the Candles in honor of Mamita Candelaria. Groups with more than 100 dancers each, perform in dance contests held during the 18 days of festivities. The festival also has pre-Hispanic origins which relate to agricultural cycles of planting and harvesting.

Boy in parade

Diablada mask represents the devil.

The Diablada, *which symbolizes the victory of good over evil, is Puno's most famous dance. A devil is pursued by angels, skeletons, and other characters.*

Waca Waca, *parodies the iconic Spanish bullfight. The men wear colorful costumes and a bull-shaped headpiece.*

Dazzling suits of lights are common.

The Aymara Love Dance *represents a courting ritual, where rows of women wildly flick their layered skirts, as groups of whistling bachelors twirl around them.*

A heart on the blouse is a part of the costume during the Love Dance.

The Festival of the Virgin of the Candles *in February, draws thousands of locals to toast Puno's patron saint.*

Llamerada, *an Aymara dance, pays tribute to llama herders with dancers dressed in silver-and gold-threaded ponchos imitating the rhythmic gait of the animals.*

Lake Titicaca ⑥

Colorful handicraft

At an elevation of 12,500 ft (3,800 m), Lake Titicaca is the highest lake of its size in the world. South America's second largest lake, it covers 3,210 sq miles (8,300 sq km), is 120 miles (194 km) long and 50 miles (80 km) wide at its broadest point. Its water level fluctuates according to the seasons, receding slightly in winter. Numerous islands are sprinkled across the lake, and the inhabitants cling to a traditional way of life centered around fishing, farming, and weaving. The Uros people live closest to Puno, on floating islands, like huge straw-like nests. They describe their buoyant life as living "between water and heaven" *(see pp150–51)*.

★ **Reed Boats**
Totora *reeds are used to build the boats, known as* caballitos.

The Yavari
This 19th-century gunboat, anchored in the Bay of Puno, houses a museum and a bed-and-breakfast taking seven guests.

Puno provides the easiest access to the lake, with boats operating tours throughout the day.

Isla Amantani, the lake's largest island, has religious centers dating back to the Tiahuanacos (500 BC–AD 900).

★ **Islas Uros**
There are more than 40 floating islands made by layering totora *reed atop root clods. New reeds are laid weekly as those below decompose.*

STAR SIGHTS

★ Isla Taquile

★ Islas Uros

★ Reed Boats

★ **Isla Taquile**
The island's red soil contrasts with the deep blue color of the lake. One of the most industrious islands, its walled paths are crowned with rustic arches and dotted with Inca and pre-Inca ruins.

The blue of Lake Titicaca highlighted against the mountains

VISITORS' CHECKLIST

Road Map E6. ✈ *from Juliaca.* 🚌 *from Cusco.* 🚗 *from Arequipa.* ⛴ *from Puno or through hotel; early morning tour (7:30am) recommended.* ℹ *in Puno.* 🎫 *fee for private boat, organized tour.* 🅿 ♿ *on some boats.* 🍴 *in Puno & Isla Taquile.* 🏧 *in Puno.* 🏨 *in Puno & Isla Taquile.* ⚓ *in Puno, Taquile, Suasi, Amantani, & Anapia Islas.*

Isla Soto lies close to where the lake reaches its greatest recorded depth of 920 ft (280 m).

Puerto Acosta

B O L I V I A

Titicaca

Isla del Sol

Isla de la Luna

Achacachi

Copacabana

Anapia

Puerto Perez

Batallas

Pucarani

Guaqui

Pomata

Juli, with its four impressive Colonial churches, confirms its past as a key religious center for Jesuits.

Pomata houses a church founded in 1700 and built from pink granite.

Isla del Sol
Located in Bolivian waters, according to legend it is the birthplace of the Sun and his son, the first Inca, Manco Cápac.

KEY

✈	Domestic airport
⛴	Ferry service
ℹ	Visitor information
▬	Major road
▭	Minor road
─	Railroad
▪▪	International border

0 km 25
0 miles 25

Isla Anapia
Located on the Bolivian border, the islanders use the neighboring island, Yupisque, for agriculture. It is inhabited by wild vicuñas.

Totora reed boat moored next to a floating island, Lake Titicaca ▷

Exploring Lake Titicaca

Enveloped in mythology, Lake Titicaca encapsulates the age-old traditions that have molded and defined the Andean region. For thousands of years, islanders have been growing potatoes and quinoa on tiered hills, fishing, weaving magical textiles, and herding llama – a lifestyle still carefully preserved. Woven textiles

Ceramic oxen on a farmstead entrance

are the main source of income. Prices are set and profits from handicraft sales are pooled and shared by the islanders. Staying with a family on an island offers a unique opportunity to experience their traditions. Archaeological sites dot the islands with the most notable on Islas del Sol and de la Luna. Ruins of an ancient temple and crop terraces, dating back 1,500 years, were found in the lake's waters in 2000.

Reed boats and the floating islands of the Uros people

🔒 Islas Uros

4 miles (6 km) from Puno. 👥 2,000. 🚤 📷 for organized boat tours. 🎫

The Uros developed their unique floating islands centuries ago to escape hostile cultures on the mainland. They consider themselves to be "the oldest people on earth." Legend says they existed before the sun, and could not drown or be struck by lightning. Mixing with the Aymaras and other tribes lost them their super-being status. They speak Aymara today.

The largest of the floating islands is estimated to be 160 years old, housing a meeting hall and a school. The islanders use the ubiquitous *totora* (a reed-like papyrus) for food and firewood – fires are carefully built on a layer of stone – as well as to make their boats, houses, and handicrafts. Most islanders earn a living from fishing and tourism.

Isla Taquile

22 miles (36 km) from Puno. 👥 2,000. 🚤 📷 🎫 🍴 🛏 📷 🎟 San Diego (St James's Day, Jul 25). 🌊

Some 350 Quechua-speaking families still live here following the Inca creed of *Ama suwa, Ama quella, Ama llullav* (do not steal, do not be idle, do not lie). There is no police force – a reflection of their belief in honesty – and problems are solved by elected community leaders at the Sunday meetings. The people wear colorful hand-woven clothes. Red knitted caps distinguish married men from bachelors who don red and white. Señoritas wear multicolored pompoms, while married women wear bright red ones on their heavy, layered skirts. With no cars, donkeys or llamas, residents carry supplies on their backs up 545 steep steps from the jetty to the hilltop village.

🏔 Isla Amantaní

25 miles (40 km) from Puno. 👥 5,000. 🚤 📷 🎫 🛏 🌊

Amantaní islanders are famous for their baskets woven from *ichu* (a native grass) and granite carvings. Sacred Inca sites crown the island's peaks. Local shamans read the future in coca tea leaves, so be sure to have a translator on hand.

🦙 Isla Suasi

43 miles (70 km) from Puno. 🚤 🎫 🌊

The only building on this small island is an ecolodge which mimics traditional architecture with its thatched roof and stone walls. It runs solely on solar power. There are protected areas for birds, as well as wild vicuñas, centuries-old tracts of natural vegetation and cultivated plots of herbs.

🏔 Isla del Sol

9 miles (14 km) from Copacabana, Bolivia. 👥 5,000. 🚤 to Copacabana. 🚤 from Copacabana. 📷 🎫 🍴 🛏 🌊

Famed as the birthplace of the Incas, the Island of the Sun is actually in the Bolivian waters of the lake.

Close to the ruin of mazes called Chinkana, is a sacred rock carved into the shape of a puma. Farther along are two large footprints, supposedly made when the Sun came down to earth to give birth to the first Incas – Manco Cápac and Mama Ocllo. An Inca stairway leads up from the water's edge at Yumani to what is known as a fountain of youth, fed by three springs. A short walk away from the steps is Plikokayna, a fortress that was probably used to watch over the Virgins of the Sun on Isla de la Luna.

🏔 Isla de la Luna

4 miles (7 km) from Isla del Sol. 🚤

The most important archaeological site on the Island of the Moon is the *aqllawasi* (monastery). In Inca times, the island housed the "chosen women," who took part in special ceremonies dedicated to the sun. The main palace, which was rebuilt in the 1960s, has some 30 rooms centered around a courtyard.

For hotels and restaurants in this region see pp273–4 and pp293–4

An Incan rock carving of a face near Chucuito, Puno

Chucuito

12 miles (19 km) S of Puno.
🏠 10,000. 🚌 🚐 from Puno 🚤 for Inca Uyo. ♿ 🍴 🏨 📷 🛍️
The town of Chucuito was capital of the province and the main tax collection center during Colonial times.

It boasts of two magnificent Colonial churches – **Nuestra Señora de la Asunción**, built in 1601 and adorned with a Renaissance façade, and **Santo Domingo** with its single stone tower, carved stone arches, and beautiful golden altar.

The walled complex of **Inca Uyo** is often described as a fertility garden. Tales abound of women sitting on top of these stones for hours in an attempt to improve their fertility. Sceptics hint that the garden is more a marketing tool than an ancient Inca relic.

🔔 Iglesia Santiago Apóstol de Pomata

67 miles (108 km) S of Puno. 🚌 🚐 from Puno ⬜ 7am–5:30pm daily. 🚤
This Dominican church surveys both town and lake from its hilltop position. Built in pink granite, it is known for its intricate sandstone façade, fusing indigenous symbols with Baroque. It is one of southern Peru's most beautiful churches. Inside are windows made from *huamanga* stone, a towering gold leaf altar adorned with coiled columns, and Cusco School paintings.

Sillustani Burial Towers ⑦

Road Map E6. 21 miles (34 km) N of Puno. 🚌 🚐 from Puno. ⬜ 7am–5pm daily. 🚤 🎫 organized tours from Puno. 📷

Standing on the shores of the pristine Laguna Umayo, Sillustani is famous for its *chulpas* (circular burial towers), some of which are more than 39 ft (12 m) high.

The Collas, who dominated the area before the Incas, buried their leaders in towers that are wider at the top than at the base. The Lagarto and Intiwatana *chulpas* are the best examples. Experts have long deliberated whether the Collas built the towers to show off their dexterity with stone, to deter tomb-raiders, or simply to honor the dead nobility.

The inside of the tombs are said to be shaped like a woman's womb with the corpses mummified in a fetal position. Some tombs have carvings of lizards, a symbol of life due to their ability to regrow their tails. Blocks and a ramp used to hoist them up demonstrate the difficulty of constructing the towers. A museum displays pieces from the Colla, Tiahuanaco, and Inca cultures.

Traditional weaver hard at work

Juli ⑧

Road Map E6. 49 miles (79 km) S of Puno. 🏠 27,000. 🚌 🚐 from Puno. ⛴️ Thursday.

The Dominicans founded Juli in 1534 and turned the settlement into their most important religious hub, a center for training missionaries for Bolivia and Paraguay.

The presence of four Colonial churches, constructed to convert the indigenous locals, has earned the town the nickname of "Little Rome." **San Juan Bautista de Letrán** dates from 1570 and has dozens of Cusco School paintings depicting the life of John the Baptist and Saint Teresa. **Iglesia de San Pedro Mártir**, completed in 1560 and remodeled in the 20th century, combines a Renaissance façade with a Baroque altarpiece and paintings by Bernardo Bitti (1548–1610). It once boasted a 400-strong Indian choir.

ISLAND HOMESTAYS

Villagers on the islands of Taquile, Amantaní, and Anapia happily share their homes and lives with visitors. Tourism on Anapia is community-based; all the money goes back into the island to improve education and strengthen local culture. Visitors help in every-day tasks – harvesting, fishing, minding cattle, building houses, or attending the local community council meeting. They may also take part in *casarasiri* (a traditional marriage ceremony) that lasts three days, or sample *huatia* (potatoes roasted in a mud brick oven along with fish or lamb). Amantaní and Taquile islands are closer to Puno and thus easier to reach. Travelers are usually welcomed with a traditional dance and eat with the family.

Women leading tourists for a homestay on Amantaní

THE INCA HEARTLAND

The Incas' innate ability to build in harmony with the environment is more than apparent in this picturesque Andean province. The Sacred Valley, which they took to be a representation of heaven on earth, is rich in nature as well as ancient history, with many Inca temples and fortresses. Of these, none is more spectacular than Machu Picchu, a UNESCO World Heritage Site.

For two centuries, Cusco and its environs were the homeland of the Incas. Myths enfold its founding as the dynasty's capital. It is said that Manco Cápac and Mama Ocllo, the children of the Sun and the Moon, set out on a quest to find a place to establish their kingdom. When they reached the valley of the Río Huantanay, Manco Cápac was able to thrust his staff into the ground until it vanished, a divine sign indicating that this was the site for the Inca capital.

Although the area was occupied by other cultures for several centuries before the Incas arrived, including the Wari in the 8th and 9th centuries, it was under Inca control that Cusco reached its peak as an administrative, religious, and military hub.

According to the 16th century writings of Garcilaso de la Vega, the son of an Inca princess and a Spanish conquistador, 13 Inca emperors ruled over the valley from the 12th to the 15th century. From here, they built the Inca Empire in less than a century. Pachacútec, the ninth Inca (r.1438-71) and a construction visionary, was responsible for fashioning Cusco into a shape resembling the sacred puma.

In 1533, Francisco Pizarro and the Spanish arrived in Cusco and following the crushing defeat of the Incas, founded their own city, turning pre-Hispanic structures into Colonial mansions. Gradually, Cusco and its surrounds became a symbol of mestizo, a blending of Colonial Spanish with Andean elements, both architecturally and culturally.

Once Pizarro left, the province reverted to being just another calm Andean domain. The rediscovery of Machu Picchu in 1911 set in motion the transformation of this remote Inca outpost to sightseer central.

Terracing under an Inca fortress, on a hillside above Pisac

◁ **Enormous stone blocks of an Inca wall, Sacsayhuamán**

Exploring The Inca Heartland

Cusco, now Peru's tourism capital, was once the majestic mountain capital of the Incas. Today, it is the ideal base to explore the various sites located in the aptly named Sacred Valley such as Pisac, Ollantaytambo, Tipón, and Rumicolca. These sites and Machu Picchu, "the city in the clouds", all showcase the Incas' amazing grasp of architecture and hydraulics. The circular terraces at Moray testify to their aptitude for agriculture, while the meticulous positioning of the giant granite blocks at Sacsayhuamán exemplifies their precise masonry skills. Spanish influence too is on display, especially in San Pedro de Andahuaylillas, a UNESCO World Heritage listed church.

LOCATOR MAP

Area illustrated

SIGHTS AT A GLANCE

Towns and Cities

Calca **10**

Chinchero **9**

Cusco pp156–63 **1**

Pisac **11**

Archaeological Sites and Ruins

Machu Picchu pp176–81 **13**

Moray and Salinas de Maras **8**

Ollantaytambo **7**

Pikillacta and Rumicolca **5**

Sacsayhuamán **2**

Tipón **4**

Tours

Inca Trail pp170–73 **12**

Tambomachay Tour p165 **3**

Church

San Pedro de Andahuaylillas **6**

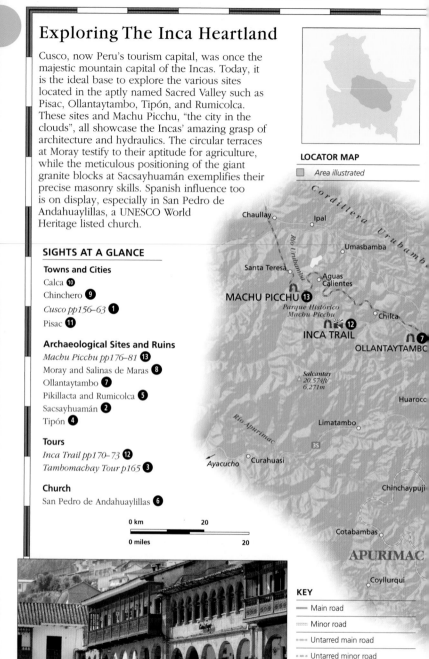

0 km 20

0 miles 20

Chaullay

Ipal

Cordillera Urubamb

Río Urubamba

Umasbamba

Santa Teresa

Aguas Calientes

MACHU PICCHU 13

Parque Histórico Machu Picchu

12

Chilca

INCA TRAIL

OLLANTAYTAMBO 7

Salcantay 20,574ft/ 6,271m

Huaroco

Río Apurímac

Limatambo

35

Ayacucho

Curahuasi

Chinchaypuji

Cotabambas

APURIMAC

Coyllurqui

KEY

— Main road

═ Minor road

▪▪▪ Untarred main road

▪═▪ Untarred minor road

- - - Track

═══ Railroad

— Regional border

△ Peak

Wooden balconies on Plaza de Armas, Cusco

Meticulously placed limestone blocks at the ruins of Sacsayhuamán

Manto

Amparaés

Lares

Challabamba

bamba

Yucay

ORAY &
ALINAS DE MARAS

10 CALCA

Paucartambo

9 CHINCHERO

PISAC

Colquepata

AYHUAMÁN
2

3 TAMBOMACHAY TOUR

San Salvador

3S

1 CUSCO

Poroy

C U S C O   Oropesa

TIPÓN **4**

Huambutio

Yaurisque

5
PIKILLACTA
& RUMICOLCA

Ccatca

Ocongate

noquite

SAN PEDRO DE
ANDAHUAYLILLAS **6**

Tinqui

Paruro

Urcos

Colcha

Quiquijana

35

bamba

Rio Santo Tomás

Acomayo

Accha

Cusipata

Pitumarca

Sangarara

Checacupe

Pomacachi

Acopia

Combapata

Raqchi

Sicuani

GETTING AROUND

Cusco has a domestic airport with daily flights
to Lima, Arequipa, and Juliaca. There is road
access from Lima, Arequipa, and Puno. Buses
run frequently to Arequipa, and then on
to Lima. There are direct services
to Puno, Pisac, and Calca. A
train connects Cusco with
Puno. Machu Picchu can
be reached on foot via
the Inca Trail or by train
then bus. Taxis can be
hired for day trips
from Cusco. Driving
can be hazardous.

SEE ALSO

• **Where to Stay** pp274–5

• **Where to Eat** pp294–5

Street-by-Street: Cusco ●

Filled with Spanish arches and squares, and wooden balconies jutting over narrow cobbled streets, the picturesque town of Cusco was declared a UNESCO World Heritage Site in 1983. Women in layered skirts, wearing stovepipe hats over long black plaits, chat in Quechua on the Cathedral steps, both fragments of the past hovering in the present. Shining examples of Spanish conquest abound in the Colonial architecture, while the precise stonework of the ancient walls is a reminder that the Incas founded the city. Despite high tourist traffic, the indigenous people ensure its Andean atmosphere is retained.

Fountain on the plaza

★ Museo de Arte Religioso
On the exterior of the museum, once an Inca palace, is the famed 12-sided stone fitting flawlessly into the wall.

★ La Catedral
The commanding Cathedral pays tribute to the Renaissance on the outside and Baroque on the inside. It was renovated from 1997 to 2002 (see pp162–3).

Museo Inka, or the Admiral's Palace, is devoted to Inca artifacts rather than naval souvenirs. It was damaged in the 1650 earthquake and was restored by a Spanish count.

TUCUMAN

PLATE

0 meters 50

0 yards 50

STAR SIGHTS

★ La Catedral

★ Iglesia de la Compañia

★ Museo de Arte Religioso

Corpus Christi Festivities
The week-long celebrations include street events when the effigies of the saints are paraded through the city.

Ceramic wall mural depicts iconic Cusqueña crafts and landmarks

VISITORS' CHECKLIST

Road Map D5. 685 miles
(1,102 km) SE of Lima.
🏚 350,000. ✈ 🚉 🚌 🛈
*Oficina Ejecutiva del Comité, Av.
Sol 103, 8am–5:30pm Mon–Fri,
8:30am–12:30pm Sat; Boleto
Turístico (Tourism Ticket) can be
bought for 16 sights.* 🍴 🛏
🎭 ♻ 🎨 *Corpus Christi (Dec)
& Easter Monday.*

Inca-built walls

Santa Catalina
*Built over the Inca ruins of the Acllawasi
(House of the Chosen Women), this convent
opened in 1610; its museum opened in 1975.*

KEY

– – – Suggested route

Iglesia La Merced
*Cusco's third most important
church, founded by Riña Sebastián de
Castañeda in 1535 on land donated
by Pizarro, was handcrafted by
local stonemasons.*

★ Iglesia de la Compañía
*Originally intended to be
Cusco's grandest church, the
Jesuits' lofty plans were
thwarted when the bishop
insisted that it not surpass
the majesty of the Cathedral.
Its ornate façade, however,
belies its secondary role.*

Exploring Cusco

Painting by local artists

In the earthquake of 1650 most of Cusco's Spanish structures were damaged but the Inca foundations remained, and under the patronage of Bishop Manuel de Mollinedo y Angulo the city was rebuilt. He also developed the Cusco art style, which can be seen in the local churches and museums. Artisans in the San Blas quarter still practice traditional kinds of handicrafts, and the churches and museums brim with centuries-old Cusco School paintings. Starting from the Plaza de Armas, Cusco's heart, all of the city's sights are in easy walking distance.

Visitors and locals relaxing at Plaza de Armas

🏛 Plaza de Armas

In Inca times, the square was mainly used for ceremonial purposes and was known as Huacaypata, meaning Warriors' Square or Square of Regrets. Inti Raymi, the Festival of the Sun, was celebrated here each year. On occasions, the mummies of the dead Incas were placed here so people could venerate them. It is said that the plaza was once covered with white beach sand, transported from the coast by llamas for the emperor's pleasure. It was then studded with tiny gold and coral sculptures to represent all the provinces.

Francisco Pizarro (see p48) claimed Cusco for Spain at the Plaza de Armas, and Túpac Amaru II (see p49), the leader of the indigenous uprising, was beheaded here in 1781.

The stone arches which grace the plaza are a reflection of the Spanish influence, along with the Cathedral and the Jesuit church of La Compañia. The latter is often mistaken for the more famous Cathedral due to its elaborate façade.

Two flags fly in the plaza, the red-and-white Peruvian national flag and a rainbow colored flag said to be the banner of the ancient Inca Empire, Tahuantinsuyu.

🏛 Museo Inka

Cuesta del Almirante 103. *Tel 084 237 380.* ☐ *8am–6:30pm Mon–Fri, 9am–4pm Sat.* 📷 *with flash.*

Built on the top of Inca foundations, the museum is also known as the Palacio del Almirante (Admiral's Palace). It is named after the original owner, Admiral Francisco Aldrete Maldonado, and is one of the finest Colonial homes in all of Cusco.

The exhibition is a must for all Inca-philes. It comprises mummies, ceramics, textiles, jewelry, metal, and gold objects. Of particular interest is the assortment – reputed to be the world's largest – of *keros*, (Inca wooden drinking cups) many of which are richly painted.

While the collection of Inca artifacts is the prime motivation for a visit, the display of textiles and ceramics belonging to earlier civilizations, a reminder of the area's long Andean history, are a bonus.

🏛 Museo de Arte Precolombino

Plaza Nazarenas 231. *Tel 084 233 210.* ☐ *9am–10pm daily.* 📷 📷 📷 *with flash.* 🍴 📷 www.map.org.pe

The former Inca ceremonial court, Kancha Inca, was transformed into a mansion for the Spanish conquistador, Alonso Díaz, in 1580. In 1850, the Earl of Cabrera took up residence here, and in 2003 it was converted into the Museum of Pre-Columbian Art.

The 11 rooms are now filled with 450 masterpieces dating from 1250 BC to AD 1532. The collection was chosen by Peruvian painter Fernando de Szyszlo and historian Cecilia Bákula from the thousands of artifacts kept in the Museo Arqueologico Rafael Larco Herrera (see p94) in Lima.

The Mochica gallery contains standout ceramic pieces. Also on display are geometrically decorated, sculptural ceramics by the Wari, and *aribalos* (monumental containers) made by the Incas. Other rooms are devoted to wooden sculptures, silver, jewelry, and gold. The museum has an impressive collection of funerary ornaments.

Colonial courtyard of the Museo de Arte Precolombino

♨ Calle Hatunrumiyoc

The street of Hatunrumiyoc is named after the famous 12-angled stone which is perfectly fitted into the right-hand side of the wall. The stone was taken from the wall of the palace of Inca Roca, the sixth Inca emperor. It is now a part of the Archbishop's Palace.

The wall is a brilliant example of the Inca's skill in polygonal polished stone masonry which they used to construct support walls.

🏛 Museo de Arte Religioso

Cnr Calles Hatunrumiyoc & Herrajes. **Tel** 084 222 781. ◯ 8–11:30am, 3–5:30pm Mon–Sat, 2–5:30pm Sun. 🎫 Boleto Turístico valid. 📷 with flash.

Housed in the Palacio Arzobispal (Archbishop's Palace), the museum displays religious paintings from the 17th and 18th centuries, including works by Diego Quispe Tito, regarded as the master of the Cusco School *(see p167)* painters.

The palace itself boasts carved cedar ceilings, Moorish-inspired doors and balcony, stained-glass windows, and a room displaying life-size models of Cusco's archbishops.

Detail on the doorway of an artist's workshop in San Blas District

The house, which once belonged to Marquis de San Juan de Buenavista, is built on top of the ancient Inca Roca palace.

♨ San Blas District

Iglesia de San Blas ◯ 10–11:30am, 2–5:30pm Fri–Wed. 🎫 Boleto Turístico valid. 📷 with flash. 🚻

Dotted with Colonial houses featuring Inca stone walls, San Blas is also known as the craftsmen's district. Once the domain of Quechua nobility, its network of narrow streets are now home to the workshops of Cusqueña artists who practice metalwork, and stone- and woodcarving.

Iglesia de San Blas, built in 1563, is the oldest parish church in Cusco. Its ornate pulpit is a fine example of Baroque woodcarving.

⛏ Koricancha and Santo Domingo

Plaza Intipampa, cnr Av. El Sol & Calle Santo Domingo. **Tel** 084 254 234. ◯ 8:30am–6:30pm Mon–Sat, 2–5pm Sun. 🎫 📷 ♿

Koricancha, meaning the "golden enclosure," was built to honor Inti or the Sun God. It was the richest Inca temple and had gold plated walls flecked with precious stones.

The garden featured life-sized gold and silver statues of animals, local trees, and corn stalks. Mummified bodies of noble Incas were kept here for ceremonies. Sadly, the temple was drained of all its treasures soon after the arrival of the conquistadors.

Girls in traditional garb

The church and convent of Santo Domingo were built on top of the Inca shrine. The building brings the two cultures together. It is difficult to imagine how the temple must have looked as so little remains of it now. However, the imposing trapezoidal architecture, pebbled floor, wall niches, and holes that are thought to be either drains or speaking tubes, hint at its past glory.

🏛 Museo de Historia Regional

Calle Heladeros, cnr of Calle Garcilazo. **Tel** 084 223 245. ◯ 8am–7pm Mon–Sat. 🎫 Boleto Turístico valid. 📷

Cusco's Regional History Museum was originally the home of the 16th-century Inca historian, writer, and poet Garcilaso de la Vega. It exhibits articles spanning the pre-ceramic era to Colonial times.

It has ancient arrowheads, Chavin, Mochica, and Chimú ceramics, a Nazca mummy, Inca musical instruments and tools, and several Cusco School paintings.

♨ Iglesia de la Compañia

Plaza de Armas. ◯ no set hours. 🎫 📷 ♿ 📷 with flash.

Constructed in 1571 on the palace of Huayna Capac, the eleventh Inca, La Compañia had to be rebuilt after the earthquake of 1650.

Considered one of the best examples of Colonial Baroque architecture in Peru, it features a spectacular carved stone façade, a 69-ft- (21-m-) high cedar altar covered in gold leaf, *huamanga (see p304)* stone windows, sculptures, and a number of Cusco School paintings.

Colonial arches of the Santo Domingo convent

Panoramic view of Cusco with the Iglesia de la Compañia in the foreground ▷

Cusco: La Catedral

Detail on a wooden altar

Construction of the Cathedral began in 1560 but took almost 100 years to complete. The church was built on top of the palace of the eighth Inca, Viracocha, using red granite slabs from the fortress at Sacsayhuamán. Two auxiliary chapels sit on either side. To the left is El Triunfo, Cusco's first church, built on top of the main Inca armoury to symbolize Spain's victory over the Incas. The 18th-century Jesús, María y José chapel is on the right. The Cathedral's Renaissance façade is in contrast with the lavish Baroque interior containing Colonial gold and silver and over 400 Cusco School paintings.

Iglesia Jesús, María y José
The façade and altar feature images of Jesus, Mary, and Joseph – the sacred family.

The chapel was built between 1733 and 1735.

★ El Señor de los Temblores
The Lord of the Earthquakes crucifix is said to have calmed the 1650 earthquake. The figure on the cross, El Negrito, has dark skin which many believe is due to candle smoke.

One of the towers, according to legend, has an Inca prince enclosed within and when it falls, he will emerge to claim his birthright.

★ Cedar Choir
The magnificently carved 17th-century choir stalls by Giménez de Villarreal features images of saints and popes.

STAR FEATURES

- ★ Cedar Choir
- ★ El Señor de los Temblores
- ★ The Last Supper

Main Altar
Fashioned from Bolivian silver, the Neo-Classical main altar weighs more than 885 lbs (400 kg). It was constructed between 1792 and 1803 by the silversmith Pinelo.

★ **The Last Supper**
Painted by Marcos Zapata (see p66) the painting has an Andean touch with Christ and his disciples enjoying a meal of roasted guinea pig, drinking chicha (corn beer) from Inca cups.

Finely carved granite altar

El Triunfo
The first Spanish church to be built in Cusco, its name itself is a constant reminder of the Spanish "triumph" over the Incas. It has an elaborately carved altar and a crypt that contains the ashes of historian Garcilaso de la Vega.

Main Entrance
These massive doors open for morning services, but the usual entrance is through El Triunfo.

Three tiers of zigzag ramparts built from huge stone blocks, Sacsayhuamán

Sacsayhuamán ②

Road Map D5. 1 mile (2 km) NE of Cusco. 🚍 from Cusco, or walk 🚶 ◯ 7am–6pm daily. 🎫 Boleto Turistico valid (see p157). ♿ only ground level. 🎭 Inti Raymi (Jun 24).

Sacsayhuamán is an impressive example of Inca military architecture. It is made up of three large terraces which overlap in a zigzag fashion. The enormous granite ramparts stretch about 985 ft (300 m), with stones as high as 17 ft (5 m), some weighing as much as 350 tonnes. So perfectly are the stones aligned that Spanish chroniclers recorded that even a fine knife could not penetrate the joints. No mud mixture was used to bind the stones together.

The ramparts feature 22 salient and re-entrant angles on each level. Such is their design that attackers trying to scale them would expose their flank to the defenders.

Thousands of men were recruited to wrestle the huge stones into place. Legend has it that about 20,000 Indians hauled the largest stone into position and

thousands were crushed to death when it toppled over at one stage.

In designing Cusco (see pp156–9), the Incas imagined it in the shape of a puma; with Sacsayhuamán representing the head and its serrated walls as the beast's teeth. Cusco was the body of the animal, while the temple of Koricancha (see p159) represented its tail.

The esplanade which runs in front of the ramparts on ground level probably functioned

Gateway made with giant stones slotted together, Sacsayhuamán

as a huge ceremonial square for religious and military events. Three towers guarded the top of the fortress; the surviving foundations are a reminder of their large size. They were linked by a series of underground passages through which all communication passed. All of Cusco's population could have been housed in the fortress if disaster struck.

During the battle of 1536 the Spanish forced the Incas back to the towers and slaughtered them. Leader Manco Inca escaped, retreating to Ollantaytambo (see p168).

The condors on Cusco's coat of arms are a macabre reference to the battle's body count, immortalizing the birds that came to feed on the dead.

Soon after their victory, the Spanish tore down many of the walls, using Sacsayhuamán as a quarry and taking the white stones to build churches and other structures in Cusco.

Opposite the hilltop fortress is Rodadero Hill, crowned by polished rocks and steps leading to an edifice shaped like a chair. From here, the Incas presided over ceremonies.

Tambomachay Tour ❸

A number of Inca sites lie on the road to Pisac, within easy reach of Cusco. The ruins of Tambomachay, Puca Pucara, Salapunco, and Qenko can be visited in a day, either by bus, taxi, on foot, or on horseback. Each of these locations is different and illustrates the artistic and architectural skills of the Incas. The shrine or *huaca* at Qenko, which is closest to Cusco, consists of a series of tunnels and a cave containing an altar, possibly used for sacrifices. At Tambomachay a spring was harnessed to form fountains, sacred to the Incas.

TIPS FOR VISITORS

Length: *10-mile (16-km) round trip.*
Tickets: *Boleto Turístico valid.*
Note: *Most visitors join an organized tour or hire taxis. Traditionally dressed locals lingering near the sites expect a tip if they are photographed.*

Puca Pucara ③
Meaning "red fort" in Quechua, this site was more likely a *tambo* or rest stop rather than a military post. The complex contains rooms, plazas, paths, aqueducts, and lookouts.

Tambomachay ④
This series of platforms, niches, and functioning fountains, testify to the Incas' worship of water as a key life force. It is believed this site honored the water deity.

Salapunco ②
Also called the Temple of the Moon or Lago, this large rocky outcrop comprises several small caves with rock carvings, platforms, and niches.

KEY

▬▬ Tour route

▭▭ Other road

──── Railroad

Qenko ①
Known as "labyrinth" in Quechua, rock channels flowed with llama blood or sacrificial *chicha* (corn beer) during ceremonies honoring the sun, moon, and stars.

0 km   1
0 miles   1

PISAC
AYACUCHO
CUSCO

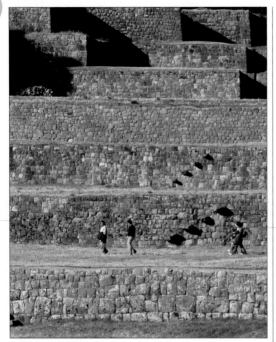

Stone terraces of the Inca ruins at Tipón

Tipón ❹

Road Map D5. 16 miles (25 km) S of Cusco. 🚌 *from Cusco.* ⏲ *7am–6pm daily.* 🎫 *Boleto Turístico valid (see p157).*

The picturesque set of stone canals, terraces, and stairways that make up Tipón are said to be part of a royal hacienda built by the eighth Inca ruler, Wiracocha, as a refuge for his father. According to experts, it was once a place of agricultural research and worship. Water is chaneled through stone structures, underground aqueducts, and decorative waterfalls, showcasing the Incas' grasp of hydraulics.

Pikillacta and Rumicolca ❺

Road Map D5. 19 miles (30 km) S of Cusco. 🚌 *from Cusco.* ⏲ *7am–6pm daily.* 🎫 *Boleto Turístico valid (see p157).*

Pikillacta, meaning the City of Fleas, was one of the pre-Inca cities built at the peak of the Wari culture. It was so named because of numerous 13-ft (4-m) enclosures that formed a protective garrison. The large complex has hundreds of mud and stone two-story buildings.

Pikillacta has an almost perfect geometrical design, divided into big rectangular blocks with long, straight streets. Walls were originally covered with mud and whitened with gypsum.

A short distance away are the remains of two imposing Inca gates called Rumicolca. Built on Wari foundations, the Inca blocks are much finer than the original Wari work. These gates acted as a checkpoint for people heading to Cusco, much like a customs office. For the people of the Quechua-speaking world, visiting Cusco was almost like making a religious pilgrimage. Standing at 12 m (39 ft), the gateway is one of the most impressive Inca constructions.

San Pedro de Andahuaylillas ❻

Road Map D5. 22 miles (36 km) S of Cusco. 🚌 *from Cusco.* ⏲ *8:30am–noon, 2–5pm Mon–Sat, 8:30–10am, 3–5pm Sun.* 🎫 ✝

Nicknamed the Sistine Chapel of the Americas, the simple mud brick façade of this 17th-century church gives no hint of the lavish treasures within.

These include a shimmering gold leaf ceiling, a mural by 17th-century painter, Luis de Riaño, depicting the paths to heaven and hell, Cusco School paintings illustrating the life of Saint Peter, and a painting of the Virgen de la Asuncion by Murillo.

The Baroque high altar is carved in cedar and covered with gold leaf, and the tabernacle is awash with silver plates. To the left of the entrance, five languages – Latin, Spanish, Quechua, Pukina, and Aymara – proclaim "I baptize him in the name of the Father, and the Son, and Holy Spirit."

Remains of the stone walls of the ancient city, Pikillacta

For hotels and restaurants in this region see pp274–5 and pp294–5

The Cusco School

Detail of gold on paintings

Hailed as one of the most important painting movements in the Americas, Escuela Cusqueña or the Cusco School of painting, grew out of the Spanish conquerors' desire to convert locals to Catholicism. Once the victory over the Incas was sealed, various Catholic orders set about winning over people who were, in general, Spanish-illiterate. They imported large numbers of European Renaissance religious paintings, including 16th-century works by Bartolomé Estéban Murillo, Peter Paul Rubens, and Francisco de Zubarán, as well as engravings and illustrations. This demand in turn drew painters to Peru in search of commissions. Representations of the Madonna, the Saints, Christ, and the crucifixion were used by priests as a kind of propaganda to illustrate their sermons.

Indigenous sensitivity in the form of local flora and fauna was introduced.

The Nativity *is a perfect example of the School's tradition whereby typical Christian images were blended with local Peruvian scenes. This painting is the representation of the birth of Chirst but the landscape is Andean; a llama and indigenous people in native headgear can be seen in the background along with angels.*

Cusco School *artists who made these paintings were largely anonymous. Paintings were produced in an industrial way, with specific artists for each phase – one for faces and hands, others for landscape and details.*

Clothing was studded with decorative ears of corn, a local crop.

Artists *depicted the archangels, armed with muskets and clad in Spanish armour, as soldiers of heaven. A symbol of both political and religious victory, the sword of the archangel defends faith but it also symbolizes the Spanish conquest of Peru.*

The Virgin of Pomata *portrays the Virgin Mary with smooth dark reams of hair like Andean women. She took on a triangular shape to represent the* apu *(sacred mountain) or Pachamama (Mother Earth), both sacred to Peruvians.*

View of town and mountains from Inca terraces, Ollantaytambo

Ollantaytambo ❼

Road Map D5. 60 miles (97 km) NW of Cusco. 🚶 *11,000*. 🚇 🚌 from Cusco. 🎊 *Fiesta de Reyes (Jan 6)*.

Spectacular Ollantaytambo is described as a living Inca town. The residents still strive to maintain ancient traditions such as tilling their fields with foot ploughs. The place takes its name from Ollanta, the Inca general who fell in love with the ninth ruler Pachacútec's daughter. He was forced to flee the city but was united with her after Pachacútec's death. Significant in Peruvian history for the greatest Inca victory over the Spanish, the town was reconquered by the Spaniards in 1537.

People have lived in these cobblestone streets since the 13th century. Originally named Qosqo Ayllu, this Inca town is divided into individual *canchas* (courtyards). Each courtyard has one entrance. A series of carved stone terraces, built to protect the valley from invaders, lead up the hillside to the fortress, **Araqama Ayllu**. The fort comprises the Temple of the Sun, the Royal Hall, or Mañacaray, the Princess' Baths, or Baños de la Princesa, and the Intihuatana, used to trace the sun's path.

Although unfinished, the Temple of the Sun is one of the finest examples of Inca stonework. Six pink monoliths,

designed to glow as the rays of the rising sun hit the structure, fit perfectly together. The T-joints, filled with molten bronze, hold the wall in place, and traces of puma symbols can still be seen on the surface. Stones for the fortress were quarried from an adjacent hillside, moved down one mountain, and up another by ramps.

Moray and Salinas de Maras ❽

Road Map D5. 31 miles (50 km) from Cusco. 🚌 🚕 from Cusco. ⏰ *7:30am–5pm daily*. 📷 for Moray.

At first glimpse Moray looks like a Greek amphitheater, but closer inspection reveals what researchers believe may have been a crop laboratory used by the Incas to find the

best conditions for allowing particular species to thrive. There are four overlapping *muyus* (slightly elliptical terraces) with each tier experiencing a different temperature due to varying levels of sun, shade, and elevation, and the largest being 148 ft (45 m) deep. Built on retaining walls filled with soil, and watered by a complex irrigation system, the 7-ft (2-m) high terraces show traces of about 250 cereals and vegetables.

The nearby Salinas de Maras (salt mines), dating back to pre-Columbian times, are in stark contrast. The natural salty water is channeled into 3,000 man-made wells and left to evaporate in the sun. Hundreds of miners work on the site even now, demonstrating their ancient working techniques.

Chinchero ❾

Road Map D5. 18 miles (28 km) NW of Cusco. 🚶 *11,000*. 🚌 🚕 from Cusco. 🛒 *Tue, Thu, & Sun*.

Dubbed the birthplace of the rainbow, Chinchero is perched about 12,375 ft (3,772 m) above sea level on the Anta plain, surveying the Sacred Valley.

The tenth Inca, Tupac Yupanqui, reportedly built his palaces here. In the mid-16th century, Manco Inca, the puppet king appointed by the Spanish conquistador Pizarro, burned down the village thereby cutting off his Spanish pursuers' supply lines. Chinchero did, however, finally succumb

Moray stone circles, believed to be an Inca crop laboratory

Women selling fresh products at Chinchero market place

to the Spanish by the end of the 16th century. Viceroy Toledo established a plantation here, putting local Indians to work on it, and built an adobe church just above the square over Inca foundations. The ceiling and walls are covered in floral and religious designs.

A massive stone wall in the main plaza, featuring ten trapezoidal niches, recalls the Incas, as do extensive agricultural terraces, seats, and stairways carved into rocks just outside the village.

Quechua-speaking locals preserve the Inca customs, wearing traditional dresses, farming the terraces, and weaving. A colorful handicraft market comes up in the square three days a week. Every Sunday, residents from the surrounding villages gather at the main plaza and exchange their agricultural products and handicrafts using a pure barter system.

Access to the ruins and the main plaza requires a Boleto Turístico, or a Tourism Ticket, available in Cusco. This ticket provides access to 16 historical sights *(see p157)*.

Calca ⑩

Road Map D5. 31 miles (50 km) N of Cusco. 🚶 20,000. 🚍 🚗 *from Cusco.* 🎭 *El Señor de Huanca (Sep 14).*

Nestled in the shadow of the Pitusiray and Sawasiray Mountains, Calca was once an important Inca administrative center favored due to its fertile soil. Today, all that remains are the maize fields and the archaeological ruins of **Huchu'y Qosqo** (Little Cusco), just outside town. Founded by the eighth Inca, Huiracocha, who spent his final days here, Huchu'y Qosqo was named after a tribe that lived here. Despite its name, the adobe brick ruins, including the remains of a three-story building, seem to bear very little resemblance to the real Cusco's streets.

Of special interest are the hot sulphur springs of **Machacancha** and the cold waters of **Minasmoqo**, considered good for health.

Pendant from Pisac market

Pisac ⑪

Road Map D5. 20 miles (32 km) N of Cusco. 🚶 10,000. 🚍 🚗 *from Cusco.* 🎭 *Tue, Thu, & Sun.*

After Ollantaytambo, the most significant Inca ruin is at Pisac. Inhabited since the 10th or 11th century, it became an important regional capital once the Incas arrived.

Researchers believe the town began as a military post to guard against invasion but grew into a ceremonial and residential center. Agricultural terraces and steep paths lead up to the hilltop fort, which has huge walls of polished stone. **Pisac Ruins** comprising military, residential, and religious buildings show that the Incas were masters at architecture, especially building in difficult places. The site's central element is the Templo del Sol, or Temple of the Sun, an astronomical observatory. The Templo de la Luna, or Temple of the Moon, a ceremonial bathing complex, and the Intihuatana, designed to track the sun's movements, are other highlights.

🎷 **Pisac Ruins**
🕙 *7am–5:30pm daily.* 🎫 *entry by Boleto Turístico (see p157).* 🎫

INCA EMPERORS

Originally, the word Inca was used only to describe the emperor. Today, however, it refers to the people. There were 13 Inca emperors beginning with Manco Cápac, called the Son of the Sun, who founded Cusco in the 12th century. The empire expanded slowly, spreading into the area around Cusco. The ninth Inca, Pachacútec (r.1438-71), pushed the empire down into Chile and captured most of the central Andes. His son, Tupac Yupanqui, extended the territory from Quito in Ecuador to Santiago in Chile. Grandson Huayna Cápac went farther north into Colombia, settling in Quito and making it the northern capital. The Inca civilization, at its peak around 1493, spanned an area of 2,983 miles (4,800 km).

Atahualpa, the last emperor of the Incas

The Inca Trail ⑫

The Incas developed an extensive network of roads, covering about 15,550–18,650 miles (25,000–30,000 km), to connect their wide ranging empire. The Cápac Ñan or Royal Road *(see p47)* comprised stone paths wide enough to accommodate two or three people as well as a llama train. Hanging bridges made of vegetable fiber spanned rivers and steep slopes were surmounted with steps and ramps. The famous Inca Trail, linking Machu Picchu with the Sacred Valley, is the best-preserved of these roads. The present day trail covers diverse landscapes and passes more than 30 Inca sites. Broken up into sections, it takes four days to complete.

Wild orchid, Inca Trail

Llactapata ①
Also known as Patallacta (Town on a Hillside) in Quechua, this city served as the local center for agricultural administration.

Intipunku ⑧
The Sun Gate is where the Incas controlled access to the city. It offers a 180-degree view of Machu Picchu. Most hikers try to get here in time to see the sunrise.

The Inca tunnel, 66-ft (20-m) long and cut through solid rock, features carved steps and polished walls. It is an amazing feat considering the lack of sophisticated mechanical drills.

0 km ———— 3
0 miles ———— 2

Rio Urubamba

Aguas Calientes

Poques
10,758 ft /
3,279m

Machu Picchu Ruins

San Miguel
9,594 ft /
2,924m

Intipata

Río Sayacmarca

Phuyupatamarca ⑦
Stairways connect the four groups of buildings built in the *pirca* architectural style (rough stones set in mud). Six water fountains and crop terraces are highlights.

KEY

🚉	Railroad station
ℹ️	Visitor information
⛺	Camping
☀️	Viewpoints
····	Other roads
——	Railroad
– –	Trail
⊦⋯⊣	Tunnel
✕	Pass
▲	Peak

Huayllabamba ②

The largest village on the trail, it is the last place to buy basic supplies such as snacks and bottled drinks. Locally brewed *chicha* (corn beer) is also readily available.

Abra de Warmiwañusca ③

This is the highest point on the trail and the hardest climb because of the lack of oxygen at this altitude. From the pass hikers can look down to the Pacaymayu (Hidden River) Valley and up to Runkurakay, which is the second pass on the trail.

Runkurakay ④

Opinion is divided on the role of this circular Inca ruin – food storehouse, watchtower, or rest stop. Its commanding position on the edge of the pass overlooking the entire area, however, suggests that it served as a watchtower. It offers superb views across the valley.

Wiñay Wayna ⑥

Resting on a series of terraces are upper and lower house clusters, interconnected by a long, steep staircase. A series of 10 fountains run from the top of the slope to the bottom, perfectly aligning with the agricultural terraces.

Sayacmarka ⑤

Carefully adapted to blend in with the natural mountain forms, this complex is made up of semicircular buildings, with a series of rooms and squares on different levels, narrow streets, fountains, patios, and canals.

Exploring the Inca Trail

Plaque marking the start of the trail

The city of the Incas, Machu Picchu, is a must on every traveler's list. One of the best ways to reach it is via the ancient Inca Trail. With paved stone paths and stairs cut into mountain-sides, the trail passes Inca citadels, such as Runturakay, Wiñay Wayna, and Phuyupatamarca, through cloud-forests speckled with orchids, across high Andean plains and up on to the oxygen-starved Warmiwañusca Pass.

At a height of 13,780 ft (4,200 m), the pass leaves many a hiker panting for breath. It is worth remembering that the Incas used to run along this trail. They used the trail to send messages across the king-dom. The *chasquis* (dispatch carriers) carried memori-zed official messages and each could cover over 250 miles (400 km) a day. Ironically, the Spanish used the same roads to infiltrate the country.

Abra de Warmiwañusca or Dead Woman's Pass

♠ Llactapata

4 miles (6 km) from KM82. 🏛 *2,000.*
Crop terraces, houses, and other edifices show Llactapata's significance in the region. At 9,843 ft (3,000 m) above sea level, it supplied Machu Picchu with maize, their staple crop.

The stone houses were believed to be occupied by the nobility and religious authorities, while the rest of the people lived in humble mud and cane homes. Pulpituyuj, the large circular tower built on a huge rock, may have served as an altar or prison. Its name comes from the Spanish word *pulpito* (pulpit) and the Quechua word *yuj*, which means a place with a pulpit.

Huayllabamba

8 miles (13 km) from KM82.
🏛 *6,000 (district).* 📷 🎭 *San Diego (Jul 25).*
Huayllabamba, which means "grassy plain" in Quechua, is the largest and the last Andean community found on this trail. At 10,040 ft (3,060 m), the village, located at the foot of a mountain, is set amid terraces of maize and potato crops. On clear days, one can see the snow-covered peak of Mount Veronica (18,640 ft/5,682 m) in the Urubamba Cordillera in the distance. Many hiking groups camp here on the first night of the trail. Inter-estingly, in Colonial times, the village resisted independence.

Andean woman at Huayllabamba

Abra de Warmiwañusca

14 miles (23 km) from KM82.
This mountain pass is 13,780 ft (4,200 m) above sea level. According to Inca mythology, the Andes were formed by giants turned into stones. This pass was perceived to be a reclining woman. The Incas believed they had to climb over her stomach to get to the other side. Warmiwañusca translates as "dead woman" in Quechua, hence the name Dead Woman's Pass.

The landscape changes here to barren and cold high plains, with the wind whistling through the pass. Hikers often place a stone on an *apacheta* (mound of rocks) located at the highest points on the trail as a payment to the Pachamama (Mother Earth).

♠ Runturakay

17 miles (28 km) from KM82
The ruins at Runturakay, discovered by explorer Hiram Bingham in 1915, have only a single north-facing entrance and exit. Some believe that Runturakay was used as a marker by travelers going to and from Machu Picchu to determine how much traveling time they had left. Others suggest that it was simply a post used to guard the road.

The round shape of the structure apparently inspired the workers employed to clean the site by Bingham to christen it Runturakay, refer-ing to its egg or basket shape.

View of terraces in the ancient town of Llactapata

For hotels and restaurants in this region see pp274–5 and pp294–5

Sayacmarka

22 miles (35 km) from KM82.

Perched high on a ridge at a height of 11,810 ft (3,600 m) above sea level, Sayacmarka can only be reached by a narrow stairway cut into the mountain. It is thought to have been a sacred ceremonial center devoted to astronomy. Sayacmarka means the "inaccessible town," in Quechua, but it did have a permanent supply of water and excellent food storehouses suggesting its importance.

Hiram Bingham named the site Cedrobamba in 1915 after discovering a cedar wood forest nearby. It was renamed in 1941 by anthropologist Paul Fejos to reflect the site more accurately.

Hikers on the narrow stairway cut into the mountain, Sayacmarka

Phuyupatamarca

25 miles (41 km) from KM82.

One of the best preserved towns on the trail, it is called the "town above the clouds" because at night the clouds settle in the ravines and the complex rises majestically above them. However, at sunrise the clouds disappear.

Hiram Bingham discovered the ruins in 1915 and christened them Qorihuayrachina. Like Sayacmarka, Paul Fejos renamed the ruins in 1941.

The curved walls and geometric terraces superbly blend with the shape of the mountains, illustrating the deep respect the Incas had for their natural environment. The ceremonial baths reflect the Inca mastery at controlling a natural force, spring water.

Path through the rocky terrain of Phuyupatamarca

Wiñay Wayna

27 miles (44 km) from KM82

This impressive Inca complex is situated at 8,860 ft (2,700 m) above sea level. The ruins were discovered in 1941 by, Paul Fejos, but it was Peruvian archaeologist, Julio C. Tello, who named it Wiñay Wayna in 1942. Meaning "forever young," Wiñay Wayna is also the name of a local orchid that blooms perennially.

Its location near a major access road and the striking architecture suggests that Wiñay Wayna was an important township for the Incas. The town is divided into four distinct sectors. There is the agricultural area with terraces, the religious or ritual area, the tower area which boasts some of the best architecture, and the urban sector. The latter is made of rectangular single- and double-story buildings with trapezoidal windows, doors and wall niches, as well as stairways and fountains. Significant sections of the complex illustrate the high-quality cut stone assembly of the Incas. It is the last ruin before Machu Picchu, which is just 4 miles (6 km) from here. It offers fantastic views of the beautiful valley and the surrounding mountains.

Aguas Calientes

5 miles (8 km) from Machu Picchu.
2,000. to Cusco. to Machu Picchu. in Town Hall. in thermal baths.

Aguas Calientes, meaning "hot springs" in Spanish, is popular amongst visitors for its natural pools. Also known as Machu Picchu Pueblo, it is the last town for visitors going to the ruins and the end of the line for travelers arriving by train from Cusco (see p176).

The town's economy revolves around tourism so there are many hotels, restaurants, and countless souvenir and handicrafts stalls. The streets are filled with vendors touting for trade. Even the railroad track changes into an open market once the train leaves the station.

For hikers with aching muscles, there are thermal pools just out of town, including a bracing one filled with icy mountain water. The pools were destroyed by floods but have been re-built.

Terraced mountainside and buildings at Wiñay Wayna

The astonishing Machu Picchu ruins bathed in sunlight ▷

Machu Picchu ❹

Llama on the mountain top

The mist-cloaked lost city of the Incas is arguably the most famous sight in all of South America. The citadel is built of rock at an altitude of 7,710 ft (2,350 m), on the saddle of a mountain flanked by sheer drops to the Urubamba Valley below. It was never sacked by the Spanish as they failed to find it, instead Machu Picchu was simply abandoned and left to nature to reclaim. The exquisite Inca stonework has withstood the ravages of time, but its function remains baffling. Experts speculate that it served as a place of worship, a sight for tracking stars, and the ninth Inca emperor, Pachacútec's country hacienda.

Sacred Rock is said to have been an altar for mountain and river gods.

★ Intihuatana
The stone was used by the Incas as a precise indicator of the two solstices, which they then used to plan agricultural cycles.

★ Sacred Plaza
The plaza is flanked by the Temple of the Three Windows on the east, the House of the High Priest to the south, and the back of the Principal Temple to the north. This fine structure was probably used for ceremonial rites.

VISITING MACHU PICCHU

Trains leave regularly from Cusco and Poroy for Aguas Calientes, a town just below Machu Picchu. Hiram Bingham, the luxury train, leaves from Poroy, a 20-minute drive from Cusco. Backpacker and Vistadome *(see p330–31)*, meant for standard tourists, leave from Cusco for a scenic journey through the Urubamba Valley to Aguas Calientes. From here a local bus zigzags up the mountains to the historical Inca site. However, the most satisfying way to visit Machu Picchu is by hiking the Inca Trail.

Train at the Aguas Calientes station

View of Machu Picchu
A spectacular view of the ruins, terraces, and stairways with Huayna Picchu forming the backdrop.

Skilled Architecture
The fine craftsmanship involved in building the structures here is evident: they are made of many-sided stone blocks fitted together flawlessly like pieces in a jigsaw and without mortar.

★ Temple of the Sun
Machu Picchu's only round building has two tower windows aligned to the points where the sun rises on the summer and winter solstices.

Agricultural terraces
were cut into the mountainside and provided food for up to 1,000 inhabitants.

STAR SIGHTS

★ Intihuatana

★ Sacred Plaza

★ Temple of the Sun

Exploring Machu Picchu

The remarkable state of preservation of Machu Picchu, with its superb interlacing masonry, satisfies even the most demanding visitor. This Inca city, comprising an upper and lower section with houses, temples, fountains, plazas, and agricultural terraces, clings to a mountain ridge, linked by scores of stairways and paths, and watered by natural springs. No other civilization has managed to assemble so many colossal stone blocks so seamlessly. Cut with stone or bronze tools, the edges of the stones were rubbed smooth until they merged together perfectly, like a jigsaw. Just how the Incas transported the granite they chiseled from the mountain remains a talking point for scholars today.

Water collects in the cut stone base of the fountains

Caretaker's Hut
This small open-fronted hut, with its spectacular view over Machu Picchu, was perfectly positioned to allow the caretaker to observe the access points to the city's south. The hut has been restored with a thatched roof, similar to how it would have appeared when the site was inhabited.

Fountains
The Incas harnessed a natural spring located on a steep slope to the north of Machu Picchu, building a 2,457 ft- (749 m-) long canal to bring the water down to the city. They channeled the water through a series of 16 fountains, often referred to as the "stairway of fountains." The water collects in the cut stone base of the fountain before going into a circular drain that delivers it to a channel leading to the next fountain. Each fountain featured a rectangular spout fashioned to produce a stream of water tailor-made to fill an *urpu* (a tall-necked, globular clay jug with a flared rim and a pointed base).

Royal Sector
The buildings in the Royal Sector, sometimes called the Group of the King, all feature considerable rock lintels, some weighing as much as three tons. These heavy structures were a feature of imperial Inca architecture.

Terraces next to the Caretaker's Hut

MACHU PICCHU SITE PLAN

1 Caretaker's Hut
2 Agricultural Sector
3 Dry Moat
4 Fountains
5 Main Fountain
6 *Temple of the Sun (see p180)*
7 Palace of the Princess
8 Fountain Caretaker's House
9 Royal Sector
10 Hut
11 Funerary Rock
12 Quarry
13 Temple of the Three Windows
14 Principal Temple
15 Sacristy
16 Intihuatana
17 Sacred Rock
18 Common District
19 Mortar Building
20 Temple of the Condor
21 Intimachay

0 meters   100

0 yards   100

Such characteristic rock lintels along with the abnormally spacious rooms, the high quality of stonework, and close proximity to the Temple of the Sun, the Sacred Plaza, and the first of the fountains, has led experts to surmise that this is where Pachacútec, the ninth Inca emperor, and other members of the Inca court lodged when they were in Machu Picchu. The entrance and exit to the Royal Palace via a single portal also signifies a high level of security. Hiram Bingham believed that the room at the front of the inner patio facing south was the Inca ruler's bedroom. It features 10 trapezoidal niches that would have housed significant ornaments. A room on the other side of the patio, with 12 niches, was thought to be the ruler's workroom.

Funerary Rock

The Funerary Rock, with its curious engraved shapes, is located near the Hut, which provides a great view of the entire area. Researchers believe it may have been used as a sacrificial altar. Llamas, the Incas' favorite offering, were probably sacrificed here. Hiram Bingham, however, suggested it was a mortuary slab on which deceased Inca nobles were laid out in the heat and cold to mummify. Just above the rock lies the upper cemetery of the complex, where Bingham uncovered a significant number of tombs.

Condor-shaped rock at the Temple of the Condor

Temple of the Three Windows

Located on the eastern side of the Sacred Plaza, the rectangular temple comprises large polished blocks flawlessly positioned together. There are three walls and the open side faces the plaza. On the opposite side, the wall has three trapezoidal windows, flanked by two niches. During the winter solstice, the first rays from the sun would come through these windows filling the room with light. At other times, there is a sweeping view on to the ruins below and across the valley. A group of stones in the center of the temple testifies to the presence of a column at some point.

Temple of the Condor

The temple earned its name from the two slabs which form the bird's stylized outspread wings and the head defined by the carved rock on the ground. Hiram Bingham tagged this area as the "prisons" during his expedition because of the dank subterranean dungeons and the niches above the building in which he believed prisoners were held and lashed. Modern day historians, however, believe that the niches were in fact altars on which mummies were placed during the ceremonies that were devoted to the condor, one of the most important Inca deities.

One of the windows at the Temple of the Three Windows

HIRAM BINGHAM (1875–1956)

Explorer, professor, and archaeologist Hiram Bingham set out as the leader of the Yale Peruvian Scientific Expedition in 1911 with a local policeman acting as guide and interpreter. While camped at Mandor Pampa, the expedition met local farmer Melchor Arteaga, who claimed that there were extensive ruins hidden on a nearby mountaintop. Bingham convinced Arteaga to show him the site by offering him one sol for his services. Bingham, Arteaga, and the policeman made the steep climb, eventually coming upon present day Machu Picchu, which despite being covered in centuries of growth, Bingham described as breathtaking.

Hiram Bingham on an expedition

The Temple of the Sun

The temple is regarded by many as having the most sublime stonework in all of Machu Picchu. Built over a large polished rock, the walls of the temple sinuously mimic its natural curve; the entire perimeter wall bends inward. It has compartments for holding offerings or idols. Archaeologists believe it served as an astral observatory, with Inca astronomers gleaning information about their crop cycles from the position of the constellations and the solstices.

Entrance to the Temple
Controlled by an Inca security mechanism, the door is the finest in the city.

Fountain caretaker's hut is a three-walled structure which was probably used to hang heavy objects.

Palace of the princess has an exclusive entrance to the temple.

Serpent Window
This window inside the temple was used to introduce snakes.

Entrance to the temple

Extraordinary stonework is a feature of all Inca structures.

The Royal Tomb
The steps represent the three levels of existence in the Inca world – the snake (underworld), puma (present), and condor (celestial world).

Window for the Solstices
This is aligned to the points where the sun rises on the summer and winter solstices, the longest and the shortest days.

A grand view of the Royal Sector on left and Temple of the Condor on right, with Common District behind

Sacred Plaza

The Principal Temple, the Sacristy, the House of the High Priest, the Temple of Three Windows, and the Intihuatana make up what Bingham called the Sacred Plaza. The Principal Temple, which faces the House of the High Priest, features the finest architecture. The two side walls have five expertly finished niches, while the back wall contains a small stone altar and seven niches. The Sacristy, which is connected to the Principal Temple, is famed for the two rocks lining the entrance, one of them is said to contain 32 angles. A stairway behind the building leads up to the Intihuatana.

Intihuatana

The Intihuatana stone indicates the precise dates of the solstices and the equinoxes, as well as other important astronomical periods. The June (winter) solstice was said to be the most important day of the year, when the sun is said to cast its longest shadow from the pillar. At this moment the sun is said to be "hitched" to the rock, hence its name "hitching post to the sun." The Incas held

ceremonies at this time, "tying the sun" to halt its northward movement. From this day onward the days become longer meaning more hours of light and more time to work the land and produce more food. Interestingly, the Intihuatana is not completely vertical but tilts 13 degrees to the north, the city's latitude.

Sacred Rock

The enigmatic carved rock, which mimics the shape of a mountain, is believed to have been used as an altar to worship the Apus, the Gods of the

Steps lead to the Intihuatana, used for astronomical purposes

Mountain, Water, and Fertility. Anthropologists believe that the rock mirrors the Pumasillo (Puma's Claw) located in the Vilcabamba Range, a peak revered by Andeans today. The Sacred Rock appeals to the gods whose form it recreates. It may also have been used as a sacrificial altar to appease the gods.

Common District

Located above the Temple of the Condor is the Common District, also known as Secular District or Industrial Quarter. It was thought to have housed the workers of the realm because the construction is inferior to that of the upper section. Bingham speculated that the two circular rocks which protrude from the floor in one of the buildings were mortars used to crush grain, but as they do not show any wear and are highly polished, this seems unlikely. They may have played a role in a ritual, being filled with offerings of *chicha* or blood, or in an astrological ceremony as the sun, moon, and some stars are reflected when the mortars are filled with water. Their real purpose, however, remains a mystery to archaeologists.

CENTRAL SIERRA

*T*he Central Sierra is an unspoiled area of remote Andean scenery, splendid Colonial towns with an ancient pre-Inca heritage, and traditional rural communities. Despite the wealth of local crafts and lively festivals, this region sees relatively few visitors. Those who do venture here will be amply rewarded by some of Peru's most attractive and pristine landscapes.

Visitors to Peru, lured by the attractions of the Amazon and Cusco regions, largely ignore the Central Sierra. Yet the area's Colonial cities rival Cusco for architecture and charm, especially 16th-century Ayacucho, with its well-preserved churches and grand mansions.

Here, you will also find ancient ruins of the Wari Empire (around AD 600–1100), which dominated the area. The Incas were greatly influenced by the Wari methods of governance and their culture.

Until the early 1990s, this region witnessed the worst of the atrocities committed by the Maoist guerrilla group, the Shining Path *(see p195)*. After the capture of their ringleaders in 1992, the group went into decline and has now all but disappeared. As memories of violence recede, the pretty villages have seen a revival and have now begun to draw travelers.

Today smaller towns, such as Lircay, where the inhabitants still wear distinctive local dresses, and Huancavelica, once a strategic Inca center, are well worth a visit. Another attraction is Huancayo, which plays host to a bustling market every Sunday, where villagers from the surrounding communities display colorful fabrics, handmade wooden ornaments, and produce from their own smallholdings.

The local population – the majority of whom are subsistence farmers – is one of the poorest in the country. Small rural communities are dotted across the neatly cultivated valleys and locals are generally welcoming and friendly. Wandering through the dusty streets and plazas is like taking a step back in time: ancient crafts and traditions are still maintained and there are hardly any tourists in the area.

Well-preserved Colonial buildings line the streets of Ayacucho

◁ **Railroad tunnel cutting through the Andes**

Exploring Central Sierra

The region provides a fascinating glimpse of rural Peru. Distinctive local artesania is on show in the adobe villages of the Mantaro Valley, such as Cochas Grande, Hualhuas, and San Agustín. Ayacucho has some wonderful examples of Colonial architecture best seen in its churches, and the Santa Rosa Convent, outside the village of Concepción is also impressive. There is evidence of pre-Inca cultures at the Temple of Kotosh, Huánuco, and the Wari Ruins, outside Ayacucho. These areas are all accessible from the region's commercial hub, Huancayo, where a dynamic Sunday market showcases the agricultural produce and craftwork from nearby villages. Huancayo is also the last stop on one of the world's highest train journeys.

SIGHTS AT A GLANCE

Towns and Cities
Ayacucho pp192–3 **7**
Concepción **3**
Huancavelica **6**
Huancayo **4**
Huánuco **1**
Palcamayo **2**
Quinua **9**

Area of Natural Beauty
Pikimachay Caves **10**

Tour
Mantaro Valley Tour **5**

Archaeological Site and Ruin
Wari Ruins **8**

San Pedro de Chonta
San Buenaventura
Río Santa Martha
Aucayacu
HUÁNUCO
Hermilio Valdizán
Puca
Monzón
Tantamayo
Chavin de Pariarca
Parque Nacional Tingo María
Tingo María
Quivilla
Ceja de la Montaña
Pachas
Chinchao
Chavinillo
Chaglla
HUÁNUCO 1
Panao
Margos
Ambo
Páucar
Yanahuanca
Atacocha
Cerro de Pasco
Colquijirca
Dique
Pari
Parque Nacional de Junín
Carhuamayo
Ulcumay
Carhuacayán
Ondores
Junín
Huasa
PALCAMAYO 2
Tarma
Paccha
La Oroya
Yauli
Lima
Piñascochas
Ac
Cochas
San de Qu
Aura
Tanta

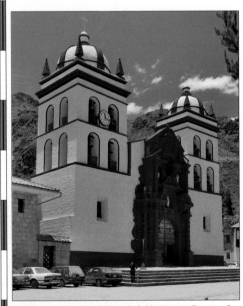

Brightly-colored façade of the Cathedral in Huancavelica, one of the best examples of Colonial architecture in the region

KEY

— Main road
⊷⊷ Untarred main road
= = = Untarred minor road
- - - Track
⊷⊷ Railroad
— Regional border

SEE ALSO

• **Where to Stay** pp275–6
• **Where to Eat** pp295–6

Andean farmers herding their flock of sheep along a mountainous path in the Huánuco area

GETTING AROUND

There are daily flights from Lima to Ayacucho and to Huánuco. Buses regularly ply the route from Lima to Huancayo (193 miles/310 km), Huánuco (230 miles/370 km), and Ayacucho (354 miles/570 km). The roads for the ten-hour journey between Huancayo and Ayacucho and the 92-mile (147-km) stretch between Huancayo and Huancavelica are in very poor condition. It is not advisable to hire a car in Central Sierra. A train also runs from Lima to Huancayo and from Huancayo to Huancavelica.

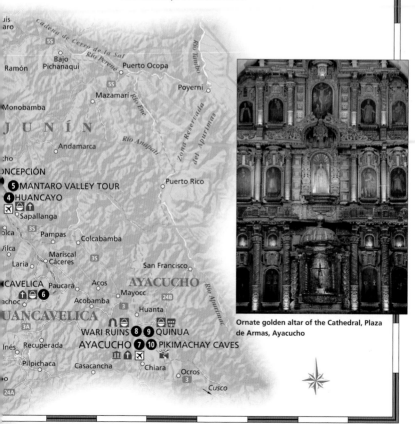

Ornate golden altar of the Cathedral, Plaza de Armas, Ayacucho

Mud moldings of crossed arms from the Temple of Kotosh, Huánuco

Huánuco ❶

Road Map C4. 280 miles (450 km) NE of Lima. 👥 190,000. ✈ 🚌 from Lima. ℹ General Prado 718, 51 2980. 📅 Town Anniversary (Aug 12–17).

This Andean town, situated at a height of 6,214 ft (1,894 m), has the best climate in Peru. The capital of its department, Huánuco lies on the banks of the Río Huallaga. Founded by the Spanish in 1541, the town still has a few examples of fine Colonial architecture. These include the Cathedral, which contains some pieces from the famous Cusco School paintings (see p167), Iglesia San Cristóbal with intricate woodcarvings, and the grand 16th-century Church of San Francisco. The town also has a natural history museum.

Just outside Huánuco lies the **Temple of Kotosh**, said to be one of Peru's oldest archaeological sites, dating from 2000–1500 BC. Although the site was rediscovered in 1935, it was not excavated until 1960, and still little is known about this ancient culture. The most important findings here are the two mud moldings, each depicting a pair of crossed arms in one of the enclosures, believed to be between 4,000 to 5,000 years old. One of these is now on display at the Museo de la Nación (see p95) in Lima. The other pair, unfortunately, has been destroyed.

The site, comprising three stone-built enclosures, is a bit overgrown, though there are a number of replicas of the mud moldings in the temple. Local guides willingly take visitors around for a small tip.

🏚 **Temple of Kotosh**
3 miles (5 km) W of Huánuco.
🕐 8am–4pm daily. 📷 🎥 🚫

Palcamayo ❷

Road Map C4. 65 miles (105 km) N of Huancayo. 👥 28,000. 🚌 from Tarma. 📅 week-long Fiesta Patronal (end of July). **www**.palcamayo.org

Palcamayo is a small town situated in a green valley. The area's main attraction is the **Gruta de Huagapo**, an enormous limestone cave considered the deepest in South America. Although speleologists have explored 9,006 ft (2,745 m) of the cave, its exact depth is still unknown.

The entrance to Huagapo, which means "cave that cries" in Quechua, is through a huge hole on the side of the mountain from which an underground river flows. The entrance leads into a giant chamber that is 99 ft (30 m) high and 66 ft (20 m) wide. Exploring the first 984 ft (300 m) of the cave is fairly straight-forward, but professional equipment, including scuba gear, is needed to go farther. The light fades and temperature drops as visitors venture deeper into the cave. Local boys act as guides, providing ropes and torches for a tip.

🏚 **Gruta de Huagapo**
2 miles (4 km) from Palcamayo.
🕐 8am–4pm daily. 🎥 📷 🚫

Cave paintings in Gruta de Huagapo, Palcamayo

Concepción ❸

Road Map C4. 14 miles (22 km) NW of Huancayo. 👥 63,000. 🚌 from Huancayo.

A sleepy village, Concepción lies in the Mantaro Valley. Just out of town is the 18th-century Franciscan **Convent of Santa Rosa de Ocopa**, which was established as a base for training missionaries heading to the Amazon. The museum in the convent exhibits indigenous artifacts and examples of wildlife, as well as old maps and photographs. The library has a fascinating collection of more than 25,000 volumes, some of which are hundreds of years old. There is also a display of Colonial religious art as well

Convent of Santa Rosa de Ocopa, Concepción

The library at the Convent of Santa Rosa de Ocopa, Concepción

as works by contemporary Huancayo-born artist, Josué Sánchez (b.1945).

The beautiful convent, with its cloisters, stone fountains, and a picturesque garden, is a lovely place to explore. Nuns give hourly tours of the premises to the interested visitors. Unfortunately they only speak Spanish.

🔒 Convent of Santa Rosa de Ocopa
4 miles (6 km) from Concepción.
🕐 9am–noon, 3–6pm Wed–Mon.
📷 Spanish only. 🔒

Huancayo **4**

Road Map C4. 224 miles (360 km) E of Lima. 🏛 430,000. ✈ 🚌 from Lima. 🛈 Casa del Artesano, Calle Real 481. 🎭 Semana Santa (week leading to Easter), Fiesta de las Cruzes (May). **www**.hyoperu.com

Situated at a height of 10,696 ft (3,260 m) in Mantaro Valley, Huancayo is a busy, modern, commercial center. It is also the trade hub for the nearby villages. For a good view of the town, the Cerrito de la Libertad hill is a short distance from the city center. Beyond the hill are the dramatic sandstone towers of **Torre Torre**.

The region is both culturally and agriculturally one of the richest in the Andes. Every Sunday, a huge market attracts villagers from surrounding communities, who come here to sell agricultural produce and local handicrafts. It is perhaps one of the most popular markets in Peru. Huancayo is also a good base from which to visit these rural communities. Each has its own traditional dress and style of dance, and are renowned for their many festivals. This is also the area to savor local culinary specialties such as *pachamanca* (marinated meat, potatoes, spices, and vegetables cooked in a hole dug in the ground and covered by hot stones).

Once home to the Wari culture, around AD 600, Huancayo was absorbed into the Inca Empire in 1460. The Calle Real, which runs through the city, was part of

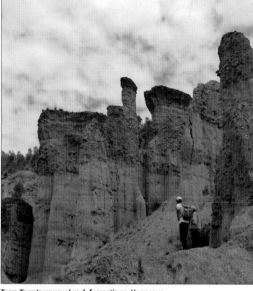

Torre Torre's unusual rock formations, Huancayo

the Cápac Ñan *(see p47)* from Cusco to Cajamarca. The city was founded by the Spanish in 1572, and a few Colonial buildings still remain, the most interesting of which is La Merced. It was in this church that the Peruvian constitution was approved in 1839. It contains a good collection of religious art from the Cusco School.

A big tourist attraction is the **Lima to Huancayo Train**, one of the world's highest train journeys. Conceived by an American, Henry Meiggs, the railroad was built between 1870 and 1908 by more than 10,000 workers, mainly brought over from China. Though passenger service has been disrupted several times, a limited service has now resumed.

Lima to Huancayo Train
Departs: *Lima*, 7am on last *Thu of each month*.
Returns: *Huancayo*, 7am Sunday.
📷 🍴 🖥 **www**.ferrocarrilcentral. com.pe

THE LIMA TO HUANCAYO TRAIN

The spectacular journey begins at sea level in Lima's Desamparados Station, and winds its way through 66 tunnels and 59 bridges. At 15,843 ft (4,829 m), the Ticlio Pass is one of the highest railroad passes in the world, and Galera, at 15,686 ft (4,781 m), one of the highest passenger stations. The passenger service is a weekend excursion, on the final weekend of the month. Its daily, regular service is used to transport minerals from Andean mines and agricultural produce from the Mantaro River Valley. This 208-mile (335-km) journey takes about 12 hours, and passes through breathtaking Andean scenery.

Thrilling route of the Lima to Huancayo train

Mantaro Valley Tour ❺

The Mantaro Valley, through which the Río
Mantaro flows, is a beautiful, verdant region
of agricultural abundance, producing corn,
potatoes, artichokes, and carrots. The area
is dotted with small adobe villages and the
population is renowned for its distinct
craftwork, music, and dance with numerous
lively festivals held throughout the year.
There are few facilities here, and very little
English is spoken, but these communities
provide a refreshing glimpse of rural
Peruvian life. All the villages are easily
accessible from Huancayo.

Cochas ①
The pre-Inca tradition of *mates burilados*
(engraved gourds) is still practised in the
twin villages of Cochas Grande and
Cochas Chico. The intricate and detailed
carvings depict stories of Andean life.

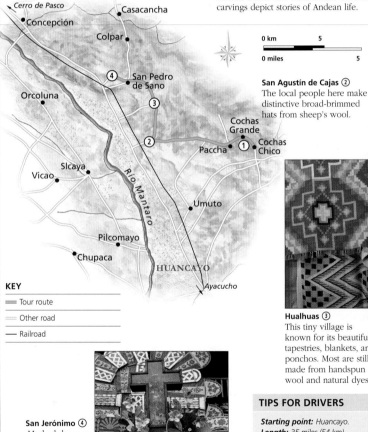

0 km   5

0 miles   5

San Agustín de Cajas ②
The local people here make
distinctive broad-brimmed
hats from sheep's wool.

KEY

▬▬ Tour route

═══ Other road

─── Railroad

Hualhuas ③
This tiny village is
known for its beautiful
tapestries, blankets, and
ponchos. Most are still
made from handspun
wool and natural dyes.

TIPS FOR DRIVERS

Starting point: *Huancayo.*
Length: *35 miles (54 km).*
Stopping-off points: *Carry
water and snacks as there is little
infrastructure along the route.
The small roadside stalls sell only
agricultural products. Good views
of the valley provide lots of
opportunities for photo-stops.*

San Jerónimo ④
Masked dancers
participate in the
festival of the patron
saint of San Jerónimo.
The village is renown-
ed for its complex
silver filigree jewelry,
on sale at the
Wednesday market.

Colonial-style buildings in the Plaza de Armas, Huancavelica

Huancavelica ⑥

Road Map C5. 92 miles (147 km) S of Huancayo. 🏘 *40,000.* 🚌 *from Huancayo.* 🚂 *from Huancayo & Lima.* 🎭 *Semana Santa & Christmas.*

This attractive town, the capital of the department of the same name, is located in a high, remote area known for mining and agriculture. At one time a strategic Inca center, the Spanish town was founded in 1571 after the discovery of vast deposits of mercury nearby. They exploited the area's mineral wealth, bringing in slaves to mine for silver and mercury. Due to gradual depletion of resources, the mines were closed in the mid-1970s. At 12,140 ft (3,700 m), the town retains a lovely Colonial atmosphere and has some excellent examples of Spanish architecture. The churches are renowned for their intricate silver altars. Each Sunday a lively market attracts villagers from the surrounding rural communities, who come in their traditional dress.

Environs
Santa Barbara, made famous by the mines nearby, is a good three-hour hike from Huancavelica, up a steep trail that reaches over 13,125 ft (4,000 m) above sea level. The walk to the mines goes over some striking terrain, past herds of alpaca and llama. Carved into a rockface,

the old entrance to one of the original 16th-century mines is still open and unguarded, but it is not advisable to enter.

Ayacucho ⑦

See pp192–3

Wari Ruins ⑧

Road Map D5. 14 miles (22 km) from Ayacucho. ◯ *Tue–Sun 10am–5pm.* 📷

Wari pottery, site museum

The road from Ayacucho on the way to Quinua passes the Wari Ruins. Built on a hill, at 8,100 ft (2,470 m), it was the

capital of the first known expansionist empire in the Andes, and covers an area of around 4 sq miles (10 sq km). Divided into five main sections, it comprises rectangular buildings set out on a grid system, a complex of streets, squares, tombs, paths, and irrigation channels. Very little restoration work has been carried out so far, and the site is therefore not much to look at. The site museum too is usually closed but some of the artifacts from these ruins are displayed at an archaeological museum in Ayacucho.

THE WARI (AD 600–1100)

The Wari founded Peru's first militaristic and urban culture, expanding their influence by conquest. They subdued the cultures of those they conquered by enforcing their own customs and forbidding any practice of the former culture. As a result, all trace of the earlier oral traditions has been lost. The Wari Empire *(see pp44–5)* lasted four times longer than that of the Incas, who went on to appropriate their road network and architectural devices, such as an advanced ventilation system and earthquake-proof housing. The reasons for their decline in AD 1100 are unclear, but it is thought that they were replaced gradually by smaller, locally dominant regional groups.

Water channel at the Wari Ruins

Farming in the Central Sierra countryside ▷

Ayacucho 🕖

Retablo depicting rural life

Founded by the Spanish in 1539, Ayacucho lies 8,950 ft (2,750 m) above sea level. A temperate climate, leafy plazas, and beautifully preserved Colonial architecture make strolling around it a pleasure. Ayacucho has a rich tradition of arts and crafts and has retained its charm and Colonial atmosphere which is visible in its wonderful church architecture. During the 1980s the city was isolated and tourism was discouraged due to terrorist activity by the Shining Path. It now plays host to the country's famous Holy Week celebrations, which attract visitors from all over Peru.

The Cathedral on Plaza de Armas, Ayacucho

🏛 Iglesia de Santo Domingo

Cnr of Bellido & 9 de Diciembre.
⬜ 6:30–8am daily. 🕇
The church has a Renaissance façade which was later embellished with columns and a balcony. The Spanish Inquisition used this balcony to hang its victims. Inside the church, there is evidence of the fusion of Andean and Catholic influences. There is a portrait of an Inca face on the gold leaf altar, and a hummingbird motif used for decorative purposes. The bells of Iglesia de Santo Domingo were rung to declare independence from the Spanish after Peru's victory at the Battle of Ayacucho in 1824.

🏛 Museo de Arte Popular

Plaza de Armas.
⬜ 10:15am–5:30pm Tue–Fri; 9:45am–12:15pm Sun.
This fascinating museum is a showcase for the traditional art of the region. There is a display of *retablos*, Peruvian term for small portable altars once used by mule drivers to bring luck. These wooden

boxes have two doors and feature elaborate depictions of religious scenes or laid-back rural Andean life, made from plaster. Some examples tell the story of political agitation and conflict during the Shining Path era.

There are also exhibits of traditional small clay churches that local women paint with designs of corn and flowers; and several examples of the *tablas de sarhua*, or illustrations on wood, depicting traditional village customs.

Detail of an angel adorning the gilt altar inside the Cathedral

🏛 Cathedral

Plaza de Armas. ⬜ 5:30–7pm daily.
🕇
Located beside the university, on the elegant Plaza de Armas, Ayacucho's 17th-century cathedral has an inauspicious pink and grey façade. The interior is impressive, with a gilded altar and ornately carved pulpit, which is best viewed when it is illuminated during the evening service. The Cathedral is the center of the famous candlelit Holy Week procession, when a crowd gathers here to follow an effigy of Christ that is carried around the city atop a white donkey. There is also a Museum of Religious Art inside the church that exhibits works brought to the country from Rome during the Colonial period.

🏛 Casa Boza y Solís-Prefecture

Portal Constitución, Plaza de Armas.
⬜ 8am–8pm Mon–Fri.
This two-story mansion, built in 1748, has been turned into government offices, which are open to the public. The interior courtyard has an

Stone fountain in the courtyard of Casa Boza y Solís-Prefecture

original stone fountain and the upper floor is decorated with beautiful glazed Sevillian tiles. Visitors are allowed to see the cell of María Parado de Bellido, a revolutionary hero who was incarcerated here before she was executed by a firing squad in 1822.

🛈 Iglesia San Francisco de Paula
Cnr of Garcilaso de la Vega & Cusco. ◷ 6:15–7.30am, 6:15–7:30pm daily. 🛈
This church is in competition with Cusco's San Blas church *(see p159)* for Peru's finest carved pulpit. The altar here is one of the few in the city not covered in gold leaf. It is considered to be the finest in the country, made from

Cedar wood altar at the Iglesia San Francisco de Paula

Nicaraguan cedarwood carved with dozens of angels. The church, built in 1674, also holds a collection of Flemish paintings.

Detail on the limestone façade of La Merced

🛈 Compañía de Jesús
28 de Julio, btwn Lima & San Martin. ◷ 9:30am–12:30pm daily. 🛈
This Jesuit church, built in different architectural styles, has a façade of flowers sculpted in red and orange stone. Inside, the gilded altar, carved wood interior, and a good collection of Colonial religious paintings and sculptures are worth seeing. Next door is the Jesuit school where Latin, music, wood-carving, and painting lessons were given to indigenous children, before the expulsion of the Jesuits from Latin America in 1767.

🛈 La Merced
Cnr of 2 de Mayo and San Martin. ◷ 6:15–7:30am daily. 🛈
Built in 1541, La Merced is the city's second oldest church. It has one nave and a simple Renaissance façade made from fading limestone, which stands in marked contrast to the later elaborate Baroque style, and is a characteristic of many of the neighboring churches. Constructed in a similar modest style, is the adjacent convent, one of the oldest in the country.

🛈 Iglesia y Monasterio de Santa Clara
Between Libertad & Nazareño. ◷ 6:30–8am daily. 🛈
The church has a simple limestone exterior and has the effigy of Jesus that is the center of worship during the famous Holy Week celebrations. It also has a beautiful, intricately carved Mudéjar-style wood ceiling.

AYACUCHO CITY CENTER

Casa Boza y Solís-Prefecture ④
Cathedral ③
Compañía de Jesús ⑥
Iglesia de Santo Domingo ①
Iglesia San Francisco de Paula ⑤
Iglesia y Monasterio de Santa Clara ⑧
La Merced ⑦
Museo de Arte Popular ②

0 meters 200
0 yards 200

Key to Symbols see back flap

Semana Santa

The most important event in the Peruvian religious calendar begins on Palm Sunday. Semana Santa, a week of festivities commemorating the trial and crucifixion of Christ, culminates in a joyous celebration of his resurrection on Easter Sunday. Spectacular celebrations are concentrated in Andean towns and villages, where the mixture of Catholic rituals and the pagan beliefs of indigenous communities combine to create a fascinating spectacle. All schools and offices are closed during Holy Week and locals exhibit their religious devotion with processions through the streets, united in impassioned prayer behind an effigy of Christ. These emotional expressions of piety are combined with a celebratory atmosphere filled with folkloric music, dance, feasts, and fireworks. The week-long celebrations present a bewitching fusion of Catholic and pre-Columbian beliefs.

Christ of the Tremors

Ayacucho *sees thousands of people descend on the town for Holy Week. City lights are dimmed while a glass coffin containing an effigy of Christ is paraded through streets strewn with roses, followed by a candlelit procession of black-clad worshippers, chanting and praying.*

Tarma *is famous for its elaborate floral carpets that cover the streets during Semana Santa. Arches, also made from flowers, add to the festive atmosphere.*

Cusqueñans *worship the Christ of the Tremors, which locals believe defended the city from an earthquake in 1650. This painting, commissioned by Alonso Cortes de Monroy, depicts the city after the earthquake and is carried along the streets of Cusco every Easter Monday.*

An effigy of Christ *is central to celebrations all over Peru. Even though each area has its own style of celebrating Semana Santa, all processions have people following the effigy in fervent prayer.*

Handmade costumes *and elaborate masks with mythological or pre-Columbian themes are common. Some outlandish get-ups are also used to poke fun at the Spanish conquistadores.*

Handmade ceramic church on a roof, Quinua

Quinua ⓿

Road Map D5. 23 miles (37 km) NE of Ayacucho. 🚌 from Ayacucho. 🛒 Sunday. 🎭 Independence Day (early Dec).

In the rolling hills 23 miles (37 km) northeast of Ayacucho (see p192–3) lies Quinua at almost 10,827 ft (3,300 m) above sea level. This beautiful little town has an attractive cobbled plaza and is famous for its ceramic crafts. The roofs of the houses in the region are adorned with small ceramic churches, decorated with painted flowers and corn. These churches are believed to be good luck charms by the locals, and are used to ward off evil spirits.

Local artisans also produce handmade guitars and alabaster figurines featuring comical bands of musicians or groups of gossiping women. The ceramics, made from the rich, red local clay, are on display at workshops and are also sold at the small Sunday market held every week.

Just outside the village lies the **site of the Battle of Ayacucho** (see p49), where Spanish royalist troops were finally defeated, after years of struggle for independence, on December 9th, 1824. This battle brought an end to Colonial rule in the country. The battlefield is a ten-minute walk from the town, and a 132 ft- (40 m-) high white obelisk commemorates the event. There is an annual week-long festival held every

December. Locals in Quinua and people all over Peru celebrate with week-long festivities that include feasting, folk music, and dance.

Pikimachay Caves ⓿

Road Map D5. 15 miles (24 km) W of Ayacucho. 🚗 organized tours from Ayacucho.

Situated close to Ayacucho, the cave is hewn out of limestone and is thought to date back to 12,000 BC. It holds evidence of long-term human occupation – the earliest in all of South America. These early inhabitants are thought to have been nomadic hunters

THE SHINING PATH

Sendero Luminoso or Shining Path, a Maoist guerilla group, was founded in the 1960s by Abimael Guzmán. It pledged to overthrow the government and return land to peasant farmers. By assassinating unpopular government officials and landowners, the movement gained sympathy initially. However, the 1980s saw a decline in the support due to their activities in rural areas, including brutal "popular trials" and the execution of peasants. By 1992, the group was waging a terror campaign, and had widespread control throughout the countryside of central and southern Peru and in Lima's shantytowns. In 1992, Guzmán was captured and imprisoned for life. Since then the Shining Path has all but disappeared.

Abimael Guzmán, founder of the Maoist Shining Path

and gatherers. Remains of ancient chopping implements, basalt, and blades have been found, along with bones of a giant sloth. It was not until 4,000 BC that agriculture was introduced, and man started cultivating crops such as beans, squash, and chilies.

Beyond the Pikimachay Caves is the **Mirador de Huatuscalla**, a remote viewpoint that looks over the confluence of the Urubamba, Cachi, and Mantaro rivers. Dramatic mountain scenery provides the backdrop to the confluence.

Tour operators based in Ayacucho can arrange personalized packaged tours for visitors going to Quinua, Pikimachay Caves, and Huatuscalla.

View of the valley from the Pikimachay Caves

CORDILLERA BLANCA

*T**he Cordillera Blanca, or White Range, so called because of its
perennial ice-capped peaks, has the greatest number of summits
over 19,700 ft (6,000 m) outside the Himalayas. These include
Peru's highest mountain, Huascarán (22,205 ft/6,768 m), and
Alpamayo (19,511 ft/5,947 m), considered one of the most beautiful
mountains in the world, thanks to its near-perfect pyramid of ice.*

This 112-mile (180-km) range in the heart of the tropical Andes is a breathtaking area of dramatic views, towering peaks, precipitous gorges, sparkling lakes, and abundant wildlife. The range runs parallel to the Cordillera Negra, forming the Callejón de Huaylas, a lush agricultural valley dotted with small villages, known for their arts and crafts, where ancient Andean ways of life persist. Villages such as Chacas are renowned for their woodcarving and carpentry. The valley is also home to relaxing natural thermal baths in Monterrey and Chancos, and a number of fascinating Inca and pre-Inca ruins, including the 3,000-year-old archaeological site at Chavín de Huántar, a major ceremonial center of the Chavín people.

Huaraz, capital of the Ancash region, is one of the most important trekking and climbing centers in Peru. Led by local guides, mule-supported treks into the Huascarán National Park are some of the most spectacular that the continent has to offer, with high-altitude camping over vertiginous passes and fantastic views of the surrounding snowy peaks. The dazzling turquoise lakes, such as Parón and Llanganuco, are the highlights of many hikes in the region. The glacial silt collected in these lakes creates a vibrant color that glows in the bright Andean sun.

The region is home to the some unusual flora, such as *Puya raimondii*, a gigantic bromeliad, which takes up to a century to reach its full height, and forests of polylepsis trees, a member of the rose family that flourishes at this altitude. While trekking through the range, visitors may also spot the Andean condor, and the camelid vicuña.

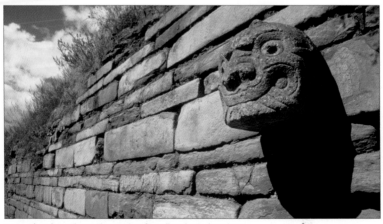

A stone face decoration on the remains of a wall at Chavín de Huántar

◁ Snowy peaks reflected in the waters of Laguna Cullicocha

Exploring Cordillera Blanca

Most visitors to the area base themselves in the towns and villages of the Callejón de Huaylas, the valley between Cordillera Blanca and Cordillera Negra. Huaraz, Caraz, Carhuaz, and Chacas are all home to local festivals, rural produce markets, and arts and crafts. From the valley many of the highlights of the region can be visited on a day trip, including the hot springs at Chancos and Monterrey, the ruins at Chavín de Huántar, the spectacular lakes of Llanganuco and Parón, and Huascarán, a UNESCO Biosphere Reserve. More adventurous travelers can use Huaraz or Caraz as a base from which to hire mules, equipment, and a guide to go for a longer hike into the mountains. The popular choices are the Santa Cruz trek, and the Olleros to Chavín trek.

SIGHTS AT A GLANCE

Towns and Cities
Caraz ❶
Carhuaz ❸
Chacas ❺
Cordillera Huayhuash ⑪
Huaraz ❼
Sechín ❿

Areas of Natural Beauty
Hot Springs of Monterrey ❻
*Parque Nacional Huascarán
  pp202–204* ❹

Cemetery
Campo Santo, Yungay ❷

Archaeological Sites and Ruins
Caral p212 ❾
*Chavín de Huántar
  pp208–209* ❽

KEY

▬▬	Highway
▬	Main road
▭▭▭	Minor road
●▬●	Untarred main road
▪▪▪	Untarred minor road
- - -	Track
▬▬	Railroad
▬	Regional border
△	Peak

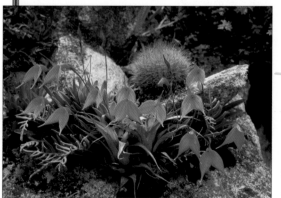

Beautiful orchid growing on the mountain slopes

0 km ————— 50

0 miles ————— 50

SEE ALSO

• **Where to Stay** pp276–7

• **Where to Eat** pp296–7

For additional map symbols *see back flap*

An awe-inspiring view of Callejón de Huaylas

Traveling on mules in the Cordillera Blanca

GETTING AROUND

Only chartered flights arrive at the airport in Anta, 20 miles (32 km) north of Huaraz. Most visitors fly to Lima and then reach Huaraz by road. Frequent buses, *colectivos*, and *combis* make the 42-mile (67-km) journey from Huaraz to Caraz, stopping at villages on the way. Two routes cross the Cordillera, one via Carhuaz and down to Chacas over the Quebrada Ulta Pass, and the other via Chavín de Huántar. The road to the north coast passes the ruins at Sechín and crosses the Punta Callan Pass at a height of 13,850 ft (4,200 m), giving fantastic views.

Enchanting view of Mount Alpamayo

Caraz ❶

Road Map B3. 42 miles (67 km) N of Huaraz, Callejón de Huaylas. 🏔 16,600. 🚌 *frequent colectivos from Huaraz & Yungay.* ℹ *Municipalidad, Plaza de Armas.* 🕒 *Wednesday.* 🎉 *Fiestas Patrias (Jul 28).*

A small, pretty town at the end of the Callejón de Huaylas, Caraz has avoided total devastation from the earthquakes and avalanches that have destroyed so much of the valley. A flower-lined road leads into town, which has a leafy Plaza de Armas.

At 7,450 ft (2,270 m), Caraz is lower than nearby Huaraz *(see p206)* and has a milder, more agreeable climate. The tourism industry is developing slowly here to accommodate trekkers and climbers – it is the starting point for the Santa Cruz Trek *(see p204)* and also for ascents of the northern part of Mount Alpamayo *(see p205)*.

There are a number of good places to stay in the area in which to stay and eat as well.

Environs

To the north, near Caraz, are the ancient ruins of **Tunshukaiko** – a platform structure thought to date back to the Huaraz culture, around 2000 BC. The setting, in a lush valley with the Cordilleras Blanca and Negra on either side, is spectacular, although there is little to see at the site.

A road runs 20 miles (32 km) east of Caraz through an impressive canyon bordered by 3,280-ft (1,000-m) high granite walls, leading to **Laguna Parón**. This lake is surrounded by snowy peaks, including **Mount Pirámide**, at a height of 19,310 ft (5,885 m). Parón is less-visited but just as spectacular as the Lagunas Llanganuco *(see p204)*.

"Sweet Caraz", icing on the cake

Campo Santo, Yungay ❷

Road Map B3. 7 miles (12 km) from Caraz. 🚌 *colectivos run throughout the day from Caraz & Huaraz.* 🕒 *8am–6pm.* 📷 💻 📦

The Callejón de Huaylas suffered more than its fair share of tragedy in the last century due to a number of devastating *aluviónes*. When the high-altitude lakes of the Cordillera breach as a result of earthquakes or excessive snow-melt, they send deadly cascades of water, ice, mud, and debris on to the villages below. In 1971 an enormous earthquake (measuring 7.7 on the Richter scale) rocked central Peru and the resulting *aluvión* wiped out the village of Yungay, burying 18,000 people.

When an enormous lump of ice and granite was dislodged from Mount Huascarán's north face by the earthquake, it hurtled down towards Yungay at over 190 mph (300 kmph), burying the entire village and sparing only 400 lives. The site, now known as Campo Santo, has been consecrated as a cemetery, which is open to visitors, and the thick layer of soil that covers the former village is adorned with paths and flowers. It is a poignant and evocative sight; the tip of

Remains of a bus after the 1971 mudslide in Campo Santo, Yungay

Well-kept gardens of the Plaza de Armas, Carhuaz

the cathedral's spire and the tops of four palm trees are all that remain of the Plaza de Armas, and there are a number of monuments marking the sites of former homes. A large statue of Christ on a nearby hillside looks over the ruined town. It was to this point that a few residents managed to climb and escape.

Other catastrophic mudslides in 1941 and 1962 have claimed around 9,000 lives.

Carhuaz ❸

Road Map B4. 20 miles (32 km) N of Huaraz, Callejón de Huaylas. ⏴ *13,000.* ⏴ *frequent colectivos from Huaraz.* ⏴ *Sunday.* ⏴ *Virgen de la Merced (end Sep).*

This quiet little town in the northern Callejón de Huaylas has a limited tourist infrastructure, although it is a stopping point for trekkers in the Cordillera Blanca. The town lies at 8,655 ft (2,638 m) and has an attractive main square and a bustling market which comes alive every Sunday morning with displays of agricultural produce and crafts from all over the region.

Each September, for ten days Carhuaz comes alive with dancing, drinking, music, and firework displays at the annual celebration of the Virgen de la Merced festival, thought to be the most raucous in the valley.

Environs
A number of good walks from Carhuaz have remained relatively unexplored as visitors favor the longer treks into Cordillera Blanca. A pretty 5-mile (8-km) walk east from Carhuaz leads to the **Baños de Pariacaca**, the bubbling hot thermal waters of the natural rock pools beside a chilly river. For the brave, these are a fun place to swim. The trail continues to the **Lakes Hike** which takes three to five hours and passes between Laguna Rajupaquinan, Laguna 513,

Condor in flight

and Lagunas Auquiscocha. The most spectacular and longest hike is to a small village called **Yanama.** This three-day trip into the Quebrada Ulta (13,780 ft/4,200 m), features fantastic views of the towering peaks of the **Parque Nacional Huascarán** *(see pp202–4).* Access to other major treks in Quebrada Ulta is from Shilla, 8 miles (13 km) east of Carhuaz. Information on these and other good hikes is available at local hostels and trekking shops.

QUISPE SISA

Born in the Ancash region, Quispe Sisa (later known as Doña Inés Yupanqui) was of noble Inca birth. When the Spanish arrived in Peru, her brother, the 13th Inca emperor Atahualpa, "gave" her to conquistador Francisco Pizarro to be his wife. Their union produced what are thought to be the country's first two mestizo children. However, they were the last in the line of Inca nobility because both died childless. The marriage of Pizarro and Quispe Sisa did not last long. He soon found a younger mistress, and she went on to marry another Spaniard and left for Spain with her daughter, who was later legitimized.

Sculpture of Quispe Sisa and conquistador Francisco Pizarro

Parque Nacional Huascarán ❹

LOCATOR MAP

☐ Parque Nacional Huascarán

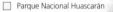

Situated in the Ancash region, the Huascarán National Park encompasses almost the entire Cordillera Blanca. This area of glaciers, turquoise lakes, and stunning mountain scenery, has 50 towering snow-capped peaks over 18,700 ft (5,700 m), including Peru's highest mountain, Huascarán *(see pp204–205)*. Declared a UNESCO Biosphere Reserve in 1977, and a World Heritage Site in 1985, the park aims to protect the region's diverse flora and fauna, its geological formations, and archaeological remains. Locals participate in the growing adventure tourism industry so that revenue is channeled to their communities.

Orchid in full bloom

★ Mount Huascarán

The highest mountain in Peru, Huascarán has two huge summits, with the southern face being higher than the northern one. Freezing temperatures, glaciers, and avalanches make it a challenging climb.

Yungay

Huascará 22,

Carhuaz

Hualc 20,095 6,125

Copa 20,295 ft/ 6,186m

Toclaraju 19,797 ft/ 6,034m

Huaraz

Ranrapalca 20,236 ft/ 6,168m

Palca 20,58 6,274

Pucaranra 20,177 ft/ 6,150m

Chinchey 20,420 ft/ 6,224m

Huantsan 20,981 ft/ 6,395m

Yanama 17,182 ft/ 5,237m

Santa Cruz Trek

This 4- to 5-day hike is one of the most spectacular in the Cordillera Blanca. The high-altitude trail passes beneath a dozen peaks, through dazzling mountain scenery and is suitable for novice hikers, as long as they are properly acclimatized.

STAR SIGHTS

★ Lagunas Llanganuco

★ Mount Huascarán

Alpamayo
Once voted the most beautiful mountain in the world, Alpamayo is not the highest mountain in Peru, but the climb to its summit is considered to be one of the most technical.

VISITORS' CHECKLIST

Road Map C4. 13 miles (40 km) from Huaraz. ⬜ *from Huaraz.* 🚌 *from Huaraz.* ℹ️ SERNANP, Federico Sal y Rosas 555, Huaraz, *043 422 086.* 📷 🅿️ *guide & mule with handler.* ⛺ *hostels & hotels in Yungay, Caraz, and Huaraz.* 🅰️ *free camping throughout the park on payment of entrance fee & guide fees.* www.sernanp.gob.pe

★ **Lagunas Llanganuco**
These two lakes lie in a narrow glacial valley east of Yungay. The dazzling turquoise waters reflect the peaks of Huascarán, Huandoy, and Chopicalqui.

KEY

ℹ️	Visitor information
══	Major road
══	Minor road
‑ ‑	Santa Cruz Trek
‑ ‑	Park boundary
▲	Peak

0 km 5
0 miles 5

The topography of the area is varied, ranging from snow-capped mountains to glaciers and high-altitude lakes. Hence the diverse flora and fauna.

Puya Raimondii in Bloom
This extraordinary plant is the world's largest bromeliad and is found in just a few isolated Andean areas.

Spectacled Bear
Ten mammal species, including the spectacled bear, can be found here along with 112 species of birds.

Exploring Parque Nacional Huascarán

Gleaming mountain peaks, jeweled turquoise lakes, fascinating archaeological sites, and unusual fauna make the Huascarán National Park an essential part of any visit to Peru. The area is attractive for hikers, climbers, and naturalists alike and is easily accessible from Huaraz *(see p206)* or Caraz *(see p200)*. Both these lofty towns have good hotels, equipment hire shops, and mountain guides, as well as a lively pre- and post-trek scene. Regular minibuses run between major villages in the valley, and the main road is in good condition. Short trips to the surrounding mountains, or longer hikes for the more adventurous climbers can be organized.

One of the many waterfalls at Lagunas Llanganuco

Santa Cruz Mountain reflected in a pool

🏃 Santa Cruz Trek

Start from Lagunas Llanganuco *(see below)* or Cashapampa, near Caraz.
🛏️ 🎒 *guides can be hired in Caraz or Huaraz.* ⛺

This is one of the most popular treks in the Cordillera Blanca. The high-altitude trail through panoramic mountain scenery passes beneath a dozen peaks which are over 18,700 ft (5,700 m) high.

The trail can begin from Lagunas Llanganuco, which are accessible from Yungay, or from Cashapampa, just beyond Caraz. For those who require mules and handlers to help with the equipment, Cashapampa is a better option.

The path is well defined, and there are a number of long but fairly gentle ascents along switchback trails, as well as some more level walking alongside rivers and across the verdant meadows in the valley.

The highest pass is Punta Unión at 15,590 ft (4,750 m). Here the Cordillera opens up in front of the trekkers to reveal a breathtaking 360-degree panorama of snowy peaks and glistening glacial lakes. Camping at this altitude is a chilly but spectacular affair. To wake up surrounded by towering ice-capped peaks and thaw out with hot coffee is a once-in-a-lifetime experience. It is a suitable trek for amateur hikers, once they are properly acclimatized and have the right equipment as well as clothing.

🏃 Lagunas Llanganuco

18 miles (28 km) E of Yungay.
🚚 *trucks & minibuses leave in the morning from Yungay's main square.*
🎫 *Huascarán National Park's entrance fee.*

These two glacier-fed lakes sit in an awesome glacial valley 12,630 ft (3,850 m) above sea level, with the peaks of Huascarán and Huandoy looming above them, covered in snow all year round. Surrounded by the rare polylepis trees, the dazzling turquoise waters glow in the midday sun.

It is best to arrive in the morning as the lakes get shady later and the afternoons often bring clouds and an icy wind. Pick-ups and minibuses from Yungay run throughout the day in the tourist high-season which lasts from May through September.

PUYA RAIMONDII

Named after the Italian scientist Antonio Raimondi (1826–1890), who discovered it, this extraordinary plant is the world's largest bromeliad and is found in just a few isolated Andean areas such as the Huascarán National Park. One of the most ancient plant species in the world, the spiky and tough *Puya raimondii* has a thick rosette of pliable, cactus-like leaves. It blooms once in its 100-year lifetime. The elongated cluster of flowers grows from a single main stem which can reach 40 ft (12 m) in height. It may yield up to 20,000 flowers, which bloom from May for about three months, before the plant withers and dies. It is often surrounded by hummingbirds.

Puya raimondii, the world's largest bromeliad

Climbing in the Cordillera Blanca

The Cordillera Blanca is a climbers' paradise, with 33 peaks over 19,700 ft (6,000 m). The views afforded by these ascents, over an expanse of pristine snow, are staggering.

Mule carrying supplies

Most climbers base themselves in Huaraz, where there are many companies who can help plan a trip to the mountains, provide experienced guides, and rent out equipment. However, it is advisable to bring your own gear for the longer expeditions. Huaraz is also a good place for acclimatization hikes, ranging from four days to a week, before any serious climb. There are a number of climbs which are best-attempted only during the dry season, between June and the end of August.

CLIMBERS' PARADISE
There are numerous treks in the area which range from short, non-technical ascents to long, highly technical ones meant for experienced and physically fit climbers. Muleteers can be hired locally, but *burros* carry equipment only until the base camp.

Specialist gear is an absolute necessity as temperatures drop dramatically at sundown and fierce winds are frequent.

Mountain biking, *such as the 6-day trip into the Ulta Valley, is both challenging and exhilarating. The highest altitude reached on the route is 16,080 ft (4,900 m).*

Spectacular views, *especially from some of the mountain summits such as the Pisco, are ample reward for the demanding climbs.*

Non-technical ascents *of 2–3 days to Urus, Pisco, and Ishinca, with good guides and equipment suit the less-experienced.*

CLIMB	CLIMB DURATION	HEIGHT	AREAS COVERED
Alpamayo	7 Days	11,950 ft (5,947m)	Huaraz, Cashapampa & Llamacorral
Chopicalqui	5 Days	20,850 ft (6,354m)	Huaraz, Lakes Chinancocha & Orconconcha
Huascarán	6 Days	22,210 ft (6,768m)	Huaraz, Musho & Huascarán
Ishinca	3 Days	18,210 ft (5,550m)	Huaraz, Pashpa & Ishinca

Stained-glass window of the Don Bosco School, Chacas

Chacas ❺

Road Map C4. 73 miles (118 km) NE of Huaraz. 🚌 from Huaraz. 🎆 Bullfight (Aug 17–18).

The rural town of Chacas is accessible by a stunning bus journey. The trip starts from Huaraz and crosses a specta-cular pass at Punta Olímpica (16,044 ft/4,890 m). The pretty Plaza de Armas plays host every August to a bullfight in which townfolk take their chances in the arena. The streets are filled with dancing and music during the festival.

The town is also home to the **Don Bosco School**, the famous woodcarving institute for underprivileged children. This cooperative, established in 1979, teaches poor children the art of woodcarving and carpentry, and the profits are used to fund medical and agri-cultural projects in the area. The beautiful designs can be seen in the church, as well as decorating many of the balconies in the village.

Hot Springs of Monterrey ❻

Road Map B4. 3 miles (5 km) N of Huaraz. 🅿️ 🍴 📷 🍽️

The hot springs of Monterrey are famous for their curative properties. The high tem-perature of the water in the springs is believed to be good for digestive and other health-related problems. Visitors can immerse themselves in the hot water of the springs. The lower pools, however, are cheaper which is why they are more crowded.

Monterrey is located at a height of 8,868 ft (2,703 m) in the Callejón de Huaylas, the beautiful valley between the Cordillera Blanca and Negra mountain ranges.

Environs

About 22 miles (35 km) farther up the valley is **Chancos**, located at the foot of Mount Copa. It has a series of small lakes and a steam bath within a cave, as well as a number of private cubicles with saunas.

Huaraz ❼

Road Map C4. 292 miles (470 km) from Lima. 🏠 80,000. 🚌 from Lima. 🚹 Plaza de Armas, 51 043 728812. 🎆 El Señor de la Soledad (around May 3), Semana del Andinismo (Jun).

Huaraz is the capital of the department of Ancash and the tourist center for visitors to the Huascarán National Park (see pp202–4) and the Callejón de Huaylas. The city was largely rebuilt after a catastrophic earthquake in 1970, so little Colonial arch-itecture remains, but the setting is spectacular.

The town is situated at an altitude of 10,142 ft (3,091 m) with the colossal peaks of the Blanca and Negra mountain ranges rising on either side. The busy main street, Avenida Luzuriaga, teems with cafés, bars, and shops that rent out hiking equipment. People from nearby communities come into town to sell local products such as cheese, honey, and sweets.

Huaraz is a sociable place with some lively nightspots, hostels, and bars.

Panoramic view of Huaraz with the Cordillera Blanca in the background

Olleros to Chavín Trek

This three-day hike, also known as the Llama Trek, follows an ancient Inca path on its way to Chavín. This area of southern Cordillera is characterized by stunning and varied scenery, from the lush valleys of the eastern slopes of the Andes, to high-altitude savannah, lakes, and snow-capped peaks. There are several passes en route with grand views of the

Sign for the three-day trek

surrounding peaks and valleys. The high point of the trek is the Yanashallash Pass, which, at 15,420 ft (4,700 m), is a tiring but rewarding climb with an inspiring view of the adjacent area. Nights are spent camping, with the imposing Mount Huantsan (20,886 ft/6,366 m) providing a constant backdrop. For information on guides and trek operators see page 311.

```
Huaraz        Huantsan
               20,886ft/
               6,366m
Olleros       Uruashraju
               18,772ft/5,722m
   Río Olleros
  Canrey     Yanashallash
   Chico      15,420ft/      Chavín
Recuay        4,700m
  Catac  Río Yanamayu
```

KEY

- - Trail route

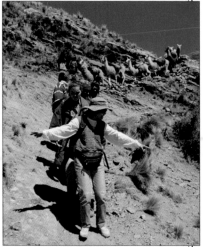

Olleros, *the starting point of the Llama Trek to the impressive ruins of Chavín, is about an hour's drive from Huaraz. Guides and animal handlers with llamas, to carry the trekking equipment, can be hired from this pretty village.*

The trail *passes through a marshy valley following, for much of the way, an Inca path alongside the Río Negro. There are a number of other ruins worth exploring en route.*

Camping spots that are flat, firm, and grassy are easily located along the trek.

Ruins of Chavín, *considered the best remaining example of the Chavín culture, are visible after descending Quebrada Huachesca.*

Independent trekkers *should carry a good map and keep an eye out for signposts. There are some areas where paths intersect and it is easy to lose the way. Good quality equipment and enough food and water are also important as there is nothing available along the route.*

Chavín de Huántar ❽

Sculpted head on the outer wall

Located in the Ancash region, halfway between the coast and the jungle, Chavín de Huántar lies at 10,335 ft (3,150 m) above sea level on the Río Mosna. Declared a World Heritage Site by UNESCO in 1985, this major ceremonial center for the Chavín people dates back to around 1300 BC. Displaying a pattern of additions and renovations, there are two distinct parts to the complex, an original temple with underground passageways and carved stelae, and a much larger and later extension, which comprises a mighty, pyramid-like building leading down to the main plaza. The construction is notable for its sophisticated masonry.

View of Chavín de Huántar with Río Mosna in the foreground

★ El Castillo
The most important building in the extension of the original temple's right wing, El Castillo is believed to date from 500–200 BC.

★ Underground Tunnels
These incredible passageways are connected by a series of ramps and stairs. They are extremely well ventilated despite there being just one doorway.

FLOOR PLAN OF THE MAIN TEMPLE

Offerings Gallery is where jars, stone objects, and human and animal remains were found.

Underground Passageways lead to the Lanzón de Chavín.

Circular Plaza is sunk below the court surface with wedge-shaped staircases leading from the east and west.

| 0 meters | 500 |
| 0 yards | 500 |

Porch of Falcons
The black and white portal on El Castillo comprises a large carved lintel spanning the cylindrical columns.

★ Lanzón de Chavín
Located between the subterranean passageways in the Main Temple, this 13-ft (4-m) granite monolith has a carving of the principal deity worshipped by the Chavín culture.

Ceiling Detail
Underground passageways and chambers are roofed with rectangular slabs resting on the top of walls or supported by stones projecting from the walls.

The original temple buildings sit to the right of El Castillo around the circular plaza.

Sunken Plaza
This large central plaza is believed to be where thousands of pilgrims gathered during important fiestas.

Low platforms flank each side of the sunken plaza.

STAR SIGHTS

- ★ El Castillo
- ★ Lanzón de Chavín
- ★ Underground Tunnels

THE CULT OF CHAVÍN (1300–400 BC)

The Chavín, the oldest major culture of Peru, dominated northern Peru with its artistic and cultural conquest more than 2,000 years before the Incas. Due to abundant agricultural production the Chavín used their free time to pursue artistic and religious practices. They had a highly sophisticated artistic style and their principal deities (anthropomorphic feline characters) were represented in stone stelae that can be found at Chavín sites.

A leopard figure etched in stone, Chavín de Huántar

Caral �ⓐ

Rediscovered in 1994, Caral is believed to date from 2600 BC, around the same period as the Egyptian pyramids were built, and long before Mexico's Aztec and Toltec structures. It was officially declared the oldest known urban center in the Americas in 2001 *(see p42)* and indicates that an advanced civilization existed in the New World 800 years earlier than previously thought. Archaeologists have unearthed 20 stone structures featuring six pyramids with ceremonial plazas, irrigation channels, and many artifacts.

Carved warrior monolith

The sunken circular plaza of the Great Pyramid

Altar of the Eternal Fire
This structure within the walled complex of the amphitheater was used for rituals.

Rectangular altar with underground ventilation.

★ **Amphitheater**
This was one of the main buildings of the city and was used for religious and political functions.

The atrium was the ceremonial courtyard with tiered seating.

GREAT PYRAMID
The complex has two components, a circular plaza and a pyramid with platforms. The leaders could survey the city from this most impressive building of Caral. It was the center of all activities.

A central stairway leads up from the circular plaza to the atrium.

CARAL SITE PLAN

Quarry Pyramid has a walk-in altar at its summit.

Pyramid of the Circular Altar was made of stones bonded with mortar, plastered and then painted white, yellow, and red.

Amphitheater

Altar of the Eternal Fire

Greater Residential Complex

Pyramid of the Huanca

Great Pyramid

Lesser Pyramid is the smallest pyramid in the complex.

Pyramid of the Gallery has a room lined with whalebone seats.

0 metres	500
0 yards	500

Road Map C4. 75 miles (120 km) N of Lima, off Panamerican Highway North, KM182. **Tel** 01 205 2500 (ext 517). ☐ 9am–5pm daily; group entries are allowed only till 4pm. 🖼 🅿 ☕ in Barranca and Huacho. ☐ www.caral peru.gob.pe/como_llegar.htm

★ **Pyramid of the Huanca**
This three-tier structure has a staircase leading up to a ceremonial area with a view of a large obelisk.

East wing had seven superimposed terraces with stairways and rooms.

STAR SIGHTS

★ Amphitheater

★ Great Pyramid

★ Pyramid of the Huanca

Sechín ⑩

Road Map B4. 3 miles (5 km) SE of Casma. 🚌 from Casma. ☐ 9am–5pm daily. 🖼 ☕ in Casma.

Thought to date back to 1600 BC, the ruins at Sechín were first excavated in 1937 by the famous Peruvian archaeologist J.C. Tello (1880–1947). The stone frieze on the outside wall of the main temple depicts a gruesome battle scene: warriors dressed in loincloths and carrying staves or clubs standing over their victims, who are shown with severed heads and limbs. It is thought that the temples were intended to commemorate an important battle but it is unknown, as yet, to which belligerent culture this complex belonged. Inside the temple, earlier mud structures are being excavated even today.

Cordillera Huayhuash ⑪

Road Map C4. 🚌 from Chiquián or Huallanca, on the bus route between Huaraz and Huánuco. 🗺 guides and mule handlers can be hired at Chiquián or Huallanca. 🄰 free.

Just 19 miles (30 km) long, this remote and pristine range incorporates dramatic mountain scenery, turquoise lakes, and rolling grasslands. There are seven peaks over 19,600 ft (6,000 m), including Yerupaja, at around 21,765 ft (6,634 m), the second highest mountain in Peru, and Siula Grande (20,853 ft/6,356 m). It was the latter where the

The awe-inspiring scenery of Cordillera Huayhuash

famous motivational speaker and mountaineer Joe Simpson (b.1960) along with fellow climber Simon Yates (b.1963) famously came unstuck. Simpson talks about the mountain in his memoir *Touching the Void*. A documentary film of the same name was shot in the area and was released in 2003 making the range famous worldwide.

There are seven other peaks over 18,000 ft (5,500 m) high. Although barely 31 miles (50 km) away, Huayhuash is very different from its more famous neighbor, Cordillera Blanca. There are no broad valleys, mountain passes are higher and more treacherous, and access is limited. At one time, the only trekking here was a 12-day loop of the range from Chiquián. Today, buses carry hikers on the dirt road from Huaraz to Huallanca, where shorter, five-day trips are possible. A period of prior acclimatization is essential.

A head carved in a wall at Sechín

THE NORTHERN DESERT

*T*his is one of Peru's richest archaeological regions. From the Moche Valley to the Túcume Valley, north of Chiclayo, monumental adobe pyramids rise majestically over farmlands. Discoveries over the last 20 years have revealed incredible treasures, such as the Lord of Sipán's tomb and Batán Grande, that confirm the historical importance and development of these people in ancient times.

Often described as South America's Egypt, this region was the cradle of the Moche, Sicán, and Chimú kingdoms, highly sophisticated pre-Columbian civilizations that flourished in the heart of one of the world's most arid strips of land. Besides the Lord of Sipán's Tomb, the area is home to many spectacular structures, including Túcume or the Valley of the Pyramids, Huaca del Sol y de la Luna (Temples of the Sun and the Moon), and Chan Chan, the world's largest adobe city and a UNESCO World Heritage Site.

The region's Colonial past can be seen in Peru's second largest city, Trujillo, founded in 1534. An elegant town with well-preserved churches and mansions, the city led the call for Peruvian independence in 1820. In 1931, after the Alianza Popular Revolucionaria Americana (APRA) was outlawed and its leader, Victor Raúl Haya de la Torre, was imprisoned by dictator Sánchez Cerro, Trujillo's middle classes staged an uprising which saw over 6,000 rebels shot dead near Chan Chan.

The Sechura Desert occupies 72,900 sq miles (188,750 sq km) from the northern coast, extending 12 to 62 miles (20 to 100 km) from the shoreline to the secondary ridges of the western Andes. In the north lies the North-western Biosphere Reserve, which includes four natural protected areas of red mangrove and Equatorial Dry Forests. To the south are a series of arable valleys that have provided food in this area since pre-Columbian times.

This territory has an exquisite culinary tradition with fish, seafood, and goat as the main ingredients of the varied spicy and richly flavored dishes. It is a prosperous region thanks to its agricultural lands where the best rice, sugar, limes, and mangoes are grown, as well as its thriving rum industry.

Colonial houses in the Plaza de Armas, Trujillo

◁ Remains of Chan Chan, the capital of the Chimú Empire

Exploring the Northern Desert

This long strip of land stretches from the mangrove forest and sunny beaches of Tumbes to the warm desert valleys south of Trujillo. The city of Trujillo is also the base for visiting sites such as Chan Chan, Huaca del Sol y de la Luna, and Huanchaco. Treasures recovered from the Moche, Sican, and Chimu cultures can also be seen in museums, a highlight being the Museo Tumbas Reales de Sipán in Lambayeque. The Northern Desert is also home to picturesque sea towns such as Huanchaco and Máncora, and Peru's most attractive beaches on the coast off Piura and Tumbes, the country's northernmost region. Here, a number of reserves protect the endangered species that live in endemic and unique ecosystems.

SIGHTS AT A GLANCE

Towns and Cities
Chiclayo ⑥
Huanchaco ④
Máncora ⑫
Trujillo pp218–21 ①
Tumbes ⑩
Zorritos ⑪

Complejo
  Arequeológico
  El Brujo ⑤
Huaca del Sol y de
  la Luna ②
Túcume ⑧

Museum
*Museo Tumbas Reales
  de Sipán pp228–31* ⑦

**Archaeological Sites and
Ruins**
Batán Grande ⑨
Chan Chan ③

SEE ALSO

• *Where to Stay* pp277–9

• *Where to Eat* pp297–9

*Map labels:*
⊠ ⑩ TUMBE
⑪ ZORRITOS
Cañaveral
⑫ MÁNCORA
Atascadero
Cerros de Amotape
Talara
Poechos
La
Lom
Negritos
1A
Sullana
Tar
Gra
Paita
Chulucana
Catacaos
Piura ⊠
La Unión
PIU
Sechura
Mor
Parachique
PANAMERICAN HIGHWAY
Bayóvar
Reventazón
*Desierto
de Sechu*
PACIFIC OCEAN

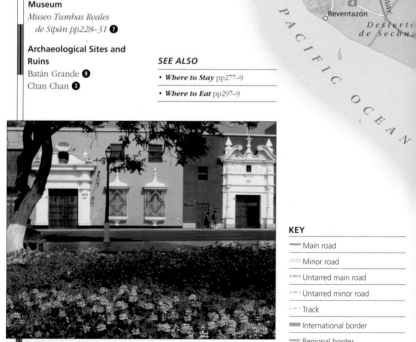

Brightly painted Colonial buildings, Trujillo

KEY

━━ Main road
┄┄┄ Minor road
▬▬ Untarred main road
▪▪▪ Untarred minor road
- - - Track
▬▬▬ International border
━━ Regional border

GETTING AROUND

The Panamerican Highway is generally in good condition, unless heavy rains occur due to El Niño. Avoid daytime driving when crossing the long desert coast, especially the Sechura Desert located between Chiclayo and Tumbes, since it has high temperatures all year round. There is a network of comfortable overnight bus services that connect all major cities and towns from Lima to the Ecuadorean border. Major airports in Trujillo, Chiclayo, Piura, and Tumbes have daily flights to Lima.

A fierce mural on the walls of Huaca de la Luna (Temple of the Moon)

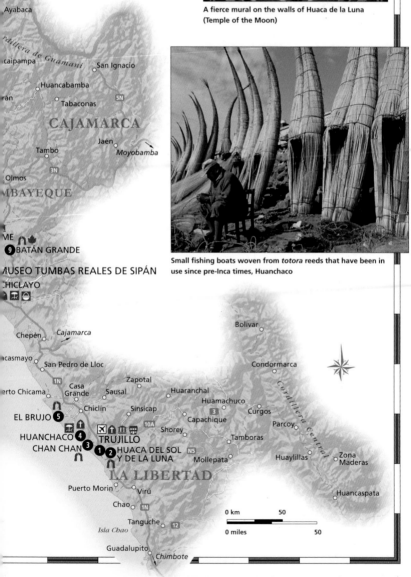

Small fishing boats woven from *totora* reeds that have been in use since pre-Inca times, Huanchaco

Ayabaca

Cordillera de Guamani
caipampa
San Ignacio
rán
Huancabamba
Tabaconas 5N
CAJAMARCA
Tambo
Jaén
Moyobamba
Olmos 3N
MBAYEQUE
ME
9 BATÁN GRANDE
MUSEO TUMBAS REALES DE SIPÁN
CHICLAYO

Chepén
Cajamarca
acasmayo
San Pedro de Lloc
Bolivar
Condormarca
erto Chicama 1N
Casa Grande
Zapotal
Huaranchal
Sausal
Huamachuco
Chiclin
Sinsicap
Capachique 3
Curgos
EL BRUJO 5
Shorey
Parcoy
HUANCHACO 4
10A
TRUJILLO
Tamboras
CHAN CHAN 3
1 2 HUACA DEL SOL
Y DE LA LUNA N5
Mollepata
Huaylillas
Zona Maderas
LA LIBERTAD
Puerto Morin
Virú
Huancaspata
Chao 1N
Tanguche 12
Isla Chao
0 km 50
0 miles 50
Guadalupito
Chimbote
Cordillera Central

Trujillo ❶

Window with ornate grill

Ranked as Peru's second largest city, though in constant rivalry with Arequipa for such a privilege, Trujillo's spring-like climate has earned it the title of Ciudad de la Eterna Primavera (the city of eternal spring). The 50 small blocks that make up the Colonial heart of the city, encircled by the Avenida España, contain most of the relevant sites worth visiting, all at walking distance. The city's historic buildings and churches are relatively well preserved. Many have been restored magnificently, highlighting the strong Colonial tones in which they were originally painted, and the blend of local and Colonial architectural styles that justify this city's reputation as the urban jewel of northern Peru.

Bright façade of the Cathedral, Plaza de Armas

🏛 Cathedral

Cnr of Independencia & Orbegoso. **Tel** 044 223 328. ⏰ 7:50–9:30am, 5:30–8:30pm Mon–Sat; 7:30am–1pm & 5:15–7pm Sun. 🚻
Museum ⏰ 8am–2pm daily. 🏷
On one side of the Plaza de Armas is the Cathedral, also known as the Basilica Menor by the locals. First built in the mid-17th century (between 1647 and 1666), it was destroyed in the 1759 earthquake and then rebuilt. It features colorful Baroque sculptures and paintings from the Escuela Quiteña, a style of painting which originated in 18th-century Quito.
The Cathedral also has a **Museum** with a number of beautiful 18th- and 19th-century religious paintings and sculptures on display.

Giant sculpture, Plaza de Armas

🏛 Plaza de Armas

Also known as Plaza Mayor, some claim it to be the largest main square in Peru. At the center of the plaza is a giant marble and bronze monument dedicated to the heroes of the Wars of Independence. The 85-ft (25-m) high and 100-ft (30-m) wide statue, designed by the German artist, Edmund Moeller (1885–1957), was inaugurated in 1927 to commemorate the city's struggle and independence from Spanish Colonial rule.
Every Sunday, a flag-raising ceremony accompanied by a parade is held on the Plaza de Armas. At certain times *marinera* *(see p28)* dancers can be seen performing here. The famous Peruvian Paso horses *(see p221)* can also be seen striding through the plaza.

🏛 Casa Urquiaga

Pizarro 446. **Tel** 044 244 841.
⏰ 9:15am–3:15pm Mon–Fri. 🏷
This magnificently restored mansion, also known as Casa Calonge, originally belonged to Bernardino Calonge, who founded the city's first bank. The grand Colonial mansion, painted royal blue with white window grills, was bought from the Urquiaga family in 1972 and is now owned by the Banco Central de Reserva del Perú. The 18th-century mahogany desk of Simón Bolívar, who lived in the

Key to Symbols *see back flap*

TRUJILLO CITY CENTER

Casa de la Emancipación ⑥
Casa de Orbegoso ⑤
Casa Urquiaga ③
Cathedral ①
Iglesia la Merced ④
Iglesia y Monasterio del Carmen ⑨
Museo de Arqueología ⑧
Museo del Juguete ⑩
Palacio Iturregui ⑦
Plaza de Armas ②

house after proclaiming Peru's independence in 1821 (*see p49*), is preserved here.

The building features three interior courtyards. The dining room is decorated with exquisite French porcelain and superb chandeliers, as

its restored dome, features beautiful and picturesque molded figures representing scenes from the life of Saint Peter Nolasco, the French founder of the Mercedarian congregation. There is also an image of the Virgin of Mercy,

VISITORS' CHECKLIST

Road Map B3. 348 miles (560 km) N of Lima. 🏙 804,000. ✈ 6 miles (10 km) NW. 🚌 from Lima. 🚉 Pizarro 402, 044 294 561. 🎭 Concurso Nacional de Marinera (Jan), Festival de la Primavera (Sep).

altarpieces painted on the walls, dating from the time before free-standing altars were used, as well as a priceless Rococo pipe organ.

🏛 Casa de Orbegoso

Orbegoso 553. *Tel 044 234 950.* ◯ 9am–1pm, 4–8pm Mon–Sat.
This outstandingly elegant 18th-century mansion, now the property of the Interbank, is still in perfect condition. Stretching around the block, it has its own plaza facing the Iglesia de San Agustín. It was the residence of Luis José de Orbegoso y Moncada, a well-known general who fought for Peru's independence and later became the President of Peru from 1834–36 and 1837–8. His government marked a low point in the country's history and he disappeared from the political scene to return to his mansion in complete disgrace.

Orbegoso's mansion has an interesting collection of glass, art, silverware, and furniture from that period. It also exhibits the general's relics and personal objects as well as the crypt where he is buried.

patron of the congregation, sculpted by Alonso de Mesa around 1603. Other interesting features include unusual

well as mirrors. It is home to some extremely fine Rococo-style furniture. Several Moche and Nazca ceramics along with many Chavín and Chimú gold ornaments are also on display here.

🏛 Iglesia la Merced

Pizarro 550. *Tel 044 201 615.* ◯ 8am–noon, 5–8pm daily. 📷 🚉
This church was designed and built around 1636 by Portuguese artist Alonso de Las Nieves. During the 1970 earthquake it suffered severe damage. The building, with

Musicians outside the 17th-century Iglesia la Merced

Exploring Trujillo

Façade detail, Monasterio del Carmen

Founded by Diego de Almagro in 1534, Trujillo became the northern coast's most important city in the 16th century. Sugar-cane landlords and rich merchants built opulent mansions during the Colonial era. Due to constant attacks by pirates, a wall was built around the 3-sq mile (8-sq km) city in the late 17th century. In 1820, Trujillo led the struggle for Peruvian independence, and since then, it has been a center of popular rebellion. Today, Trujillo is an oasis of green surrounded by abundant rice and sugar-cane fields, and with fascinating Moche and Chimú archaeological sites nearby.

🏯 Casa de la Emancipación

Pizarro 610. **Tel** 044 207 778.
🕘 9:15am–12:45pm, 4–6:30pm Mon–Fri; 9:30am–12:30pm Sat.
One of the most historically significant buildings in the city, this was the place where Trujillo's independence from Spanish rule was planned, declared, and spearheaded by the Marquis of Torre Tagle in 1820. Also known as Casa Rossel-Urquiaga, after the family that owned the house from 1884 to 1944, it was the first seat of government and Congress in Peru.

In the mid 20th century, BBVA Banco Continental bought and restored the building as its head office in the city. The main court-yard and entrance exhibit a symmetrical and austere design and the wide gallery contains impressive marble flooring. There are a few interesting 18th-century murals depicting peasant life. The plans and the history of the house are displayed along-side permanent exhibitions

on the life of iconic poet César Vallejo (1892–1938) and Bishop Baltazar Martínez de Compañón y Bujanda (1737–97), who, as he moved around his diocese, painted numerous watercolors that reveal the customs and lifestyle of the period.

🏯 Palacio Iturregui

Pizarro 688. **Tel** 044 244 434.
🕘 11am–6pm Mon–Sat. 🚫
Occupied today by the Club Central, an exclus-ive social center for Trujillo's upper classes, this early 19th-century Neo-Classical mansion was home to General José Manuel Iturregui y Aguilarte, father of Peruvian independence. He bought it from the Marquises of Bellavista in 1841. Situated two blocks east of the Plaza de Armas, the so-called palace has three large patios encircled by beautiful halls and galleries embellished with gold moldings on the ceilings, tall,

Frieze reproduction, Museo de Arqueología de la Universidad

slender interior columns, and an open roof. There is restricted access, however, with only some parts open to tourists.

🏛 Museo de Arqueología de la Universidad de Trujillo

Junín 682. **Tel** 044 249 322. 🕘 8:30am–2:30pm Mon–Fri; 9am–noon Sun. 📷 🎫 🏠 www.unitru.edu.pe/cultural/arq/munt.html
Housed in what was once a splendid 17th-century Colo-nial mansion, the Museum of Archaeology of the University of Trujillo is remarkable for its large and comprehensive collection of thematic exhibits covering 12,000 years of the northern coast's history. This building has had many owners, including the Risco family who lived here until 1984, which is why it is also known as the Casa Risco. After several years of state ownership, the mansion was handed over to the University of Trujillo in 1995, providing a permanent exhibition space for its large archaeological collection, begun in 1939.

Moche ceramic

Textiles, ceramic and metal objects, and other artifacts are on display. The most impres-sive are the Moche finds exca-vated from the Huaca de la Luna (see p223).

🛐 Iglesia y Monasterio del Carmen

Cnr of Colón & Bolívar. **Tel** 044 256 155. 🕘 9am–1pm Mon–Sat. 📷 🎫 🕘 7–7:30am Sun.
This church and monastery was founded in 1759, though some historians claim it was established in 1724. Occupy-ing an entire block, this is the biggest religious complex in

The historic Casa de la Emancipación

the city. Although severely damaged by earthquakes in 1759 and later in 1970, the complex has survived. Today, it is referred to as the "jewel of Colonial art in Trujillo".

The church and monastery houses the most important collection of Colonial art in Trujillo. The Pinacoteca Carmelita (Carmelite Painting Gallery) exhibits about 150 Baroque and Rococo paintings, most of them dating from the 17th and 18th centuries. Some of the finest examples include Flemish paintings, such as the *Last Supper* (1625), by Otto van Veen (1556–1629), one of Rubens' teachers, and the sculptured image of Joseph and Jesus crafted by Quiteño artist, Manuel Chili "Capiscara", in the late 18th century. At the end of the Pinacoteca, a room demonstrates the paintings' restoration process, although all explanations are in Spanish.

The church has other marvelous features, particularly the breathtaking central gilded altar, considered a masterpiece of the Churrigueresque style in Peru, created in 1759 by Fernando Collado de la Cruz, a free black Peruvian. Floral murals in soft pastel shades line each side of the single dome nave, with exquisite altars on either side and a fine gold-leaf pulpit.

The monastery has two cloisters, the processional and the recreational, both boasting superb vaulted arches and painted wooden columns. A fair portion of the convent's art collection is kept here, but it is not open to the public.

THE PERUVIAN PASO

With Spanish horses such as the Berber, Spanish Jennet, and Andalusian as part of its lineage, the Peruvian Paso is an extraordinary, gentle creature. As an important Paso breeding stronghold, Trujillo hosts frequent festivals and competitions. The Paso horse has a unique gait: *paso llano*, a cross between a walk and a canter. This specially-bred characteristic enables the horse to cover long distances in a short period without tiring. The gait is inbred and requires no training. The gait of the purebred foals can be seen within a few hours of their birth. Another fundamental virtue is *término*: a loose action in which the front legs are rolled out as the horse strides forward, giving the mount balance.

The unique Paso horse

🏛 Museo del Juguete

Independencia 705. **Tel** 044 282 828. ⬤ 10am–6pm daily. 📷 🚫 🖥 www.angelmira.com

Inaugurated in 2001, this museum exhibits an unusual and fascinating collection of toys put together by Trujillo-born painter, Gerardo Chávez (b.1937). With about 1,000 pieces, including a 2,500-year-old Vicus whistle, pre-Columbian Chancay ragdolls, genuine 18th-century French biscuit dolls, post-war metal cars, and battalions of diminutive tin soldiers, the museum aims to become the biggest private toy collection in Latin America. It is sponsored by Espacio Cultural Angelmira, headed by Chávez, which is located on the first floor, where a very discreet and smartly decorated café-bar offers drinks and snacks.

Numerous ceramics on display, Museo José Cassinelli

🏛 Museo José Cassinelli

Avenue Nicolás de Piérola 601. **Tel** 044 203 433. ⬤ 9am–1pm, 3–6pm Mon–Sat & 9am–1pm Sun; can vary. 📷 🎫 by appointment.

Few could imagine that under a gas station there existed a "museum" of sorts. Owned by José Cassinelli Mazzei, a man of Italian descent born in Trujillo, this collection of artifacts reflects his abiding passion for pre-Columbian history. Despite its unusual setting, having Cassinelli, called "Pepe" by his friends, guide and explain the detail of each piece can be an unforgettable experience.

The collection of about 1,000 pieces includes ceramic whistling pots and other objects from the Chimú, Moche *(see p222)*, Vicus, and Recuay cultures.

Imposing façade of the Iglesia y Monasterio del Carmen

Moche Art

The Moche culture developed along the northern coast of Peru between 200 BC and AD 700. Archaeological sites reveal that their culture was sophisticated, however, they left no written records. Most of the information about the Moche society and religion is based on the illustrations found on their pottery. Their artifacts document a society which was highly class-based.

A Moche warrior

These pieces depict everything from sexual acts to warriors, deities, and humans as well as hunting, fishing, war, and elaborate ceremonies. The predominant medium of the Moche was clay, however, copper, silver, and gold were also used. They were highly skilled in techniques of metalworking as finds from the Lord of Sipán's *(see pp228–31)* burial site reveal.

Stone inlay *was an integral part of Moche art. Semi-precious stones such as lapis lazuli, shells, and metals were used to make mosaics, on discs made of gold, showing mystical creatures.*

Ulluchu man *is a 2-ft (0.6-m) high, gilded gold piece with the head and legs of a human and the caparace, legs, and claws of a crab. The odd-looking deity was found inside the Lord of Sipán's tomb.*

MOCHE POTTERY

There are two distinct types of pottery. One takes the form of animals or gods and is globular. The other shows elaborate scenes from battles or religious sites.

Black color vessels were rare; red was the predominant color.

Stirrup-shaped handles were a distinct feature.

Molds *were used for mass production of pottery, bricks, and vessels. Makers' marks were very important and can be seen in a number of bricks.*

Personal ornamentation was important as the large bracelets show.

Portrait vessels *were made to order for men of social importance, emphasizing their most dominant characteristic.*

Erotic figures *of the Moche culture are famous for their explicit representation of sexual acts.*

Daily life, *scenes of significant events, as well as ceremonies were captured in ceramic by Moche artists.*

View of the Huaca del Sol from the top of Huaca de la Luna

Huaca del Sol y de la Luna ❷

Road Map B3. 3 miles (5 km) SE of Trujillo along Panamerican Highway, detour on unpaved road. 🚌 🚗 *from Trujillo.* ◯ *9am–4pm daily.*
📷 ✏️ 🏪 🚻

This archaeological complex includes two pyramids. The impressive Huaca del Sol (Temple of the Sun), at 148 ft (45 m), is the largest pre-Columbian adobe structure in the Americas. According to the Spanish chronicler, Antonio de la Calancha, it was built with 140 million blocks, by almost 200,000 workers around AD 500.

Close by is the Huaca de la Luna (Temple of the Moon), a smaller structure that contains six levels, built on top of the other during a 200-year span. It has interconnected rooms, and inner patios, with friezes of anthropomorphic figures.

Chan Chan ❸

Road Map B3. 3 miles (5 km) W of Trujillo. 🚌 🚗 *from Trujillo.*
◯ *9am–4pm daily.* 📷 ✏️ 🏪 🚻

A part of the UNESCO World Heritage List since 1986, this enormous site covering almost 11 sq miles (28 sq km) is considered the largest adobe city in the world and one of Trujillo's major attractions. Chan Chan was built between AD 1100 and 1300 as the capital of the Chimú Empire (*see p45*) and

residence of the Tacaynamu dynasty. At the height of its glory, this pre-Columbian metropolis had a population of 100,000, comprising civilians, military personnel, as well as skilled artisans. The Chimú sovereigns surrendered to the Incas after a siege around 1470.

The complex is made up of nine sectors or citadels. The best preserved and most visited is Ciudadela Tschudi. A marked route leads through an amazing complex of large sunken plazas, chambers, restored corridors, temple cloisters, residential areas, and military barracks. Most have friezes depicting seabirds, fish, and other sea creatures. Unfortunately, many structures have been damaged by floods caused by El Niño in 1925, 1983, 1997, 1998, and 2003 as well as invaders and *huaqueros* (tomb-raiders).

Environs
Located about 2.5 miles (4 km) northwest of Trujillo, **Huaca El Dragón** is by far the best restored structure of the Chan Chan complex. It is also called Huaca Arco Iris (rainbow) after motifs found on its inner walls that can be traced back to the Nazca, Wari, or Tiahuanaco cultures. There is a small site museum too.

Between Chan Chan and Trujillo is **Huaca Esmeralda**, discovered in 1923. Excavations have revealed a temple enclosed by a defensive wall. It was probably part of the Chan Chan complex.

Maze of walls of the audience hall at Chan Chan

Huanchaco ❹

Road Map B3. 7 miles (12 km) NW of Trujillo. 🏠 *38,000.* ✈️ *from Lima.* 🚌 🚗 *from Trujillo.* 🎭 *Festival del Mar (Jul).* **www**.turismohuanchaco.com

The best beach resort near Trujillo retains its quiet fishing village ambience. Although the water is too cold for swimming, it is perfect for surfers all year round. The town's 16th-century past is visible in the Baroque-style church of Virgen del Perpetuo Socorro, built in 1540 above a pre-Columbian temple, and various Colonial mansions. The major attractions, however, are the sea rafts or *caballitos de totora* which translate literally as reed horses. Locals still use them and are the only ones who can build these vessels, first used by the Moche culture some 2,500 years ago.

Sea rafts stacked in rows along Huanchaco beach

Complejo Arqueológico El Brujo ❺

Road Map B3. 28 miles (45 km) NW of Trujillo, off Panamerican Highway toward Magdalena de Cao. 🚗 *from Trujillo.* ◯ *9am–5pm daily.*

In 2006, archaeologists announced the discovery of a well preserved and tattooed 1,500-year-old mummy of a young woman. She was found in a mud-brick pyramid called Huaca Cao Viejo, a part of the El Brujo Moche complex. In the tomb with La Señora de Cao (The Lady of Cao), were funeral objects such as gold sewing needles, weaving tools, and metal jewelry.

For hotels and restaurants in this region see pp277–9 and pp297–9

Gallery display at the Museo Tumbas Reales de Sipán, Lambayeque

Chiclayo ⑥

Road Map B3. 124 miles (200 km) N of Trujillo. 🏚 798,500. ✈ from Lima. 🚌 from Lima & Trujillo. 🎉 Señor Cautivo de Monsefú (Sep). **www**.lambayeque.com

Founded in the mid-16th century as a rural Indian village that connected the Colonial towns of Zaña and Lambayeque with the port of Pimentel, Chiclayo is a commercial hub and northern Peru's second largest city after Trujillo. Major attractions here are the Neo-Classical style cathedral, built in 1869, and the Mercado Modelo (Central Market). The market is considered one of the most interesting in Peru, offering everything from herbs and healing charms used by *curanderos* and *brujos* (witchdoctors and healers), to mats, hats, woven straw baskets, and other products. Chiclayo serves as the most convenient starting point to visit all major archaeological and historical features in the area.

Gold jewelry, Museo Tumbas Reales de Sipán

Environs
About 6 miles (10 km) north of Chiclayo lies the 17th-century Colonial town of **Lambayeque**. It still retains houses with distinctive wooden balconies and wrought-iron, grillwork windows. Examples of fine architecture can be found along Calle 8 de Octubre or Calle 2 de Mayo, where Casa de la Logia o Montjoy boasts a 210-ft- (64-m-) long balcony, said to be the longest in Colonial America. The other big attractions here are the museums. **Museo Tumbas Reales de Sipán** is a state-of-the-art museum that exhibits the fabulous discovery of the Lord of Sipán's tomb *(see pp228–31)*. The **Museo Arqueológico Nacional Brüning** displays a fine collection of Sicán, Moche, Chimú, and Lambayeque archaeological artifacts collected by German engineer, Hans Heinrich Brüning (1848–1928), and acquired by the Peruvian government in 1921.

Pimentel, 6 miles (10 km) west of Chiclayo, has a nice beach with good waves for surfing. This coastal town has an old pier, which locals claim is one of the longest in South America, from where cotton and sugar were exported. The ghost town of **Zaña**, 32 miles (51 km) southeast of Chiclayo, was founded in 1563. The ruins of churches and buildings show evidence of this town's former opulence. Attacked by English buccaneers Edward Davis and Francis Drake, a flood destroyed Zaña in 1720 and it was abandoned.

Another museum worth a visit is **Museo Nacional de Sicán** in Ferreñafe, 11 miles (18 km) northeast of Chiclayo. On display here are golden artifacts, ceramics, and other utensils; found in the tombs at Batán Grande, they rival the Sipán finds.

🏛 **Museo Arqueológico Nacional Brüning**
Av. Huamachuco, Cuadra 8, Lambayeque. **Tel** 074 282 110.
⏰ 9am–5pm daily. 📷 🎫 🚻

🏛 **Museo Nacional Sicán**
Av. Batán Grande, Cuadra 9, Ferreñafe. **Tel** 074 286 469.
⏰ 9am–5pm Tue–Sun. 📷 🎫 🚫 📷 🚻

Museo Tumbas Reales de Sipán ⑦

See pp228–31.

THE PERUVIAN HAIRLESS DOG

Known as *perro sin pelo*, this ancient breed can be traced back to pre-Columbian times. Ceramic hairless dogs from the Vicus, Moche, Chimú, and Chancay cultures have been excavated along the north and central coast, offering evidence of its Peruvian origins. The Inca kept them as pets to please the Sun God and Moon Goddess. The Spanish conquest nearly caused the breed's extinction, but fortunately they survived in rural areas, where people believed in their magical forces. Smart, independent, and good with children, the breed's lack of hair has given them a reputation for being clean even though the skin has to be taken care of. The dogs vary in size from 10 inches (25 cm) to 26 inches (65 cm).

Peruvian hairless dog, declared a national heritage in 2000

Diorama of a shaman, Museo de Sitio Túcume

Túcume **8**

Road Map B3. 21 miles (33 km) NE of Chiclayo on the Old Panamerican Highway to Piura. **Tel** 074 830 250. from Chiclayo and Lambayeque. 8am–5pm daily. www.tucume.com

Also known as the Valley of the Pyramids, this site is located in the plains of Túcume, in the Lambayeque Valley. The area was developed as the capital of the Lambayeque culture, which existed between AD 1000 and 1375. The settlement was occupied by the Chimú from 1375 to 1450, until the Incas conquered the Chimú kingdom and inhabited the city until 1532.

Replica of a frieze, Túcume pyramid

Túcume consists of 26 major adobe pyramids about 131-ft (40-m) high and other lesser buildings constructed around Cerro Purgatorio. This excellent 646-ft- (197-m-) high promontory lookout is also known as Cerro La Raya, after a sting ray fish that, according to legend, lives within it.

Túcume is thought to have been a center of pilgrimage which had high priests with great understanding of agro-astrology. The most relevant investigations carried out here were conducted between 1988 and 1994 by Thor Heyerdahl (1914–2002), the Norwegian ethnographer and explorer who led an expedition on a *kon-tiki* (balsa raft) from Peru to Polynesia in 1947. His studies concentrated on three major structures: Huaca Larga, Huaca 1, and the Templo de la Piedra Sagrada (Temple of the Sacred Stone). Heyerdahl discovered evidence of a pre-Columbian maritime culture, confirming theories that inspired his journey across the Pacific Ocean.

Excavations have yielded details about the functioning and lives of the inhabitants. Evidence of the Chimú and Inca occupations of the region has been found in dedicatory offerings, burials, and ceramics. In Huaca Larga, for example, archaeologists found the lavish burial of a prominent Inca general. Some archaeologists believe that the fire that razed central Huaca Larga coincided with the beginning of the Colonial period in Peru. The **Museo**

de Sitio Túcume, built in 1991, exhibits the works of Heyerdahl and American archaeologist, Wendell C. Bennet, who was the first to scientifically excavate the site in 1936. Also on display are elements of the local *curanderismo* (the ancient art of healing), still performed around the site.

Museo de Sitio Túcume
At the entrance of the site. **Tel** 074 830 250. 8am–5pm daily. www.tucume.com

Batán Grande **9**

Road Map B3. 24 miles (38 km) NE of Chiclayo on the road to Ferreñafe. from Chiclayo. home stay. www.darwinnet.org

An interesting blend of nature and history, Batán Grande consists of around 20 adobe pyramids in the heart of an ancient forest of *algarrobo* (mesquite) trees. Between 1978 and 2001, Japanese archaeologist, Izumi Shimada unveiled many tombs from the middle Sicán period (AD 900–1100). Some of the best gold artifacts found here are displayed at the Museo Nacional Sicán in Ferreñafe. The Sicán culture, which in Muchik language means "Temple of the Moon," arose after the Moche fell, but they left in the 12th century.

The **Santuario Histórico Bosque de Pomac**, protected since 2001, is home to 11th-century mesquite trees and 70 bird species.

Carob tree in the protected forest, Santuario Histórico Bosque de Pomac

Human-shaped vessels found at the excavated site of the Lord of Sipán's tomb ▷

Museo Tumbas Reales de Sipán 🄬

Detail on a gilded rattle

The pyramid-shaped Museum of the Royal Tombs of Sipán was inaugurated in 2002. Designed by architect Celso Prado Pastor, it is inspired by Huaca Rajada, a Moche mausoleum where the Lord of Sipán was buried 1,700 years ago. The pre-Columbian sovereign's tomb was discovered in 1987 by archaeologist Walter Alva and was dubbed "the richest tomb of the New World". This museum of monumental proportions has three floors and is divided into ten thematic sectors. The exhibits include 1,400 objects of gold, silver, copper, bronze, precious stones, and ceramics of extraordinary beauty and artisanship.

Pottery and Ceramics
The reconstructed old Lord of Sipán's tomb, which contains the pottery that was discovered.

★ **Fully Costumed Moche High Priest**
A human-sized mannequin of the high priest wearing a Mochica ceremonial outfit and jewelry. He watched over religious worship and rituals.

The High Priest's Tomb has been reconstructed here. He was second in the hierarchy during the Lord of Sipán's reign.

The Octopus Pectoral
This impressive breastplate made of gilded copper and silver is shaped like the tentacles of an octopus that surround a funeral mask.

★ **Lord of Sipán's Burial Chamber**
This replica has been reconstructed exactly as it was found by archaeologists. The servants were buried along with the Lord (see p231).

First Floor

Image of Ai Apaec
The principal god of the Moche people, Ai Apaec, is also known as the Decapitator.

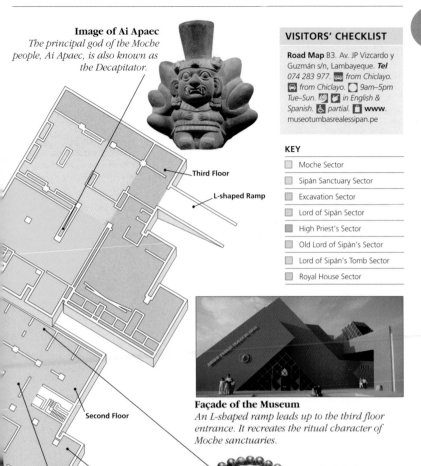

Third Floor

L-shaped Ramp

Second Floor

Funeral ornaments
that covered the Lord of Sipán's face, including those covering his eyes, nose, and mouth.

Open square pit
from where the Lord's funeral chamber can be seen.

VISITORS' CHECKLIST

Road Map B3. Av. JP Vizcardo y Guzmán s/n, Lambayeque. **Tel** 074 283 977. 🚌 from Chiclayo. 🚐 from Chiclayo. ⏰ 9am–5pm Tue–Sun. 🎧 🎫 in English & Spanish. ♿ partial. 🌐 www. museotumbasrealessipan.pe

KEY

☐ Moche Sector

☐ Sipán Sanctuary Sector

☐ Excavation Sector

☐ Lord of Sipán Sector

☐ High Priest's Sector

☐ Old Lord of Sipán's Sector

☐ Lord of Sipán's Tomb Sector

☐ Royal House Sector

Façade of the Museum
An L-shaped ramp leads up to the third floor entrance. It recreates the ritual character of Moche sanctuaries.

Lord of Sipán's Earring
The earring has a turquoise inlay deer figure with gold detailing. This is one of the three striking earrings discovered.

★ Peanut Necklace
This 20-piece gold and silver necklace made from peanut-shaped pieces symbolizes Mochica duality.

STAR EXHIBITS

★ Fully Costumed Moche High Priest

★ Lord of Sipán's Burial Chamber

★ Peanut Necklace

GALLERY GUIDE
The visit unusually begins on the third floor with a video presentation of the Huaca Rajada excavations and Moche culture. A recreation of the original site and the repository is on the second, while the first floor focuses on the tombs of the Lord of Sipán and seven others.

Exploring Museo Tumbas Reales de Sipán

Entering one of Latin America's biggest museums through the apex of the building on the third floor, enables the visitor to experience seeing a tomb the way an archaeologist does: working down from the top, beginning with the most recent, general features, digging down to ever older, more specific findings, and ending at the dream find – an undiscovered royal tomb.

Gilded banner showing figure with turquoise bracelets

Third Floor
The entrance features a dark-glass antechamber which blocks UV rays and allows the eyes to adjust to the muted, sepulchral lighting. After a video presentation which is optional, the museum's **Moche Sector** gives an overview of that culture. It is followed by the **Sipán Sanctuary Sector** which details Sipán as an ancient site and explains life in the village today. Highlights on this floor include a fabulous collection of ceramics

Golden funerary mask

depicting various aspects of Moche life such as people working, playing musical instruments, making love, and so on. Plants and animals were also popular subjects for Moche potters, along with their many gods and related religious ceremonies.

Second Floor
Much of this floor is dedicated to the **Lord of Sipán Sector**, where some of the most dazzling finds of the tomb are displayed. There are splendid

adornments for the face and body of the Lord of Sipán, who archaeologists believe was a warrior-priest of high rank, including ear ornaments and a gold peanut necklace (see p229). Made principally of gold, silver, copper, and turquoise, this veritable treasure trove has been exhibited around the world. Equally interesting finds include funerary offerings such as over 1,100 miniature ceramic pots containing food and other items. The tomb of the guardian, discovered in a sitting position, is displayed here along with finds from the **High Priest's Tomb**.

First Floor
Finally, at the base of the museum, the **Lord of Sipán's Tomb** is displayed in all its splendour. The Lord was flanked by two warriors, one of whom was buried with his dog. The bodies of two young females were interred at his head and feet, and a small boy was found in a niche above the burial. One of the men and the women were missing their left feet – the reason for the amputation still remains a mystery. Two sacrificed llamas complete the burial entourage.

Nearby, another, older tomb was discovered. It contained a senior warrior-priest, dubbed the **Old Lord of Sipán**, who was buried along with several exceptionally well-crafted pieces including an octopus pectoral (see p228), a necklace of linked spiders, and an anthropomorphic crab, all displayed here.

On show today is a precise reproduction of the tombs with the original pieces.

A recreation of the Lord with his entourage

HUAQUEROS AT SIPÁN

In Sipán, the *huaqueros* (robbers of *huacas* or shrines) first found a tomb in the pyramid known today as Huaca Rajada. In February 1987, the local police chief called Walter Alva to report that 33 antiquities had been found with a *huaquero*. Tense days followed and a *huaquero* was killed by the police. The villagers swore revenge but the situation was defused when local and international agencies provided financial backing and Alva hired *huaqueros* to work as excavators and guards. Four months later Alva came across the untouched tomb of the Lord of Sipán.

Excavation work at Huaca Rajada

For hotels and restaurants in this region see pp277–9 and pp297–9

Lord of Sipán's Burial Chamber

On the fiber-glass first floor lies a replica of the Lord of Sipán's coffin, which was surrounded by several other burials and offerings within a much larger burial chamber. The Lord was first clothed in a simple white undergarment and the body then adorned with splendid treasures of precious metals and gems combined

Mask of the Lord of Sipán

with artistic ceremonial offerings. It was then wrapped in multiple shrouds and placed in a wooden coffin along with gold, silver, and copper ornaments. From his copper-sandaled feet to his feathered headgear, the ceremonial burial of the Lord clearly indicated his high stature in the Moche world.

Ornaments made of feathers and copper resembled fans.

Eleven pectorals *made of colored shells and copper beads were found in different layers.*

Outer shirt was covered with gilded copper platelets and was decorated with cone-shaped tassels.

Fabric banners of gilded copper platelets, showing figures with turquoise-bead bracelets, were placed above and below the body.

Golden copper necklace *shows smiling faces, symbolizing life. The teeth are made of shell.*

Back flaps *were normally decorated with the image of the Decapitator, a Moche god.*

Strapping made of copper, fastened the contents of the coffin together.

KEY TO LAYERS

1 Coffin lid
2 Fabric banners
3 Pectoral
4 Outer shirt
5 Feather ornaments
6 Necklaces
7 Inner garment
8 Gold rattle
9 Ingots
10 Ceremonial sandals
11 Gold headdress
12 Support frame
13 Back flap
14 Headdress ornament
15 Copper strips
16 Three shrouds
17 Miniature shield
18 Pointed darts

Northern Beaches

Fishing raft under sail

Tumbes, the northernmost regional capital city of Peru, about 19 miles (30 km) away from the Ecuadorean border, is the starting point for traveling over 90 miles (150 km) to some of the finest beaches in the country. This relatively un-explored region has good waves to surf, attractive fishing villages, superb and spicy local food, unique wildlife enclosed in four protected areas, and the only stretch of Peruvian coast where the sea is really warm all year round.

Santuario Nacional Manglares de Tumbes ①
The reserve is known for its red mangrove forest which houses 200 species of birds and 40 varieties of plants.

Map of the Northern Beaches region

PACIFIC OCEAN

Santuario Nacional Manglares de Tumbes ①
Puerto Pizarro
Tumbes ② X Pedro Canga
Bocapán
Punta Sal ④ ③ Zorritos
Canoas   Pampa El Toro
Reserva Nacional de Tumbes ⑩
Catrina
Cap. Hoyle
⑤ Máncora Férnandez
⑥ Vichayito
Los Organos
Nuro
Atascadero
⑦ Cabo Blanco
Coto de Caza El Angolo ⑧
Parque Nacional Cerros de Amotape ⑨
CERROS DE AMOTAPE

0 km   20
0 miles   20

Tumbes ②
This coastal city, with airport facilities, is the starting point for traveling down to the northern beaches. A number of wildlife reserves can also be visited from here.

Zorritos ③
This old fishing village used to be the favorite of the Tumbes aristocracy during the early 20th century.

Punta Sal ④
The ideal spot for well-to-do Peruvians, this resort has extensive sands and warm waters. It is safe for swimming, fishing, and diving.

Máncora ⑤
The most-visited coastal resort with a lovely beach, Máncora is very popular with surfers, both local as well as foreign.

Vichayito ⑥
Located south of Máncora, it is a chic resort with stylish hotels built in front of a peaceful beach. Great spots for diving and kite-surfing have made it popular.

For additional map symbols see back flap

Reserva Nacional de Tumbes ⑩
The Tumbes National Reserve
protects endemic species that
have adapted to the hot and
humid tropical conditions of
the surrounding area.

Parque Nacional Cerros de Amotape ⑨
This park protects 225,607
acres (91,300 ha) of
Equatorial Dry Forest and a
major part of the North-
western Biosphere Reserve.

Coto de Caza El Angolo ⑧
A permit from SERNANP
allows hunting in this
enclosed zone. There is
just one small lodge in
the Sauce Grande.

KEY

— Major road

— Minor road

- - Park boundary

—·· International border

Cabo Blanco ⑦
This was a popular resort
during the 1950s, mainly due
to the presence of writer
Ernest Hemingway and for
its sport fishing. Deep-sea
fishing is also possible here.

Banana harvest on the shores of Río Tumbes, Tumbes

Tumbes ⑩

Road Map B2. 90 miles (140 km) N
of Talara. 👥 *93,000.* ✈ 🚌 *from*
Lima. 🎉 *San Pedro in Puerto Pizarro*
(Jun 28–29).

Tumbes is a small, peaceful
city which was originally
inhabited by the Tallanes,
related to the coastal tribes of
Ecuador. The Spanish conquistadores arrived here in 1527.
The city was also the point of
dispute in a border war with
Ecuador between 1940 to 1941
that was finally won by Peru.

Environs
Located about 8 miles (13 km)
northeast of Tumbes, the
**Reserva de Biósfera del
Noroeste** (Northwestern
Biosphere Reserve), covering
702 sq-miles (1,818 sq-km),
comprises four protected
areas best accessed through a
paved road along the Tumbes
River by the town of Limon.

Zorritos ⑪

Road Map A2. 16 miles (28 km)
SW of Tumbes. 👥 *14,000.* 🚌
🚗 *from Tumbes.*

The area's biggest fishing
village, Zorritos has some great
beaches favored by locals. It is
good for fishing and because
it is home to many migratory
birds, it is a favorite with bird-
watchers too.

Environs
About 6 miles (9 km) south
of Zorritos, at KM1232 of the
Panamerican Highway is
Bocapán, the turnoff to the
hot springs of **Hervideros** and

the main access road to the
**Parque Nacional Cerros de
Amotape** (Amotape Hills
National Park). Created in
1975, the park conserves the
extreme northern environ-
ment of Peru and protects
many endangered animals,
including the Tumbes
crocodile *(Crocodylus acutus)*
and the South American river
otter *(Lutra longicaudis).*
Visitors need to get per-
mission from the National
Institute of Natural Resources,
SERNANP to enter the park.

Máncora ⑫

Road Map A2. 14 miles (23 km) S
of Punta Sal. 👥 *9,000.* 🚌 🚗 *from*
Tumbes. **www**.vivamancora.com

Máncora is without doubt the
trendiest beach town in all
of Peru and attracts a mixed
and colorful crowd. Young
surfers, gringo backpackers,
and well-to-do Limeños, all
head for this town for its
enchanting beaches, mainly
Las Pocitas, 3 miles (5 km) to
the south. It is a great surfing
destination too, easily rivaling
those of Brazil and Ecuador.
It is renowned for its lively
bars and clubs, especially in
the summer months.

Environs
About 7 miles (11 km) to the
east are the **Baños de Barro**,
natural hot springs with
sulfurous waters believed to
have curative properties.
Beyond is the **Coto de Caza
El Angolo** (El Angolo
Enclosed Hunting Zone),
where hunting is allowed
with a SERNANP permit.

THE NORTHERN HIGHLANDS

*D*ominated by the great Amazonian rivers of Marañon and the Huallabamba, which cut through the towering Andes, the Northern Highlands is an ideal destination for the intrepid traveler. This remote, agriculturally rich, and extremely picturesque region is also well known for its vibrant tradition of crafts, a legacy that dates back to the pre-Inca Chachapoyan civilization.

Peru's Northern Highlands remain firmly off the beaten track. Yet this is one of the most exciting regions in the country. The provincial capital, Cajamarca, is renowned for its elegant Colonial architecture. From here, routes lead over the mountains to the beautiful cloud-clad region of Chachapoyas, with its famed ruins of Kuélap, and on to the jungle towns of Tarapoto and Yurimaguas in the Amazon, or else north towards Ecuador via Jaén, or south to Cajabamba.

The spectacular ruins of Kuélap are testimony to the skills of the Chachapoyas culture, which reached its "classic" period around AD 800 and grew to occupy a huge swathe of the northern Peruvian Andes. The wide range of habitat and climate allowed Chachapoyans to cultivate an extensive range of crops. They were skilled agriculturalists, carving terraces into mountain slopes and covering low-lying areas with intricately drained field systems. They were expert weavers as well and samples of their superb textiles are now on view at the Museo Leymebamba.

The great Amazonian rivers, Marañon and Huallabamba, which rise here less dramatically than in the Cordillera Blanca. The area's remoteness has its advantages as well as disadvantages. On a positive note, there is an intrepid feel to exploring this hinterland, where tourists are few and far between and rural life continues as it has done for centuries. On the downside, infrastructure is creaky: buses are shabby, flights infrequent, journeys slow, and luxury hotels non-existent. One needs time and patience to explore the region in any depth, but the rewards outweigh the trials and tribulations.

An Andean weaver at work, Cajamarca, provincial capital of the Northern Highlands

◁ View of the lush green vegetation in the Cordillera Central

Exploring the Northern Highlands

This remote area sees few tourists and rural life continues as it has done for centuries. Heading inland from the coast, several routes connect the verdant countryside. The northernmost road loops up from Chiclayo to Jaén. From there, visitors can head south to Chachapoyas, past the Kuélap ruins, Gocta Falls, and on to Cajamarca. Most travelers with little time make a beeline for Cajamarca on the central route via an improved road from Pacasmayo (north of Trujillo) which winds its way up the beautiful Río Jequetepeque Valley. Cajamarca can be used as a base for visiting the thermal baths at Los Baños del Inca, the aqueduct at Cumbemayo, and the burial niches at Ventanillas de Otuzco. The southern route cuts east from Trujillo via Huamachuco and Cajabamba, then north to Cajamarca – or even south to the Cordillera Blanca.

LOCATOR MAP

■ *Area illustrated*

SIGHTS AT A GLANCE

Towns and Cities
Cajamarca pp238–9 **①**
Karajía **⑨**
Levanto **⑧**
Leymebamba and La Laguna de los Cóndores **⑤**

Los Baños del Inca **③**
Revash **⑥**
Ventanillas de Otuzco and Combayo **④**

Archaeological Sites and Ruins
Cumbemayo **②**
Kuélap pp244–6 **⑦**

Area of Natural Beauty
Cataratas Gocta **⑩**

```
0 km          25
0 miles        25
```

Jaén
Chama

Río Chama

Santo Domingo

Cutervo

Cochabamba

3N   La

Santa Cruz

Catache

La Florida

San Miguel
De Pallaques

Sa
Pal

Río Jequetepeque   CUMBEMA

Tembladera

Contumaza

Pacasmayo,
Trujillo

San Benito

Casc

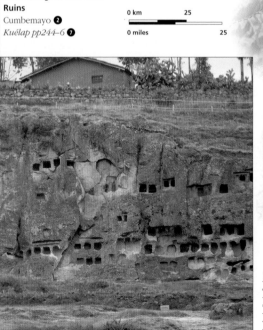
Burial niches carved into the mountains, Otuzco

KEY

━━ Main road

═══ Untarred minor road

- - - Track

━━ Regional border

Model of the Karajía statues displayed in the Leymebamba Museum

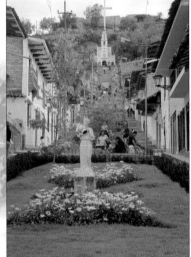

Stairs leading up the Santa Apolonia hill to the small chapel, Cajamarca

GETTING AROUND

There are only a few daily flights from Lima to Cajamarca (the region's sole airport with scheduled flights), so plan in advance. By bus, it takes up to 14 hours direct from Lima to Cajamarca via Trujillo and Pacasmayo. From Trujillo, it takes about 7 hours by bus to Cajamarca; from Chiclayo, it takes about 6 hours. Going via Huamachuco and Cajabamba, the journey takes two days. To get to Chachapoyas from Cajamarca, the journey is done in two legs: first to Celendín where you change and then take another bus. Check bus timings before starting since they are infrequent. Most of the roads except the road from Pacasmayo are in poor condition. With public transport erratic and uncomfortable, consider renting a high-clearance 4WD car in Lima, Trujillo, or Chiclayo.

SEE ALSO

• **Where to Stay** pp279–80

• **Where to Eat** pp299–300

Cajamarca ❶

Carving, Apolonia

Laid out in a traditional Spanish grid plan, the provincial Andean capital of Cajamarca has been a favorite haunt of travelers since Inca times. This is where the Inca emperor Atahualpa was captured by conquistador Francisco Pizarro. Its Colonial- and Independence-era architecture rivals that of Cusco and Arequipa for elegance. The main thoroughfare is Amalia Puga, with the Plaza de Armas at the city's historic heart. Cajamarca also makes a very pleasant base from which to explore the countryside renowned for its cheese and other dairy products. The best time to visit is during what is considered Peru's most raucous celebration, Carnaval, when the city pulsates with music, fireworks, and parades.

Beautiful interior of Iglesia de San Francisco

Baroque architecture of the Cathedral, Plaza de Armas

🏛 Museo Arqueológico

Del Batán 289. ⏱ 8am–2:30pm Mon–Fri. 🌐 pub hols. ▨

Run by Cajamarca University, the Archaeological Museum consists of an informative run-through of archaeological finds in this north Andean region from around 3,000 years ago to the recent past. The display ranges from ceramics and textiles to black-and-white photographs and mummies, drawings of the Cumbemayo petroglyphs *(see p242)* and a collection of carved stones. Of note are the paintings by local artist, Andres Zevallos. The center also stocks good leaflets on the sights in the area.

🔒 Cathedral

Plaza de Armas. ⏱ 7am–7pm. ▨ 🔔 7 & 8am.

On the northwest of the Plaza de Armas – with its lawns, benches, and imaginatively-trimmed topiary – rises the Cathedral. Begun in the 17th century, it was not consecrated until 1762. Its fine carved-stone

façade is a beautiful example of the Baroque style championed in Colonial Peru. The main altar is in the imposing Churrigueresque style, covered tip-to-toe with gold leaf. The walls of the Cathedral incorporate a large amount of Inca masonry.

🔒 Iglesia de San Francisco

Plaza de Armas. ⏱ 3–6pm. 🏛 museum only. ▨ ♿

The church and convent of San Francisco, erected in the 17th and 18th centuries, rivals the Cathedral with its Neo-Classical appearance. The priests left the belfries half-done to dodge the tax levied by Spanish authorities on religious buildings and they were only completed in 1951. This Franciscan church catered to the poor and non-whites and is also known as Iglesia de los Indios (Indians' Church). It has a fine altar, catacombs, and a religious art museum. To the right of the church is the **Capilla de la Virgen de**

Dolores, the city's prettiest chapel, housing a statue of the town's patron saint, La Virgen de los Dolores, which is carried around the town during religious celebrations.

🚪 Ransom Chamber

Amalia Puga 722. ⏱ 9am–1pm, 3–6pm Mon–Fri; 9am–12:30pm weekends. 🌐 public hols. ▨ ▨

An unpretentious house, the Ransom Chamber is nonetheless a worthy port of call when visiting Cajamarca. It is the only remaining Inca building in the town, displaying their typical, earthquake-proof trapezoidal niches and doors, and some original masonry.

However, the 17-ft (5-m) wide and 22-ft (7-m) long chamber has far more historical significance than its appearance suggests. There are two historical versions regarding its use. One claims that the room was the place where Atahualpa, the last sovereign Inca ruler, was held captive by the Spaniards following his downfall. The other says it was the room which the Inca promised to fill with gold up to the height of his outstretched arm and

Original Inca masonry still on view, Ransom Chamber

twice with silver as ransom for his freedom. The chamber is decorated with murals by two famous local artists, Camilo Blas and Andres Zevallos.

🏛 El Complejo de Belén
Calle Belén. ⬜ 9am–1pm, 3–6pm Mon–Fri; 9am–12:30pm weekends. ⬤ public hols. 🖼 🖼
This Colonial-era complex spreads across a group of buildings with several handsome patios and a number of institutions. These include the tourist office, the Institute of Culture (INC), part of the university administration, a small medical museum, two former hospitals, and one of Cajamarca's finest churches, the **Iglesia Belén**.

The church is regarded as one of Peru's best examples of the Baroque style, with its beautifully carved wooden pulpit, extravagant gold-leaf altars, and a delightfully ornate cupola complete with oversized cherubs holding an elaborate centerpiece made up of flowers.

The interesting **Museo Arqueólogico y Etnográfico** lies across the street (at Junín y Belén) from the rest of the complex, in what once served as the Women's Hospital and

VISITORS' CHECKLIST

Road Map B3. 532 miles (856 km) N of Lima. 🚗 190,000. ✈ 2 miles (3 km), 076 822 523. 🚌 from Lima & Trujillo. 🛈 El Complejo de Belén, Calle Belén 631; 076 822 997. 🎉 daily. 🎭 Carnaval (before Lent). **www**.cajamarcaperu.com.pe

morgue. The museum houses a wide collection of objects, with ceramics and weavings from the surrounding region as the highlight. Some jungle items are also on display.

🌿 Cerro Santa Apolonia
SW of Plaza de Armas. 🖼 🖼
The hill of Santa Apolonia overlooks Cajamarca's historic heart, making it a great spot for getting a feel of the city. The hill can be explored via a series of walks through gardens with native plants, leading up to the peak from where the Spaniards, under Francisco Pizarro, aimed their cannons on the Inca army below. Also located here are the remains of Chavín- and Inca-era stone carvings. One of the rocks, popularly known as the Silla del Inca (the Seat of the Inca), is shaped like a throne and the Incas are said to have reviewed their troops from here.

Ornate cupola with cherubs, Iglesia Belén

CAJAMARCA CITY CENTER

Cathedral ②
Cerro Santa Apolonia ⑥
El Complejo de Belén ⑤
Iglesia de San Francisco ③
Museo Arqueológico ①
Ransom Chamber ④

0 meters 100
0 yards 100

Key to Symbols see back flap

Central Market
Museo Arqueológico ①
Maj Gen Fap A R Iglesias
Colectivos a los Baños del Inca
Cathedral ②
PLAZA DE ARMAS
Iglesia de San Francisco ③
Ransom Chamber ④
El Complejo de Belén ⑤
Museo Arqueológico Y Etnográfico
Cerro Santa Apolonia ⑥

The strange window-like cliff necropolis at Otuzco ▷

Shepherdess in the Cumbemayo mountains near Cajamarca

bus ride from Cajamarca. The baths date back to pre-Inca times. It is believed that the last Inca, Atahualpa, and his army had camped at the baths when Spanish conquistador, Pizarro, arrived giving the place its name.

The resort is popular at the weekends, but it is probably best avoided then as it can be quite an experience sharing the bath with dozens of strangers. There are various pools at varying temperatures and prices. The best time to visit is in the morning when they are the cleanest. The complex has a modest restaurant and hotel, and is equipped with a sauna. The recreational complex is a huge attraction.

Cumbemayo ❷

Road Map B3. 13 miles (20 km) SW of Cajamarca. 🚌 *from Cajamarca.*
☑ 🅰

The mountainous region of Cumbemayo, situated to the southwest of Cajamarca *(see pp238–9)*, is famous for the canal and aqueduct carved from rock and pieced together by deft stonemasons with great skill. The structure is thought to be about 2,000 years old and perhaps had ritual as well as practical significance, due to the great effort that went into its construction. It originally carried water from the Atlantic watershed over to the Pacific side through an intricate system of tunnels and canals, some of which are still in use.

To one side of the aqueduct is a rock, shaped like a face, into which a man-made cave has been carved. Inside the cave, with the aid of a torch, one can make out 3,000-year-old petroglyphs which bear feline features. This is a hallmark of the Chavín style which dominated this part of Peru at that time. There is a small museum at the site, but sometimes the guardian of the museum may have to be located to get it opened.

On the way from Cajamarca, before Cumbemayo, an odd natural rock formation known

as the **Bosque de Piedras** (Stone Forest), is clearly visible. The limestone rock masses have eroded, forming tapered shapes which are reminiscent of the human form, thus giving it their Spanish name, *los frailones* (the big monks).

Los Baños del Inca ❸

Road Map B3. 3 miles (5 km) E of Cajamarca. 🚌 🚐 *from Cajamarca.* ⏰ *5am–6:45pm daily.* 🖼 🍴 🔲 🍽 🅰

A pleasant way to spend an afternoon is to wallow in the thermal baths at the Baños del Inca, just a short taxi or

Ventanillas de Otuzco and Combayo ❹

Road Map B3. 5 miles (8 km) NE of Cajamarca. 🚐 🚐 *from Cajamarca.* ⏰ *8am–6pm daily.* 🖼 🅰 *not official.*

One of the oldest cemeteries in Peru, the Ventanillas de Otuzco date back about 3,500 years. The necropolis comprises a series of burial niches carved into the volcanic rock of the cliff, some of which are decorated with carvings. The chieftains of Cajamarca were buried in these niches. From a distance, they look like windows, hence the Spanish name *ventanillas* (little

Hot spring pools at Los Banos del Inca, near Cajamarca

Ancient burial niches in the cliff face at Otuzco

windows). An extensive collection of these niches can be found at Combayo, located 18 miles (30 km) southeast of Cajamarca. Both the sites can be visited on a tour from Cajamarca. Otuzco is a 90-minute walk from Los Baños del Inca.

Leymebamba and La Laguna de los Cóndores ❺

Road Map B3. 50 miles (80 km) SE of Chachapoyas. 🛶 🛆

The small and attractive market town of Leymebamba, about an 8- to 10-hour drive from Cajamarca, is not covered by most travel itineraries of Peru. However, the surrounding countryside is wonderful for exploring on foot as well as on horseback. Close to the town are many small archaeological sites of tourist interest, including **Museo Leymebamba**, built and run by the community.

The museum is located at San Miguel, the site of the original Leymebamba town which was evacuated following a yellow fever epidemic in the 1600s. It houses the amazing archaeological finds from the nearby Laguna de los Cóndores. The mummies and artifacts recovered from the cliff tombs in 1997 were moved to the museum to protect them from *huaqueros* (tomb-raiders). The Leymebamba museum and all the materials used in its construction, such as timber,

stone and *tapia* (mud walls), were made by local crafts-people using traditional construction techniques.

Among the 5,000 artifacts on display are almost 150 well-preserved mummies, and there is an ethnographic display on life in the region. The museum also has a colorful orchid garden housing more than 100 native species of beautiful flowers. The town has very basic facilities, and is best visited on a day trip from Chachapoyas. The trip to the Laguna, however, is for the adventurous as the route on foot or horseback climbs up to 12,139 ft (3,700 m) before descending to the spellbinding lake. There is a basic lodge here with minimum facilities, and if you bring food, the family will

Karajia-style statue, Museo Leymebamba

cook it for you. The journey takes about 10 to 12 hours so it is best to plan it as a three-day trip.

🏛 **Museo Leymebamba**
Av. Austria s/n, San Miguel, Leymebamba. ⬜ 9:30am–4:30pm Tue–Sun. ⬤ public hols. 📷 📹
www.centromallqui.org.pe

Revash ❻

Road Map B3. 37 miles (60 km) S of Chachapoyas, nr Santo Tomás. 🚐 🚗 from Chachapoyas. 📷

Named for the Revash culture, contemporary with the Chachapoyans *(see p246)*, this site is famed for its *chullpas* (funerary chambers). These small, multi-hued buildings perch precariously on ledges high up on the limestone cliffs. They are made from mud and stone walls, then plastered over and painted, and topped with peculiar gabled roofs. The *chullpas* have been looted, but a dozen burials and accompanying funerary offerings were discovered by archaeologists. A variety of pictographs can be seen on the cliff behind the structures.

There are daily minibuses from Chachapoyas to Santo Tomás. Visitors can disembark at the Santo Tomás turnoff. Allow 3 hours for the steep climb up to the ruins. Near Santo Tomás, the village of Yerbuena has a busy Sunday market.

Building on the central square of the highland town of Leymebamba

Kuélap 🛈

Rhomboid carving on Kuélap houses

The imposing fortress of Kuélap is the main attraction of the Chachapoyas region. It ranks among the finest and most impressive ruins in Peru. The structure occupies a perfect vantage point, set on a dramatic ridge high above the Río Utcubamba amid verdant, rolling countryside. Reclaimed by the surrounding forest for more than 300 years, it wasn't until 1843 that the site was rediscovered by a local judge, and it wasn't truly explored until the late 19th and early 20th centuries. Local experts claim the fortress contained three times more stone than the Great Pyramid at Giza in Egypt.

Bromeliads
The cloudforest is ideal for bromeliads and orchids to thrive. They can be seen growing on the ruin walls.

Outer Wall of Fortress
The huge perimeter wall, made of giant limestone blocks, was perhaps built for defense purposes. In some places the wall reaches a height of 36 ft (11 m) and encircles the entire site.

El Tintero
On the southern side of the citadel, a mysterious inverted cone-shaped structure, El Tintero (inkwell) rises 18 ft (5.5 m) high.

STAR SIGHTS

★ Circular Houses

★ Main Entrance

★ Torreón

★ Main Entrance
The funnel-shaped defensive entrance is still used today. There are only three entrances to the fortress.

VISITORS' CHECKLIST

Road Map B3. 58 miles (93 km) from Chachapoyas. 🚌 from Chachapoyas to Tingo, then a 4-hour walk up. 🕐 8am–2pm 🎫 🛒 from Chachapoyas. 🍴 ⛺ www.kuelap.org

Surrounding Area

Located on a limestone ridge which runs north-south, the fortress was built to maximize the natural topography of the area against enemy raids.

Restoration Work

A recovery project to restore some of the ruins has been going on at the site since 1999.

★ Torreón

The great tower at the northern end is one of the main features at the ruin. It's a D-shaped lookout tower.

★ Circular Houses

Hundreds of round stone houses are scattered randomly throughout the site. They were once about 13-ft (4-m) high and had thatched roofs.

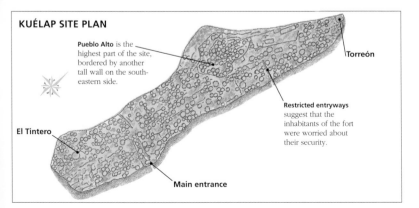

KUÉLAP SITE PLAN

Pueblo Alto is the highest part of the site, bordered by another tall wall on the south-eastern side.

Torreón

Restricted entryways suggest that the inhabitants of the fort were worried about their security.

El Tintero

Main entrance

Exploring Kuélap

Ceramics discovered in Kuélap indicate that the area had been inhabited since AD 500, but the majority of construction occurred between AD 900 and 1100. The result is a fortress bigger than any other single structure in Peru. The complex had an outer wall protecting over 400 circular houses, thought to have been home to 3,500 people. It also had terraces, outlying settlements, and burial areas outside the main walls. When the Incas arrived around 1470, they found that Kuélap, full of fierce Chachapoyan warriors, was no easy place to conquer. They were unable to conquer the fort properly and only five Inca buildings have been found among the hundreds of structures in the fortress.

One of the unrestored entrances to Kuélap.

Main Entrance

There are actually three main entrances, all very similar to each other, however, only one is in use today. The funnel-shaped entrance leads into the fortress and becomes narrower the farther in one goes, until eventually it is wide enough for only one person. The solid walls rise high above the head. The construction of the entrance is a clear pointer to the fact that no one could have gained entry into the fortress without the inhabitants allowing them admission.

El Tintero

It is the most popular structure within the walls. The word means "inkwell" because of the structure's shape, an inverted cone, not because of any reference to ink since the Chachapoyans did not have a written language. Early surveys gave a variety of functions to this building, ranging from a water reservoir to a jail – even a torture chamber and a cemetery. However, studies now suggest that the building had astronomical functions,

since the small entrance lines up with the sun at the most favorable times for planting crops. In reality, the purpose of this strangely shaped structure still remains a mystery. A small human face carved in low relief into a limestone block can be seen on the eastern side of El Tintero.

Circular Buildings

Unlike almost all other buildings in Peru, the Chachapoyans left circular structures for posterity to admire and ponder over. No one knows why they were circular. A few have been restored in Kuélap and elsewhere. Most researchers agree that the buildings had steep, conical thatched roofs designed to ward off torrential cloudforest downpours. In Kuélap, some of the buildings have walls 20 inches (50 cm) thick. The apparently random order of these buildings is quite deceptive. Archaeologists claim the design is quite rational, with the buildings being distributed either along corridors or arranged with the patios facing each other.

Torreón

This 23-ft (7-m) high tower at the north end of Pueblo Alto gave views in every direction. Archaeologists found an arsenal of broken stone axe heads and 2,500 stones piled on the floor, of a perfect size to fit in the slingshots that defenders would have used.

Water Channels

Stone channels have been found leading archaeologists to believe they may have led to a spring at the top of the ridge, which must have provided the fortress with a permanent source of water.

THE CHACHAPOYA PEOPLE

The name Chachapoya is commonly believed to come from the conflation of two Quechua words, *sacha* and *puyu*, literally forest-cloud. The Chachapoyans were famous for their white skin and beauty. They were a fierce community and it took the Incas many men to conquer the region. They were also famous shamans, known as great sorcerers and herbalists. The people were skilled agriculturalists and also renowned for their weaving. The finds displayed at the Museo Leymebamba testify to the beauty of the imagery and the wide variety of techniques used, including plain weaves, tapestry, brocades, and embroidery on a single textile. They also produced a wide range of pottery.

Chachapoya people from the Cruzpata village

For hotels and restaurants in this region see pp279–80 and pp299–300

A view of the sleepy town of Levanto

Levanto ⑧

Road Map B3. 14 miles (22 km) S of Chachapoyas. 🚌 🚐 *from Chachapoyas.*

An original and unrestored Inca road joins Chachapoyas with Levanto, which was first settled by the Spanish in 1532. Despite its history it remains a small village with only a few remnants of its Colonial past.

A few miles away is the overgrown site of **Yalape** (built AD 1100–1300) which has classic circular buildings embellished with geometric friezes, and the remains of an irrigation system. This is part of the second largest known Chachapoyan fortress after Kuélap, with other sites nearby.

Most visitors make it a day trip, arriving by the morning bus uphill from Chachapoyas and returning along the Inca road downhill on foot.

Karajía ⑨

Road Map B3. 30 miles (48 km) NW of Chachapoyas, near Luya. 🚌 *from Chachapoyas.* 📷 🚐 *Luya.*

Oversized, colorfully painted vertical sarcophagi made of earth, wood, and straw, decorated with faces, were the final resting places of important members of the famous Chachapoyan culture. Many of these coffins have been discovered and the ones found at Karajía are the easiest to visit from Chachapoyas. The site is reached by minibuses from Chachapoyas to Luya, from where it is a 3-hour hike. Tours from Chachapoyas are also available. Karajía is a 45-minute walk from Cruzpata.

Environs

Gran Vilaya, a three-day trek from Karajía, is a large area with some 30 archaeological sites. The best way to explore them is by taking an organized tour from Chachapoyas.

Cavernas Quiocta near Lamud can be combined with a visit to Karajía. Located one-and-a-half hours by road from Karajía, this series of caves contain Inca remains, pools, and splendid geological formations. Visitors need to ask for a guide in Lamud.

Cataratas Gocta ⑩

Road Map B2. Near San Pablo. 🚐 *from Chachapoyas or Pedro Ruíz.* 🚶 🏕 *camping allowed but no facilities.*

In 2002 it was discovered that this huge waterfall, hidden in the cloud forest and known only to the locals, was one of the highest in the world. Stefan Ziemendorff, a German hydro-engineer saw the falls on the Río Cocahuayco and did preliminary measurements – an astounding 2,531 ft (771 m) in height. Initially, the fall was touted as the third highest in the world, but sceptics have pointed out that it is a two-tiered fall. However, the two tiers are close enough to one another and the World Waterfall Database considers them to be one waterfall, and rates them among the top ten in the world.

Gocta is on the east of the main Chachapoyas-Pedro Ruíz road. Taxis from either town can be taken for San Pablo, where informal guides take visitors on a trail which lasts 1–2 hours to a view of the upper falls. En route, views of both tiers are available. To see the falls from the bottom, it is necessary to backtrack and take another taxi to the smaller hamlet of Cocachimba, and walk about 3 hours through the cloud forest.

The magnificent Cataratas Gocta, rated amongst the world's highest

THE AMAZON BASIN

The fabulous Amazonian rainforest is home to more species of animals than any other area on earth. This is where visitors may see monkeys and macaws, army ants and armadillos, thousands of butterfly species, 900 bird species, and a variety of trees and plants. National reserves protect the flora and fauna, and provide inaccessible areas where indigenous tribes live untouched by the 21st century.

The original rainforest inhabitants are separated into dozens of groups speaking distinct languages, but united by an ability to thrive in this difficult environment. Using local materials, people still build thatched wooden houses along constantly shifting riverbanks, carve canoes, and hunt using blow pipes and poison-tipped darts.

Little is known about their history. At the height of the Inca Empire, the upper Amazon Basin was incorporated into Antisuyo (the empire's eastern quarter) and the Indians traded scarlet macaw feathers and jungle fruits for metal tools. After the conquest, the Spaniards concentrated on the coastal and highland regions. A few ill-fated Amazonian expeditions were foiled by the Indians. The Spaniards' greatest impact was in the unintended introduction of diseases, to which natives had no resistance. Millions died of smallpox, influenza, or other illnesses.

In the 16th century, Colonial outposts were established in places such as Moyobamba, but the Amazon was not permanently occupied until a few missions were built in the 18th century. With the 1870s rubber boom the population exploded. Four decades later, the boom collapsed and the once-opulent towns survived by logging, exploitation of jungle crops, and export of animals for zoos.

The discovery of oil in the 1960s fueled another population boom, soon followed by a nascent tourism industry. Slowly, cities such as Iquitos, Pucallpa, and Puerto Maldonado gained renewed importance, and mestizo *ribereños* (river-dwellers) began to clear forests for agriculture.

Although over half of Peru lies in the Amazon, barely 5 percent of the population lives there. Visiting this wilderness, where few roads penetrate, can be a thrilling adventure.

The jaguar, the most prized wildlife sighting in the Amazon

◁ **Misty view of the dense Amazon rainforest canopy**

The Amazon Basin

The rainforest is the overwhelming attraction, with jungle towns being essential gateways. River travel is customary and is a highlight of a visit. For premium wildlife viewing, a tour and rainforest lodge stay is ideal. In the south lies the Reserva de la Biosfera de Manu, difficult and expensive to reach but one of the world's most protected rainforest reserves. Nearby, the Ríos Tambopata and Madre de Dios converge at Puerto Maldonado, a remote jungle town with access to some of Peru's best rainforest lodges. The central part has the best road links with Lima and offers opportunities for those on a tight budget; reasonably priced tours can be taken from Chanchamayo, Tarapoto, and Yarinacocha. Iquitos, the area's most interesting city, is located in the north. It can be reached by riverboat from Pucallpa or Yurimaguas, and offers access to the Amazon's longest canopy walkway.

SIGHTS AT A GLANCE

Towns and Cities

Iquitos ❶

Moyobamba and Alto Mayo ❼

Oxapampa ⓬

Pevas ❷

Pucallpa ❾

Tarapoto ❽

Ucayali River Towns ❹

Yurimaguas ❻

Areas of Natural Beauty

Chanchamayo Region ⓫

Reserva de la Biosfera de Manu ⓭

Reserva Nacional Allpahuayo-Mishana ❸

Reserva Nacional Pacaya-Samiria ❺

Ríos Tambopata and Madre de Dios Area pp262–3 ⓮

Yarinacocha ❿

SEE ALSO

• *Where to Stay* pp280–81

• *Where to Eat* pp300–01

Children of the Bora tribe paddling in a dugout canoe

0 km 150

0 miles 150

Do
uray Copal Urco
Vidal

Francisco
de Orellana
2 PEVAS

T O Mazán *Río Amazonas*

IQUITOS 1 ☒

3 RESERVA NACIONAL
ALLPAHUAYO-MISHANA
Nauta

4 UCAYALI RIVER
equena TOWNS

VA NACIONAL
AYA-SAMIRIA

Leticia,
Colombia

Tabatinga,
Brazil

GETTING AROUND

Iquitos, Peru's major Amazon city, is
the world's largest with no access by
road, and can only be reached by
river or air. Other cities with regular
flights from Lima include Pucallpa,
Tarapoto, and Puerto Maldonado.
Traveling between areas nearly
always necessitates a return to Lima.
Almost all Amazonian national parks
and jungle lodges are best reached
by a combination of air and river
travel. The Chanchamayo area is the
most accessible by road from Lima
(8 hours) but gives the scantest
taste of the Amazon Basin.

Chapawanqi Falls near Tarapoto

NACOCHA
☒
PUCALLPA

to
re
Puerto
Putaya

San Luis

aya
esta
UCAYALI
Río Ucayali
Atalaya
Puerto
Varadero
Río Curanja
Cocama
Alerta
Esperanza
Río Yaco

l
in
nal
Shepahua
Río Las Piedras
Noaya
26B

MADRE DE DIOS
Fitzcarrald
Río Manu
RESERVA DE LA
BIOSFERA
DE MANU
13
Manu
Providencia
Río Manuripe
Soledad

Madre de Dios
Río Madre de Dios
Puerto
Maldonado ☒
14
RÍOS TAMBOPATA
AND MADRE DE
DIOS AREA
Río Heath
Parque Nacional
Bahuaja-Sonene

KEY

— Main road

▪▪▪ Untarred main road

▪ ▪ ▪ Untarred minor road

- - - Track

▬▬ International border

▬▬ Regional border

A dry season view of Belén Village along Río Itaya, Iquitos

Iquitos ❶

Road Map D2. 373 miles (600 km) NE of Pucallpa. 450,000. from Colombia only. from Lima. from Pucallpa or Yurimaguas. Plaza de Armas, Napo 232, 065 236 144. Founding of Iquitos (Jan 5), San Juan (Jun 24). **www**.iquitos-peru.com

Jesuit missionaries founded this major Amazonian port in 1757. Iquitos led a precarious existence until the rubber boom of the 1880s changed it from a village of 1,500 to a city of 25,000. The rubber export to Europe made it more connected to that continent than to Lima, and the city soon boasted opulent houses, decorated with tiles from Portugal, Spain, and Italy. Calle Prospero, south of Plaza de Armas, is lined by these old tiled buildings.

A block east is the Malecón Tarapacá, the river boulevard built during the rubber boom. One side has river views, while the other has tiled buildings and the **Amazon Museum**. The Museum provides a chance to view the interior of a late 19th-century building with photographs and paintings of early Iquitos. The most interesting exhibits are life-sized statues of indigenous tribespeople made of molds obtained by plastering live models.

The boulevard's north end becomes Malecón Maldonado, where weekend nights are busy with locals watching street performers. To the south is the outdoor Belén market, which stretches for many blocks. Famous for its huge variety of jungle produce, on sale are dozens of fresh fish, thick home-rolled cigars, illegally hunted jaguar skins, live turtles, and caiman steaks. Ask for the Pasaje Paquito, an alley filled with unique medicinal products "guaranteed" to treat all kinds of ailments.

Behind the market is **Belén Village**, where thousands of people live in wooden huts which float for over half the year when the river rises during the rainy season. Locals offer boat tours to see, what they call, the Venice of the Amazon.

The absence of roads connecting Iquitos to the rest of the world gives it a sassy, friendly atmosphere. Iquiteños' infectious friendliness is unparalleled. The city is frenetically noisy because of the numerous motorcycles. Three-wheeled *motocarros* or motorcycle rickshaws outnumber other vehicles and it is an inexpensive and popular mode of public transport.

Motocarro on the road

🏛 **Amazon Museum**
Malecón Tarapacá 386. **Tel** 065 234 221. ◯ 8am–1pm, 3–6pm Mon–Fri, 8am–1pm Sat.

Pevas ❷

Road Map D2. 90 miles (145 km) downriver from Iquitos. 3,000. from Iquitos. daily.

The oldest town on the Peruvian Amazon, Pevas today is made up of wooden structures, many with thatched roofs. Founded by missionaries in 1735, the town sadly has no buildings left of that era. Most of the friendly inhabitants are mestizos or natives of the Bora, Huitoto, Yagua, or Ocainas groups. The most famous resident of the town is artist, Francisco Grippa, whose unique works can be seen in the towering hilltop studio and gallery where he lives. Visitors are welcomed and served beer and bananas, instead of wine and cheese.

CANOPY WALKWAY

In the 1990s, biologists at Explorama's Field Station constructed the canopy platforms linked by hanging bridges near the Río Napo, 100 miles (160 km) from Iquitos, to study life on the treetops. It is one of the world's longest canopy walkways with 14 platforms supporting a 550-yard (500-m) long series of suspension bridges, 115 ft (35 m) above the ground. The walkway, approached via a staircase, gives a superb view of the rainforest canopy. It is a highlight of any Amazon visit and the chances of seeing unusual birds, lizards, and orchids are excellent.

Canopy walkway enclosed in see-through netting

River Travel

It is impossible to visit the Amazon Basin without getting on a boat. Other than expensive cruises designed for tourists, the possibilities are endless and range from a 10-minute ferry crossing of the Río Madre de Dios at Puerto Maldonado to a week or more on a commercial boat from Yurimaguas or Pucallpa to Iquitos and beyond. Boarding a boat opens the traveler's eye to local life: be it on a tiny canoe or a majestic three-decked vessel, the *ribereños* (river-dwellers) can be seen traveling, working, cooking, washing, fishing, and getting on with life.

Typical riverboat

Iquitos to the Pacaya-Samiria area is the most common route taken by tourists. Boats stop at the national park and take a week to return. Another week-long cruise goes to the border and back.

TIPS FOR TRAVELERS

Commercial routes: *Pucallpa to Iquitos (3–6 days), Yurimaguas to Iquitos (2–4 days), and Iquitos to Brazil/Colombia border (2–3 days).*
Getting there: *Destination and departure date is written in front of each boat. Tours can also be arranged (see p311).*

Río Ucayali *is longer than the Marañón. With more villages to stop at, the opportunity to befriend local travelers is far greater.*

Mazán — Brazil/Colombia Border
Iquitos
Santa Rosa
Miraflores
Parinari
Nauta
Lá Libertad — Río Marañón
Requena
Lagunas — Pacaya-Samiria Reserve
Santa Cruz
Iberia
Yurimaguas — Río Ucayali — San Roque
Navarro — Dos de Mayo
Orellana
Inahuaya
Contamana
Paoyhan
Yarinacocha — Pucallpa
Campo Verde

0 km 100
0 miles 100

Nauta *is located on Río Marañón, which meets Río Ucayali to form the Amazon. Travelers can take a bus from here to Iquitos.*

Dugout canoes *are the main means of travel for the locals, especially those living in remote areas. They are used for myriad jobs: river taxis, fishing, cargo, as well as selling food.*

KEY

🚤 Riverboat boarding point
🚌 Bus station
═ Minor road

White quartz sand soil visible in a forest clearing

Reserva Nacional Allpahuayo-Mishana ❸

Road Map D2. 16 miles (25 km) from Iquitos. 🚌 🚐 ✈ *from Iquitos.* **Tel** *065 265 515.* ℹ *Oficina IIAP, Av. A Quiñones KM2.5, Iquitos.* 📷 ✍

The Allpahuayo-Mishana Reserve is known for its unusually high levels of biodiversity. Covering an area of 142,520 acres (57,677 ha), the reserve is home to flora and fauna found nowhere else. It is a region of diverse soil-types ranging from the remarkable white-sand jungles to clay licks, which are a concentration of minerals deposited by rivers. It was officially recognized as a reserved zone in 1999 making it Peru's only protected white-sand forest.

Bird-watchers are drawn to the 500 species found here, four of which are found only in the reserve – the Allpahuayo antbird, the ancient antwren, the Mishana tyrannulet, and the vibrantly colored pompadour cotinga.

Allpahuayo-Mishana also has a record number of 120 species of reptiles and 83 species of amphibians. About 150 mammal species, including the rare equatorial saki monkey and the Lucifer titi monkey, have also been spotted here. The 65 bat species found here make for the highest bat density in Peru. New plant and insect species are still being discovered as scientists comb through these protected riches that are unique in the Peruvian Amazon. Though easily accessible by bus along the Iquitos-Nauta Road, the infrastructure within the reserve is limited. Visitors should carry water, mosquito repellents, and wear sturdy footwear.

Ucayali River Towns ❹

Road Map C3. Btwn Pucallpa & Iquitos. 🚢 *from Iquitos or Pucallpa.*

For decades, the main water-way linking Iquitos (*see p253*) with the rest of Peru has been along the Río Ucayali from Pucallpa. Two- and three-decked riverboats ply the river between Pucallpa and Iquitos, delivering everything from motorcycles to medical equipment, to the villages and small towns in-between. The riverboats also provide passenger transport to locals, most of whom hang their own hammocks on the second or third deck, while hot, stuffy cabins with a couple of bunk beds are also available for extra charge. Basic on-board meals are also provided on these boats. The boats stop frequently at the many small villages along the river. Passengers in a hurry can get a speed boat for a choppy ride, however, the slow riverboats are much more fun. The trip from Pucallpa to Iquitos, with the current, takes around four days, while the return, against the current, can take as long as six days. The faster *expreso* boats take one or two days to ferry passengers.

The main towns on the route are **Contamaná** and **Requena**, both of which have basic hotel and restaurant facilities. Contamaná, located 267 miles (430 km) from Iquitos, is known for its hot springs and a macaw clay lick that can be reached by car via a 14-mile (22-km) dirt road.

A growing town, Requena lies 100 miles (160 km) from Iquitos. It boasts of a small cathedral and Laguna Avispa, which is at a distance of 5 miles (8 km) by boat. This is a popular spot with the locals for fishing, both with lines and nets, and swimming in the calm, warm lake waters. Bird-watchers enjoy the small Laguna Avispa, not for any rare species, but for chances to observe some of the best-known Amazonian birds in their natural surroundings. Watching long-toed jacanas running speedily over the tops of the water lillies and other aquatic vegetation is a beautiful sight for any bird-lover. Female jacanas mate with several partners, moving on after each laying and

Pompadour cotinga

Harbor at Requena, one of the towns on Río Ucayali

Shoreline forest, lit by sunlight, inside Reserva Nacional Pacaya-Samiria

leaving the males to take on the majority of hatching duties, a feature which is extremely rare among birds.

Reserva Nacional Pacaya-Samiria ❺

Road Map C2. 190 miles (306 km) SW of Iquitos. 🚌 *Tel* 065 223 555. 🛈 *SERNANP, Calle Jorge Chavez 930, Iquitos.* 📷 📋

Lying mainly in the crook of the Ríos Ucayali and Marañón, this 8,031-sq-mile (20,800-sq-km) reserve is Peru's largest. Officially, it is inhabited by almost 450 species of birds, 102 species of mammals, and 256 species of fish, some of which are on the endangered list. This protected wildlife reserve includes jaguars, several species of monkeys, two types of turtles, giant river otters, and the huge paiche fish which, at over 7 ft (2 m) in length, is one of the largest freshwater fish in the world.

Even after the region was declared a reserve in 1982, the Indian and mestizo communities have been allowed to continue living here as before. Today, the 42,000 people living in the reserve, belonging to 94 different communities, survive on hunting, fishing, and gathering.

Entrance to the reserve is not easy for tourists. A paid permit is officially required ahead of time from SERNANP. Tourists are stopped for checking at ranger stations along the rivers, although gun-toting locals are allowed to pass through. The best option is to take a local guide from a small town such as Lagunas, on the Río Huallaga, or join an organized tour from Iquitos and stay at the private Pacaya-Samiria Jungle Lodge on the banks of the Marañón.

A tour boat on the Río Yanuyacu in Reserva Nacional Pacaya-Samiria

Yurimaguas ❻

Road Map C2. 240 miles (390 km) from Iquitos. 🏠 *35,000.* 🚌 *from Tarapoto.* 🚢 ⛪ *Fiesta de la Virgen de las Nieves (Aug 5–15).*

Founded by a Jesuit priest in 1710, the city derives its name from two indigenous groups, the Yoras and the Omaguas. These groups no longer exist though there are reports that some Omaguas still live in the more remote jungle regions.

It remained a tiny outpost until the rubber boom, and the tilework from its early days can be seen along the east end of Avenida Arica. Life in Yurimaguas still revolves around the colorful river port. The frenetic 20th-century growth visible in Iquitos and Pucallpa has passed the town by.

Popularly known as the Pearl of Huallaga, Yurimaguas is the main port on the Río Huallaga. It is the last motor-able point with onward transport possible only by boat or chartered light aircraft. Despite being closer to Iquitos, Yurimaguas has been the forgotten option, while Pucallpa has long been considered the shortest and best route from Lima to the Amazon. Highways from the coast through Tarapoto to Yurimaguas are being paved and improved and locals hope that the city will now become more important.

RIVER DOLPHINS

Two species of dolphin live in the fresh waters of the Amazon. While the smaller grey dolphin (*Sotalia fluviatilis*) is found throughout the Amazon and parts of the Atlantic Coast, the larger pink dolphin (*Inia geoffrensis*) is found only in the Amazon. Predominantly found in northern Peru, dolphins are spotted near tributaries where the merging waters attract fish on which they feed. An ideal place to see the dolphins is in their natural habitat at the Muyuna Amazon Lodge (*see p280*), near Iquitos. Tribal folklore of Peru abounds with stories revolving around the pink dolphin. The stories vary but are united by the common thread that dolphins change into handsome young men.

Pink river dolphin, a species exclusive to the Amazon

Old bridge over Río Mayo near Moyobamba

Moyobamba and Alto Mayo ❼

Road Map C3. 99 miles (160 km) E of Chachapoyas. 🏠 35,000. 🚌 from Chachapoyas. **www**.moyobamba.com

Located on the edge of the Amazon Basin, the small town of Moyobamba was established by the Spaniards soon after the conquest of the region in the 1540s. Despite devastating earthquakes in 1990, 1991, 2001, and 2005, it has recovered and provides good access to the high subtropical jungle. The locals proudly call it the City of Orchids.

Moyobamba is the oldest city in Peru's Amazon region and, according to some, it was Tupac Yupanqui *(see p169)* who penetrated this area and made it a base from which the Incas made incursions into the surrounding areas. The name Moyobamba derives from the Quechua word *muyupampa*, which means a "circular plain."

Located on the upper Río Mayo basin, known as Alto Mayo, Moyobamba's main attractions are essentially water-related. The hot springs, popular with the locals, are just to the south of town and can be reached on foot or by a *motocarro* (a motorcycle rickshaw). Just an hour's drive from Moyobamba are the **Cataratas del Gera**, most popular amongst the many falls in the region.

Tarapoto ❽

Road Map C3. 72 miles (116 km) from Moyobamba. 🏠 100,000. ✈ 🚌 from Moyobamba or Chiclayo. 🚌 🎉 *Fiesta Patronal (mid-Jul)*, *Aniversario de Tarapoto (Aug 20)*. **www**.tarapoto.com

The friendly and bustling town of Tarapoto is the largest and fastest growing city in the Department of San Martín. Located at a height of 1,181 ft (360 m), it is a place for fishing, swimming, and relaxing. Also dubbed as the Land of Waterfalls, it has some of the finest falls in the entire country. The Río Mayo, 19 miles (30 km) away, offers white-water rafting options to adventurous visitors from June to October.

Tarapoteños enjoy a good party, and their festivals feature street dances, folk music, costumed processions, and plenty of food. Among its many sought-after local drinks is *uvachado*, which is made by soaking grapes in a cocktail of sugarcane alcohol, cinnamon, and honey for a month.

Environs

The famous Quechua-speaking hillside town of **Lamas** is located 18 miles (28 km) northwest from Tarapoto. The town is not built on the banks of any river, which is rare in the Amazon jungle. Recovering from the devastation of the 2005 earthquake, the village eagerly welcomes travelers interested in visiting the museum or experiencing the traditional dance, music, and folklore, seeing the thatch and mud-wall architecture, or buying arts and crafts. The colorful annual fiesta is held in late August. Guided tours are available from Tarapoto.

Of the many lakes in this area, the **Lago Sauce** is the most popular. Getting there is half the fun as taxis and minibuses have to cross the Río Huallaga on a balsa raft midway through the 32-mile (52-km) drive. A fish hatchery ensures abundant angling opportunities. Other relaxation comes in the form of boating and swimming. Hotel and camping facilities are available.

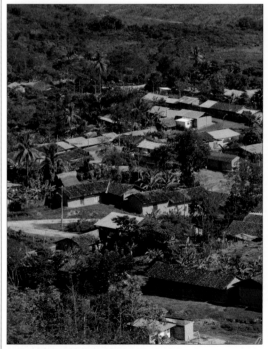

A view of the peaceful town of Lamas near Tarapoto

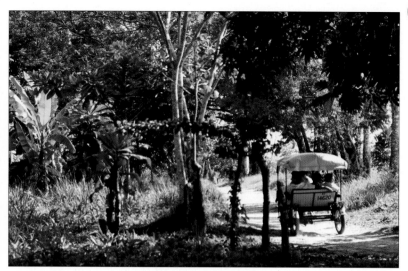

Visitors enjoying a *motocarro* ride through the mud streets around Pucallpa

Pucallpa ⑨

Road Map C3. 178 miles (288 km) NE of Lima. 🚏 *290,000.* ✈ *from Lima & Iquitos.* 🚐 *from Lima.* 🚤 *from Iquitos.* 🎭 *San Juan (Jun 24), Fiestas Regionales (Aug 20–22).* **www**.pucallpa.com

A late-blooming city of the Peruvian Amazon, Pucallpa is now amongst its fastest growing. In 1900, it had a population of just 200. The highway from Lima came in 1930, changing Pucallpa into a major logging center of the country. Recent exploration for oil, gas, and gold has further boosted the city's economy, making Pucallpa the most important port on the Río Ucayali.

Not attractive in the traditional sense, Pucallpa is a city of modern buildings encircled by mud streets. Most travelers move on to nearby Yarinacocha or take a boat for a trip to Iquitos.

For artistically inclined visitors, an essential stop is the gallery in the **Home of Agustín Rivas**, a famous local woodcarver, whose pieces grace many public buildings in the town. Another is **Usko Ayar**, where shaman and painter Pablo Amaringo teaches, works, and exhibits his esoteric and visionary pieces inspired by rainforests.

🏛 **Home of Agustín Rivas**
Tarapaca 861. **Tel** 061 571 834.
🕐 10am–noon, 2–5pm Mon–Sat.

🏛 **Usko Ayar**
Sánchez Cerro 465. **Tel** 061 573 088. 🕐 10am–5pm Mon–Fri.
🌐 **www**.pabloamaringo.com

Yarinacocha ⑩

Road Map C3. 6 miles (10 km) NE of Pucallpa. 🚐 🚐 🚗 *from Pucallpa.*

Just 6 miles (10 km) northeast of downtown Pucallpa, this lovely, tranquil oxbow lake is a world away from city bustle. *Cocha* is the Quechua Indian word for lake, so the locals simply call it Yarinacocha.

Visitors arrive at **Puerto Callao**, a ramshackle lakeside village to the south. It has several basic hotels and many inexpensive restaurants. Worth a visit is the thatched warehouse called Maroti Shobo, which sells renowned Shipibo Indian ceramics with their characteristic geometric designs. This cooperative shop collects handmade pieces from about 40 Shipibo villages of the region.

Boats are readily available for those wanting to see the dolphins in the lake. Trips are organized to visit the verdant

Chullachaqui botanical garden, which includes a 45-minute boat ride followed by a 30-minute hike. Sloths and green iguanas can be spotted here.

Several Shipibo villages can be visited, of which **San Francisco** and **Santa Clara** to the west are the best known. The Shipibo is a matriarchal society and many continue to live traditionally in thatched, open-sided huts that are raised on stilts.

Adventurous overnight expeditions, during which travelers can sleep in Indian huts, can be arranged with the help of local guides. The few lodges offering comfortable accomodation are a short boat ride away.

Sloth climbing a tree in the Chullachaqui botanical garden

Macaws at the clay licks in Reserva de la Biosfera de Manu ▷

Andean spectacled bear can be spotted in Yanachaga Chemillén

Chanchamayo Region ⓫

Road Map C4. 190 miles (305 km) NE of Lima. 👥 *30,000.* 🚌 *from Lima.*

The Yanesha and Ashaninka indigineous groups were the first inhabitants of this region, named for the Río Chanchamayo, when the valley was mainly a cloud forest zone. Since then much of the land has been cleared and the region is now famous for its coffee and fruit plantations. The small towns of **La Merced** and **San Ramón** are excellent bases for visiting the nearby area, which is known for its picturesque landscape. The region is full of rivers, waterfalls, and fruit orchards.

La Merced is the larger of the two towns, with a better choice of restaurants and accommodation. It is the gateway for transportation to Puerto Bermúdez and Oxapampa, and for visiting remote Ashaninka villages such as **Marankiari Bajo**, 16 miles (26 km) from La Merced. The drive to Puerto Bermúdez takes around 8 hours by bus.

Environs

Parque Nacional Yanachaga Chemillén covers an area of 47 sq miles (122 sq km) and protects several ecological zones, including the famous cloud forests of Peru, which are home to the endangered Andean spectacled bear. It has a ranger station 5 miles (8 km) outside Oxapampa and some basic camping areas between Oxapampa and **Pozuzo**.

Pozuzo, settled in 1857 by Austrian and German families, is the real heart of the Teutonic settlement. Reached by a serpentine, unpaved 50-mile (80-km) road which passes through a section of the Chemillén National Park, Pozuzo is surrounded by steep hills and waterfalls. The road is sometimes closed by landslides in the rainy season.

Pozuzo's founding is celebrated with German music, dancing, costumes, and food.

🦋 **Parque Nacional Yanachaga Chemillén**
Tel *063 462 544.* 🏛 *SERNANP, Jr. Pozuzo Cuadra 3 s/n, Oxapampa.* 🔲 *www.sernanp.gob.pe*

Marankiari Bajo
*Carretera tramo vial La Merced a Satipo KM26. **Tel** 063 811 254.* 📷 🎊 *July 25–30.* 🚐 🔲 *www.rcp. net.pe/ashaninka*

Oxapampa ⓬

Road Map C4. 50 miles (80 km) SW of Chanchamayo. 👥 *10,000.* 🚌 🚐 *from Chanchamayo.* **www.** oxapampaonline.com

Calling itself the geographical center of Peru, Oxapampa is a popular logging, ranching, and coffee-growing hub. Founded in 1891 by German settlers from Pozuzo, it has a hint of the Teutonic life in most of its festivals and architecture. Occasional blonde-haired, blue-eyed Peruvians attest to its original heritage. Connected to Chanchamayo by unpaved road, Oxapampa retains a friendly frontier atmosphere, as yet the town is little-visited.

THE ASHANINKA

The Ashaninka is the largest Amazonian indigenous group in Peru, with 55,000 members living in over 200 communities along several central Amazonian rivers. They depend mainly on subsistence agriculture, using age-old slash and burn techniques. Most of them do not speak Spanish and retain a traditional lifestyle. Their recent history is frightful. During the 1980s, the Sendero Luminoso *(see p195)* forcefully recruited Ashaninkas. In turn, the Peruvian army entered Ashaninka lands in pursuit of the guerillas, and the tribespeople

Ashaninkas use native fruits to color their faces

were caught between the two. Since the capture of Sendero leaders in the 1990s, peace has returned to the tribe. They have begun claiming title to their land to protect themselves from incursions by oil and logging companies. Today, several communities have ecotourism projects and welcome visitors who stay in villagers' homes, learn about traditional customs, enjoy local music, and buy crafts. The Albergue Humboldt *(see p281)* hotel in Puerto Bermudez organizes tours to visit Ashaninka communities.

Reserva de la Biosfera de Manu ⑬

This UNESCO World Heritage Site covers almost 7,700 sq miles (20,000 sq km) of the Manu Basin. It drops vertiginously from 1,120 ft (4,000 m) above sea level north of Cusco, through remote cloud forests containing some of the most diverse bird populations on earth, to lowland rainforests which are home to various Indian groups and a proliferation of jungle flora and fauna. The reserve has

Sulphur butterfly on an orchid

three zones. Over 80 percent of the reserve lies in the intangible zone, the abode of natives who have almost no contact with the outside world; travelers are prohibited. The reserved zone allows tourism *(see p309)* and camping on beaches is permitted with authorized guides. The multiple use zone is where the one road from the highlands enters, and has several villages and cloud forest lodges.

CLOUD FOREST

The wide-ranging elevations create ideal environments for birds and new species are discovered here often. Mixed feeding flocks of dozens of bird species are a highlight and hikers on precipitous trails are rewarded with sightings of woolly monkeys and brown capuchins.

Toucans *live in groups and are mainly fruit eaters but may use their bill against small prey.*

Paradise tanager *is a beautiful, bright bird popular for its seven-colored plumage.*

Woolly monkeys *live in groups and have a prehensile tail which can be used to hold objects.*

Giant katydid *is one of the thouands of insect species found in Manu.*

RESERVED ZONE

This is the relatively flat rainforest of the Río Manu. Canopy platforms and towers are available for visitors, and over a dozen monkey species roam the forests here. Meandering in huge curves, the river sometimes leaves behind oxbow lakes known as cochas.

Hoatzins *and horned screamers, both known for their ornate head plumes, live around oxbow lakes.*

Oxbow lakes are the haunt of the rare giant river otters and some spectacular waterbirds.

Río Manu flows across the reserve which is home to a vast variety of flora and fauna.

Ríos Tambopata and Madre de Dios Area ⑭

The beautiful rivers, pristine lakes, and primary rainforests of southeastern Peru are teeming with wildlife. This is the most biodiverse area of Peru's Amazon and has the highest concentration of jungle lodges, staffed by naturalist guides and reached only by river. Most of the land south of Río Madre de Dios is protected by national parks. The vibrant frontier city of Puerto Maldonado sits conveniently at the confluence of the Madre de Dios and Tambopata rivers, and is the best base for visiting the area. Most visitors reach Puerto Maldonado on daily flights from Cusco. However, there is also an unpaved 310-mile (500-km) road which takes two to six days from Cusco depending on the season.

Barred leaf frog on stem

A family of capybaras, the world's largest rodents

PERU

Río Madre de Dios

Río Inambari

Laberinto

26B

Río Carama o Malinowski

Mazuco

TAMBOPATA NATIONAL RESERVE

Río Tambopata

★ **Reserva Nacional Tambopata**
The reserve has many lodges and some of the largest clay licks. With over 600 species of birds, 1,200 species of butterflies, and many mammals, it provides excellent access to the rainforest.

CARLOS FITZCARRALD (1862–97)

Fitzcarrald made a fortune during the rubber boom in the 1880s. He discovered that the Ucayali and Madre de Dios river basins were separated by a short finger of the Andean foothills. Enslaving hundreds of indigenous people, he moved a steamship piece by piece over the isthmus, and traveled down Madre de Dios past what would later become Puerto Maldonado. Werner Herzog's film, *Fitzcarraldo* was inspired by his story.

Scene from the film *Fitzcarraldo* (1982)

STAR SIGHTS

★ Reserva Nacional Tambopata

★ Puerto Maldonado

★ Clay Licks

★ **Puerto Maldonado**
After the rubber boom, this town with a population of 40,000, turned to logging, rainforest agriculture, and gold panning. The market has Brazil nuts, coffee, and tropical fruits on sale. A 98 ft- (30 m-) high tower provides views of the ubiquitous corrugated-metal roofed buildings.

VISITORS' CHECKLIST

Road Map E5. 37 miles (60 km) SW from Puerto Maldonado. ✕ from Lima. 🚌 from Cusco. 🚤 from Puerto Maldonado. 🛏 in Puerto Maldonado. ⛺ organized through tour operators.

Las Piedras

(26B)

Lago Valencia

Puerto Maldonado

Lago Sandoval

nfierno

Río Heath

BAHUAJA-SONENE NATIONAL PARK

opata

Río Madre de Dios flows from the highlands near Manu Biosphere Reserve into Bolivia. A major trade route, it has a lot of traffic, gold dredging, and settlements.

Lago Sandoval
Surrounded by towering palms, this lake is home to the endangered giant river otters. One-day trips are possible.

BOLIVIA

Río Heath is slowly being discovered and is becoming popular for ecotourism.

Río Tambopata is a tributary of Río Madre de Dios. The river is most likely to yield wildlife sightings.

KEY

✕	Domestic airport
🚤	Riverboat boarding point
▬	Minor road
▬ ▬	Park boundary
▬ ▪	International border

★ **Clay Licks**
Riverside mud cliffs with abnormally high salt content attract hundreds of parrots and macaws who nibble on the clay to obtain essential minerals. The brilliantly colored macaws and parrots make it a spectacular sight indeed.

TRAVELERS' NEEDS

WHERE TO STAY 266–281

WHERE TO EAT 282–301

SHOPPING IN PERU 302–305

OUTDOOR ACTIVITIES 306–311

SPECIALIZED HOLIDAYS 312–313

WHERE TO STAY

Despite Peru's large variety of archaeological and natural treasures, it's only in the last ten years that tourists have begun visiting the country in considerable numbers. Consequently, there's no shortage of good quality accommodation but the standard can fluctuate, especially in more remote areas. Price is not always

Signage at a hotel in Peru

a reliable indicator of quality or facilities. Hotels are usually the best bet; *hostales* have fewer facilities and campgrounds exist solely on treks. Room rates soar during local festivals, national holidays, and the high season, when advance bookings are a good idea as demand is huge. For detailed listings refer to pages 270–81.

A double room at the Sheraton Lima *(see p270)*

BOOKING

It is advisable to book your accommodation well ahead of your visit, especially if you are traveling during the high season from June to August. In cities such as Cusco, Lima, Arequipa, and Trujillo it is difficult to get reservations during the festivals of Inti

Raymi, Semana Santa *(see p194)*, and Fiestas Patrias when demand is very high.

If you have made the reservations using the Internet, do expect to pay for the privilege. Often, walk-in rates are cheaper, however, a reservation removes the need to trudge unknown streets trailing heavy bags.

HOTEL CHAINS

International chains such as the **Swissôtel**, **Sheraton**, Hilton, and **Marriott**, have properties in Lima, with tariffs in the high-end range. Restaurants, bars, swimming pools, and fitness centers are all standard. Some, such as the Sheraton and Marriott, also have casinos.

The **Orient Express Hotels** group operates five deluxe hotels in Peru – the Miraflores Park in Lima *(see p271)*, one in the heart of the Colca Canyon, one in the Sacred Valley, the Monasterio in Cusco, and the Sanctuary Lodge in Machu Picchu; the latter garners a high room tariff more for its position as the only accommodation on the mountain, rather than for its facilities. Top-end hotels charge an 18 percent sales tax on their room rates, but they

Mountains form the backdrop to the Sanctuary Lodge, Machu Picchu *(see p275)*

◁ Local women selling handicrafts at the Cruz del Condor, Canyon Country

A well-equipped bathroom, Casa Andina Private Collection *(see p273)*

will refund this to foreigners who can prove that they live outside Peru. Some charge a 13 percent service tax also.

Generally, apart from the Novotel in Cusco, regional cities are the domain of hotel chains such as **Casa Andina** and **Libertador**, as well as **Sonesta Posada del Inca**, all of which run mid-level and more expensive properties. The Casa Andina Private Collection properties, in Cusco, the Sacred Valley, Puno, and on Lake Titicaca's Suasi Island, are the upmarket version of their hotels, while the Libertador's more exclusive properties, in Puno, Arequipa, and Cusco are linked with the Summit luxury hotels chain. They also have hotels in Lima.

Hotel logo painted on tiles

MID-RANGE ACCOMMODATION

Standards do vary and despite ritzy reception areas, rooms in these hotels can sometimes be a letdown in comparison to their European, Asian, or North American counterparts. Private bathrooms, cable TV, minibars, telephones, and in warmer climates, fans or air conditioning are normally the rule, although remote jungle lodges may be the exception.

Lima, Cusco, and Arequipa have a wide range of options available. In remote areas, the best hotel in town may bill itself as a four- or five-star but don't be surprised if the facilities are just mid- to low-range.

BUDGET ACCOMMODATION

There are innumerable inexpensive hotels in towns across Peru, but before you commit yourself, always ask to see the room. That way you can avoid a room on the noisiest street in town or the windowless one. While 24-hour hot and cold water is required by law for *hostales* and hotels from one star up, the supply of hot water is often limited. Some turn it on only at part-icular times of the day, or may need notice to do so. Ask before you check in. You may also be asked to place toilet paper in a basket to avoid blocking the drain.

A *hostal* is not the same as a hostel in English. Instead, it denotes a small hotel or inn that is usually cheaper than a hotel and has fewer facilities. By law, *hostales* must have no less than six rooms.

The word *albergue* was traditionally used to describe shelters, such as those run by a religious order, or a simple guesthouse, but today the term encompasses a range of accommodation options in rural Peru. From coastal cabanas to smart hotels, their uniting feature is their local ambience and location.

Conventional *albergues*, similar to bed-and-breakfasts, still exist in Peru. Those that meet the minimal government regulations imposed upon them – such as separate toilet for guests or emergency exits – are permitted to display a sign. Economical *pensiones* and *hospedajes* (guesthouses) are found throughout the major cities and towns. Often they do not display signs but rely on word of mouth.

YOUTH HOSTELS

Peru's more than 30 youth hostels offer accommodation with dormitory, single, twin or *matrimonial* (double rooms), some with private bathrooms. They usually have a bar, café, kitchen, and many have a computer with Internet access. The **Asociación Peruana de Albergues Turísticos Juveniles** (Peruvian Association of Youth Hostels) has information on hostels.

La Gruta Hotel, Arequipa *(see p273)*

Machu Picchu Pueblo Eco, Inca Heartland (see p274)

JUNGLE AND ECO LODGES

There are a range of options at varying prices in Peru's jungles, and advance reservations are recommended. River transport is included as lodges are usually a few hours upriver; some tours and guides are also part of the package. Most lodges have offices in the capital city of Lima, and some in Madre de Dios have offices in the beautiful city of Cusco.

Ceiba Tops, run by **Explorama**, is more of a resort than a lodge. Located near Iquitos, it has luxury rooms with screened windows, satellite TV, swimming pool, and large bathrooms with hot showers, while the Wasai Maldonado Lodge in Puerto Maldonado *(see p281)* offers stilted wooden bungalows and a fine jungle introduction on the Río Madre de Dios. Rustic options abound around Madre de Dios, with palm-thatched roofs, cold water, mosquito nets, and kerosene lanterns or candles. The focus here is on nature and wildlife, rather than luxury.

In keeping with government regulations, ecolodges must be constructed of natural material from the area. They should be built in harmony with the environment and preferably use natural energy sources such as solar or wind.

HOMESTAYS

Travelers can stay in the homes of villagers on the islands of Taquile, Amantani, and Anapia on Lake Titicaca *(see p147)* for a small price. Conditions, however, are no-frills. **All Ways Travel**, which promotes social development with these communities, organizes stays on the islands. Vicos, near Huaraz, is the first Peruvian community to own the title to their lands. Ten families host travelers and tourists who then live and work alongside locals for stays of between two to five days. You can book your stay with them through **Centro Yachaqui Wayi**.

Some families in Cusco also offer homestay programs. Contact **Homestay in Cusco** for details.

SPECIALIST HOLIDAYS

Many tour operators who concentrate on holidays in Peru also offer specialist tours *(see pp311–12)* for those interested in a particular activity. Trekking, rafting, mountain-biking, bird-watching, butterfly-watching, culinary tours, camping high up in the Andes as well as in the Amazon Basin, and jungle trips to Iquitos in the north or Manu in the south, are some of the options. Several jungle tour operators have interests in lodges and tours are all-inclusive – food, lodging, guide. For example, **Inkanatura Travel** is the profit-making branch of the Peru Verde or Green Peru conservation program, which part-owns Manu Wildlife Centre *(see p261)*.

Trekkers camping during their journey through the Cordillera Blanca

Inner courtyard, Hotel Monasterio, Cusco *(see p275)*

PRICES

Hotel rates in Lima and other high tourist traffic areas, such as Cusco and Iquitos, are more expensive than in the rest of Peru. Whatever the star rating of a hotel, prices will rise in the peak season from June to September and for important festivals such as Inti Raymi in Cusco, Easter Week in Ayacucho, or national holidays such as Fiestas Patrias.

GRADING

Peruvian hotels are graded using the international star system, however, the standards within a rating can vary significantly. Establishments are awarded stars on the basis of meeting certain criteria such as providing color TV, parking, washing, and ironing services, rather than for the levels of luxury they provide.

The Peruvian government requires signage to be put up to identify accommodation types: H for hotel, Hs for *hostal*, R for resort located in a holiday area, such as on a beach or river, AH for Apart Hotel with kitchen facilities, E for ecolodge which promotes ecotourism, and A for *albergue*.

DISABLED TRAVELERS

Only the more upmarket, modern or recently renovated hotels cater to travelers with disabilities, and most of these are located in Lima, Cusco, Trujillo, Iquitos, and Aguas Calientes. A few jungle lodges have facilities for disabled clients. Telephones for hearing impaired travelers are almost unknown in Peru. However, some hotels are moving to instal visual alarms and expand facilities for disabled clients. The hotel staff, in general, will do whatever is possible to assist any disabled clients.

DIRECTORY

HOTELS

Casa Andina
Tel 86 220 4434
(toll-free US),
888 350 6263
(toll-free Canada),
08 082 343 805
(toll-free UK).
www.casa-andina.com

Libertador
www.libertador.com.pe

Marriott
Tel 01 217 7000.
www.marriott.com

Orient Express
Tel 800 237 1236
(toll-free USA & Canada),
20 7960 0500 (UK).
www.orient-express.com

Sheraton
Tel 01 315 5022.
www.sheraton.com.pe

Sonesta Posada del Inca
www.sonesta.com/
corporate/south-america.
asp

Swissôtel
Tel 01 611 4400.
http://lima.swissotel.com

YOUTH HOSTELS

Asociación Peruana de Albergues Turísticos Juveniles
Avenida Casimiro Ulloa 328, San Antonio, Miraflores. **Map** 4 C1.
Tel 01 446 5488. www.
hostellingperu.com.pe

JUNGLE AND ECO LODGES

Explorama
Tel 065 252 530, 1800 707 5275 (toll-free US, Canada).
www.explorama.com

Inkaterra
Tel 1 800 442 5042
(US and Canada),
0 808 101 2224 (UK),
610 0410 (Lima).
www.inkaterra.com

HOMESTAYS

All Ways Travel
Casa de Corregidor,
Calle Duestua 576,
Puno.
Tel 051 353 979.
www.titicacaperu.com

Centro Yachaqui Wayi (Vicos)
Jr. Gabino Uribe 650, Huaraz.
Tel 043 422 6538.
www.yachaquiwayi.org

Homestay in Cusco
Tel 084 242 562.
www.homestayincusco.com

SPECIALIST HOLIDAYS

Inkanatura Travel
Manuel Bañon 461,
San Isidro, Lima.
Map 2 C2.
Tel 01 440 2022 /
422 8114.
www.inkanatura.com

Choosing a Hotel

Most of the hotels and resorts in this guide have been selected across a wide price range for facilities, good value, and location. The prices listed are those charged by the hotel, although discounts may be available through agencies. The hotels are listed by area. For map references for Lima, see pages 104–111.

LIMA

BARRANCO The Point
Malecón Junín 300 **Tel** *01 247 7997* **Rooms** *11*   **Map** *4 C4*

With the motto "for backpackers by backpackers," The Point is known for its cheery, social atmosphere, weekly barbecues, and get-togethers in the guests-only Pointless Bar. It has dorms as well as private rooms with shared bathrooms. **www.thepointhostels.com**

BARRANCO Hospedaje California
Martinez de Pinillos 129 **Tel** *01 477 0772* **Rooms** *7*

Self-contained apartments in a 1906 *casona*, noted for its architectural restoration. High ceilings, original woodwork, and well-equipped rooms with queen-size beds, full bathrooms, and kitchen facilities. The hotel has a games and billiards room and ample tiled patio. Cheaper rates for long-term stays. **www.hospedajecalifornia.com**

BARRANCO Casa Victor Delfín
Calle Domeyer 366 **Tel** *01 247 5522* **Rooms** *5*   **Map** *5 D4*

The former home of Peruvian sculptor Victor Delfín *(see p79)* is now a super stylish bed-and-breakfast. Delfín's exotic artworks, however, still adorn the house and clifftop garden with its sea views. Rooms are white and airy, and very comfortable. **www.secondhomeperu.com**

CENTRAL LIMA Hotel Kamana
Jirón Camaná 547 **Tel** *01 426 7204* **Rooms** *42*   **Map** *1 E1*

Within walking distance of the city's historical churches, Government Palace, and cathedral, the Hotel Kamana provides spacious rooms with private bathrooms. Facilities include a snack bar, 24-hour room service, laundry service, and Wi-Fi. Breakfast is included. The friendly staff can arrange taxi pick-ups. **www.hotelkamana.com**

CENTRAL LIMA Hotel España
Jirón Azangaro 105 **Tel** *01 427 9196* **Rooms** *22*   **Map** *1 F2*

The Hotel España is a 19th-century home full of paintings, plants, sculptures, and character. The rooftop garden is home to tortoises and birds. Next to San Francisco Convent, it has dorms and private rooms with shared bathrooms. Rooms are basic but snug, although sometimes noisy. **www.hotelespanaperu.com**

CENTRAL LIMA Hotel Maury
Jirón Ucayali 201 **Tel** *01 428 8188* **Rooms** *76*   **Map** *1 F1*

Famed as the hotel in which the potent pisco sour *(see p289)*, the most popular drink of Peru, was invented, Hotel Maury offers clean, comfortable rooms with free Wi-Fi, just a block away from Plaza de Armas. The restaurant serves international cuisine and an American-style breakfast.

CENTRAL LIMA Gran Hotel Bolívar
Jirón de la Unión 958 **Tel** *01 619 7171* **Rooms** *99*   **Map** *1 E2*

Built in 1924, the venerable Bolívar stands guard over Plaza San Martín. Rooms retain an old-world grandeur, and the Presidential Suite, despite its name, is a bargain. There's a stately old bar famed for its pisco sour, and a domed stained-glass rotunda that is perfect for afternoon tea. **www.granhotelbolivar.com.pe**

CENTRAL LIMA Sheraton Lima
Paseo de la Republica 170 **Tel** *01 315 5000* **Rooms** *431*   **Map** *1 E3*

Sitting at the entrance of Lima's historic center, the Sheraton is the only modern luxury hotel in the downtown area. Rooms have city views and all the modern comforts. Folkloric shows are held on Friday nights. The hotel provides a free shuttle service to Miraflores. **www.sheraton.com/lima**

MIRAFLORES Hostal El Patio
Diez Canseco 341 **Tel** *01 444 2107* **Rooms** *17*   **Map** *4 B1*

All rooms of this urbane *hostal*, in the heart of Miraflores, open on to a delightful plant-filled patio with a tinkling fountain. Rooms are charming, spotless, and come with full baths. Suites comprise separate living room and bedroom, while mini suites have a kitchenette. **www.hostalelpatio.net**

Key to Symbols *see back cover flap*

MIRAFLORES Pariwana Backpacker Hostel

Av. Larco 189 **Tel** *01 241 3701* **Rooms** *19*

Map 4 B1

Run by the team from the ever popular Loki in Cusco *(see p274)*, this super convivial *hostal* opposite Parque Kennedy *(see p78)* has an expansive, sun-filled rooftop terrace, dorms, and private rooms with top-notch bathrooms, TV room, free Internet, and a restaurant/bar in which a nightly get-to-know-you dinner is held. **www.lokihostel.com**

MIRAFLORES Hostal Torreblanca

Av. José Pardo 1453 **Tel** *01 447 0142* **Rooms** *30*

Map 4 B1

Only 328 ft (100 m) from Lima's coastline, Colonial-style Torreblanca has spacious, carpeted rooms, some with fireplaces and wooden ceiling beams, all with cable TV. The *hostal* also offers a 30-day free baggage storage service. The on-site restaurant serves an array of traditional Peruvian dishes. **www.torreblancaperu.com**

MIRAFLORES Hotel Antigua

Av. Grau 350 **Tel** *01 241 6116* **Rooms** *35*

Map 4 A1

This vibrant pink mansion, built in 1918, has rooms with handcrafted furniture, Peruvian art and antiques, and deluxe baths with Colonial tiles and brass fittings. Suites contain Jacuzzis and kitchenettes. It has an elegant garden and balconies, cable TV, and a gym. **www.peru-hotels-inns.com**

MIRAFLORES NM Lima Hotel

Av. Pardo y Aliaga 300 **Tel** *01 612 1000* **Rooms** *68*

Map 2 C4

Classy, contemporary hotel within easy walking distance of the ancient Huaca Pucllana *(see pp80–81)* adobe pyramid, and the pretty Bosque El Olivar or olive grove *(see p83)*. The hotel offers a creative, calm atmosphere, and a sunny outdoor patio. **www.nmlimahotel.com**

MIRAFLORES Sol de Oro Apart Hotel

Calle San Martín 305 **Tel** *01 610 7000* **Rooms** *83*

Map 4 B2

This modern five-star Apart Hotel has one- and two-room suites with kitchen facilities, making it ideal for anyone planning a long stay. The complex also houses a gym, sauna, and Turkish bath, along with a business center. Computer rental can be organized. **www.soldeoro.com.pe**

MIRAFLORES JW Marriott

Malecón de la Reserva 615 **Tel** *01 217 7000* **Rooms** *300*

Map 4 B2

Set on the cliffs of Miraflores, opposite Larcomar shopping center *(see p79)*, the glass-fronted Marriott has panoramic ocean views from each of its five-star rooms. The higher you go, the better it gets. It also offers an open-air tennis court and a swimming pool. **www.marriott.com.pe**

MIRAFLORES Miraflores Park

Malecón de la Reserva 1035 **Tel** *01 610 4000* **Rooms** *82*

Map 4 B2

The cost of a standard room at this luxury hotel starts at more than 1,000 neuvo sols and climbs; prices befitting a member of the Orient Express group. Set in a park overlooking the Pacific, almost all rooms enjoy an ocean view. Great vistas, too, from the rooftop pool. **www.mira-park.com**

SAN ISIDRO El Olivar

Pancho Fierro 194 **Tel** *01 712 6000* **Rooms** *134*

Map 2 C3

El Olivar is located just across from Lima's centuries-old olive grove. Rooms can be a little ordinary so be sure to ask for one overlooking the grove. The indoor and outdoor pools on the rooftop have superb views. The restaurant draws rave reviews but the lobby could do with a spruce-up. **www.sonesta.com/peru_lima/**

SAN ISIDRO Foresta Hotel & Suites

Av. Libertadores 490 **Tel** *01 630 0000* **Rooms** *50*

Map 2 C3

Located in a mainly residential area of San Isidro and just 10 minutes away from the historical center of Lima, the Foresta is renowned for its friendly service. Rooms are modern, clean, and practical. Suites have kitchenettes. The third floor is non-smoking. **www.foresta-hotel.pe**

SAN ISIDRO Country Club

Calle Los Eucaliptos 590 **Tel** *01 611 9000* **Rooms** *75*

Map 2 A3

Built in 1927, this deluxe hacienda-style hotel boasts antique furnishings, Colonial paintings on loan from the Museo Pedro de Osma *(see p90)*, and a lobby crowned with a stained-glass dome. Befitting its name, it looks onto Lima's most exclusive golf course. Rooms are plush with marble bathrooms. **www.hotelcountry.com**

SAN ISIDRO Los Delfines

Calle Los Eucaliptos 555 **Tel** *01 215 7000* **Rooms** *198*

Map 2 A3

Two important long-term guests – Yaku and Wayra who live in a rather restricted pool area – are responsible for the hotel's name: The Dolphins. Guests can watch their underwater antics from the groovy Oceanus Lounge, or above surface from the hotel lobby. **www.losdelfineshotel.com**

SAN ISIDRO Swissôtel Lima

Vía Central 150, Centro Empresarial Real **Tel** *01 611 4400* **Rooms** *244*

Map 2 B3

This elegant, modern hotel in the heart of Lima's business district has a spa, sauna, indoor pool, and beauty salon. Rooms are equipped with marble baths and high-speed Internet, the latter making it a favorite with business travelers. **lima.swissotel.com**

THE SOUTHERN COAST

CHINCHA ALTA Wakama
Panamerican Highway South, KM178.5 **Tel** *998 386 154* **Rooms** *20*
Road map *C5*

Beach lovers will swoon over these rustic bamboo and eucalyptus bungalows with palm thatched roofs and uninterrupted views of lapping ocean waves. There is also bird-watching, mountain-biking, horse-riding, games for children, massages, Afro-Peruano shows, and hammocks for lazing the day away. **www.wakamaecoplaya.com**

HUACACHINA Casa de Arena
Av. Angela de Perotti s/n **Tel** *034 215 439* **Rooms** *30*
Road map *C5*

This lively *hostal* is popular with international backpackers intent on surfing the sands. There are free sand-boarding lessons, dune-buggy tours, free massages, a volleyball court, and regular evening barbecues. Staff can also organize pisco tasting tours. **www.globehostels.com/arena/**

HUACACHINA Hostería Suiza
Malecon Huacachina **Tel** *056 238 762* **Rooms** *22*
Road map *C5*

Hostería Suiza is run by a local woman who happens to be the daughter of Swiss hoteliers. The rooms are simply and cheerfully decorated. A shady verandah overlooks the pool and there are wonderful views of the lagoon from the breakfast room. **www.hosteriasuiza.com.pe**

ICA Hotel Sol de Ica
Calle Lima 265 **Tel** *056 218 931*
Road map *C5*

The modern building, a former state tourism hotel, has been decorated with country touches to make it a very pleasant place, with additional grounds for gardens and a swimming pool. Rates include a buffet breakfast and entry to the sauna. **www.hotelsoldeica.com**

ICA Las Dunas
Av. La Angostura 400 **Tel** *056 256 224* **Rooms** *106*
Road map *C5*

Set right in the middle of sand dunes, this hotel has tennis courts, a 121-ft (37-m) waterslide, a small golf course, horse-riding and, of course, sand-board rental. Rooms have cooling red tile floors and ceiling fans. Flights over the Nazca Lines *(see pp126–7)* are available from the airport next door. **www.lasdunashotel.com**

NAZCA Hotel Alegria
Calle Lima 168 **Tel** *056 522 702* **Rooms** *43*
Road map *C5*

Just five minutes' from the airport, this hotel has easy access to all Nazca attractions. Rooms are clean and comfortable, some have fans, others have air conditioning. Prices include airport or bus transfer. There is Internet access, an on-site travel agency, plus a bag minding service for non-guests. **www.nazcaperu.com**

NAZCA Hotel Majoro
Panamerican Highway South, KM452, Vista Alegre **Tel** *056 522 490* **Rooms** *70*
Road map *C5*

A convent built in 1698 by Augustine monks, it became privately owned in 1910 and has been fully renovated. The hotel includes 75 acres (31 ha) of grounds, a swimming pool, and access to sand-boarding, dune-buggy rides, and flights over the Nazca Lines. **www.hotelmajoro.com/hotel.html**

NAZCA Casa Andina
Jirón Bolognesi 367 **Tel** *056 523 563* **Rooms** *60*
Road map *C5*

Located just one block from the main plaza, the Casa Andina offers all the mod-cons, including cable TV, comfortable beds, swimming pool, sun-bathing terrace, and Internet access, along with a number of non-smoking rooms. **www.casa-andina.com**

NAZCA Nazca Lines Hotel
Jirón Bolognesi s/n **Tel** *056 522 293* **Rooms** *78*
Road map *C5*

This white hacienda with palm-shaded pools offers an ideal escape from dusty plains. The hotel's Maria Reiche planetarium, run by the Instituto Peruano de Astronomia, presents a talk about the Nazca Lines and starry night skies most evenings. **reservas@derrama.org.pe**

NAZCA Hotel Cantayo Spa and Resort
Nazca **Tel** *056 522 264* **Rooms** *40*
Road map *C5*

Rising from the ruins of an old hacienda (original floor tiles and arches remain), this is a spiritual retreat-cum-resort spa. Rooms have all the creature comforts, including king-size beds with alpaca wool blankets, but no TV. Yoga and meditation, horse-riding, massages, sand-boarding, and 4WD safaris are offered. **www.hotelcantayo.com**

PARACAS El Mirador
Carretera a Paracas, KM20 **Tel** *056 545 086* **Rooms** *35*
Road map *C5*

Perched on Paracas Bay, El Mirador is ideally positioned for organizing boat trips to the Ballestas Islands *(see p120)* as well as the Paracas National Reserve *(see p123)*. The rooms are comfortable and have great views of the garden, the pool or the boats and bay. **www.elmiradorhotel.com**

CANYON COUNTRY

AREQUIPA Colonial House Inn

Calle Puente Grau 114 **Tel** 054 223 533 **Rooms** 12   **Road map** D6

This sprawling centuries-old house has a reputation for having some of the most helpful staff around. Rooms are rustic and spacious, and there is a great rooftop terrace for breakfast. It also provides a library and book exchange, and common sitting room with Internet access. **www.colonialhouseinn-arequipa.com**

AREQUIPA La Casa de Melgar

Calle Melgar 108 **Tel** 054 222 459 **Rooms** 30   **Road map** D6

With its thick *sillar* walls and vaulted ceilings, this was home to Arequipa's bishop in the 19th century. Rooms today have a funky monastic feel, comprising wooden chairs, dressers, and corner closets. It has three indoor patios, a common TV room, and a cosy café. **www.lacasademelgar.com**

AREQUIPA La Gruta Hotel

Calle la Gruta 304, Selva Alegre **Tel** 054 224 631 **Rooms** 12   **Road map** D6

All rooms in this 1970s building have large windows overlooking the leafy garden, plus cable TV and Wi-Fi Internet. Suites have a fireplace and private access to the garden. Airport transfer and breakfast are included in the room tariff. The staff is friendly and helpful. **www.lagrutahotel.com**

AREQUIPA Sonesta Posada del Inca

Portal de Flores 116 **Tel** 054 215 530 **Rooms** 58   **Road map** D6

The hotel's privileged location on the main plaza means that it is within minutes of the city's major sights. Rooms are modern and have a small interior patio. Lunch and dinner are served on the balcony which looks out on to one of the prettiest plazas in Peru. **www.sonesta.com**

AREQUIPA Hotel Libertador

Plaza Bolivar s/n, Selva Alegre **Tel** 054 215 110 **Rooms** 88   **Road map** D6

Arequipa's only five-star hotel is housed in a Republican-style building erected in the 1940s. Rooms are spacious, with dark wood furniture and huge bathrooms. There is an ample garden as well as outdoor pool and playground. Offers an excellent view of the three volcanoes that surround the city. **www.libertador.com.pe**

CHUCUITO Taypikala Hotel

Panamericana Sur, KM18 **Tel** 054 355 887 **Rooms** 49   **Road map** E6

Just 15 minutes from Puno, on the shores of Lake Titicaca, this roadside hotel festooned with jagged faux rocks and models of condors and pumas is impossible to miss. There are lake views from the garden, terrace and some rooms, while other rooms have garden vistas. All feature copies of local rock art. **www.taypikala.com**

COLCA CANYON La Casa de Mamayacchi

Arequipa s/n, Coporaque **Tel** 054 241 206 **Rooms** 25   **Road map** D6

Located in the tiny village of Coporaque, famed as the place where an Inca emperor built a house entirely of copper for his wife, this charming lodge has superb views of the canyon's volcanoes. The lounge area with its roaring log fire is the perfect spot to curl up with a book. **www.lacasademamayacchi.com**

COLCA CANYON Las Casitas del Colca

Carretera Yanque s/n **Tel** 01 610 8300 / 054 959 672 480 **Rooms** 20   **Road map** D6

The 20 spacious *casitas* in this luxury eco-lodge have private terraces with a hot tub and views over the Colca Canyon. There is a spa and four massage rooms. Treks, horse-riding, and visits to see soaring condors are also possible. Solar panels power the hot water on this estate. **www.lascasitasdelcolca.com.pe**

ISLA SUASI Casa Andina Private Collection

Isla Suasi **Tel** 01 213 9739 (Lima) **Rooms** 24   **Road map** E6

Built of local stone, adobe, and *totora* reed, the hotel has the small island of Suasi all to itself. All rooms have views of Lake Titicaca. The two-room Andean Cottage boasts stone fireplaces, as well as a private beach, pier, and terraces. Canoeing and trekking facilities are available. **www.casa-andina.com**

LAMPA La Casona de Lampa

Jirón Tarapaca 271 **Tel** 054 345 844 **Rooms** 10   **Road map** E5

Set in the Plaza de Armas of the pink city of Lampa, the 300-year-old *casona* has been home to the Frisancho family for 170 years. Rooms are clean and simple with Colonial flourishes. The hotel has sun-drenched patios and a communal sitting room. **http://espanol.geocities.com/lacasonalampa**

PUNO Hotel Arizona

Jirón Ancash 333 **Tel** 051 368 355 **Rooms** 8   **Road map** E6

Set in a modern building with a striking green façade, this friendly hotel is a backpacker's delight. Rooms are clean, comfortable, quiet and secure, and the owners are flexible when it comes to rates. The hotel provides daily airport pick-ups. **hostal.arizona@hotmail.com**

PUNO Plaza Mayor Hostal

Jirón Deustua 342 **Tel** *051 513 9237* **Rooms** *34* · **Road map** *E6*

Roomy modern bathrooms and box-spring beds with chintzy bedspreads guarantee a good night's sleep after a day on the lake. As it is right in the center of town it can be noisy, so light sleepers should ask for a room away from the main road. Free pick-up from bus station. **www.plazamayorhotel.com**

PUNO Sonesta Posada del Inca

Sesquicentario 610, Sector Huaje **Tel** *051 364 111* **Rooms** *62* · **Road map** *E6*

Just 3 miles (5 km) from the main plaza, this hotel nestling on the shores of Lake Titicaca has modern facilities and rooms with a view. The Yavari, the lake's oldest steamship-turned-museum, is berthed just outside in Puno Bay with access provided by a 131-ft- (40-m-) pontoon. The captain happily gives tours. **www.sonestaperu.com**

PUNO Hotel Libertador

Isla Esteves **Tel** *051 367 780* **Rooms** *123* · **Road map** *E6*

All rooms in this expansive hotel, set on its own island, have views over Lake Titicaca. The Libertador has all the comforts expected of a five-star hotel, with prices to match. A walk leads down to the water's edge, where a herd of alpacas can often be found grazing. The hotel also has a private dock. **wwww.libertador.com.pe**

THE INCA HEARTLAND

AGUAS CALIENTES Machu Picchu Pueblo Eco

Aguas Calientes Train Station **Tel** *084 211 122/211 123* **Rooms** *86* · **Road map** *D5*

Nestled amid a rainforest, the habitat of remarkable wild orchids and vibrant hummingbirds, this is the most elegant eco option around. Rooms are stylishly rustic, many with fire places, all with pristine white sheets and organic bathroom goodies. Nature walks with expert guides can be arranged. **www.inkaterra.com**

CUSCO Casa Grande

Santa Catalina Ancha 353 **Tel** *084 264 156* **Rooms** *21* · **Road map** *D5*

Just two minutes walk from the Plaza de Armas, this charming courtyard hotel is the epitome of cheap and cheerful. The staff almost bend over backwards to help. Visitors need to pay a little more for rooms with bathrooms on the upper floor. Rooms downstairs have shared bathrooms and less sunlight.

CUSCO Loki Hostel

Cuesta Santa Ana 601 **Tel** *084 243 705* **Rooms** *42* · **Road map** *D5*

Housed in a restored 450-year-old house, affable Loki is run by four backpackers who fell in love with Peru. Some five blocks from the main plaza, it has a bar, kitchen, courtyards, dorms and private rooms, Internet access, and a reputation as a great place to meet people. Breakfast until 1pm is an added attraction. **www.lokihostel.com**

CUSCO Amaru Hostal

Cuesta San Blas 541 **Tel** *084 223 521* **Rooms** *27* · **Road map** *D5*

Situated in the artists' neighborhood of San Blas, this Colonial townhouse offers panoramic city views. Rooms are clean with rustic furniture and polished wooden floors. There is a cheery café, TV room, library with book exchange, and sun-filled garden. **www.amaruhostal.com**

CUSCO Los Aticos Pardo

Av. Pardo 675 **Tel** *084 231 710* **Rooms** *5* · **Road map** *D5*

This small, centrally located, family-run *hostal* has 24-hour kitchen facilities with free tea, coffee, and fruits. Two family rooms feature a kitchenette and are suitable for long stays. A sunny patio allows relaxation and there is Internet access. **www.losaticos.com**

CUSCO Hostal Corihuasi

Calle Suecia 561 **Tel** *084 260 502* **Rooms** *20* · **Road map** *D5*

Corihuasi, meaning "golden house" in Quechua, seems to exude an old world charm. A renovated 18th-century house, constructed over Inca crop terraces, it has quirky old furniture and paintings, woven bedspreads, and loads of verandahs. Ask for a room with a good view. **www.corihuasi.com**

CUSCO Hostal Rumi Punku

Calle Choquechaca 339 **Tel** *084 221 102* **Rooms** *28* · **Road map** *D5*

Rumi means "stones" and *punku* "doorway", referring to the impressive Inca entrance-way that leads to two Colonial buildings with their flower-filled courtyards. Simple rooms with wooden floors, a garden, cosy lounge, rooftop terraces, and a café with a view add to the charm. **www.rumipunku.com**

CUSCO Casa Andina Private Collection

Plazoleta de Limacpampa Chico 473 **Tel** *084 232 610* **Rooms** *72* · **Road map** *D5*

This restored 16th-century Colonial house, with elegant suites, king-size beds, and sitting rooms, faces the tiny plaza. Local artisans sit and weave in the sun-filled inner courtyard. Wi-Fi service and computers with free Internet access are available in the lounge. **www.casa-andina.com**

Key to Price Guide *see p270* **Key to Symbols** *see back cover flap*

CUSCO Hotel Monasterio

Calle Palacios 136, Plazoleta Nazarenas **Tel** *084 241 777* **Rooms** *126*

Road map *D5*

Undoubtedly Cusco's most luxurious hotel with prices to match. Set in a restored 400-year-old monastery, rooms encircle a stone courtyard adorned with an old cedar tree. Expect Colonial paintings, carved furniture, and five-star comforts. Oxygen can be pumped into some rooms for altitude sickness. **www.monasterio.orient-express.com**

MACHU PICCHU Sanctuary Lodge

Machu Picchu **Tel** *01 610 8300* **Rooms** *31*

Road map *D5*

Although comfortable, the rooms of this ex-scientists' hut are no match for their extravagant price tag. However, the sight of sunrise and sunset over Machu Picchu is impossible to match. Two rooms with views of the ruins are pricier. It has an orchid garden and a sunny outdoor patio. Rates include meals. **www.machupicchu.orient-express.com**

OLLANTAYTAMBO El Albergue

Ollantaytambo Train Station **Tel** *084 204 014* **Rooms** *8*

Road map *D5*

Rooms in El Albergue, the town's oldest *hostal*, are spacious, with whitewashed walls, simple wooden tables and bedheads, and paintings by owner Wendy Weeks. Fresh garden flowers and handwoven textiles add to the mix. A wood-fired eucalyptus steam sauna provides an ideal end to a day of hiking. **www.elalbergue.com**

URUBAMBA La Quinta Eco Hotel

Calles Arenales 105 **Tel** *084 201 448* **Rooms** *20*

Road map *D5*

Every room in this eco-friendly hotel has balconies with views of the surrounding countryside. Most of the food in the restaurant is home grown on their farm. The hotel also offers massages, sauna, bike hire, and live folkloric shows. Mystic sessions with Andean priests, known as *k'eros*, can be arranged. **www.laquintaecohotel.com**

URUBAMBA Monasterio de la Recoleta

Jiron Recoleta s/n **Tel** *084 201 419* **Rooms** *30*

Road map *D5*

This tastefully restored 15th-century building was the first Catholic monastery in the Cusco region. It has a restful large courtyard garden with a fountain, and attractive rooms. There is a good on-site restaurant and the Lobby Bar is a great place to socialize and listen to modern Andean music. **www.hotelessanagustin.com.pe**

CENTRAL SIERRA

AYACUCHO Hotel San Francisco de Paula

Jirón Callao 290 **Tel** *066 527 247* **Rooms** *36*

Road map *D5*

Hotel San Francisco de Paula is a popular hotel in a quiet but central location. The rooms are clean and comfortable, if a little dark, with cable TV and a minibar (in double rooms only). There is a nice, Colonial patio, and the rooftop breakfast bar has superb views of the city. **www.sanfranciscodepaula.com**

AYACUCHO Hostal Tres Máscaras

Tres Máscaras 194 **Tel** *066 312 921* **Rooms** *18*

Road map *D5*

Ideally located in Ayacucho's historic center, the rooms in this attractive, Colonial building are basic but clean. Some have private bathrooms and hot water is available. A lovely patio is filled with plants and caged birds, and there are parking facilities. **hostaltresmascaras@yahoo.com**

AYACUCHO Hotel El Marqués de Valdelirios

Alameda Valdelirios 720 **Tel** *066 318 944* **Rooms** *14*

Road map *D5*

This grand Colonial mansion has been thoughtfully decorated with local artworks, flowers, and beautiful wood furnishings. Rooms are warm, spacious and comfortable and breakfast is served in an imposing dining area. It is located across the river, a good 15-minute walk from the center of town.

AYACUCHO Hotel Santa Rosa

Jirón Lima 166 **Tel** *066 312 083* **Rooms** *14*

Road map *D5*

Hotel Santa Rosa occupies an historic 17th-century building with a lovely, leafy courtyard. Rooms are clean and spacious with en suite bathrooms and hot water, and there is a roof terrace with great views over the city. It has a good, reasonably priced restaurant, and helpful staff.

AYACUCHO La Crillonesa

Calle El Nazareno 165 **Tel** *066 312 350* **Rooms** *36*

Road map *D5*

Beautifully decorated with local arts and craftwork, this hotel has a roof terrace with views over the town. Rooms are simple but comfortable with en suite bathrooms and hot water. The staff can provide helpful local information. Located just behind the market, it is a short, safe walk from the center of town. **www.hotelcrillonesa.cbj.net**

AYACUCHO La Posada de Santa Ines

Jirón Chorro 139 **Tel** *066 319 544*

Road map *D5*

A pleasant, clean, and comfortable hotel with a roof terrace and a small pool. Rooms are simple, light and have en suite bathrooms with hot water. Located just behind the Mercado 12 de Abril, a short walk from the town center. The friendly staff speak limited English. **posada_staines@hotmail.com**

AYACUCHO Plaza Hotel

Jirón 9 de Diciembre 184   **Tel** *066 312 202*   **Rooms** *84*   **Road map** *D5*

The hotel occupies a colonnaded Colonial building in the center of the town. Plaza Hotel has a wonderful atmosphere which makes it a perfect place for longer visits. Most rooms are laid out around a flower-filled central courtyard. It is the most popular place to stay in Ayacucho. **hplaza@derrama.org.pe**

HUANCAVELICA Hotel Presidente

Plaza de Armas   **Tel** *064 452 760*   **Rooms** *45*   **Road map** *C5*

Probably the best hotel in Huancavelica at present, Hotel Presidente is right in the middle of town. An attractive stone structure, it has light and airy rooms with en suite bathrooms and free Wi-Fi Internet. Room tariffs include a breakfast buffet. Friendly staff. **www.hotelpresidente.com.pe**

HUANCAYO Hotel Confort

Ancash 237   **Tel** *064 233 601*   **Rooms** *114*   **Road map** *C4*

The hotel has a very central location, a block from the Plaza de Armas. Rooms are basic but clean and comfortable with en suite bathrooms. It can get very noisy at night so try to get a room away from the main street. The staff is friendly, helpful, and speak English.

HUANCAYO Hotel Santa Felicita

Giráldez 145, Plaza Constitución   **Tel** *064 235 285*   **Road map** *C4*

A fairly plain hotel with simple rooms, however, Hotel Santa Felicita has a great location overlooking the plaza. Some rooms can be very noisy, so ask for a room away from the square when booking. All rooms have en suite bathrooms, with hot water. Breakfast is included in the rates. **irmalegui@hotmail.com**

HUANCAYO Hotel Turismo

Jirón Ancash 729   **Tel** *064 231 072*   **Rooms** *70*   **Road map** *C4*

Conveniently located just two blocks from the Plaza de Armas, this hotel occupies a beautiful Colonial building. Common areas are grand and all rooms are of a good standard. Visitors can exchange money at the reception. Breakfast is included in the rates. **www.hotelpresidente.com.pe**

HUÁNUCO Grand Hotel Huánuco

Jirón Dámaso Beraún 775, Plaza de Armas   **Tel** *062 514 222*   **Rooms** *31*   **Road map** *C4*

This grand, Colonial-style building is located on the town's main square. There is a pretty courtyard and a good-sized pool. All rooms are spacious and simply decorated with high ceilings. The staff can provide helpful information about the region. **www.grandhotelhuanuco.com**

CORDILLERA BLANCA

CARAZ Grand Hostal Caraz Dulzura

Jirón Saenz Pena 212   **Tel** *043 391 523*   **Rooms** *12*   **Road map** *B3*

Ten blocks from the Plaza de Armas, this modern hotel has simple, spacious rooms that surround an interior patio and there are splendid views of the mountains. The owner is friendly and can help arrange trips into the surrounding area. Luggage storage for trekkers available. **www.hostalcarazdulzura.com**

CARAZ O'Pal Sierra Resort

Carretera Caraz, KM266, Pativilca   **Tel** *043 391 015*   **Rooms** *16*   **Road map** *B3*

This is an idyllic spot with bungalows and rooms set amid lush gardens in the mountains outside Caraz. White-washed, peg-tiled cabins can accommodate up to 5 people (price indicated is for a room), and some have their own kitchen and living area. Staff members are helpful. **www.opalsierraresort.com**

CARHUAZ El Abuelo

Jirón 9 de Dieciembre 257   **Tel** *043 394 456*   **Rooms** *8*   **Road map** *B4*

The rooms in this modern hotel are comfortable, and there is a terrace overlooking a colorful fruit and vegetable garden. Meals are prepared from their own produce, and there is a fantastic café and ice cream parlour just down the road, owned by the same people. **www.elabuelohostal.com/**

CHACAS Hostal Pilar

Jirón Ancash 110   **Tel** *043 723 813*   **Rooms** *15*   **Road map** *C4*

This pretty little hotel has rooms around a tiled, flower-filled courtyard in central Chacas. Light and spacious rooms have been tastefully furnished with local works of art and iron-framed beds. There is a good restaurant and the guests are well looked after by the friendly and efficient owner, Pilar. **www.huaraz.com/pilar**

CHAVÍN Hostal Inca

Jirón Wiracocha 170, Plaza de Armas   **Tel** *044 754 021*   **Rooms** *17*   **Road map** *C4*

The small, family-run hotel in the heart of Chavín, makes for a good base from which to explore the nearby ruins. Pleasant, clean, and simple rooms overlook a central courtyard. Tiled floors and stone paving can make it quite cold at night, but each room has hot water and a good-size bathroom. **www.huaraz.com/hotelinca**

Key to Price Guide *see p270* **Key to Symbols** *see back cover flap*

HUARAZ Albergue Churup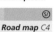
Jirón Amadeo Figueroa 1257, Soledad **Tel** *043 424 200* **Rooms** *16*   **Road map** *C4*

This is a family-run hotel that has expanded over the last few years. Common areas are spacious and there is a rooftop terrace. The living areas have open fires and there is a sauna. Breakfasts are excellent and the area is safe and quiet. They also have a tour operator, Churup Adventures, which can arrange trips in the area. **www.churup.com**

HUARAZ Edward's Inn
121 Av. Bolognesi **Tel** *043 422 692* **Rooms** *16*   **Road map** *C4*

A popular, friendly *hostal*, Edward's Inn is set in a low-rise modern building with clean, bright rooms, most of which have mountain views. Often full of trekkers and climbers, it is a sociable spot, and you can arrange tours and treks in the Huascarán National Park from here. **www.edwardsinn.com**

HUARAZ The Way Inn
Jirón Buenaventura Mendoza 821 **Tel** *043 943 466 219* **Rooms** *7*   **Road map** *C4*

The inn has a dormitory as well as individual rooms over three storys. There is a communal kitchen, lounge, and space for washing, plus an open bar. The Way Inn Lodge, with rustic accommodation and camping, is 10 miles (15 km) outside Huaraz in the mountains around Llupa. Transfers are available from the *hostal*. **www.thewayinn.com**

HUARAZ Hostal Colomba
Jirón Francisco de Zela 278 **Tel** *043 421 501* **Rooms** *20*   **Road map** *C4*

This old hacienda has been remodeled and modernized. The rooms are located around the bungalow's neat, manicured lawn. Spacious, light-filled rooms have good, modern bathrooms. There is a tiny gym and a games room, and a small late 19th-century chapel in the hotel grounds. **www.huarazhotel.com**

HUARAZ Andino Club Hotel
Pedro Cochachin 357 **Tel** *043 421 662* **Rooms** *60*   **Road map** *C4*

Part of the Libertador chain, this is the best and most expensive hotel in Huaraz with efficient service and a good restaurant. Rooms with balconies, which are more expensive, have a view over the town and into the Cordillera Blanca. There is also a tour operator on site, which can arrange trips into the mountains. **www.hotelandino.com**

MONTERREY El Patio de Monterrey
Carretera Huaraz–Caraz, KM206 **Tel** *043 424 965* **Rooms** *29*   **Road map** *B4*

Located close to the Monterrey Hot Springs (*see p206*), this hotel occupies a two-story Colonial-style building, with balconies and attractive gardens. Rooms are airy and nicely decorated and it is a good idea to request a balcony room. The friendly staff speak some English. **www.elpatio.com.pe**

THE NORTHERN DESERT

CHICLAYO Hotel Paraíso - Chiclayo
Av. Pedro Ruiz 1064 **Tel** *074 228 161* **Rooms** *70*   **Road map** *B3*

Located five blocks away from the main square, across the Parque Obrero, the hotel has standard and executive rooms with additional Wi-Fi facility in the latter. The hotel has a 24-hour cafeteria, parking, lockers, auditorium, business center, and a boutique store. **www.hotelesparaiso.com.pe**

CHICLAYO Garza Hotel
Av. Bolognesi 756 **Tel** *074 228 172* **Rooms** *94*   **Road map** *B3*

Conveniently located halfway between the main square and the airport, this hotel offers an attractive and varied culinary deal: Coffee Hour (Wed–Fri), daily breakfast buffet, and a Sunday buffet with a number of Peruvian and regional dishes. Highly recommended for food-lovers. **www.garzahotel.com**

HUANCHACO La Casa Suiza (or Heidi's House)
Los Pinos 451 **Tel** *044 461 285* **Rooms** *9*   **Road map** *B3*

Heidi Statcher, originally from Switzerland, moved into Huanchaco in 1980s and established this small, family-style *hostal*. There are shared rooms, some with private bathrooms, Wi-Fi Internet, barbecue area, book exchange, table games, and surfing equipment. The *hostal* offers breakfasts and laundry service. **www.casasuiza.com**

HUANCHACO Hotel Bracamonte
Los Olivos 503 **Tel** *044 461 162* **Rooms** *28*   **Road map** *B3*

Hotel Bracamonte is the oldest and one of the best places to stay at in Huanchaco, with a friendly and safe atmosphere. There is also a camping site for the adventurous, book exchange, children's playground, pool, foosball, and other table games. **www.hotelbracamonte.com.pe**

HUANCHACO Huanchaco International
Autopista a Huanchaco, KM 13.5 (Playa Azul) **Tel** *044 461 754* **Rooms** *24*   **Road map** *B3*

Owned by a Belgian-Peruvian couple, this hotel is a 10-minute walk south of Huanchaco, across the road from the beach. The rooms have cable TV, fans and direct-dial phones. Bungalows have a private terrace with splendid ocean views. The hotel also provides laundry and taxi services. **www.huanchacointernational.com**

MÁNCORA Sol y Mar Lodging Restaurant

Av. Piura 419 **Tel** *073 258 106/258 070* **Rooms** *70*   **Road map** *A2*

This is the oldest and biggest lodging in Máncora. Popular among backpackers and surfers, it has single, double, and triple rooms with hot water in the bathrooms. There is a children's playground. The restaurant turns into a disco-bar playing reggae and salsa rhythms during the evening. **www.vivamancora.com/solymar**

MÁNCORA Punta Ballenas Inn

Panamerican Highway North, KM1164 **Tel** *073 258 136* **Rooms** *10*   **Road map** *A2*

This highly recommended inn is located within walking distance south of Máncora by the Old Panamerican Highway. It has suites and airy rooms with ocean view terraces, hammocks, minibar, cable TV, and fan. There is a reading area with books in Spanish and English, sauna, massage service, gym, and Internet. **www.puntaballenas.com**

MÁNCORA Sunset Residenza & Ristorante

Av. Antigua, Panamerican Highway North, KM196 **Tel** *073 258 111* **Rooms** *6*   **Road map** *A2*

The owners prefer to call their place a boutique-hotel with warm and personalized service. The rooms have private bathrooms and hot water. The restaurant serves homemade pasta, Italian cuisine, and superb seafood. Airport transfer and excursions to Máncora and other nearby attractions are also offered. **www.hotelsunset.com.pe**

MÁNCORA Las Arenas de Máncora

Av. Antigua, Panamerican Highway North, KM1213 **Tel** *073 258 240* **Rooms** *19*   **Road map** *A2*

This hotel has been a member of the Libertador Hotel since 2005. The first class accommodation and service blend perfectly with the exquisite fish and seafood gourmet cuisine. It has packages for couples with horseback-riding, therapeutic massages, and all beverages included. **www.lasarenasdemancora.com**

PUNTA SAL Hotel Caballito de Mar

Panamerican Highway North, KM1187 **Tel** *01 241 4455 (Lima), 072 540 058 (Punta Sal)* **Rooms** *24* **Road map** *A2*

Located by the beach, this is the best mid-price hotel in Punta Sal. There are 24 bungalows overlooking the ocean with all the services. Owned by Manolo and Michelle, a young Peruvian couple, this place features sports such as snorkeling, surfing, and horseback-riding upon request. **www.hotelcaballitodemar.com**

PUNTA SAL Punta Sal Club Hotel

Panamerican Highway North, KM1192 **Tel** *01 422 7855 (Lima), 072 540 088 (Punta Sal)* **Rooms** *55* **Road map** *A2*

This seaside resort hotel is located near sandy beaches and warm waters with an ideal average temperature almost all year round. The hotel offers very good accommodation and activities including a deep-sea fishing, day trip on a fully equipped boat with a specially trained crew. **www.puntasal.com.pe**

TRUJILLO Hotel San Martín

San Martín 749 **Tel** *044 252 311 / 221 369* **Rooms** *150*   **Road map** *B3*

The façade looks more like a government building than a budget hotel. Located three blocks away from Trujillo's main square, the rooms have basic amenities such as cold and hot water, phone, and TV. The place has a small bar, cafeteria, and a conference room. It is usually quite a busy place. **www.deperu.com/sanmartin**

TRUJILLO Hotel Paraíso – Trujillo

San Martín 240 **Tel** *044 200 073* **Rooms** *30*   **Road map** *B3*

Situated two blocks away from the main square, this mid-price hotel offers a good deal. Rooms have cable TV, room service, and Wi-Fi Internet. Other amenities include: a 24-hour cafeteria, laundry, lockers, parking, business center, and rent-a-car service. **www.hotelesparaiso.com.pe**

TRUJILLO Hotel El Brujo

Santa Teresa de Jesús 170, Urb. La Merced **Tel** *044 223 322* **Rooms** *47*   **Road map** *B3*

This is a modern three-star hotel located southwest of downtown Trujillo, in a very quiet neighborhood. It has a variety of rooms, including suites. Their services include: elevator with Braille system, 24-hour room service, Wi-Fi Internet, business center, auditorium, and transport services and tours. **www.elbrujohotel.com**

TRUJILLO El Gran Marqués – Hotel & Spa

Díaz de Cienfuegos 145–147, Urb. La Merced **Tel** *044 481 710* **Rooms** *50*   **Road map** *B3*

A main feature of this hotel, situated a few miles away from the historic center, is the Tussen spa. Dry and steam saunas, treatment cabins, Spanish showers, exfoliation with chocolate mud, massages, manicure and pedicure among other amenities are available. **www.elgranmarques.com**

TRUJILLO Gran Hotel El Golf de Trujillo

Los Cocoteros 500, Urb. El Golf **Tel** *044 484 150* **Rooms** *120*   **Road map** *B3*

This is the largest hotel complex in the entire Northern Desert region. The elegantly decorated and furnished suites and rooms have all amenities. The hotel has a pharmacy, children's playground, fronton court, sauna, gym, rent-a-car service, and airport transfer facility. **www.granhotel.pe**

TUMBES Hotel Costa del Sol

Av. San Martín 275 **Tel** *072 523 991* **Rooms** *54*   **Road map** *B2*

The hotel is two blocks away from the main square of Tumbes. It has smoking and non-smoking rooms with soundproof windows, Internet connection, cable TV, security box and a minibar. Other features include sauna, massage room, casino, gym, fully equipped business center, and a parking lot. **www.costadelsolperu.com**

Key to Price Guide *see p270* **Key to Symbols** *see back cover flap*

VICHAYITO El Mirador de Vichayito

Av. Antigua, Panamerican Highway North, KM1155 **Tel** *01 271 6751/9823 3264 (Lima)* **Rooms** 10 **Road map** A2

El Mirador is probably the best of the lodges located in Vichayito. All ten suites and a private cabin have three bedrooms, a fully equipped kitchen, dinning area, TV room, two bathrooms, furnished terrace, and a swimming pool. It also has a restaurant. Ideal for families or big groups. **www.elmiradordevichayito.com**

ZORRITOS Costa Azul Hotel & Spa

Faustino Piaggio 115 **Tel** *01 9823 8040 / 9735 8904 (Lima), 072 544 268 (Zorritos)* **Rooms** 24 **Road map** A2

Costa Azul has a number of rooms in various sizes with modern designs and a relaxing ambience, overlooking the ocean. It also has a spa with massage room, steam bath, Spanish shower, mud and chromo therapy, and hydro massage. **www.costaazulperu.com**

THE NORTHERN HIGHLANDS

CAJAMARCA Hostal Portada del Sol

Pisagua 731 **Tel** *076 363 395* **Rooms** 18 **Road map** B3

The rooms in this refurbished Colonial house offer polished wood floors, balconies, and period furnishings surrounding a stone courtyard with a fountain. The helpful owners also have a similarly priced 15-room country hacienda, 4 miles (6 km) from town (same contacts). Transfers and breakfasts are included. **www.hostalportadadelsol.com**

CAJAMARCA Los Pinos Inn

La Mar 521 **Tel** *076 365 991* **Rooms** 22 **Road map** B3

Each room is different in this attractive hotel with Colonial tilework around a central flagstone courtyard. Public areas feature antique iron candelabras and lamps, while the rooms are good-sized with pleasing wooden headboards and colorful bedspreads. Continental breakfasts are included. **www.lospinosinn.com**

CAJAMARCA El Portal del Marqués

Jr del Comercio 644 **Tel** *076 368 464* **Rooms** 20 **Road map** B3

This central hotel housed in a Colonial mansion has carpeted rooms and exhibits original local art in the rooms and public spaces. Their restaurant is locally popular and well recommended. The hotel also features Internet cabins, a bar, and casino. **www.portaldelmarques.com**

CAJAMARCA AREA Hotel & Spa Laguna Seca

Baños del Inca, 4 miles (6 km) from Cajamarca **Tel** *076 584 300* **Rooms** 40 **Road map** B3

Built near the thermal baths where Inca Atahualpa camped before his capture, this hotel offers in-room thermal waters as well as outdoor pools, Turkish baths, and Jacuzzis. Spa treatments and massages are available, and local tours by foot, bicycle, car or horse can be arranged. Rates include use of pools. **www.lagunaseca.com.pe**

CAJAMARCA AREA Posada del Puruay

3 miles (5 km) N of Cajamarca **Tel** *076 367 028* **Rooms** 14 **Road map** B3

A sumptuously restored 19th-century mansion, this is the area's best hotel. Set in elegant, expansive gardens, it is ideal for walks and horseback rides; one ride is included in the rates, along with airport transfers and breakfast. The huge rooms and suites have period furnishings and modern conveniences. **www.posadapuruay.com.pe**

CELENDÍN Hostal Celendín

Unión 305 **Tel** *076 555 041* **Rooms** 23 **Road map** B3

Located on the Plaza de Armas, this friendly *hostal* is at the center of the action. A pleasing, tiled Colonial courtyard is surrounded by simple rooms with TV. Some rooms boast plaza views. Hot water is available but can be slow. The restaurant is among the town's best and serves local specialties including *cuy (see p285)*. **www.hostalcelendin.pe.nu**

CHACHAPOYAS Hotel Revash

Grau 517 **Tel** *041 477 391* **Rooms** 15 **Road map** B3

Right on the Plaza de Armas, this old-fashioned hotel is named for a nearby archaeological site. Its owner, Carlos Burga, is a well-known local guide. A few rooms have plaza views, others open on to a tree-filled courtyard oozing with rustic charm. All rooms have hot showers. Breakfast is available. **www.chachapoyaskuelap.com.pe**

CHACHAPOYAS Casa Vieja Hostal

Chincha Alta 569 **Tel** *041 477 353* **Rooms** 12 **Road map** B3

This converted mansion has attractive, individually decorated rooms, all with hot showers and one with a fireplace. Continental breakfast service is offered. The hotel has a library with information and Internet connection. All the usual local archaeological tours can be arranged. **www.casaviejaperu.com**

CHACHAPOYAS Hotel Gran Vilaya

Ayacucho 755 **Tel** *041 477 664* **Rooms** 23 **Road map** B3

This modern and rather bland hotel caters to business people and international tour groups. It is considered the best in town and has an office for Vilaya Tours (www.vilayatours.com), which is the most expensive and upscale local tour operator. **www.hotelvilaya.com**

CHACHAPOYAS AREA Hostal Estancia Chillo

29 miles (46 km) en route to Cajamarca **Tel** *041 832 140* **Rooms** *17*   **Road map** *B3*

A working farm, this remote, rustic but comfortable hacienda includes three daily meals in its rates. Hot showers and electricity are available. The owner, Spanish-speaking Oscar Arce, is very knowledgeable about the area and arranges guided tours and expeditions to all the local archaeological sites. **www.estanciachillo.com**

KUÉLAP AREA Marvelous Spatuletail Lodge

Choctámal **Tel** *041 478 838* **Rooms** *7*   **Road map** *B3*

This small lodge is popular with international birding groups as well as travelers looking for comfort near Kuélap, which is a 40-minute drive away. The lodge has balconies on both sides, built to give good views of birds and scenery. Breakfast is provided. **www.marvelousspatuletail.net**

LEYMEBAMBA La Casona

Amazonas 223 **Tel** *041 830 106* **Rooms** *14*   **Road map** *B3*

This hotel oozes small-town Peruvian charm with its whitewashed walls, wooden balconies, blue painted window frames, flower-filled courtyard, and tiled roof. Local archaeological excursions with guides and, if necessary, animals can be arranged. Laundry services are available after a muddy trek. **www.casonadeleymebamba.com**

THE AMAZON BASIN

CHANCHAMAYO REGION Hotel El Refugio

Ejército 490, San Ramón **Tel** *064 331 082* **Rooms** *21*   **Road map** *C4*

This is the nicest hotel in the San Ramón-La Merced region. The hotel features a botanical garden which attracts the general public. Rooms are well ventilated with fans, and vary from standard rooms to bungalows. All have hot showers and cable TV, and include breakfast in the rates. **www.hotelelrefugio.com.pe**

IQUITOS Hospedaje La Pascana

Pevas 133 **Tel** *065 231 418* **Fax** *065 233 466* **Rooms** *18*   **Road map** *D2*

This popular cheap hotel has small rooms with fans and cold showers, arranged along a plant-filled garden with shaded tables. Away from the street, the hotel is quiet and offers breakfast service, a book exchange, tour agency, luggage storage, and is a good place to relax and meet other travelers. **www.pascana.com**

IQUITOS Hostal Ambassador

Pevas 260 **Tel** *065 233 110* **Rooms** *24*   **Road map** *D2*

The rates, which include free airport transfer and Continental breakfast, make this an excellent choice for budget travelers. Although the rooms are bland, the beds are comfortable enough and the staff friendly. The front desk can arrange jungle tours. **www.paseosamazonicos.com/hotel_ambassador.html**

IQUITOS Hotel Victoria Regia

R Palma 252 **Tel** *065 231 983* **Rooms** *45*   **Road map** *D2*

This modern hotel is considered the second best in town. Set on a residential side street about four blocks from the main plaza, it offers cool, spacious rooms and a handful of suites. Most units overlook the indoor pool. The hotel is affiliated with its own jungle lodge and tours can be arranged. **www.victoriaregiahotel.com**

IQUITOS Hotel El Dorado Plaza

Napo 258 **Tel** *065 222 555* **Rooms** *65*   **Road map** *D2*

Right on the Plaza de Armas, this is Iquitos's most luxurious hotel. A Jacuzzi, sauna, 24-hour room service, breakfast, and airport transfer are available at no extra charge. Sizable rooms have plaza views (with soundproof windows) or pool views. The hotel has a casino and the restaurant is among the best in town. **www.eldoradoplazahotel.com**

IQUITOS AREA Muyuna Amazon Lodge

87 miles (140 km) upriver on Río Yanayacu **Tel** *065 242 858* **Rooms** *16*   **Road map** *D2*

Rooms in stilted, thatched bungalows with a balcony and hammock offer an authentic jungle experience. Locals staff the lodge and welcome visitors. Rates include boat transfers, meals, and bilingual guided tours that include a unique opportunity to see and listen to river dolphins *(see p255)* using underwater microphones. **www.muyuna.com**

LAGO SANDOVAL Sandoval Lake Lodge

20 miles (30 km) from Puerto Maldonado **Tel** *01 440 2022 (Lima)* **Rooms** *25*   **Road map** *E5*

Arriving at this lovely lodge is half the fun – a one-hour ride down Río Madre de Dios, followed by a 2-mile (3-km) hike on a boardwalk through the forest to Lago Sandoval. Dugout canoes paddle across the beautiful lake to the lodge, built on a hilltop overlooking the water. **http://www.inkanatura.com/sandovallakelodge.asp**

LAKE YARINACOCHA Pandisho Ecolodge

3 miles (5 km) from Puerto Callao **Tel** *061 591 517* **Rooms** *8*   **Road map** *C3*

This rustic lodge provides various jungle adventures including hikes, canoe rides, night excursions, camping, and even *ayahuasca* ceremonies *(see pp22–3)*. Rates per night vary by the number of nights stayed. Two rooms have private bath, others are shared, and meals, transfers, and some excursions are included. **www.amazon-ecolodge.com**

Key to Price Guide *see p270* **Key to Symbols** *see back cover flap*

MANU BIOSPHERE RESERVE Manu Lodge

Cocha Juarez Lake, 0.6 miles (1 km) from Río Manu **Tel** *084 252 721* **Rooms** *12*

Road map *E4*

This well-established lodge is the only permanent one within the reserve. Rooms are screened with mosquito netting; cold showers and toilets are shared. Manu Lodge can be booked only as part of a complete transportation, meals, and guides package. A tented camp on raised platforms is also available. **www.moyobamba.net**

MOYOBAMBA Country Club Hostal

Manuel del Aguila 667 **Tel** *094 562 110* **Rooms** *20*

Road map *C3*

Half a block from the Plaza de Armas in the heart of town, this inexpensive hotel has tidy, tiled rooms with cable TV and hot showers. The hosts are friendly and helpful, and a travel agency is on the premises. A large garden and a small pool add a relaxing touch in this steamy, high-jungle city. **mmenesesm@terra.com.pe**

OXAPAMPA Albergue Turistico Bottger

Mariscal Castilla, 6ta Cuadra **Tel** *063 462 377* **Rooms** *6*

Road map *C4*

The steep-roofed, wood-paneled rooms hark back to the first settlers of this town. This small, family-run *hostal* is just a five-block walk from the Plaza de Armas and has beautiful views of the surrounding mountains. Rates include a full breakfast. **www.oxapampaonline.com/bottger**

PUCALLPA Hotel Sol Del Oriente

San Martín 552 **Tel** *061 575 154* **Rooms** *42*

Road map *C3*

This is clearly Pucallpa's best hotel. The more expensive rooms boast a Jacuzzi and there is one suite in the hotel. The tiled public areas are spacious, shaded and cool, pleasantly decorated with palms and life-sized wooden carvings of Indians and animals. A mini-zoo features Amazonian animals. **www.soldelorientehoteles.com**

PUERTO BERMÚDEZ Albergue Humboldt

Puerto de la Rampa **Tel** *063 963 722 363* **Rooms** *8*

Road map *C4*

A ramshackle building perched on the banks of the Río Pachitea, it is the center for visiting the Ashaninka villages and surrounding rainforest. Accommodations are basic, with shared cold showers, and a choice of beds, hammocks, or camping, and food is included in the rates. Electricity is on from 8am to 11pm. **www.alberguehumboldt.com**

PUERTO MALDONADO Hotel Don Carlos

León Velarde 1271 **Tel** *082 571 029* **Rooms** *31*

Road map *E5*

Located 0.6 miles (1 km) southwest of town, this hotel has wood-paneled or tiled rooms, some with a view of the Río Tambopata. All have a TV and mini-fridge. Rates include airport transfer and Continental breakfast; other meals and room service are available. **www.hotelesdoncarlos.com**

PUERTO MALDONADO Wasai Maldonado Lodge

Plaza Grau, Puerto Maldonado **Tel** *082 572 290* **Rooms** *18*

Road map *E5*

Stilted, thatched, wooden bungalows overlooking the Río Madre de Dios provide a fine jungle introduction in the most popular hotel in town. Lush gardens with a waterfall tumbling into a small pool are featured. The related Wasai Tambopata Lodge, with 20 rooms on the Río Tambopata, provides jungle excursions. **www.wasai.com**

RÍO HEATH Heath River Wildlife Center

3 hours boat ride S of the Madre de Dios **Tel** *01 440 2022 (Lima)* **Rooms** *10*

Road map *E5*

This lodge is located on the Río Heath, which separates Peru from Bolivia in an intriguing, little-known area which features both rainforest and pampas. Clay licks reached by camouflaged rafts attract macaws, and Ese'eje Indians welcome visitors to their village. **www.inkanatura.com/heathriverwildlifecenter.asp**

RÍO TAMBOPATA Picaflor Research Center

74 km up Río Tambopata **Tel** *084 572 589* **Rooms** *6*

Road map *E5*

This private research center accommodates up to 6 tourists in single rooms (doubles on request) and includes transport from Puerto Maldonado airport, meals, and guided excursions. This is a great option for small groups who want privacy over luxury, yet want to learn about the Amazon. **picaflor_rc@yahoo.com**

RÍO TAMBOPATA Tambopata Research Center

8 hours boat ride up the Río Tambopata **Tel** *01 421 8347 (Lima)* **Rooms** *13*

Road map *E5*

This rustic lodge, with shared cold showers, is remoter than other lodges on the river. One of the Amazon's largest clay licks is nearby, and the possibilities of spotting wildlife in this area are above average. Some mammals forage in the forest directly in front of the rooms, which have large unglassed windows and mosquito nets. **www.perunature.com**

TARAPOTO Hotel Río Shilcayo

Pasaje Las Flores 224 **Tel** *042 522 225* **Rooms** *38*

Road map *C3*

This hotel is among the best in the region. Set in pleasant, flower-filled grounds, it provides guests with a choice of standard rooms or private bungalows with patios and a hammock. The restaurant, bar, pool, and outdoor games attract locals at weekends. A sauna is also on the premises. **www.rioshilcayo.com**

YURIMAGUAS Hostal El Naranjo

Arica 318 **Tel** *065 352 650* **Rooms** *40*

Road map *C2*

This is the most attractive of the handful of accommodations in this small town, and is the most pleasant place to spend a day or two while waiting for a riverboat to leave for Iquitos. The owners are friendly and the location is a block from both the Plaza de Armas and the central market. **www.hostalelnaranjo.com**

WHERE TO EAT

Peruvian cuisine is said to be one of the world's finest. French culinary master Auguste Escoffier (1846-1935) ranked it third behind French and Chinese food. The country's huge biodiversity produces an assortment of fresh ingredients from the mountains, the jungle, and the coast, and its cultural

Signage of a popular restaurant in Cusco

mix, a hybrid of Andean and Spanish traditions with Japanese, Chinese, and African influences, lends the cuisine its distinctive edge. *Cocina criolla* is the coastal Creole cooking, *nikkei* refers to Peruvian-Japanese fusion, and *novoandina* is the new Andean cooking that melds native ingredients with new recipes.

RESTAURANTS AND BARS

Lima offers the greatest choice of places to eat, with something to suit every taste. There are elegant restaurants headed by lauded chefs as well as traditional family-run eateries, and no shortage of restaurants and bars offering a fixed-price *menú*, usually a *causa* (cold potato salad) or soup, main course, a small dessert, and a drink. Arequipa is also famous for the standard and variety of its restaurants and produce.

Cebicherías are the place to try seafood, *anticucherías* specialize in grilled kebabs, *pollerías* serve roast chicken, *sanguicherías* offer Peruvian-style sandwiches, *picanterías* are traditional home-style restaurants found in Arequipa, while *chifas* fuse Peruvian and Chinese flavors. The country has the highest number per capita of Chinese restaurants in Latin America. Buffets are a popular option in both *chifas* and Creole restaurants, with Sundays drawing large family groups.

Welcoming entrance of La Trattoria del Monasterio, Arequipa (see p293)

Huariques (hiding places), which are usually known only to locals, hence the name, are small family-run establishments in which the cook has perfected one or two signature dishes, perhaps a *cebiche (see p284)*, a sandwich or a spicy one-pot stew, and their modest appearance belies the quality of the food. It is advisable to go with someone in the know.

CHAIN RESTAURANTS

Most of the principal US fast food chains are represented in Peru, including Pizza Hut, KFC, McDonald's, Burger King, and Dominos. There are, however, a number of homegrown alternatives including Bembos (hamburgers), D'nnos (pizza), and Pardo's (roast chicken).

Lima's upmarket café chains, San Antonio, La Baguette, and Café Café, serve sandwiches, salads, and hot meals from morning to night, while T'anta offers more expensive and substantial meals. *Cebicherías* Punta Sal, Señor Limon, and Segundo Muelle have several branches across the city.

FOOD HYGIENE

Health standards can vary, especially outside major cities, and it is worth taking a few precautions. Avoid salads and uncooked vegetables in all but the best restaurants and cafés; creamy mayonnaise is a favoured dressing and as it is

Busy hour at *cebicheria* La Mar in Miraflores, Lima *(see p291)*

often prepared well ahead, it is best to steer clear of it. Peruvians tend to eat *cebiche* for lunch when they believe it is at its freshest.

Avoid undercooked meat. Remember to peel all fruit, or wash it in a bacterial disinfectant available from supermarkets. Open air markets and street stalls should be treated with caution, especially homemade ice-cream vendors who are known to refreeze thawed wares. Drink only purified water, canned or bottled carbonated drinks, spirits, or hot drinks.

Streetside fruit stall displays its abundant produce, Trujillo

EATING HOURS

Restaurants in general don't open before 8am, so early risers in search of *desayuno* (breakfast) should head for an international hotel or highend restaurant. Breakfast consists of bread, jam, and coffee, although on weekends, most families will sit down to a *tamale* (steam-cooked corn dough with or without filling), *chicharrón* (fried pork rind) with Creole onions.

Almuerzo (lunch) is eaten late, usually from 1:30pm. Most *cebicherías* only open for lunch. For many Peruvians, it is the main meal of the day and consists of a fish or meat dish with rice. *Lonche* is the Peruvian version of English afternoon tea but with more substantial food than delicate cakes and sandwiches. Lamb *brochettes*, *empanadas*, tripledecker sandwiches, door-stop cake wedges or pie, and a pisco sour or thick hot chocolate are the norm. Some Lima restaurants offer special promotions for *lonche*.

Peruvians rarely make *cena* (dinner) reservations earlier than 9pm. If invited for drinks or dinner, locals seldom arrive on time, displaying a more relaxed Latin attitude.

PAYING AND TIPPING

Restaurants in Peru are required to publish their prices, including taxes and a 10 percent service charge, but they don't always do so. The service charge is indicated by the words *propina* or *servicio* near the bottom of the bill. Things such as bread or live entertainment can incur an extra charge. Peruvians don't normally tip and you are not obliged to, but for good service, add 5–10 percent to the 10 percent already charged. Credit cards are accepted and many restaurants accept payment in US dollars.

ALCOHOL

Restaurants and cafés usually have licenses to sell alcohol, and top-end restaurants have good international wine lists. Naturally, Argentinian and Chilean labels are prominent, along with local Peruvian brands. Bringing your own is not generally an option, although some top-end restaurants will allow it if wine is not readily available and will charge a corkage fee.

Sale of alcohol is not permitted, even in supermarkets, during federal and local elections due to a *ley seca* (the dry law), which runs from Thursday night through to Sunday night.

Rosa Nautica restaurant in Miraflores, Lima *(see p291)*

WHEELCHAIR ACCESS

Few restaurants in Peru make special allowances for wheelchair users. Access is difficult and assistance is required. Toilets that can accommodate a wheelchair are rare.

CHILDREN

The majority of Peruvian restaurants welcome children, especially family-run ones. Most well-off parents, however, bring their nannies along to take care of them. Usually, there is little room for strollers. Child portions are not common but staff are happy to provide an extra plate so children can share.

SMOKING

Most restaurants and cafés have separate smoking and non-smoking areas.

Barman stirs up drinks at Rojo Bar, Hotel Maury, Lima *(see p270)*

The Flavors of Peru

Peruvian cuisine is one of the world's most varied and delicious. Staples such as potatoes, corn, peanuts, chilies, quinoa, and fresh seafood pre-date the Incas, while chicken, beef, pork, citrus fruits, olives, wine, cinnamon, and cloves came courtesy of the Spanish. The blending of Spanish, African, and Andean ingredients resulted in what's known as *comida criolla* (Creole food). Later waves of immigrants, including Chinese, Japanese, and Italians, added their own flavors. Peru boasts some 400 versions of the iconic dish *cebiche*, a testament to its culinary creativity.

Quinoa

Ripe corn cobs in different colors piled on a roadside stall

PERUVIAN PRODUCE

Peru is home to 84 of the world's 114 biological zones, which results in a cornucopia of fresh ingredients. The Pacific Ocean is the source of superb fish and seafood. From the Andes come an astonishing range of potatoes and peppers. Wild mushrooms are grown in the Sacred Valley. The Amazon

harvest includes bananas and manioc. Juicy prawns are caught in the Arequipa rivers. Mangoes, asparagus, limes, and black scallops, all thrive in the northern valleys and lakes.

Top Peruvian chef Gaston Acurio claims to be able to choose from 60 different varieties of fresh fruit and vegetables and 70 different types of seafood when he visits a Lima market. While

the cuisine varies from region to region, reflecting local produce and culinary traditions, the use of native *aji* (dried Peruvian chilies) and aromatic herbs such as coriander, basil, *hierbabuena* (mint), and oregano, is a common thread. Ancient ceramics, with their images of native fruit and vegetables and daily cooking rituals, detail Peruvians' enduring love for preparing food.

Avocado · Prickly pears · Maracuya · Limes · Papaya · Ca gooseberr

Bananas

Selection of luscious Peruvian tropical fruits

PERUVIAN DISHES AND SPECIALTIES

Chilies

Peruvian meals begin with *piqueos* (snacks) such as *anticuchos* (grilled beef heart kebabs marinated in vinegar), *conchitas a la parmesana* (scallops with Parmesan), *humitas* (savory mashed corn steamed in corn husks), *causa* (cold mashed potato), or *tiradito* (similar to *cebiche*). *Pachamanca* may feature pork, lamb, beef, potatoes, broad (fava) beans, and corn wrapped in banana leaves, buried in a pit with white hot rocks, and steamed. Other main dishes include *adobo* (a pork stew with corn beer and spices, cooked in a clay pot), and Chinese-influenced *chaufa* (beef, rice, onions, tomatoes, peppers, and soy sauce). For dessert, the caramel-flavored fruit *lúcuma* is delicious in mousses or ice cream, while *picarones* (sweet pastries dunked in sugar syrup) are a popular treat.

Cebiche *is chunks of raw fish marinated in lime juice, onions, and chilies, served with corn and sweet potato.*

Traders thronging the lively and vibrant market stalls in Cusco

LEGACY OF THE INCAS

Inca dishes have survived through the centuries. *Pachamanca* (the Peruvian underground barbecue) and *carapulca* (dehydrated potato stew with pork), are cooked much as they were 500 years ago. The ancient Peruvians freeze-dried potato to make *chuño*, and llama and alpaca meat to produce *charqui*, akin to a beef jerky. Both remain popular today.

Maiz (corn) is still a mainstay of the Peruvian diet. In pre-Hispanic times, as today, it was toasted, boiled, or made into *humitas* (mashed corn dumplings). *Cuy* (guinea pig) has been an essential source of protein in Central Peru for 5,000 years. "Raise guinea pigs and eat well," proclaims an Inca saying. *Cuy* is omnipresent

at Andean fiestas, and is still used by healers to diagnose illnesses. Peruvians consume some 22 million *cuys* a year.

In upmarket restaurants throughout Peru, new uses are being found for the ancient grain quinoa, known to the Incas as the "mother

Tending a *pachamanca*, underground barbeque

of all grains." Today, its mild, nutty flavor may turn up in dishes like *quinoto* (risotto) or *arroz con leche*, a type of rice pudding.

OUT OF AFRICA

Cinnamon and cloves, synonymous with Creole desserts, were brought to Peru by the Spanish but they initially came from the Moors who occupied southern Spain for 700 years. Later, African slaves in the kitchens of Peru's plantation houses made the most of discarded ingredients, such as filleting and marinating beef hearts to make the now ubiquitous *anticuchos* (kebabs), and creating *tacu-tacu* (spicy fried patties) as a way of using leftover beans and rice.

THE STORY OF CEBICHE

Pre-Hispanic cultures started Peru's *cebiche* tradition – "cooking" their fish using the juices and flesh of the *tumbo* (a type of passionfruit). Later, the Incas marinated fish in *chicha* (corn beer), and also salted their catch for transport into the mountains. The Spanish brought lemons and onions to the dish. The Japanese popularized scallops and prawns so much that they now rival Peruvian *corvina* (sea bass) and *lenguado* (sole) as *cebiche* staples. Peruvians hail the leftover *cebiche* juice, called *leche de tigre*, as the perfect cure for a hangover.

Lomo saltado *features strips of beef, sautéed with onions, chilies, garlic, tomatoes, spices, and fried potatoes.*

Rocotos rellenos *are hot red peppers stuffed with meat, tomatoes, raisins, and olives, served with a spicy sauce.*

Suspiro a la limeña *is a blend of condensed milk, egg yolks, cinnamon, and port, topped with meringue.*

Flavors of Peru: The Potato

As Francisco Pizarro navigated the Andes intent on conquering the Incas, he probably gave little thought to the *papa* (potato) plant he trampled beneath his feet. Yet it was to be one of the most significant treasures the Spanish uncovered in Latin America. The potato is thought to have reached Europe in the 1560s on board Spanish galleons. A dozen ancient varieties still grow in the Canary Islands, relics of that first voyage. Europe now grows the highest number of potatoes, but Peru has the most varieties and has been dubbed the "Potato Capital of the World."

Sweet potatoes

Cooking potatoes on an open fire in Arequipa province

GOLD OF THE ANDES

The potato was first domesticated more than 6,000 years ago near Lake Titicaca, where the greatest diversity of wild species is still found. The Incas cultivated more than 1,000 varieties and, of the 3,000 types currently identified, hundreds are still common in Andean markets. The potato is known by countless names in the Andes. To people in the highlands each potato is distinct – they will eat one kind for breakfast, a different one for lunch, and yet another for dinner. Like their ancestors before them, they revere the earth and, for them, the potato is its consummate blessing. Centuries ago, harvested potatoes were reburied among hot stones as an offering so that Pachamama (Mother Earth) could eat before the farm workers. This gave rise to the method of roasting food underground, still in use today, the *pachamanca*.

Andeans have also found many non-dietary uses for the potato, from curing ulcers and dissolving kidney stones with raw potato juice, to soothing burns with raw potato compresses, and even patting on a mashed potato beauty mask at night.

But, most importantly, no Peruvian meal is complete without a potato, whether it be starter, main course, side dish, or even dessert.

Luntus
Yana allkkay warmi
Milagro
Puka pina
Puku tarma
Waka kkallu
Yana warmi

Some of the many varieties of Peruvian potato

PERUVIAN POTATO DISHES AND SPECIALTIES

For Limeños summer wouldn't be summer without a *causa rellena*. Cold, mashed yellow potato is layered with avocado, mayonnaise, poached fish or chicken, and topped with prawn tails. *Causa de pulpo* is stuffed with octopus in olive mayonnaise, and *causa verde* is tinted green with spinach and parsley and layered with crab meat. *Papa a la huancaína* pairs potatoes with a spicy cheese sauce garnished with black olives and hard-boiled egg. Creole influence is apparent in *papa rellena*, which is served with a *salsa criolla* of sliced onions, vinegar, and chili. African cooks influenced one of Peru's preferred sweet treats, *picarones*, replacing the wheat flour with mashed sweet potato and pumpkin and dipping them in a cinnamon-orange syrup.

Paprika

Papas rellenas, *potato croquettes, are filled with meat, egg, olives, tomatoes, onions, and paprika.*

Reading the Menu

The list below gives the most common dishes and main ingredients, in alphabetical order, that visitors are likely to encounter on a Peruvian menu, both in Lima and regionally. However, not all dishes will be available in every region. *Cuy* (guinea pig) for example, is a specialty of the Central and Southern Highlands, while fish dishes will feature more strongly (and be better and fresher) near the coast. General vocabulary that will be useful when eating out can be found in the *Phrase Book* on pages 350–52.

Cilantro (coriander)

Aji de gallina chicken stew made with milk, Parmesan, bread, chilies and walnuts.
Ajis chilies, including *amarillo* (yellow), *panca* (purple), *mirasol* (orange).
Albahaca basil.
Alfajores wafer-thin discs of shortbread dusted with icing sugar, filled with caramelized condensed milk or honey.
Anticuchos beef heart kebabs.
Arroz con camarones river prawns with rice, seasoned with chili, paprika, and coriander.
Arroz con pato duck and rice cooked with beer.
Caldo de cabeza ram's head soup flavored with mint and chili.
Cancacho roasted pork or lamb marinated in chili and oil.
Cancha fried corn kernels.
Carapulcra boiled, dehydrated potato stew with pork, chicken, chilies, garlic, and spices.
Cau-cau tripe stew with potatoes, mint and *palillo* (a turmeric-like spice).

Field workers prepare a meal of maize and potatoes

Causa rellena *(see opposite)*.
Chicharrones pork rinds fried in their own fat.
Chicharrones de pescado fried pieces of fish.
Chifles fried banana chips.
Chimichurri olive oil, parsley, and garlic sauce.
Chirimoya custard apple.
Choclo corn on the cob.
Chuño lawa beef soup with rice, *garbanzos* (chickpeas), and dehydrated potatoes.
Chupe de camarones chowder of river prawns, fish, milk, eggs, potatoes, chilies, and oregano.
Chupe de cangrejo crab chowder.
Conchitas negras black scallops.
Cuy chactado guinea pig fried under a stone.
Escabeche fish or chicken marinated in vinegar and steamed with onions.
Juane rice (seasoned with *palillo*) and chicken or fish cooked in banana leaves.
Lechón suckling pig.
Mani peanuts.
Maracuya passionfruit.
Mariscos shellfish.
Mazamorra morada purple corn pudding.

Mero grouper fish.
Ocopa boiled potatoes with cheese sauce, lima (butter) beans, onions, olives, and *rocoto*.
Palta avocado.
Parihuela de mariscos seafood soup.
Pesque de quinoa mashed quinoa with milk and cheese.
Picante de cuy guinea pig stew with peanuts and chilies.
Pollo a la brasa spit-roasted chicken.
Pulpo al olivo octopus in black olive mayonnaise.
Rocoto hot, red pepper.
Salsa criolla *(see opposite)*.
Seco de cabrito stew of roasted kid marinated in corn liquor, with beans.
Solterito salad of cheese, lima beans, red onions, black olives, corn, and *rocoto*.
Sopa a la criolla mildly spicy noodle soup with beef, milk and peppers, often with a fried egg on top.
Tacu-tacu "pancake" of fried pork-flavored beans and rice, topped with steak, onion, salsa, and sometimes a fried egg.
Timbuche concentrated fish and coriander broth.
Tiradito very thin slices of raw fish, doused in lime juice and chili salsa.
Tres leches three layers of sponge cake soaked in condensed and evaporated milk and cream or milk.
Tumbo type of passionfruit.
Tuna prickly pear fruit.
Turron de Doña Pepa aniseed-flavored layered biscuit in fruit syrup.
Yuca cassava root.
Zapallo pumpkin.

Deep-fried *cuy* (guinea pig), the centerpiece at a village fiesta

What to Drink in Peru

The wide variety of drinks on offer in Peru range from the non-alcoholic, blindingly yellow Inca Kola to the national favorite, the potent pisco sour, a cocktail invented in the early 20th century in Lima's Maury Hotel's Rojo Bar. As a rule, never drink tap water and avoid fruit juices and other drinks in places where cleanliness levels are suspect. It is better to stick to pre-packaged drinks. Bottled *agua sin gas* (still water) or *agua con gas* (sparkling water) are readily available in reliable shops.

Classic poster of Coca wine, a popular tonic in the 1870s

BEER

Cerveza (beer) has existed in Peru for hundreds of years. Home brewed *chicha* (corn beer) is often sold at markets or during festivals. There are *chicherías* (corn beer bars) in northern towns. Other forms include *chicha de molle*, made from pepper tree seeds, and *chicha de siete semillas*, made from corn, wheat, barley, and chickpeas. The best-known beer brands of Peru are Cristal, Cusqueña, and Pilsen. Sweet dark beer, called *malta or cerveza negra*, is also available all over the country.

Cristal and Cusqueña beer

OTHER ALCOHOLIC DRINKS

Pisco is the undisputed king of Peruvian alcohol, appearing in the celebrated pisco sour, as well as variations such as a piscopolitan (with cranberry juice), *algarrobina* (with carob syrup), and pisco puro (straight). Other drinks include *masato*, made from fermented yuca, with sweet potato or with some sugar.

Pisco sour   Piscopolitan

WINES

The first vineyards in Peru were planted in the 1550s. Grapes from the principal vineyards *(see p122)*, located near Ica on the Southern Coast, go into making pisco. However, the vineyards of Tacama and Tabernero are also serious about wine-making. Tacama has had a French wine-maker at the helm of the harvest since 1961 and several wines from both producers have garnered international praise. Ocucaje also makes wine. Naturally, given the proximity, Chilean and Argentine imports abound.

Wine from Tacama

COLD DRINKS

The bubble-gum flavored Inca Kola has been Peru's top-selling drink since 1935. But there are others, including Real Kola. Almost as popular is *chicha morada*, a non-fizzy drink made from boiled purple corn, apple peel, pineapple, and cloves. *Ponche*, common in the Central Highlands is a milk-based drink flavored with sesame seeds, spices, nuts, and grated coconut. *Chapo*, a banana and sugar juice, is a favorite in the jungles of Peru.

Inca Kola bottle

HOT DRINKS

Matés (herbal teas), served black with lemon and sugar, are more popular than plain tea in Peru. *Manzanilla* (camomile) and *anís* (aniseed) are quite prevalent in the towns and cities of the country. *Maté de coca* (coca leaf tea) is believed to help in altitude sickness and is considered emblematic of the highlands. *Café americano* (medium- to low-strength filter) or instant coffee is common, although espressos and cappuccinos are also available in most major cities.

Coffee   Coca tea   Camomile

Pisco: Peru's Miracle Drink

Hailed as the miracle of the desert, pisco is Peru's national drink. Writer Ricardo Palma dubbed it as his "rousing pick-me-up." When Peruvian wine exports were banned by Spain, wine-makers here began to increase production of grape brandy, shipping it from the port of Pisco. Exports reached their height in the 17th–18th

Traditional wine vessel

centuries. Pisco is considered a symbol of Peruvian resilience. Despite the Spanish embargo, the Chilean army's systematic destruction of cellars during the War of the Pacific *(see pp50–51)*, and failed agrarian reforms in the 1970s which saw some vines cut up for firewood, pisco has survived. As the Peruvians say, "Pisco is Peru."

HOW PISCO IS MADE

Pisco, a clear grape brandy or *aguardiente*, is distilled from fresh grape must in stills. The final product should be transparent without any kind of additives. It takes almost 13 lb (6 kg) of grapes to make one bottle of pisco.

Grapes *were brought from the Canary Islands to Peru's arid south coast. Aided by the knowledge of ancient peoples who had worked out how to irrigate the desert, locals started making pisco.*

Pisco *in Quechua means bird and a valley. The potters who made the large conical vessels, in which the liquor was, and sometimes still is, stored, were also called piscos.*

Distillation *takes place in steel or copper stills. Then pisco is aged in clay barrels or other neutral containers for three months. No distilled water is added to alter its consistency.*

Bottling *is done with the same level of alcohol as when it was produced, officially 38-48 percent. The flavor comes from the fruit itself; there is no aging in oak barrels.*

Pisco *was recognized to be of Peruvian origins in 2005 by the World Intellectual Property Organization after a prolonged dispute with Chile.*

HOW TO DRINK PISCO

Pisco can be chilled and sipped straight. However, most Peruvians prefer it in the form of the pisco sour. All you need is three parts pisco mixed with lime juice, sugar syrup, egg white, ice cubes, and some Angostura bitters. Just bear in mind that the bitters are to be added right at the end. Peruvians are very serious about their national drink and the national Pisco Day is celebrated on February 8, every year.

Pisco sour

Choosing a Restaurant

The restaurants in this guide have been selected across a wide range of price categories for their good value, quality of food, and atmosphere. In some parts of Peru, there are few restaurants that can be recommended. In such cases, places that offer good value have been suggested. For map references for Lima, see pp104–111.

PRICE DETAILS
The price ranges are for a meal for one, including tax and service charges and a glass of house wine.
Ⓢ under 35 nuevo soles
ⓈⓈ 35–80 nuevo soles
ⓈⓈⓈ 80–120 nuevo soles
ⓈⓈⓈⓈ 120–150 nuevo soles
ⓈⓈⓈⓈⓈ over 150 nuevo soles

LIMA

BARRANCO Antica Trattoria

ⓈⓈ

Calle San Martín 201 **Tel** *01 247 3443*   **Map** *4 C4*

This huge restaurant with wooden beams has a rustic and relaxed atmosphere. It serves up appetizing pizzas, home-made pastas, and robust Italian classics such as osso bucco (veal shank) with polenta (ground maize). It is the ideal starting point for a night of bar-hopping in Barranco or other branches in Lima.

BARRANCO LA 73

ⓈⓈ

Av. El Sol Oeste 175 **Tel** *01 247 0780*   **Map** *4 C3*

With its London tube-style tiles and art posters, LA 73 (named after the bus stop opposite) looks more like a fish and chip joint than a new Andean eatery. Alongside salads and sandwiches is grilled tuna, beef with mashed potatoes, and *churros* (fried dough) coated in hot chocolate.

BARRANCO Cala

ⓈⓈⓈ

Playa Barranquito, Costa Verde **Tel** *01 252 9187*   **Map** *4 C4*

With a slick decor and a view overlooking the ocean and surfers at play, Cala complements its prime position with classy food. Start with martinis, popcorn prawns, and Thai salsa and move on to *robalo* fish with Creole risotto. The bar downstairs is a trendy watering hole.

CENTRAL LIMA L'Eau Vive

ⓈⓈ

Jirón Ucayali 370 **Tel** *01 427 5612*   **Map** *1 F1*

Run by a French order of nuns, all proceeds go to charity. There are several airy dining rooms with the nicest reserved for à la carte diners. Duck in orange sauce and rabbit with mustard are good choices. As an added bonus, the nuns sing "Ave María" every night. The lunch menu is a bargain.

CHORRILLOS Sonia

ⓈⓈ

Jirón Agustin Lozano La Rosa 173 **Tel** *01 467 3788*

Diners sit at wooden tables under a bamboo roof, amid fishing paraphernalia and photographs of the owner, Sonia, with celebrities. Expect absolutely fresh fish, including *cebiche (see p285)*, fried calamari, sea bass, and crab stew and oodles of rice. Inca Kola is the tipple of choice with *cebiche*.

LA VICTORIA Sankuay

ⓈⓈⓈ

Calle Leon 114, Santa Catalina **Tel** *01 470 6217*

There are no menus at the 10-table restaurant, also called Chez Wong, that chef Javier Wong runs from his home. *Lenguado* (sole) – "the best fish created" – is a favorite, and may be teamed with melon, pineapple, and cinnamon, stir-fried with chilies, sliced paper-thin and served raw, or starring in a classic, unadorned *cebiche*.

MIRAFLORES Bircher-Benner

Ⓢ

Av. Larco 413 **Tel** *01 446 5791*   **Map** *4 B1*

Despite the abundance of good restaurants in Lima, this unassuming vegetarian eatery is always packed. People come for the fish-free *cebiche* of mushrooms and orange sweet potato, soy *lomo saltado* (a spicy dish traditionally made with meat, onions, chips, and chili) eaten with chunky fresh fruit salads, and creamy yoghurt with honey.

MIRAFLORES Arugula

ⓈⓈ

Calle San Fernando 320 **Tel** *01 444 0132*   **Map** *3 F5*

Expect both modern Mediterranean food and a touch of Asia in this sun-filled corner eatery, with its vibrant tiled floor, wooden tables, and warm welcome. Choose from rich four-cheese tortellini, sesame-coated tuna perched on soy-dressed salad, and for dessert, crème brûlée.

MIRAFLORES Wa Lok

ⓈⓈ

Av. Angamos Oeste 700 **Tel** *01 447 1314*   **Map** *2 C5*

With its distinctly hybrid Cantonese-Peruvian cooking, Wa Lok has legions of fans. Diners keep coming back for the crispy-skinned roast duck, the stir-fried abalone, whole fried fish, and *chaufa*, which is fried rice prepared in a typical Peruvian style.

Key to Symbols *see back cover flap*

MIRAFLORES Brujas de Cachiche

⑨⑨⑨

Calle Bolognesi 460 **Tel** *01 447 1883*

Map *4 A1*

Some dishes here are made according to ancient Peruvian recipes. The *anticuchos* (beef heart kebabs) and *cabrita norteña* (goat stew with beans and rice) are hugely popular. The restaurant's name refers to a southern village said to be full of *brujas* (witches and sorcerers).

MIRAFLORES Huaca Pucllana

⑨⑨⑨

General Borgoño, Cuadra 8 **Tel** *01 445 4042*

Map *2 C4*

At night the illuminated ruins of the pre-Inca Huaca Pucllana provide a memorable backdrop to the stylish food served here, including bite-sized scallops dotted with Parmesan, trout with artichokes, and chicken stuffed with Andean cheese. If time is short, squeeze in a late-afternoon drink on the terrace.

MIRAFLORES La Mar

⑨⑨⑨

Av. La Mar 770 **Tel** *01 421 3365*

Map *2 B5*

No reservations allowed at this modish, lunch-only eatery. So expect to wait unless you get here at noon. There are classic and contemporary *cebiches*, along with *tiraditos* (thinly sliced raw fish), *causa* (mashed potato with seafood), and whole baby sole in black butter with capers.

MIRAFLORES La Trattoria di Mambrino

⑨⑨⑨

Calle Manuel Bonilla 106 **Tel** *01 446 7002*

Map *4 B1*

Consistently rated as Lima's best Italian restaurant, thanks to the succulent spaghetti with *langostinos* (lobsters), pappardelle with rabbit ragout, and wood-fired pizzas. Don't miss the extravagant desserts prepared by TV chef Sandra Plevisani, Lima's dessert queen.

MIRAFLORES Pescados Capitales

⑨⑨⑨

Av. La Mar 1337 **Tel** *01 421 8808*

Map *2 B5*

The name of this lunch-only restaurant is a play on the words *pescados* (fish) and *pecados* (sins). The menu echoes the "deadly fins" theme with "Wrath" (octopus with bubbling butter), "Impatience" (tuna with chickpea and avocado salad), and "Greed" (huge sea bream with mashed potatoes). Great *cebiche* is served here.

MIRAFLORES Rosa Nautica

⑨⑨⑨

Espigón 4, Circuito de Playas **Tel** *01 447 0057*

Map *4 B2*

The location is what makes Rosa Nautica so appealing. Built on a pier jutting out into the Pacific, this Lima stalwart serves up seafood to the sound of crashing waves. The sautéed sea bass with crayfish and mushroom sauce is a winner, so too is the tuna with avocado risotto.

MIRAFLORES Scena

⑨⑨⑨

Calle Francisco de Paula Camino 280 **Tel** *01 241 8184*

The perennially entertaining Scena, an amalgam of *escena* (stage) and *cena* (dinner), dishes up sweet potato gnocchi and goat's cheese, trout stuffed with mushrooms, and crème brûlée to the accompaniment of performances by acrobats, magicians, puppets, and tightrope walkers.

MIRAFLORES Astrid y Gastón

⑨⑨⑨⑨

Calle Cantuarias 175 **Tel** *01 242 4422*

Run by celebrity chef Gastón Acurio and his wife Astrid, this is Lima's most renowned *novoandino* eatery. This award-winning restaurant champions local flavors – roasted guinea pig with pecan and pisco sauce, risotto with black scallops, and duck with *lúcuma* (eggfruit).

MIRAFLORES Rafael

⑨⑨⑨⑨

Calle San Martín 300 **Tel** *01 242 4149*

Map *4 B2*

This chic restaurant is all about sophistication, from its Zen-like ambience to the cool, contemporary food. Chef Rafael Osterling's spaghetti with marinated lobster in garlic confit is simply addictive, and meat fans queue up for the most succulent baked goat in Madeira.

MIRAFLORES Rodrigo

⑨⑨⑨⑨

Calle Francisco de Paula Camino 231 **Tel** *01 446 0985*

Chef and owner Rodrigo Conway's sleek European lounge-style restaurant dips into Mediterranean, Basque, French, and Peruvian traditions. Dishes include foie gras-filled quinoa cannelloni, prawns sautéed in vanilla oil, and tuna with oranges and Grand Marnier. A DJ spins out tunes after midnight.

MIRAFLORES Costanera 700

⑨⑨⑨⑨⑨

Av. El Ejército 421 **Tel** *01 421 4635*

Map *2 B5*

Locals joke that the "700" is an indication of the meal price. But Humberto Sato's Japanese-Peruvian fusion cuisine is worth a splurge. Try *tako ankake* (octopus with sweet and sour plums) or *chita a la sal* (sea bream baked in a salt crust), served flambé courtesy of a last-minute coating of rum.

SAN ISIDRO Segundo Muelle

⑨⑨

Av. Canaval y Moreyra 605 **Tel** *01 717 9996*

Map *3 D3*

Immensely popular with locals, this informal lunch-only place offers fresh fish at reasonable prices. Try the tasty scallop *cebiche*, and wok-fried Chinese vegetables with fish, calamari, and prawns. There are two other branches of this restaurant in San Isidro.

SAN ISIDRO T'anta

Calle Pancho Fierro 117 **Tel** *01 421 9708*

This airy café with a sunny enclosed terrace caters to Lima's upwardly mobile with a range of tapas, *empanadas* (a stuffed pastry), sandwiches, and salads. More expensive are the mains such as lamb shanks in red wine. Lush desserts are also on offer. The restaurant has other branches in Lima.

SAN ISIDRO Fusión

Calle Choquehuanca 714 **Tel** *01 422 7600*   **Map** *2 B3*

Tucked away in the heart of the Lima business district, this fashionable eatery is a hit with affluent locals who have a taste for the contemporary. Chef Rafael Piqueras' *cebiche* martini, fish with passionfruit, wasabi and chili, and cheesecake with banana ice cream keeps the customers coming back.

SAN ISIDRO Malabar

Camino Real 101 **Tel** *01 440 5200*   **Map** *2 B3*

A striking portrait of two nude female swimmers greets diners on entry, showing that chef Pedro Miguel Schiaffino, while serious about his food, has a sense of humour. Italian and Peruvian flavors mix in dishes such as spicy red peppers stuffed blood sausage, and duck breast with chocolate and chilis.

SAN ISIDRO Casa Hacienda Moreyra

Av. Paz Soldán 290 **Tel** *01 444 3979*

Lima's Spanish legacy is on show in this imposing terra-cotta-colored Colonial mansion. Book a balcony table overlooking the Moorish courtyard fountain, or a table inside, surrounded by 18th-century art, and dine on calamari stuffed with red pepper and prawns, tender veal fillet, and caramelized apple pancakes.

THE SOUTHERN COAST

CHINCHA ALTA Casa Hacienda San José

Panamerican Highway South, KM203 **Tel** *01 441 0209*   **Road map** *C5*

This elegant restaurant is famous for its plentiful Creole buffets on Sundays. Chef Celina Reyes' specialties include *causa* (mashed potato) layered with vegetables, chicken and rice, and custard apple tart topped with meringue. There are Afro-Peruvian dance performances, too.

CHINCHA ALTA Wakama

Panamerican Highway South, KM178.5 **Tel** *01 998 386 154 (Lima)*   **Road map** *C5*

Located on Wakama Beach, between Chincha and Cañete, this breezy restaurant, part of the Wakama Ecoplaya, offers sea views and fresh seafood, including grilled octopus, freshly caught clams with pasta, as well as tasty pizzas. Creole music and dance performances also take place. Do remember that it is open from November to April only.

HUACACHINA Hotel Mossone

Balneario de la Huacachina s/n **Tel** *056 213 630*   **Road map** *C5*

The restaurant in this Colonial-style Hotel Mossone, with its graceful columns and arches, serves up a range of Peruvian and international dishes. The emphasis is on fresh seafood and Creole flavors. Its location gives the visitor a feel of an oasis within an oasis.

ICA Pizzeria Venezia

Calle Lima 230 **Tel** *056 232 241*   **Road map** *C5*

Simple pizzas loaded with cheese, homemade pastas, including gnocchi made with yellow Peruvian potatoes, and meat and fish dishes, rounded off with a scoop of ice cream, are the flavor of the day at this popular Italian-Peruvian eatery located just a few steps from the Plaza de Armas.

ICA Plaza 125

Calle Lima 125 **Tel** *056 211 816*   **Road map** *C5*

As the name indicates, this popular family pitstop sits right on Ica's main plaza. It serves good grilled meats, including hamburgers, barbecued chicken, Peruvian sandwiches, salads, and regional specialties such as hearty *adobos* (stews). Breakfast is also available.

ICA El Otro Peñoncito

Calle Bolivar 255 **Tel** *056 233 921*   **Road map** *C5*

Ica's most upmarket restaurant serves up Peruvian Creole favorites such as *aji de gallina* (creamy chicken stew), as well as good seafood, pasta, and meat options on linen-covered tables. The family makes its own pisco and the bartender's pisco sour is a knockout.

NAZCA Restaurante Farita

Calle Arica 415 **Tel** *056 523 944*   **Road map** *C5*

Farita specializes in Peruvian favorites such as *chicharrones* (pork rinds fried in their own fat), duck with rice and *carapulcra* (boiled, dehydrated potato stew with pork, chicken, chilies, garlic, and spices), as well as a coastal Creole favorite *escabeche pescado* (fish cooked in vinegar with onions), and usually served cold.

Key to Price Guide *see p290* **Key to Symbols** *see back cover flap*

NAZCA El Portón

Calle Ignacio Morseski 160 **Tel** *056 523 490* — **Road map** *C5*

Hailed by many as home to the best pasta in Nazca; the lasagne packed with local seafood only confirms their reputation. Creole dishes also feature *aji de gallina*, and *seco de cabrito* (goat stew), alongside plump pizzas, and Italian-inspired salads.

NAZCA Cantayo Spa and Resort

Hotel Cantayo Spa and Resort, Nazca **Tel** *056 522 345* — **Road map** *C5*

Housed in Nazca's best hotel *(see p272)*, this restaurant is known for its use of organic produce, delicious home-made pastas, and freshly caught seafood. They also do a mean *pachamanca*, Peruvian barbecue where meat and vegetables cooked in an underground pit.

NAZCA Nazca Lines Hotel

Jirón Bolognesi s/n **Tel** *056 522 293* — **Road map** *C5*

This excellent restaurant in the Nazca Lines Hotel *(see p272)* serves up a fine *cebiche* (dish of raw marinated fish) and other fresh seafood either on the breezy, polished patio framed by white colonnades overlooking the garden, or in the more formal dining room, with its linen-covered tables and polished wooden chairs.

PISCO Don Manuel

Jirón Comercio 179 — **Road map** *C5*

Pisco's best restaurant specializes in grilled fish and *mariscos* (shellfish) and does a good *cebiche corvina* (chunks of local sea bass marinated in lemon juice with a touch of chili and onion). There are grilled meat options including steak with french fries, as well as Creole-style dishes, all washed down with pisco sour. The lunch menu is a bargain.

CANYON COUNTRY

AREQUIPA Lakshmivan

Calle Jerusalén 402 **Tel** *054 228 768* — **Road map** *D6*

Vegetarians are spoilt for choice at this appealing garden eatery. The fare on offer includes soups, soy and tofu hamburgers, spinach lasagna, paella, as well as an extensive array of salads. For breakfast fans, there is homemade muesli and bread, yoghurt and fruits.

AREQUIPA El Turko II

Calle San Francisco 315 **Tel** *054 203 862* — **Road map** *D6*

Chef Ibrahim Veyssal offers a taste of Turkey in rural Peru. Sample rice-filled vine leaves, eggplant dip, hummus, falafel, lamb grilled in kebabs and roasted with herbs, all in the unique ambience created by volcanic stone walls and wooden floors. The smaller and cheaper café (El Turko I) is just down the street.

AREQUIPA La Cantarilla

Calle Tahuaycani 106, Sachaca **Tel** *054 251 515* — **Road map** *D6*

Arequipa's best loved open air restaurant is like a bastion of local flavors. Juicy *camarones* (river prawns) are used in soups, starters, and the main course. *Queso helado* (milky cinnamon and coconut ice cream) is definitely the preferred choice of dessert.

AREQUIPA Mixto's

Pasaje La Catedral 115 **Tel** *054 205 343* — **Road map** *D6*

Located on the pedestrian alley behind the Cathedral, Mixto's eclectic menu runs from *cebiche* (dish of raw marinated fish) and pizza to pasta and salads, along with Spanish tortillas. The view of the Cathedral from the balcony upstairs enhances the charm of the meal.

AREQUIPA Sol de Mayo

Calle Jerusalén 207, Yanahuara **Tel** *054 254 148* — **Road map** *D6*

Relax in the umbrella-shaded courtyard of one of Arequipa's best traditional restaurants and enjoy *rocotos rellenos* (spicy red peppers stuffed with meat), and *ocopa* (boiled potatoes with cheese sauce), and of course, *camarones* prepared in myriad ways.

AREQUIPA Tradición Arequipeña

Av. Dolores 111, J.L.B. y Rivero **Tel** *054 426 467* — **Road map** *D6*

The flavors of Arequipa take center stage here. *Camarones*, along with other *chupes* (seafood) and *pebres* (meat) soups, and hearty mains including *adobo Arequipeño* or pork marinated in *chicha* (corn beer) are served here. The flower-filled courtyard is a perfect setting for outdoor dining.

AREQUIPA La Trattoria del Monasterio

Santa Catalina 309 **Tel** *054 204 062* — **Road map** *D6*

The cosy stone-walled restaurant with brightly colored paintings and murals serves sophisticated Italian fare, including spaghetti with Arequipa's famous *camarones*, osso bucco, risotto, and chubby tortellini filled with ricotta and asparagus.

AREQUIPA Zig Zag

Zela 210 **Tel** *051 206 020* **Road map** *D6*

Located in a narrow Colonial house, this pretty restaurant boasts an iron staircase designed by Frenchman Gustave Eiffel. The cuisine is a blend of the Andes and the Alps. Specialties include carpaccios of ostrich, trout, and alpaca as well as fondues and stone-grilled steaks and seafood.

PUNO Casa del Corregidor

Jirón Deustua 576 **Tel** *051 365 603* **Road map** *E6*

Housed in one of Puno's oldest Colonial buildings, which is now a cultural institute, this informal café is an ideal spot for a toasted sandwich, accompanied by coffee and cake. The center also has a library, an art gallery, and a shop in the courtyard that sells locally made handicrafts.

PUNO La Casona

Jirón Lima 517 **Tel** *051 351 108* **Road map** *E6*

Decorated with paintings from the Cusco School *(see p167)* and the odd antique, La Casona bills itself as a museum-restaurant. The menu veers between traditional and modern – from guinea pig and *pesque de quinoa* (mashed quinoa with cheese and milk) to trout from the nearby Lake Titicaca.

PUNO La Fonda de Santiago

Jirón Libertadad 414 **Tel** *051 975 3188* **Road map** *E6*

Modern Peruvian dishes – *causa* with freshly caught kingfish, alpaca steak, and lamb chops with pumpkin ravioli – are the hallmark of this breezy restaurant run by the effervescent Margarita. The outdoor patio is ideal for casual summer eating, while the second floor is both cosy and classy.

PUNO Los Uros Restaurant

Hotel Libertador, Isla Esteves s/n, Lake Titicaca **Tel** *051 367 780* **Road map** *E6*

Dine on freshly caught *pejerrey* (kingfish) in black butter sauce, trout with almonds, or alpaca chops with quinoa risotto while gazing over Lake Titicaca from Puno's most upscale restaurant. Boats glide past en route to Los Uros, the floating reed islands on the lake.

THE INCA HEARTLAND

AGUAS CALIENTES Indio Feliz

Lloque Yupanqui Lote 4–12 **Tel** *084 211 090* **Road map** *D5*

Good value food served in a bright and cheery atmosphere. There are a variety of options to choose from – soups, salads, local trout with lemon, and soothing apple pie. Flowers on the table, classical music, and a fire during the winters, adds to the homely feel.

AGUAS CALIENTES Michuna Wasi

Aguas Calientes **Tel** *084 211 032* **Road map** *D5*

The glass-walled restaurant in this mountainside hotel offers marvelous views of the briskly flowing Río Urubamba below and the steep Andes rising behind. The food served here is modern Peruvian – avocado salad, corn chowder, and *lomo saltado* (a spicy dish made from sliced beef, onions, chips, and chili).

CUSCO Kin Taro

Calle Heladeros, Plaza Regocijo **Tel** *084 226 181* **Road map** *D5*

The decor might be a bit shabby at first glance but the simple Japanese food is anything but. Opt for miso soup, sashimi, sushi, or any of the loads of tofu dishes. The meal can be washed down with a glass or two of the famous Japanese drink, sake. Bargain lunch menu.

CUSCO Paddy's Irish Pub

Calle Triunfo 124 **Tel** *084 247 719* **Road map** *D5*

Overlooking the plaza, Paddy's dishes up great pub grub, including steaming shepherd's pie, hearty casseroles and curries accompanied by crusty baguettes, and to top it off, a helping of rib-sticking bread and butter custard. Great value means that it is always busy.

CUSCO Green's Organic

Calle Tandapata 700, San Blas **Tel** *084 243 379* **Road map** *D5*

Totally organic produce is the selling point of this second-floor eatery. Food has a Peruvian-British focus, and runs from chicken curry with perfumed rice to alpaca steak with elderberries. Local trout is also available. Sunday roasts are popular, so reserve a table in advance.

CUSCO Jacks' Café

Calle Choquechaca 188 **Tel** *084 254 606* **Road map** *D5*

With its warm woody interior, racks of glossy magazines, and modern art, Jack's is a comfortable place at any time of the day. Sup on scrambled eggs with roast tomatoes, generous steak sandwiches, vegetable burgers, pastas, or tasty green chicken curry.

Key to Price Guide *see p290* **Key to Symbols** *see back cover flap*

CUSCO Olas Bravas
Av. de la Cultura s/n, Mariscal Gamara **Tel** *084 439 328* **Road map** *D5*

Fresh seafood, such as scallops, prawns, and fish, are flown in daily from Lima, making this restaurant (open from 9am–5pm) the Inca capital's best bet when one needs to satiate a seafood craving. Olas Bravas also serves some great *cebiches (see p285)* at very reasonable prices.

CUSCO Pacha Papa
Plazoleta San Blas 120 **Tel** *084 241 318* **Road map** *D5*

Set in the courtyard of an old Colonial house in San Blas, the informal Pacha Papa specializes in traditional food cooked in an outdoor adobe oven, and in clay pots. Try roasted guinea pig or the highly popular *olluco con charqui* (Andean tuber and potatoes stewed with dried alpaca meat).

CUSCO Baco
Calle Ruinas 465 **Tel** *084 242 808* **Road map** *D5*

Large, modern space with dark wood, leather lounges, and modern art, it serves gourmet pizzas with smoked trout and fennel, Argentinian steaks, and a sustaining barbecued antipasto platter. There is also a great selection of cocktails and a decent list of local and imported wines.

CUSCO Cicciolina
Calle Triunfo 393 **Tel** *084 239 510* **Road map** *D5*

Locals dub this as Cusco's classiest fine-dining option. The second floor restaurant is divided into a tapas bar and dining room. Food is a fusion of Mediterranean, particularly Italian, and Peruvian. It has an extensive South American wine list. The first floor bakery is open for breakfast.

CUSCO Incanto
Calle Santa Catalina Angosta 135 **Tel** *084 254 753* **Road map** *D5*

Clean modern lines – light wood tables, striking flower arrangements, and abundant use of white – have endeared this restaurant to upscale locals and visitors alike. The food is "new Peruvian" with lots of pastas, salads, steaks, and wickedly sweet desserts.

CUSCO Map Café
Casa Cabrero – Museo de Arte Precolombino, Plazoleta Nazarenas **Tel** *084 242 476* **Road map** *D5*

The new merges with the old in this striking glass restaurant located in the distinguished Colonial courtyard of the Museum of Pre-Columbian Art. The elegant food matches the surroundings – alpaca *tonnato* (alpaca in tuna sauce), yellow potato gnocchi with spicy prawn and pepper sauce, and rosy sesame-crusted tuna with chilies.

CUSCO Tunupa
Portal Confituria 233, Plaza de Armas **Tel** *084 252 936* **Road map** *D5*

The sprawling Tunupa is a tourist haven because of its abundant Peruvian buffet tables and live music along with dance performances. A cosy fire in the dining room upstairs is a bonus in winter, while tables on the narrow balcony overlook the plaza, which is particularly pretty at night.

OLLANTAYTAMBO Mayupata
Jirón Convención s/n **Tel** *084 204 009* **Road map** *D5*

Overlooking the Río Patacancha, this restaurant turns out sparkling fresh trout *cebiches*, crispy-crust pizzas, generous burgers, and good Peruvian standbys such as *lomo saltado*. Owner Raul Palma, apart from being a food lover, is a storehouse of information about the area.

CENTRAL SIERRA

AYACUCHO El Monasterio
Jirón 28 de Julio 178 **Tel** *066 312 343* **Road map** *D5*

This little *pollería* serves large portions of excellent roast chicken and chips. It is also a pleasant place to sit, as it is located in the Colonial courtyard of Ayacucho's Centro Cultural. It is a very reasonably priced restaurant and is quite popular in this area.

AYACUCHO La Casona
Jirón Bellido 463 **Tel** *066 312 733* **Road map** *D5*

A good selection of well-cooked and nicely presented Andean specialties is on offer at this popular eatery. Tender grilled meats, trout, and oven-baked pork are some of the favorites. The seating is around a pretty courtyard and the service is friendly and efficient.

AYACUCHO Los Portales
Portal Unión 33 **Road map** *D5*

This restaurant has an extremely central location. Los Portales serves excellent local dishes as well as snacks, sandwiches, and tortillas around a pleasant courtyard. A popular lunch venue, it also transforms into a cheesy disco over the weekends.

AYACUCHO Mercado de Abastos Carlos F Vivanco

Mercado Central **Road map** D5

The Central Market is a great place to sample some of the local dishes, and very cheaply. There are numerous stalls offering specialties of the region including some fantastic meaty stews. Be sure to pick a popular stall where you can see that the cooking conditions are sanitary. It is a perfect spot for watching people, far from the tourist crowd.

AYACUCHO Mia Pizza

San Martín 420 **Road map** D5

This is a long-standing restaurant that serves great pizzas, pastas, salads, and snacks. In the evenings it transforms into a live music and karaoke venue. It is popular with the local young crowd as well as tourists, attracted by the reasonable prices and lively atmosphere.

AYACUCHO Urpicha

Jirón Londres 272 **Tel** *066 813 905* **Road map** D5

This lovely little restaurant, in a lovely Colonial building, is decorated with local artworks and has a plant-filled courtyard. Only traditional Andean food is served, including some excellent pork and chicken dishes, and the popular *puca picante* (a stew of pork, peanuts, and potatoes). The Urpicha platter gives a sample of the house specialties.

HUANCAVÉLICA Mochica Sachún

Jirón Virrey Toledo 303 **Tel** *064 752 613* **Road map** C5

This busy local spot has an excellent value lunch menu, which usually offers some sort of soup, a simple main course, with rice and meat, plus a dessert. Portions are not huge but the three dishes should fill you up and cost only a small sum. The service is fairly slow, but the atmosphere is cheerful.

HUANCAVÉLICA Polleria Joy

Calle M. Segura **Road map** C5

This is the place to come to for good grilled chicken and chips at very reasonable prices. Not a lot of atmosphere but the helpings are large and are great value for money. Beer and soft drinks are also served here. Its central location is ideal for an evening spent watching people.

HUANCAVÉLICA La Olla de Barro

Av. Agustín Gamarra 305 **Road map** C5

There are some hearty portions of good local dishes on offer here, including a filling, tasty *el patachi* (meat stew), as well as trout and guinea pig. They also serve pastas, meats, and sandwiches. The atmosphere is pleasant and the service is good.

HUANCAYO Koky

Puno 298 **Road map** C4

You can find some fantastic pastries in this unassuming little *panadería* (bakery). There is not much table space but the place is warm and friendly. Breakfast, which includes yoghurts and muesli, as well as good sandwiches and coffee, is also available here.

HUANCAYO La Cabaña

Av. Giraldez 652 **Tel** *064 223 303* **Road map** C4

This is a busy night spot with live folk and popular music on Thursday, Friday, and Saturday. It has fun decor, a lively atmosphere, and friendly staff. The menu offers excellent pizzas, sandwiches, and *calentitos* (sweet, deep-fried snacks). This venue is popular with the local crowd.

HUÁNUCO Pizzeria Don Sancho

General Prado 645 **Tel** *062 516 906* **Road map** C4

A vast range of oven-fired pizzas as well as pancakes and sandwiches and some delicious puddings make this a popular hangout spot with tourists and young locals. An ideal place to meet other travelers. The service is friendly and the food is very good value for money but it opens only after 6:30pm.

CORDILLERA BLANCA

CARAZ Café de Rat

Jirón Sucre 1266, Plaza de Armas **Road map** B3

This friendly little restaurant is situated on the Plaza de Armas, with a balcony overlooking the square. Popular with hikers and climbers, the café has a library and serves good fresh coffee, as well as a range of tasty pizzas and pancakes. A good place to get information on treks and climbing routes.

CARAZ Café la Terraza

Jirón Sucre 1107 **Road map** B3

Located just half a block away from the Plaza de Armas, this is the place to come to for a great lunchtime menu that is also excellent value for money. Pizzas, sandwiches, and homemade ice cream are served. Both the atmosphere and the service are good.

Key to Price Guide *see p290* **Key to Symbols** *see back cover flap*

CARAZ Jeny

Daniel Villar, Plaza de Armas

Road map *B3*

This long-standing Caraz eatery serves up some great roast chicken, along with a variety of rice and meat preparations. The food at Jeny is economical and the restaurant is ideally located for watching people strolling through the main square.

CARAZ La Punta Grande

Daniel Villar 595

Road map *B3*

A short walk from the town center, La Punta Grande is a good place to try the traditional highland dishes. Their specialties include hearty soups and stews, and *cuy* (guinea pig). There is a nice leafy garden that makes it a popular local spot for lunch.

CARHUAZ Café el Abuelo

Plaza de Armas **Tel** *043 394 149*

Road map *B4*

A small café on the Plaza de Armas serving breakfasts, sandwiches, fresh coffee, and ice cream. The organic ingredients are from the garden at the El Abuelo *(see p276)* and the ice cream is homemade – there are some interesting flavors, including pisco sour.

CARHUAZ La Punta Olímpica

Av. La Merced 500

Road map *B4*

This lively restaurant specializes in fish dishes and *comida criolla* (Creole food), including *ají de gallina* (creamy chicken stew), *anticuchos* (marinated beef heart kebabs), and *lomo saltado* (spicy dish made from sliced beef, onions, chips, and chili). They have live local music during the weekends.

HUARAZ Café Andino

Jirón Lucar y Torre 530 **Tel** *043 721 203*

Road map *C4*

This eatery has exposed brickwork, open fireplaces and a balcony with views over the Andes. Fresh juices, coffee, and a snacky lunch and dinner menu with salads, pizzas, and sandwiches are on offer. It also has an extensive library and board games, and is a popular meeting spot for hikers. The American owner advises on trekking in the area.

HUARAZ Crêperie Patrick

Av. Luzurriaga 422 **Tel** *043 426 037*

Road map *C4*

This French-run restaurant serves a huge variety of fantastic sweet and savory pancakes. There are also local trout and meat dishes, fondues, salads, and pastas on the menu. It also has one of the better wine lists in Huaraz. The service is good and the atmosphere is intimate and lively.

HUARAZ Pachamama

San Martín 687 **Tel** *043 424 200*

Road map *C4*

This large, Swiss-run restaurant has an extensive menu – all dishes are made from organic produce. There is a pretty patio with an art gallery which hosts live local and international music shows. There are pool and table tennis tables and the owners willingly provide information on trekking.

HUARAZ Pizzeria Piccolo

Jirón Julian de Morales 632 **Tel** *043 509 210*

Road map *C4*

This popular little place serves a good breakfast, with fresh coffee, muesli, and eggs, along with an inviting array of cakes and puddings. Pizzas are good and varied. There are two terraces for outdoor drinking and eating. Pizzeria Piccolo also has a delivery service.

HUARAZ Bistro de Los Andes

Jirón Julio de Morales 823 **Tel** *043 426 249*

Road map *C4*

One of the most popular eateries in Huaraz, with both locals and tourists. There is a varied menu, including traditional Peruvian, French, and vegetarian dishes. The local trout is fantastic. The owner speaks English and French, and the food is consistently good. Open for breakfast, lunch, and supper.

HUARAZ Monte Rosa

Jirón Jose de la Mar 661 **Tel** *043 421 447*

Road map *C4*

Inviting and cosy, this two-story restaurant is a great post-hike venue, with a well-stocked bar and lively atmosphere. Monte Rosa's menu offers pizzas, pastas, fondues, as well as local Peruvian dishes. Mountaineering gear can be hired from the adjacent shop.

THE NORTHERN DESERT

CHICLAYO Bar Restaurant Romana

Av. Balta 512 **Tel** *074 223 598*

Road map *B3*

A block from the main square, this popular restaurant is ideal for the adventurous. Sandwiches, salads, juices, soups, chicken, pork, and beef dishes, seafood, pastas, and desserts are available. The *chirimpico* (stewed goat tripe and organ meat, seasoned with coriander), *chicha* (corn beer), and *ají* (peppers) is a traditional breakfast.

CHICLAYO Fiesta Restaurant Gourmet

Av. Salaverry 1820 **Tel** *074 201 970*   **Road map** *B3*

This top-end gourmet chain opened in 1983 and has two other restaurants in Lima and Tacna. Their specialty is the traditional cuisine of Lambayeque, featuring home-raised duck and baby goat, cooked with spicy age-old recipes. The wine selection includes good Chilean, Argentinian, and Spanish brands. The food is highly recommended.

HUANCHACO Otra Cosa – Vegetarian Restaurant

Av. Víctor Larco 921, Urb. El Boquerón **Tel** *044 461 346*   **Road map** *B3*

Origianlly opened by Dutch couple, Janeeke Smeulders and Peter den Hond, this is the town's only vegetarian restaurant. The energizing breakfasts and nutritious lunches and dinners are economical. The place also runs a voluntary work agency and an alternative tourism project center.

HUANCHACO Huanchaco Beach

Av. Víctor Larco 602 **Tel** *044 46 1484 / 50 1706*   **Road map** *B3*

This three-story, blue-painted restaurant is a good option for great fish and seafood treats. *Cebiche a la crema de ají rojo*, a variant of the traditional Peruvian dish made with marinated fish and a red pepper sauce, is excellent. There are more than 50 other seafood choices including crab, shrimp, prawns, and octopus.

HUANCHACO Lucho del Mar

Av. Víctor Larco 600, on the cnr with Túpac Amaru **Tel** *044 461 484*   **Road map** *B3*

Huanchaco boasts great places to enjoy a sumptuous lunch and Lucho del Mar is one such eatery. The windowless restaurant has a casual ambience. The menu has almost all the Peruvian fish or seafood dishes imaginable and the food is quite extraordinary. Highly recommended.

HUANCHACO Restaurant Big Ben

Av. Víctor Larco 836, Urb. El Boquerón **Tel** *044 461 378 / 461 869*   **Road map** *B3*

Opened in 1979, Big Ben is one of the oldest restaurants in the city. Featuring a three-story set of sunshade terraces, it overlooks the ocean. Specialties include *conchitas a la parmesana* (Parmesan grilled scallops), or the *parihuela* (a tasty soup with crab, fish, shellfish, and seaweed), very popular among Peruvians as a cure for hangover.

LAMBAYEQUE El Rincón del Pato

Av. Augusto B. Leguía 270 **Tel** *074 282 751*   **Road map** *B3*

If the Sipán Museum (*see pp228–9*) is the sole reason to visit the small town of Lambayeque, the ideal complement is lunch at this restaurant. Duck cooked in various ways is the specialty. Try the *arroz con pato* (stewed duck with coriander-flavored rice) or *pato arvejado* (duck ragout), or the fish and chicken dishes.

MÁNCORA Angela's Place

Av. Piura 396 **Tel** *073 258 603*   **Road map** *A2*

Angela Schwitzberger came from Austria in 2000 and settled down here, selling home-made whole grain bread and pastries on her bike. Today, her place is an excellent option for vegetarians and non-fish eaters, the exception being goulash (a beef stew from her homeland). The atmosphere is friendly and Angela always welcomes newcomers.

MÁNCORA Casa de Playa Restaurant

Av. Antigua, Panamerican Highway North, KM1216 **Tel** *073 258 005*   **Road map** *A2*

This hotel's restaurant is reputed to be one of the best in the area, with a great view of the ocean and a laidback atmosphere. Specialties include grilled octopus with balsamic dressing, *cebiche*, tuna carpaccio with capers and Parmesan lobster, along with salads, fish, risottos, pastas, and other delicacies. The wines are pretty good too.

MÁNCORA Pizzeria Ristorante Volentieri

Talara 331 **Tel** *073 258 139*   **Road map** *A2*

Married to a Peruvian, Italian born Antonio Ortenzio started his business in 2003 delivering pizzas. Two years later he opened his *ristorante* adding to his numerous pizzas, lasagna, tagliatelle, ravioli, and gnocchi. It is famous among Italian food-lovers, locals, and travelers. Three blocks away from the Panamerican Highway, this place is a good treat.

MÁNCORA Turismo Restaurante Espada

Av. Piura 501 **Tel** *073 258 304*   **Road map** *A2*

Máncora has a number of seafood restaurants situated along the Panamerican Highway. Their doubtful quality has now changed and the owners are concerned about good service. Espada is a good example of this process, with its impressive list of fish and seafood dishes, which have earned international gastronomic awards.

TRUJILLO Chifa Ah Chau

Gamarra 769 **Tel** *044 243 351*   **Road map** *B3*

A plain doorway with a hand-painted sign leads to a long corridor with curtained doorways on both sides, each leading to a private eating booth panelled in fake, funky, plastic wood. Called a *chifa* (Chinese restaurant), it serves Chinese food with a Peruvian touch. Big portions, exquisite flavors, and great value.

TRUJILLO Café Restaurant El Romano

Pizarro 747 **Tel** *044 252 251*   **Road map** *B3*

This long-established café-restaurant is three blocks from the main square. It has a well-earned reputation for the best, hot, steamy espresso and capuccino. A wide variety of meals at good prices are served including sandwiches, salads, soups, Peruvian dishes, and desserts.

Key to Price Guide *see p290* **Key to Symbols** *see back cover flap*

TRUJILLO Chelsea Pub Restaurant

Estete 675 **Tel** *044 257 032*   **Road map** *B3*

More than an English pub, this eclectic restaurant overwhelms a diner with its diverse foods. For lunch: seafood, beef, steak, pasta; and for dinner: smoked salmon, pork, sole, grilled meat, kebabs, ribs, salads, and more. There is a piano bar (Thu–Sat), and live music (Fri–Sat) with two big bands, one for each evening. It's a place to dance and party.

TRUJILLO El Mochica

Bolivar 462 **Tel** *044 293 441*   **Road map** *B3*

According to renowned Peruvian chef Gastón Acurio this is "an ideal place to discover grandmother's cooking". *Sopa shambar* (tasty, thick soup of wheat, vegetables, and pork), served only on Mondays, *tallarines con pichones* (spaghetti with stewed baby pigeons), a delicacy seldom found elsewhere, and other meat and fish options are available.

TRUJILLO El Romano Criollo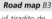

Estados Unidos 162, Urb. El Recreo **Tel** *044 244 207*   **Road map** *B3*

The popular Romano Criollo offers more than 200 dishes of traditional Peruvian and regional cuisine. This very welcoming restaurant is located south of downtown and serves the simply delicious iconic dish *cabrito a la norteña* (boneless baby goat meat stewed with herbs) served with cooked beans and rice.

TRUJILLO Restaurant Marisquería Los Herrajes

Av. Salvador Lara (ex 9 de Octubre) 893, Urb. Las Quintanas **Tel** *044 204 846*   **Road map** *B3*

Marisquería is the term given to a seafood restaurant and Los Herrajes is just that, owned by the Goicochea Cruz family, which started reviving the forgotten traditional recipes of Northern Peru. Just away from downtown, this restaurant has great *cebiches*, cold and hot entrées, deep fried fish, soups, and many delicious seafood dishes.

TRUJILLO Squalo's

Calle Cienfuegos 250, Urb. La Merced **Tel** *044 295 134*   **Road map** *B3*

A member of the Romano Group, Squalo's specializes in fish and seafood. Try the generous portions of *tiradito de pescado y camarones a las 4 cremas* (sashimi-style raw fish with prawns, bathed in a creamy *ají* pepper sauce) or *chicharrón de pescado en salsa de pulpa de cangrejo* (deep fried fish chunks with crab meat sauce).

TUMBES Restaurant Turístico Latino

Bolivar 163, Plaza de Armas **Tel** *072 523 198*   **Road map** *B2*

Though not the best in the Tumbes region, neither is this restaurant one of the *huariques* (holes-in-the-wall). Restaurant Turístico Latino serves a wide variety of Peruvian food. You can choose between sitting inside or outside on the shaded pavement. The fare is not bad at all.

THE NORTHERN HIGHLANDS

CAJAMARCA Cascanuez

Puga 554 **Tel** *076 366 089*   **Road map** *B3*

This is the best place in town for a sweet tooth. Pastries and pies are homemade, and good coffee is served. Sandwiches and a short menu of local main courses can provide a complete meal, but Cajamarqueños are known to drop in after lunch or dinner for dessert, or for an afternoon pick-me-up.

CAJAMARCA Salas

Puga 637 **Tel** *076 342 2867*   **Road map** *B3*

Salas has been the mainstay of Cajamarqueño dining for over six decades. The place offers a real local experience. A huge menu features the obligatory *cuy* (guinea pig), the infrequently seen *sesos* (cow brains) served in an omelette, *tamales* (steamed corn dough with or without filling), and straightforward chicken and chips.

CAJAMARCA El Batán

Del Batán 369 **Tel** *076 346 025*   **Road map** *B3*

This delightful restaurant-cum-art-gallery in a renovated 18th-century mansion is just two blocks from the Plaza de Armas. As with most of Cajamarca's better restaurants, the set menu offers an inexpensive choice – ask for it. Local folkloric musicians perform on Friday and Saturday evenings. Closed on Mondays.

CAJAMARCA El Cajamarqués

Amazonas 770 **Tel** *076 342 128*   **Road map** *B3*

With whitewashed walls and beamed ceilings, this is Cajamarca's most traditional upscale restaurant. The adjoining courtyard has caged birds, which attract diners waiting for their meals. The menu offers both Peruvian and international selections, weighted towards the meaty side as is found in most of Cajamarca's restaurants.

CAJAMARCA El Querubino

Puga 589 **Tel** *076 340 900*   **Road map** *B3*

Tiled and brightly painted, just steps away from the Plaza de Armas, this is among the most stylish and popular eateries. The meaty menu includes sweetbreads made of pancreas for adventurous diners looking to experiment with local cuisine. International fare includes seafood and a reasonable wine list. Music is acoustic and non-intrusive.

CHACHAPOYAS El Tejado

Grau 534 **Tel** *041 477 554*   **Road map** *B3*

This second floor restaurant with creaky wooden flooring and beamed ceiling feels like it belongs on the Plaza de Armas, which it overlooks. Extremely inexpensive set lunches bring in knowledgeable local diners. The menu is mainly Creole, with several good chicken dishes.

CHACHAPOYAS Matalacha

Ayacucho 616 **Tel** *041 478 325*   **Road map** *B3*

The menu tends strongly towards local dishes, including *cuy* and some with Amazonian influences such as *juanes* (rice with chicken or fish steamed in banana leaves) as well as a few international ones. The restaurant is brightly lit and popular with locals and the occasional tour group.

LEYMEBAMBA Cely's

La Verdad 530   **Road map** *B3*

First known as a pizza place, Cely's has expanded its menu to include a variety of chicken and pasta dishes, along with Peruvian cuisine. With local arts and crafts on its walls, this is considered the best restaurant in the Leymebamba area. The helpful owners will cook up vegetarian dishes on request.

THE AMAZON BASIN

IQUITOS Ari's Burger

Próspero 127 **Tel** *065 231 470*   **Road map** *D2*

This brightly lit place on the east corner of the Plaza de Armas is nicknamed "gringolandia" for its popularity with travelers. Plenty of American choices, as well as some local dishes and good ice creams grace the varied menu. With two walls open to the street, it almost provides outdoor dining. Early breakfast is also offered.

IQUITOS Huasaí

Fitzcarrald 131 **Tel** *065 242 222*   **Road map** *D2*

Huasaí is the local name for the tree which yields the heart of palm, and true to its name the menu has a vegetarian section. An inexpensive set lunch draws the local downtown business crowd to the handy location, a half block from the Plaza de Armas. Check the chalkboard for daily specials. Regional breakfasts and dinner grills are also on offer.

IQUITOS Chifa Wai Ming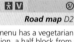

Plaza 28 de Julio, San Martín 464 **Tel** *065 233 391*   **Road map** *D2*

Chifas (Chinese restaurants) are found throughout Peru, often offering the best vegetarian option for travelers. Iquitos is no exception, and the nice-looking Chifa Wai Ming located on the Plaza is surely one of the best of the city's many eateries.

IQUITOS El Mesón

Malecón Maldonado 153 **Tel** *065 231 857*   **Road map** *D2*

Well-prepared wild game, including peccary, venison, agouti, and alligator, is the highlight at this riverfront restaurant. However, avoid turtle, which is endangered. Many tamer local dishes are also served, along with simple options such as pastas. Those on a budget will enjoy the inexpensive daily set lunch menu.

IQUITOS Fitzcarraldo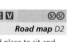

Napo 100 **Tel** *065 243 434*   **Road map** *D2*

The most upscale of a block of riverfront restaurants along the pedestrian Malecón, this is a good place to sit and watch the action on a Saturday night. The attractive, old-fashioned building dates from the rubber-boom days. Food includes salads, pizzas, and local and international dishes.

IQUITOS Gran Maloca

Sargento Lores 170 **Tel** *065 233 126*   **Road map** *D2*

This beautiful, tiled building from the rubber-boom era offers a rarity in Iquitos – air conditioning. The food is top-notch, with several local fish and wild game dishes prepared with flair and style. International food with an Amazonian twist and traditional Peruvian dishes appear on the menu as well.

IQUITOS Yellow Rose of Texas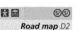

Putumayo 180 **Tel** *065 231 353*   **Road map** *D2*

This Texan restaurant/bar serves the best BBQ ribs in town, as well as Mexican, English, Italian, and Peruvian food. Comfortable wooden Adirondack armchairs and cheeky saddle stools, a variety of bar games, street-side and indoor garden seating, and 24-hour service make it popular with travelers.

LA MERCED Shambari Campa

Tarma 389 **Tel** *064 532 842*   **Road map** *C4*

On the north side of the Plaza de Armas, this long-established restaurant features interesting old photographs (and graffiti) dating back several decades. It's a hole-in-the-wall, but also the best in town, which yields an interesting ambience. The menu is extensive, the set-lunches are cheap, and the service lackadaisical.

MOYOBAMBA La Olla de Barro

Pedro Canga 383 **Tel** *042 563 450* **Road map** *C3*

Centrally located a block from the Plaza de Armas, this is the best and most typically Amazonian restaurant in town. The name means "pot of clay" and traditionally prepared jungle dishes such as grilled venison or stewed paca are a highlight. Local fruits are used in cooling juices, and vegetarian and Italian dishes are also available.

OXAPAMPA Oasis

Bolognesi 120 **Tel** *063 762 206* **Road map** *C4*

This is the best option in the center of town, with a simple albeit varied menu which is influenced more by Peruvian-style Chinese (mainly rice dishes) and Italian cuisine than by Teutonic cooking. The main dishes at Oasis are very well-prepared and filling.

OXAPAMPA El Trapiche

Mullembruck C-1 **Tel** *063 462 551* **Road map** *C4*

On the town's outskirts, this rambling wooden building offers verandas and outdoor gardens for breakfast, lunch, and dinner. The menu is meaty, and emphazises grilled and smoked Austro-German preparations. On weekends, Peruvian-style *pachamancas* (barbecue) draw the local populace.

PUCALLPA Don José's

Ucayali 661 **Tel** *061 572 865* **Road map** *C3*

It's been here for longer than any restaurant in downtown. Nothing fancy, just good basic food, with an emphasis on freshly prepared cold fruit juices to take the edge off Pucallpa's heat. Michael Palin, of *Monty Python* fame, ate here while doing his "Full Circle" around the Pacific, and he claims that it improved his perception of Pucallpa.

PUCALLPA El Alamo

Carretera Yarinacocha 2650 **Tel** *061 571 510* **Road map** *C3*

Take a cab to this restaurant, located a short distance from the center en route to Yarinacocha. It's one of Pucallpa's best upscale options, offering international cuisine whilst being mindful of local dishes. A crispy heart of palm salad is recommended as an Amazonian starter, then you are on your own. It's all good.

PUERTO MALDONADO Chez Maggy

Carrión 271 **Tel** *082 572 082* **Road map** *E5*

On the southwestern side of the Plaza de Armas, this pizza joint is a favourite of travelers and locals alike. The oven-baked, thin-crust pizzas are excellent, and are a better choice than the pastas. The place is open for dinner only – the wood-burning oven makes it too hot at lunchtime. Musicians often show up on Saturday night to pass the hat.

PUERTO MALDONADO El Califa

Piura 266 **Tel** *082 571 119* **Road map** *E5*

This ramshackle building on the edge of town is only a few blocks from the center and is famed for its regional specialties. Try grilled wild venison, fried bananas, heart of palm salads, and *juanes* (rice with chicken or fish steamed in banana leaves). The place is especially popular with locals at lunchtime.

PUERTO MALDONADO La Casa Nostra

Velarde 515 **Tel** *082 572 747* **Road map** *E5*

Of several cafés along the 5th block of Velarde, this place is especially recommended for its large and delicious tropical fruit juices. It also attracts travelers looking for breakfast, and has a good selection of light meals and snacks such as *tamales* (steamed corn dough with or without filling), stuffed potatoes, and desserts.

PUERTO MALDONADO Wasai Lodge

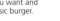

Billinghurst at Arequipa **Tel** *082 572 290* **Road map** *E5*

Breakfast, lunch, and dinner are offered at this restaurant, considered to be the best in town. It is located in the town's best hotel *(see p281)*, overlooking the Río Madre de Dios. Sit upstairs for the best river views. The menu features both international and local dishes, with Amazonian fish a specialty.

TARAPOTO El Brassero

Lamas 231 **Tel** *042 522 700* **Road map** *C3*

This dinner-only restaurant features a fine variety of inexpensive grilled meats – you choose what you want and the friendly owners will grill it for you. Ribs are the specialty, but children are catered to with the basic burger. Often, the owner will sit down and have a chat, especially with international travelers.

TARAPOTO Real Grill

Moyobamba 131 **Tel** *042 522 714* **Road map** *C3*

This locally popular place on the north side of the Plaza de Armas has a huge and varied menu which should please everyone. Local dishes, Chinese, Italian, seafood, sandwiches, and breakfasts are featured. Outdoor tables give a view of the noisy action on the plaza.

YARINACOCHA Along the Waterfront

Puerto Callao **Road map** *C3*

Locals (and a few international tourists) flock to the beautiful lake. Many eateries provide food in semi open-air stalls on the lakefront, with good fresh fish being the highlight. Wander around, see what's on offer, and grab a bench to lunch on the catch of the day. It's fun, funky, filling, and inexpensive.

SHOPPING IN PERU

Peruvian crafts are exquisite and few visitors leave without a souvenir. Upscale boutiques in the larger cities stock stylish silver jewelry and elegant alpaca shawls and jumpers, while street stalls in small northern beach towns brim over with shell necklaces and sarongs. Craft markets in Peru are loaded with alpaca knits, pottery, ceramics, handwoven textiles, baskets, and painted and carved wood.

A handmade doll

There are separate markets for fruits and vegetables. Bargaining is acceptable at street stalls but not in established shops. When buying directly from craftsmen, remember that profits are already low. Although illegal, piracy of DVDs, books, CDs, alcohol, and branded clothes is rampant, especially in Lima. It is illegal to export archaeological or valuable historical artifacts.

Shop filled with products in a handicraft market in the Inca Heartland

OPENING HOURS

As a general rule, shops, shopping centers, and handicraft markets are open daily, from 9am to 8pm. Small boutiques and shops may close for lunch, between 1 and 3pm. Large supermarkets, which exist only in Lima *(see pp100–101)* and in summer at Asia Beach, about 62 miles (100 km) south of Lima, do not close for lunch, remaining open until 10pm.

PAYMENT AND PRICES

Major credit cards such as VISA, MasterCard, and to a lesser extent, American Express, are accepted in larger shops in major cities. However, most market stall-holders prefer to be paid in cash, either soles or US dollars. Credit cards may be rejected in small villages or rural areas, so always remember to carry cash. Stalls selling large ticket items in tourist centers accept payment by credit card. Some businesses add a surcharge of up to 12 percent for credit card purchases. Always check

before paying. A value added tax (IGV) of 19 percent is added to all services and goods. A certain amount of bargaining is expected at craft markets. Local artisan cooperatives, such as those on Taquile Island on Lake Titicaca *(see pp146–7)*, have fixed prices with profits shared amongst the villagers. In other village co-ops, a portion of the profit goes directly to the craftsmen. In general, large galleries and shops arrange the shipping.

Designer handbags

Samples of handwoven textiles with traditional patterns

GENERAL STORES

Shopping malls, department stores, expensive boutiques, and supermarkets are Lima-centered. There is just one department store outside Lima, Saga Falabella in Arequipa.

Towns are the domain of craft markets, small shops, and produce markets. Clothing boutique, Alpaca 111 *(see p101)*, and silverware shop, Ilaria *(see p101)*, operate branches in top-end hotels in the provinces, such as Cusco and Puno, and some airports.

CLOTHING

Alpaca clothing abounds in the form of jumpers, coats, shawls, caps, and gloves. Garments are also available in soft baby alpaca and vicuña, considered to be the world's finest wool. Arequipa is the center of the wool industry, and has no shortage of shops.

Imported designer labels can be found at a few select boutiques in Lima. Max Mara has its own shop in San Isidro and Hugo Boss has one in Jockey Plaza. Department stores Ripley's and Saga Falabella stock a range of less expensive clothing, including popular surf labels, jeans, and mid-level brands. Designer labels available on the streets are certain to be fakes.

Expert tailors can whip up a suit in a week, and shops in the center of Lima can make leather jackets in various colors in the same time. The district of Gamarra is full of cheap fabrics, dressmakers, and tailors, as well as racks of ready-to-wear clothing. It is a poor neighborhood and travelers should exercise care.

Villages in the highlands near Cusco are the best places to buy embroidered clothing or textiles. The straw hats of Celendin, near Cajamarca, are considered the best in the entire country.

CRAFT MARKETS

The largest selection of handicrafts from across the country can be found in the strip of mini-malls that make up the indigenous markets in Miraflores (*see p77*) in Lima.

The daily market in Pisac (*see p169*), near Cusco, is one of the best known, with Sunday being the busiest day. Colorful stalls fill the main plaza and adjacent streets, offering rugs, hats, alpaca ponchos, musical instruments, jewelry, and *mates burilados* or engraved gourds (*see p304*).

Chinchero market in the Sacred Valley is a mix of a fruit, vegetable, and handicraft market. Artisans sporting traditional felt hats, with a secret fold that doubles as a purse, line their wares of painted wooden plates, hand-woven textiles, dolls, and colorfully beaded hats on the ground and weave while they wait for customers. Andean condor feathers are sometimes on sale, but it is illegal to buy or sell them.

Textiles and ceramics made by the Shipibo community are a specialty of the Mercado

Hand-painted carved wooden plates, Chincero, Inca Heartland

Artesanal de San Juan in Iquitos (*see p252*). The Shipibo community that lives along the Ucayali River in Peru's Amazon region, is known for their geometric designs.

In the northern surfing town of Máncora, street stalls are piled high with jewelry, beach-wear, shell chimes, wooden carvings, and chandeliers.

REGIONAL PRODUCTS

Every region in Peru has its specialties and, often, it is more interesting and much cheaper, in terms of quality and variety, to buy locally.

Ayacucho's Barrio Santa Ana (*see pp192–3*) is filled with craft workshops devoted to weaving tapestries and carving *huamanga* stone. The town is also famous for its *retablos*, or the boxes depicting events and customs.

Quinua is known for its *iglesias de quinua* (miniature clay chapels) which Andeans

put on their roofs for good luck. The pottery of Pampa, Pucará, and Chulucanas is also renowned.

Entire villages within the Mantaro Valley focus on one particular craft: Silver filigree in San Jerónimo de Tunán, woollen tapestries in Hualhuas, and engraved gourds in Cochas Grande and Cochas Chico.

The San Blas quarter in Cusco is home to candle-makers and the famous woodcarvers responsible for richly painted statues of the popular long-necked Virgins, saints, and chubby cherubs.

Colorful tapestry depicting a local vegetable market

FOOD AND DRINK

Olive oils and juicy olives from Ica and Tacna can be bought from small local shops, markets, and super-markets. The grape brandy, Pisco (*see p289*), which originates in both areas, is found in supermarkets and *vinotecas* (bottle shops), as well as individual wineries.

Anis Najar, a liqueur made from aniseed oil, along with La Iberica's chestnut marzipan fashioned into mini fruit, are Arequipa specialties. They are sold in shops in the center of the city and at the airport.

Ajis (dried Peruvian hot chilies) can be found in fruit and vegetable markets such as Lima's Mercado Surquillo, while jars of chili salsa are available at supermarkets.

Tourist browsing through a local indigenous craft market

Buying Peruvian Folk Art

Wooden mask

Folk art is an essential part of the country's religious, ceremonial, and everyday life with techniques passed down from generation to generation. Artisans use symbols and geometric designs in textiles as well as ceramics, and carve vivid portraits of rural life on to *mates burilados*. Textiles and clothing are made using alpaca wool, woven and spun by women in the highlands. Gold- and silversmiths create artifacts using old models and techniques. Spanish influence is evident in religious wooden carvings with Baroque flourishes and the depiction of the divine and daily life in *retablos*.

Detail on a handcarved gourd, *mates burilados*

MATES BURILADOS

Gourd carving has existed for many centuries in Peru. Different styles and techniques were developed as a result of trade between villages. The green outer skin is removed and the gourd is sun-dried. A design is then sketched on the gourd and carved by hand using a small wooden chisel. The uncarved area is finally burnt to get the colored effect.

HUAMANGA STONE CARVINGS

Statues made of Ayacucho's white alabaster, known as *piedra de huamanga*, became popular during Colonial times. The reason for this popularity was a shortage in porcelain and marble. Early works were religious in nature but now they encompass a range of different subjects.

White alabaster statue

RETABLOS

Retablos are filled with figures made of potato dough. The upper level represents heaven while the lower level depicts earthly events showing daily activities. *Costumbrista retablos* portray bullfights, dances, condor hunts, markets, religious festivals, and scenes showing the making of musical instruments and hats. The upheaval in Ayacucho, the home of *retablos*, especially during the time of the violent Sendero Luminoso (Shining Path) guerrillas (*see p195*), is portrayed in *Testimonials*. The Jimenez family *retablistas* (*see p89*) from Ayacucho, are one of the leading exponents.

WOODWORK

Churches and convents built in the Colonial era created a demand for elaborate woodwork including pulpits, choir-stalls, and religious statues. The craftsmen in the San Blas (*see p159*) district of Cusco still produce fine examples of local Baroque carving.

The town of Molinos near Huancayo (*see p187*) is famous for its wooden utensils and carved toys including animals, imaginary creatures, and acrobats.

Sarhua in the Ayacucho department is renowned for its *tablas* (painted boards) containing text and illustrated stories depicting everyday practices and customs. Originally the stories were drawn on the roof beams in homes. Masks are an integral part of most festivals of Peru, especially during the colorful and dynamic Virgen de la Candelaria (*see p145*) celebrations of Puno.

SILVERWORK

Artisans in the departments of Junín, Huancavelica, Cusco, and Ayacucho produce a range of silverwork, from religious icons to ornate frames. *Tupus*, or elaborate pins, are used to fasten shawls, a tradition left over from the Colonial era.

The town of Catacaos, in Piura department, is famous for its delicate silver filigree. Silver and gold are thinned out, and the super-fine threads curled and beveled into jewelry and figures.

TEXTILES

Weaving is Peru's oldest art form, dating back some 3,000 years. At one point, woven clothes were used as a form of payment to Inca rulers. The best weavers are found

Colorful *retablo* depicting everyday life in a Peruvian village

Textiles and handicrafts on sale in a roadside marketplace, Inca Heartland

in Ayacucho, Puno, Cusco, Junín, Apurímac, and Lima. Each village has its own technique and pattern, producing a rich variety of *chullos* (woollen caps with earflaps), bags, ponchos, scarves, rugs, and garments.

Weaving is largely done by women, but the men of Taquile Island are famous for their *chullos* and *chullis* (cummerbunds). Weavers of Ayacucho specialize in weft and warp textiles featuring abstract patterns. The weavers of Hualhuas make tapestries and rugs from hand-spun wool. Yarn is traditionally dyed using indigenous plants and insects. Pink cochineal is extracted from drying insects that feed on cacti.

Women in the village of Chucuito in Puno come from a long line of knitters. Today, they are known for their beautiful finger puppets, depicting the wildlife of Peru, such as condors, llamas, pumas, and even pop cultural icons such as Spiderman.

Arpillera or *tapiz* is the term applied to appliquéd tapestries made by Peruvian women. Some of these record village events while others portray idyllic scenes from the urban and traditional life of the ordinary people of Peru.

Local weavers give daily demonstrations in the Centre for Traditional Textiles of Cusco, showing how ancient techniques have been revived. The sales revenue from these products goes to the villagers who produce the brilliant textiles.

BASKETS

Colorful baskets woven from native reeds of the area are produced mainly in the departments of Cajamarca, San Martín, and Piura. Cusco is also famous for its brightly colored woven baskets. These baskets are easy to carry and can be used for decorative purposes. They are the perfect souvenirs of Peru.

POTTERY

Pottery is one of the most common crafts practiced in the country. In the Northern Desert, Chulucanas potters do not use the potter's wheel, instead they hand-turn the clay, using a wood paddle and stone to make thinner pieces. The vases are then smoked in burning mango leaves to give them light and dark contrasts.

The traditional geometric patterns of the Shipibo potters living in Peru's Amazon region are said to be copied from the skin of the giant anaconda, and astrological signs.

Painted porcelain plates from Pucara

The *torito* (Pucará bull), which is a hollow ceramic flask shaped like a bull, made by the potters in the Puno area, is an essential ritual part of the cattle branding ceremony. It is filled with *chicha (see p288)* and buried as an offering to the gods for increased herds. Other variations of *toritos* are made by potters in areas such as Cajamarca, Ancash, and also Ayacucho.

LEATHER

Leather chests, armchairs, and riding apparel with Baroque motifs were first made during Colonial times. Armchairs, tables, and chests bearing traditional patterns are still made today. Leather horses are the main feature of Puno.

CANDLES

An immense number of colorful, decorated candles are produced in areas such as Cusco, Ayacucho, Huaraz, Arequipa, and Lima. Festooned with articles such as flowers, leaves, angels' faces, and geometric patterns, they are used during religious festivals.

Elaborately decorated candles on sale in a local shop

OUTDOOR ACTIVITIES

Peru offers a multitude of outdoor activities to suit everybody's interests, abilities, fitness, and wallet. One highlight is a trek, a multiday camping and hiking expedition surrounded by the world's highest tropical mountains. Others include mountaineering, river rafting, mountain-biking, surfing, or watching wildlife in the Amazon Basin. Sand-boarding,

an unusual sport, is possible only in the huge dunes around Huacachina on the south coast. From the hundreds of outfitters and travel agencies that exist, we have selected ones that provide several kinds of services. Many visitors start with the South American Explorers (SAE), based in Lima or Cusco, which has information related to outdoor activities.

Surfer with board

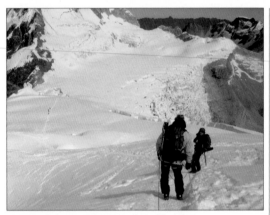

Mountain climbers on a glaciated peak, Cordillera Blanca

TREKKING AND MOUNTAINEERING

Trekking and mountaineering are extremely popular among visitors to Peru, especially during the dry season from May to September. The best base for trekking in the Andes is Huaraz. Nearby, Cordillera Blanca contains scores of glaciated mountains and is the best-known trekking area. The highlight is Huascarán, which at 22,205 ft (6,768 m) is the world's highest tropical mountain. With trails crossing passes at up to 16,405 ft (5,000 m) and camping spots commonly around 13,124 ft (4,000 m), these adventures are for fit, acclimatized visitors with good equipment. Both day trips and overnight treks, ranging from three to 12 days, can be arranged. More strenuous treks, lasting for 14 days, circumnavigate Cordillera Huayhuash, Peru's second highest range.

Mountaineers have a choice of towering icy summits, ranging from the relatively easy Pisco to the symmetrical Alpamayo, or the challenging Artesonraju. All require technical ice- and snow-climbing equipment, which can be rented in Huaraz. The climbing season is from June to August. Some visitors opt to back-pack alone while others hire guides, cooks, or *arrieros* (donkey drivers). Reliable information is available from the **Casa de Guías**, headquarter of the Peruvian Mountain Guide Association. Many rental places such as **MountClimb** and **Andean Kingdom** rent and sell gear and also arrange reasonably priced tours. **Peruvian Andes Adventures** is a top-notch outfitter in Huaraz with English- and German-speaking guides specializing in

Mountaineering gear

trekking and mountaineering. **Skyline Adventures** arranges treks, climbs, and mountaineering courses. **La Cima Logistics**, headquartered in Huaraz's Café Andino, specializes in personalized information and arrangements in the Cordillera Huayhuash. **Pony's Expeditions** in the village of Caraz, 42 miles (67 km) north of Huaraz, is a great choice for the north end of the Cordillera Blanca.

Cusco, with its fabled Inca Trail *(see pp170–73)* to Machu Picchu, is also the center for several other marvelous treks. As the Inca Trail is now highly regulated, trekkers need to plan their trips months in advance in order to obtain a permit during the dry season. Other treks are equally gorgeous and require less advance notice. The six-day circuit of Ausangate (20,906 ft/ 6,372 m) with glorious mountain views, huge herds of alpacas, and natural hot springs, is highly recommended. Several treks often end up at Machu Picchu via routes other than the more famous Inca Trail. Ecologically-minded **Ecoinka** offers their comfortable tented Camp Veronica with excellent meals, hot showers, sauna, and views of the glaciated Veronica (18,865 ft/ 5,750 m), as a base camp to the Inca Trail, a llama trek, and other trips in the surrounding region.

Explorandes is a local pioneer and offers first-class trips. **Amazonas Explorer** organizes high-quality

A trekkers' camp at Laguna Carhuacocha in Cordillera Huayhuash

trekking, mountain-biking, and rafting trips. Fully guided expeditions of the highest distinction, including international guides, and first-class hotels, are arranged by **Wilderness Travel**, which has been trekking in Peru since the 1970s. **High Places** and **Wildland Adventures** are two other preferred international outfitters. Of dozens of mid-range local trek operators, **SAS Travel**, **Q'ente Adventures**, **Liz's Explorer**, and **Inca Explorers** are recommended.

The Arequipa area offers some unique adventures. A trek into two of the world's deepest canyons, the Colca *(see pp142–3)* and the Cotahuasi *(see p144)*, can be arranged. Both have great scenery, condor-spotting opportunities, and remote villages. Among the best outfitters is **Colca Trek**, run by Vlado, an experienced English-speaking local guide.

Another special experience is climbing the arid Volcán Misti (19,101 ft/5,822 m) which dominates Arequipa's skyline. Some of the best guides are with **Zárate Adventures**, who pioneered climbing in the area and also offer ascents of higher peaks.

MOUNTAIN-BIKING

The mountain trails with their jaw-dropping scenery are the perfect getaway for adventure lovers. They provide a stark contrast to the flat desert of the Panamerican Highway. Single track dirt roads criss-cross the Andes, and a vehicle or a donkey are required to take you up for a descent of 9,843 ft (3,000 m). Rental bikes are quite good, but if you require top-of-the-line wheels, bring your own. Most international airlines allow passengers to carry them.

In Huaraz, **Mountain Bike Adventures** is the best choice, with short trips and multiday

expeditions throughout the Cordillera Blanca region. The friendly English-speaking owner, Julio, is a fine guide and bike mechanic and knows the sport inside out.

In Cusco, a good choice for planning your trip is **Ecotrek Peru** which has one- to six-day trips, some visiting Inca sites. The international outfitter, **BikeHike Adventures**, offers multisport excursions as their name implies. **Backroads** is a highly reputable company which arranges premier bike and trek tours in the Sacred Valley. A list of international biking outfitters offering luxurious personalized tours is available online on the **Adventurebiketours** website.

Hikers in Urubamba valley, near Maras, Inca Heartland

Mountain-biker on a rugged mountain trail

Rafters in action during a white-water rafting expedition

RIVER-RUNNING

The rugged high Andean rivers are the best place for white-water kayaking and rafting. Trips range from a few hours to over a week of descending through mountain canyons into the Amazon rainforest *(see p256)* and camping in the wilderness. Outfitters can be found in Arequipa and Huaraz, but Cusco has the best selection.

Short floats can be done in Class II and III rapids on the Río Urubamba in the Sacred Valley *(see p168)*, while longer trips descend the Ríos Tambopata *(see p262–3)* and Apurímac into the Amazon with rapids reaching Class IV and some very challenging Class V ones. Most are navigated by rafts with experienced guides; kayakers can also join a rafting expedition.

Companies with an emphasis on white-water trips include **Mayuc**, which has pioneered river-running and includes descents of the Colca Canyon as well as trips to the Cusco area. Also recommended is **Southern Rivers Expeditions**, which runs the Cotahuasi Canyon. Check with trekking companies as some of them also arrange personalized river-running.

SURFING

With almost 1,864 miles (3,000 km) of Pacific coastline, Peru offers great waves. The far north has the best and warmest conditions, with sea temperatures around 70°F (21°C) for most of the year. Temperatures at the beaches

around Lima *(see p99)* drop to as low as 56°F (13°C) in the coldest months of April to December, when wet suits are mandatory. For an overview of dozens of surfing beaches, visit the website **Perú Azul**. For information about the competitive surfing scene go to the website of **Bodyboardperu**. The beaches in Peru are dry desert, unlike typical tropical beaches.

Lima fronts on to numerous beaches, on the Coste Verde, and surfers are seen through the year in Miraflores *(see p79)*. To avoid the crowds, surfers head to Punta Hermosa, about 25 miles (40 km) south of Lima, where several good breaks are found and international competitions are held. **Peru Surf Guides**, a local surfboard shop, sells, shapes, rents, and repairs boards, and doubles as a surfers' information center.

Puerto Chicama, near Trujillo and 380 miles (610 km) north of Lima, has the longest lefts in the world, but the infrastructure is limited to basic hostels. May to August are the best months for wave action. Farther north, at 721 miles (1,160 km) north of Lima, the pretty village of Máncora has warmer water, good surfing, and a variety of hotels in all classes. Check the Viva Máncora website *(see pp232–3)* for surfing conditions, which are best from November to February.

The challenging sport of kitesurfing is popular in Paracas, 149 miles (240 km) south of Lima. **PeruKite** offers equipment and lessons.

SCUBA DIVING

The waters off Peru are marked with cold currents and steep drop-offs. As a result, the long Pacific Coast does not offer coral reefs, but it has its own attractions for divers. Prime among these is Paracas *(see p123)*, where divers can swim with sea lions in their natural habitat. The warmest waters are near the Ecuadorian border, where fish are more visible. **Peru Divers** is an experienced company which sells gear, arranges tours, and provides international PADI certification courses for much less than what you would pay in Europe or North America.

Scuba diver

Surfers riding the fast waves of the Pacific Ocean

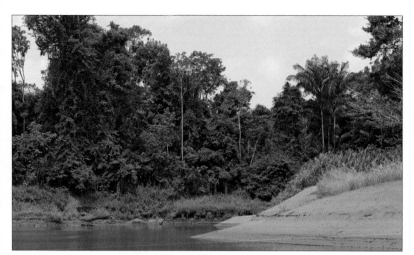

Forest along an Amazonian riverbank inside Reserva Nacional Pacaya-Samiria *(see p255)*

RAINFOREST EXPLORATION

A wildlife-watching expedition into the Amazon rainforest is an all-time adventure for those visiting Peru. Most visitors to the Amazon Basin will see sloths, monkeys, parrots, dolphins, piranhas, and a vast array of insects and plants, depending on the part of the basin they visit.

In the southern rainforests, riverside cliffs of salt-laden mud attract macaws and parrots intent on feeding on the minerals. Soon after dawn, large flocks of the colorful birds arrive to squabble and squawk over a particular area – a sight which delights bird-watchers and photographers alike. On a longer trip into remoter areas of the rainforest, glimpses of jaguars or tapirs are feasible. A good look at capybaras, anteaters, armadillos, giant river otters, and peccaries is possible as well.

Wildlife-watching is not the only highlight of the rainforest. The sounds of the jungle, from the dawn bird chorus to the nighttime frog, toad, and insect concertos, are hauntingly beautiful. Also, visiting an Indian village or climbing into the canopy are unforgettable experiences that visitors cherish for a lifetime.

Agouti, Amazon

From Iquitos, visitors can take a cruise of several days on a small ship featuring private, air-conditioned cabins and a naturalist guide with **Amazon Tours & Cruises**. The most expensive and luxurious trips are with **International Expeditions**. **Green Tracks** emphasizes biology on some of their voyages. Budget travelers can ride as hammock passengers in cargo boats *(see p253)* leaving regularly from the major ports of Iquitos, Pucallpa, or Yurimaguas. Camping in the Amazon Basin is very popular in the Manu area *(see p261)*, where **Manu Ecological Adventures** has set up semi-permanent campsites in prime locations. **Manu Expeditions** offers tours with a mixture of camping and lodge nights and is known for its expertise in bird-watching. A good mid-priced company is **Pantiacolla Tours** which camps on different beaches. Visitors need to bear in mind that even though these are camps, the logistics of getting into such remote areas means that the expeditions are not cheap, and independent travelers are not allowed.

Another option for rainforest exploration is to stay in a lodge, such as Manu Lodge *(see p281)*. Some of these lodges have canopy platforms or walkways which are an adventure in their own right. Others, such as the Heath River Wildlife Center, provide a closer view of the riverside clay licks covered with hundreds of spectacularly colorful macaws and parrots.

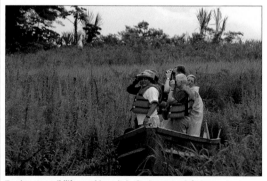

Tourists on a wildlife-watching trip in the Amazon rainforest

Visitors enjoying a hang gliding flight over the Costa Verde, Lima

HANG GLIDING AND HOT-AIR BALLOONING

Adrenaline-pumping aerial adventures such as hang gliding and hot-air ballooning are recent additions to the Peruvian sports scene. Professional as well as amateur pilots glide by the Larcomar Mall *(see p79)* in Lima, around the Paracas Peninsula, and in the Sacred Valley area near Cusco. Facilities for tandem flights with experienced pilots, as well as training courses, are available from **PerúFly** or from **Viento Sur**, which has rentals for licensed pilots. Ballooning is gaining popularity in the Cusco area, where **Globos de los Andes** provides professional services to visitors.

HORSEBACK RIDING

Peru is famous for its *paso* horses *(see p221)*, which have been bred for 400 years to produce the smoothest gait in the world. **Cabalgatas** offers exhibitions and horseback tours using these horses. **Equitours** is a recommended international wrangler offering tours in the Sacred Valley. Several trekking companies also offer riding, but not always on *paso* horses. Beware that some horses offered cheaply are poorly looked after.

SAND-BOARDING

The unusual sport of sand-boarding is a cross between snow-boarding and surfing with a huge sand dune thrown in. It is a popular pastime as the sand never melts and enthusiasts do not need to wait for the perfect wave. Sand-boarding is possible at any time, in any season, which makes it appealing for Peruvians.

Rain is almost unheard of in the coastal desert of Peru and even bad weather cannot stop the action. In the 1980s, the heart of the sand-boarding scene was the desert-lake oasis of Huacachina, a tiny village a 4-hour drive south of Lima. During earlier days, boards looked like short surfboards, candles were used as wax, and riders sat or lay on the boards as they rode down the sand dunes encircling the lake.

Extreme boarders use equipment looking more like snowboards, with foot bindings allowing a controlled ride. More than 40 countries now boast boardable dunes, and sand-boarding competitions are held for international experts who ride, jump, spin, somersault, and flip their way down the dunes. Companies do not offer organized trips but a handful of hotels and shops in Huacachina offer old-fashioned and modern boards for rent. Boarders trudge slowly up the dunes, slipping back two steps for every three made forward, or they hire a driver and beach buggy to take them to the top. This is repeated for as long as their energy lasts.

Huacachina remains the favored spot and is the easiest place to rent a board for about US$3 a day. Today dunes near Huacachina *(see p121)*, Trujillo *(see pp218–20)*, and even in the environs of Lima, are attracting boarders. See the **Peru Adventure Tours** website for information.

Horseback riding

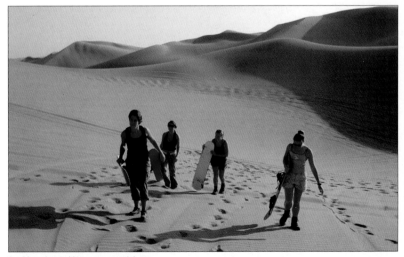

Sand-boarders trekking across sand dunes

DIRECTORY

GENERAL TOUR ADVICE

SAE Clubhouse
Calle Piura 135, Lima.
Tel 01 445 3306.
www.saexplorers.org

Peru Adventure Tours
www.peruadventures
tours.com

TREKKING AND MOUNTAINEERING

Amazonas Explorer
Collasuyo 910, Miravalle,
Cusco. *Tel 084 252 846.*
www.amazonas-explorer.
com

Andean Kingdom
Luzuriaga 522, 2nd floor,
Huaraz. *Tel 043 425 555.*
www.andeankingdom.
com

Casa de Guías
Parque Ginebra 28 G,
Huaraz.
Tel 043 421 811.
www.casadeguias.com.
pe

Colca Trek
Jerusalén 401-B,
Arequipa.
Tel 054 206 217.
www.colcatrek.com.pe

Ecoinka
Maruri 288, Oficina 404,
Cusco.
Tel 084 224 050.
www.ecoinka.com

Explorandes
Garcilaso 316-A, Cusco.
Tel 084 238 380.
www.explorandes.com

High Places
Tel 0845 257 7500.
www.highplaces.co.uk

Inca Explorers
Calle Ruinas 427, Cusco.
Tel 084 241 070.
www.incaexplorers.com

La Cima Logistics
Lucar y Torre 530,
3rd floor, Huaraz.
Tel 043 721 203.
www.cafeandino.com

Liz's Explorer
Calle del Medio 114 B,
Plaza de Armas, Cusco.
Tel 084 246 619.
www.lizexplorer.com

MountClimb
Mariscal Cáceres 421,
Huaraz.
Tel 043 426 060.
www.mountclimb.com.
pe

Peruvian Andes Adventures
José Olaya 532, Huaraz.
Tel 043 421 864.
www.peruvianandes.
com

Pony's Expeditions
Sucre 1266, Caraz.
Tel 043 391 642.
www.ponyexpeditions.
com

Q'ente Adventures
Garcilaso 210,
Oficina 210b, Cusco.
Tel 084 222 535.
www.qente.com

SAS Travel
Portal de Panes 167,
Plaza de Armas, Cusco.
Tel 084 255 205.
www.sastravelperu.com

Skyline Adventures
Tel 043 427 097. www.
skyline-adventures.com

Wilderness Travel
Tel 510 558 2489.
www.wildernesstravel.
com

Wildland Adventures
Tel 206 365 0686.
www.wildland.com

Zárate Adventures
Santa Catalina 204,
Oficina 3, Arequipa.
Tel 054 202 461.
www.zarateadventures.
com

MOUNTAIN-BIKING

Adventure-biketours
www.perubikingtours.
com

Backroads
Tel 510 527 1555.
www.backroads.com

BikeHike Adventures
Tel 604 731 2442.
www.bikehike.com

Ecotrek Peru
Canchipata 560, San Blas,
Cusco. *Tel 084 247 286.*
www.ecotrekperu.com

Mountain Bike Adventures
Lucar y Torre 530, Huaraz.
Tel 043 424 259.
www.chakinaniperu.com

RIVER-RUNNING

Mayuc
Portal Confiturías 211,
Plaza de Armas, Cusco.
Tel 084 232 666.
www.mayuc.com

Southern Rivers Expeditions
Plateros 361, Cusco.
Tel 084 255 049.
www.southernrivers.net

SURFING

Bodyboardperu
www.bodyboardperu.
com

Perú Azul
www.peruazul.com

PeruKite
Tel 01 975 570 690.
www.perukite.com

Peru Surf Guides
Contact: Raul Delgado.
Tel 997 753 573. www.
perusurfguides.com

SCUBA DIVING

Peru Divers
Santa Teresa 486,
Chorrillos, Lima.
Tel 01 251 6231.
www.perudivers.com

RAINFOREST EXPLORATION

Amazon Tours & Cruises
Requena 336, Iquitos.
Tel 065 231 611.
www.amazontours.net

Green Tracks
Tel 970 884 6107.
www.greentracks.com

International Expeditions
Tel 205 428 1700.
www.ietravel.com

Manu Ecological Adventures
Plateros 356, Cusco.
Tel 084 261 640. www.
manuadventures.com

Manu Expeditions
Pardo 895, Cusco.
Tel 084 226 671.
www.manuexpeditions.
com

Pantiacolla Tours
Saphi 554, Cusco.
Tel 084 238 323.
www.pantiacolla.com

HANG-GLIDING AND HOT-AIR BALLOONING

Globos de los Andes
Avenida de la Cultura
220, Oficina 36,
Cusco.
Tel 084 232 352.
www.globosperu.com

PerúFly
Jorge Chavez 666,
Miraflores, Lima.
Tel 01 444 5004.
www.perufly.com

Viento Sur
Tel 084 201 620.
www.aventurasvientosur.
com

HORSEBACK-RIDING

Cabalgatas
Tel 01 221 4591.
www.cabalgatas.com.pe

Equitours
Tel 307 455 3363.
www.ridingtours.com

SPECIALIZED HOLIDAYS

Peru, with its rich culture and biodiversity, is becoming a hotspot for those looking beyond conventional travel. Specialized activities such as butterfly- and bird-watching are increasingly popular. Staying with and working in the fields with an Andean community can be a life-changing experience. Learning the secrets of Peruvian

A Batesia butterfly

cuisine, one of the most varied in the world, is possible through culinary courses or tours around local markets and gourmet restaurants. Lessons in complex Peruvian dances can be a thrill in a group or individual classes, while Spanish and Quechua lessons will always improve your chances of meeting Peruvians and enjoying both the social and cultural life.

Bird-watching, a fast growing tourist attraction in Peru

BIRD-WATCHING

Peru ranks first in the world for bird species, with more than 1,800 of them. However, bird-watching is small here in comparison to neighboring countries, but is increasing fast with new companies emerging, led by a conservation-minded generation of local and foreign experts.

Kolibri Expeditions offers trips to various destinations with mid-budget alternatives. **Rainforest Expeditions** has many programs for bird-lovers. Bird-watching expeditions from three to eight days within the Tambopata National Reserve (*see pp262–3*), are available. A six-night program, dedicated to observing parrots and macaws at the clay licks is also offered. **Manu Expeditions** (*see p311*) has excellent guides with a varied combination of programs. **Gran Peru** is headed by Peruvian ornithologist, Thomas Valqui. He leads tours

mainly to the Tambopata and Manu regions and into the Northwestern Biosphere Reserve, home to no less than 1,400 bird species.

Another company focused in this area is **Ultimate Voyages**. **Birding Ecotours** provide tailor-made expeditions all around Peru for clients with particular birding interests. **Tanager Tours**, has birding programs in the Colca Canyon (*see pp142-3*) and other areas in Southern Peru.

Alejandro Tello, an expert ornithologist, often works as a freelance guide for some of the companies mentioned above, but can also arrange personalized expeditions. For more information about bird-watching in Peru consult the **Birdingperu** website or the bird-watching webpage of the **PromPerú** website.

White-breasted kingfisher

BUTTERFLY-WATCHING

Two major companies offer packages for butterfly-lovers in order to explore some of the 3,700 species existing in Peru. Manu Expeditions has a 17-day tour into some of the most pristine cloud forest spots in the Manu National Park, where butterflies can be spotted at diverse altitudes and habitats. A three-day package tour into the historic Machu Picchu sanctuary (*see pp176-81*) is also a good opportunity to watch butter-flies in the awe-inspiring scenery of the Inca citadel.

Rainforest Expeditions has a three-night program that is combined with other tropical rainforest explorations in the Tambopata National Reserve.

MUSIC AND DANCE

Afro-Peruvian music and dance with its combination of Peruvian sounds and deep African influence attracts many travelers to Lima. The **Centro Cultural de la Pontificia Universidad Católica del Perú**, offers dance workshops and *cajón* (*see pp28–9*) lessons by María del Carmen Dongo, a res-pected percussionist who also offers lessons at her own school **Zonarte – Escuela de Percusión**.

For those with a major interest in Latin rhythms, **El Sol – Escuela de Español** offers dance classes every Thursday afternoon. They include salsa, *merengue*, and other groovy beats, taught by expert Latino dancers and trainers.

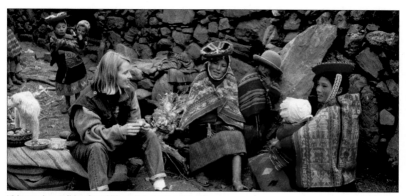

Visitors enjoy traditional rural life with Andean communities

COMMUNITY-BASED TOURISM

Sponsored by **The Mountain Institute**, community-based tourism aims to re-evaluate Andean culture and tradition.

Tilling the land and dyeing wool are part of the home-stay experience in Vicos or Humacchuco, two Quechua communities in the Cordillera Blanca *(see pp202–3)*. Similar options are available in Lake Titicaca *(see p147)*.

ETHNIC AND MEDICINAL TRADITIONS

Etnikas Travel offers one-week retreats promoting the alternative healing traditions of Amazon and Andean shamans in the Sacred Valley. In Iquitos, **Latitud Sur** gives visitors the opportunity to help preserve primary forests and the ancient knowledge of medicinal herbs on tours into the Pacaya-Samiria Reserve.

CULINARY TOURS AND COURSES

Lima Tours *(see p327)* offers a six-day tour that combines sightseeing and Peruvian gastronomy in Lima and Cusco with visits to a selection of exquisite restaurants and countryside mansions. One-day tours within Lima that include a visit to a local market, lessons in making

cebiche (see p284), and dinner at one of Lima's finest restaurants are also offered.

Le Cordon Bleu Peru offers an intense five-day course where popular Peruvian recipies can be learnt.

SPANISH AND QUECHUA CLASSES

El Sol – Escuela de Español, **Instituto Cultural Peruano Norteamericano**, and **Máximo Nivel Executive Language Center** offer various levels ranging from one to 20 weeks and up to a year. **Centro de Idiomas PUCP** also offers Spanish for foreigners and has one of the best Quechua learning programs in Peru.

DIRECTORY

BIRD-WATCHING

Alejandro Tello
Tel 01 9665 6589.
ateguevara@yahoo.com

Birding Ecotours
Tel 01 420 4448. www.
birdingecotours.co.za

Birdingperu
www.birdingperu.com

Gran Peru
Tel 074 977 1575.
www.granperu.com

Kolibri Expeditions
Tel 01 476 5016.
www.kolibriexpeditions.com

PromPerú
www.perubirdingroutes.com

Rainforest Expeditions
Tel 01 421 8347 (Lima),
084 24 6243 (Cusco),
082 52 2575 (Puerto Maldonado). www.
perunature.com

Tanager Tours
Tel 054 42 6210.
www.tanagertours.com

Ultimate Voyages
www.ultimatevoyages.com

MUSIC AND DANCE

Centro Cultural de la Pontificia Universidad Católica del Perú
Tel 01 616 1616. www.
cultural.pucp.edu.pe

El Sol – Escuela de Español
www.elsol.idiomasperu.com

Zonarte – Escuela de Percusión
www.cajonperu.com

COMMUNITY-BASED TOURISM

The Mountain Institute
www.respons.org

ETHNIC AND MEDICINAL TRADITIONS

Etnikas Travel
www.etnikas.com

Latitud Sur
www.latitudsur.com

CULINARY TOURS AND COURSES

Le Cordon Bleu Peru
Tel 01 242 8222.
www.lecordonbleu
peru.edu.pe

SPANISH AND QUECHUA CLASSES

Centro de Idiomas PUCP
Tel 01 431 0052 /
423 8078. www.pucp.
edu.pe/eculpub/cipuc

Instituto Cultural Peruano Norteamericano
Tel 01 706 7000.
www.icpna.edu.pe/ingles

Máximo Nivel
www.maximonivel.net

SURVIVAL
GUIDE

PRACTICAL INFORMATION 316–325

TRAVEL INFORMATION 326–333

PRACTICAL INFORMATION

In the last ten years Peru has made great progress in its tourism industry and today, it is much easier to travel around the country. There are some expert tour operators offering a range of options, from ecotourism and outdoor adventure to gastronomy and mysticism. Tourist offices, known as iPerú, are located in

Tourist office symbol

the larger cities, while in smaller towns, visitors can often obtain information from the *municipalidad* (town hall). Facilities in the more remote areas, however, may still be somewhat limited. Life is a bit laidback in Peru and everything takes a little longer, be it restaurants, offices, or shops, so bear in mind that patience is indeed a virtue.

June to August, the best time to visit Machu Picchu

WHEN TO GO

Most people visit Peru in winter, from June to August, when the weather is dry and sunny in the highlands and jungles. Prices for hotels rise during this period.

The wettest months are from December to March, which means muddy paths and cloudy skies for trekkers along with the water hampering outdoor activities.

The central and southern desert coast is shrouded in mist in winter, but sunny during the rainy season in the highlands. The north coast, however, has sun year round.

May, September, October, and November are good times to visit – the weather is fine, tourist routes are less crowded and prices are lower.

VISAS AND PASSPORTS

Citizens of Australia, Canada, New Zealand, South Africa, UK, USA, and most European and Latin American countries do not require a visa to visit Peru. The maximum stay is

90 days, although this can be extended at a *migración* (immigration) office in major cities. On arrival, visitors get a 30- or 90-day stamp on their passport and an embarkation card that has to be returned on leaving the country. All visitors should have a passport valid for six months from the date of travel.

OPENING HOURS

Museum opening hours can vary, but are generally 10am to 5pm. Many post offices and banks are open all day while government offices open from 9:30am to 5pm, Monday to Friday. Shops and government offices usually close for lunch.

Entrance to a post office with the distinctive Serpost logo

CUSTOMS INFORMATION

Peru allows duty-free import of three liters of alcohol, 400 cigarettes or 50 cigars, and gifts worth up to US$300 or equivalent in other currencies. It is illegal to take out pre-Columbian artifacts, Colonial art, and animal products from endangered species, unless accompanied by documentation from Peru's National Institute of Culture (INC) indicating that the object is a reproduction. Coca leaves and coca tea are legal in Peru but not in most other countries.

At Lima international airport, all travelers press a button before exiting the baggage claim area; a green light means go, a red light means your baggage will be searched. Visitors are allowed to bring a laptop, camera, bicycle, and sports gear for personal use.

LANGUAGE

Spanish and Quechua are the official languages of Peru but Spanish is the most widely used. Aymara, spoken mainly around Lake Titicaca, is also recognized by the state, along with 48 other native languages. English is spoken and understood by workers in tourism-related industries, and by members of Peru's upper socio-economic class. Outside large cities people have only a basic knowledge of English.

SOCIAL CUSTOMS

Peruvians are polite, and a bit formal. A handshake is exchanged at the beginning and end of a meeting. People who know each other greet with a

◁ **A solitary boat winds its way through the *totora* reeds of Lake Titicaca**

Wear non-revealing clothes when visiting churches

single kiss. When addressing people, use their title *(señor, señora, señorita)* or their professional title. Personal space is not a respected commodity – the buses as well as the streets are crowded.

Wearing revealing clothes or shorts in a church is considered disrespectful. Topless bathing should be avoided.

Observe signs that prohibit photography. Photography of airports, military bases, places near high-tension towers, and police stations is forbidden. Some indigenous people do not like to be photographed so ask permission first.

WOMEN TRAVELERS

It is generally safe for women to travel alone but be warned that Peruvian men are persistent in their attention. It is common for men to stare, offer *piropos* (unsolicited comments or come-ons), whistle, and catcall. Peruvian women ignore them, so do the same. Fair, blonde women come in for most attention. Wearing a wedding ring or traveling in a group can be a disincentive. Do not flag taxis in the street, avoid walking alone on tourist trails or dark streets, and stay in centrally located hotels.

DISABLED TRAVELERS

While facilities for disabled people are improving, they are still inadequate. Wheelchair ramps and disabled toilets are rare. Only high-end hotels such as the Marriott, Sonesta, and Casa Andina have specially designed rooms for disabled travelers. Many archaeological sites are accessible but only with some assistance.

TIME

Five hours behind Greenwich Mean Time (GMT), Peru is in the same time zone as the east coast of the USA (and an hour during US daylight saving time). Peru only has one time zone, and daylight saving is not in use.

ELECTRICITY

The electric current outlets are 220 volts and 60 cycles AC. There are two-prong outlets that accept both flat and round prongs. Some large hotels also have 110-volt outlets.

TOURIST INFORMATION

The official tourism body, **PromPerú**, has small offices called iPeru in Arequipa, Ayacucho, Cusco, Huaraz, Iquitos, Lima, Puno, and Trujillo. Brochures, maps, and information are available. iPeru also has a 24-hour information hotline to assist travelers. Visitors can file a complaint at iPeru offices or get advice on what to do if documents have been lost or stolen.

DIRECTORY

EMBASSIES AND CONSULATES

Australia (Australian Consulate General)
Av. Victor Andrés Belaúnde, 147 Edificio Real Trés, Of 1301 San Isidro. **Map** 2 B3. **Tel** 01 205 4012. www.australia.org.pe

Canada
Bolognesi cnr Berlin, Miraflores **Map** 4 A1. **Tel** 01 319 3200. www.lima.gc.ca

South Africa
Av. Victor Andrés Belaúnde, 147 Edificio Real Trés, Of 801 San Isidro. **Map** 2 B3. **Tel** 01 612 4848.

United Kingdom
Torre Parque Mar (Piso 22) Av. Jose Larco, 1301 Miraflores. **Map** 4 B2. **Tel** 01 618 2000. www.ukinperu.fco.gov.uk/en

USA
Av. La Encalada, Cuadra. 17 s/n Surco. **Tel** 01 434 3000. http://lima.usembassy.gov

TOURIST INFORMATION

PromPerú
Tel 01 574 8000 (24-hour) www.peru.travel/en

WEBSITES

Gastronomy
www.perumuchogusto.com

General
www.saexplorers.org

News
www.peruviantimes.com

In Spanish
www.mcultura.gob.pe (Ministerio de Cultura)

Women travelers looking at articles in a local market

Personal Security

Tourist police badge

Crime is not a major threat for visitors to Peru, although, it is important to be alert and take precautions. Theft and pick-pocketing are common in the main tourist cities and on long-distance bus routes. Always keep cash in a moneybelt under your clothes and do not wear expensive jewelry. Use ATMs during the day when there are more people around. Avoid walking alone on deserted stretches at night and always remain careful. Do not hail taxis on the street as they are not reliable, instead use radio taxis. Carry copies of important documents, such as your passport and visa, all the time.

A woman officer at a tourist police station

POLICE

Peruvian police are generally helpful, especially in larger cities. They are allowed to check your visa and passport, so always carry some identification. A certified copy of the photograph and visa page of the passport is also acceptable. The officers can be recognized by their dark-green uniforms. If a policeman tries to solicit a bribe, politely refuse or suggest a visit to the nearest police station. Police officials are paid poorly and bribes can be as little as S/5 or an Inca Kola.

If, for some reason, you are held by the police, do not make a statement or sign any document without seeing a representative from your embassy or consulate. Also, insist on the services of a reliable translator.

Tourist policeman on a motorcycle

The government has set up tourist police, or *policía de turismo,* offices in a number of cities such as Ayacucho, Cajamarca, Chiclayo, Cusco, Huancayo, Huaraz, Iquitos, Ica, Lima, Nazca, Puno, Tacna, and Trujillo, as well as a 24-hour hotline for visitors. Tourist police offer emergency assistance, and also register complaints about tourist operators, airlines, customs, or police officials. The tourist police officers speak English as well as Spanish. They can be easily distinguished from normal police by their white shirts. Keep in mind that the men in brown uniforms standing outside private homes, apartments, offices, and shops are private security guards or vigilantes. They are not affiliated to the Peruvian police or military and are not authorized to hold or question visitors.

GENERAL PRECAUTIONS

Be alert and aware of your surroundings at all times, especially on busy city streets and markets, airports, and bus terminals. Pickpockets are common in buses and *combis* and in crowded marketplaces. Baggage theft is rife on long distance bus trips.

For a safe and happy trip bear in mind some general guidelines on safety. Do not carry your wallet or passport in your back pocket. Keep expensive cameras out of view. In restaurants or cafés, hold your bag, or use the "leashes" on the table or chairs which can be attached to the bag handle.

Most cases of thefts involve momentary distraction – spilling something on your clothes, spitting, or a sudden fall are all possible diversions.

Make copies of important documents such as passport and airline tickets. Use safety deposit boxes for your valuables where available.

Never accept drinks from strangers, especially in nightclubs; there have been cases of drinks being laced with tranquilizing drugs.

DRUGS

Possession of, or trafficking in, illegal drugs is considered an extremely serious offence in Peru. If arrested on drug charges, there is a protracted pretrial detention in poor prison conditions. A minimum sentence can lead to a lengthy imprisonment of several years, and there is no bail for drug trafficking offences. Avoid conversations about drugs with people you have just met and under no circumstances accept presents from strangers. There are lots of scams involving drugs and people posing as police, whose sole aim is to relieve you of your money.

LOST AND STOLEN PROPERTY

If your belongings are lost or stolen, notify the police within 24 hours as you will need an official report to claim your insurance. If your passport is misplaced or stolen, contact your embassy or consulate immediately. Report lost credit cards to the relevant company *(see p322)*.

TAXIS

Signs at Lima airport warn travelers to use official airport taxis only. Thieves working in conjunction with unlicensed drivers have been known to smash windows and grab bags when the taxi stops or slows down in heavy traffic. Visitors must avoid taking street cabs, especially at night. Telephone-dispatched radio-taxis are more expensive than the regular taxis but are far more trustworthy. Ask your restaurant or hotel to arrange one.

STREET HAZARDS

Earthquake safe zone sign

Most roads in Peru have inadequate traffic signs and markings and lack guard rails. Peruvian drivers, particularly taxi and *combi* drivers, disobey stop signs and traffic lights, disregard traffic lanes, and never stop for pedestrians, so be extra careful while crossing roads. They are also known for their hostile attitude – speeding buses, minibuses, taxis, and cars are part of the normal landscape. A 2005 university survey of 640 taxi drivers in Peru found that almost 40 percent of them showed psychopathic attributes including "agressive, anxious and anti-social behavior."

When walking, always keep a lookout for uneven pathways and potholes. Driving at night is not recommended because, apart from the risk of robbery, lighting is also inadequate. The potholes are unmarked, pedestrians and animals may be wandering on roads, and obstacles, such as rocks or truck tyres, are difficult to spot due to poor visibility.

NATURAL DISASTERS

Earthquakes are common in Peru and small tremors are frequent. In case of an earthquake, move away from windows or weighty objects and take shelter under a doorway or a strong table if you are indoors. Never take refuge under a staircase during an earthquake and do not use elevators. If outdoors, stand clear of electric wires and poles and any tall structures. Quickly move to the safe zones identified easily by the green-and-white earthquake symbols. Most hotels and office buildings in Peru have these signs indicating safe areas.

Avalanches, landslides, and mud slides are common in the highlands. They destroy roads and railroad lines during rainfalls every year.

DIRECTORY

EMERGENCY NUMBERS

Ambulance (SAMU)
Tel 117.

Police
Tel 105.

Fire Brigade
Tel 116.

Tourist Protection Hotline
Tel 01 574 8000 (Lima),
084 237 364 (Cusco).

Tourist Police Headquarters
Jirón Colon 246, Miraflores.
Tel 01 243 2190.

Tourist Police Lima
Jirón Moore 268,
Magdalena del Mar.
Tel 01 460 0844.

Tourist Police Cusco
Calle Shapy 510.
Tel 084 249 654.

Typical pedestrian and traffic movement in a busy plaza, Cajamarca

Health Precautions

Logo of a *botica*

When traveling to Peru, pack a small medical kit of essentials before you leave home. This should include things of everyday need such as bandages, tweezers, scissors, tape, anti-bacterial ointment, and insect clothing spray. Although Peruvian pharmacies are well stocked, explaining what you need if you don't speak Spanish, can be a trial. It is sensible to carry prescription or allergy medicines and water purification tablets, if visiting remote areas. If you wear contact lenses, do not forget to bring the solution. The sunlight can be severe in high altitudes, so bring a sunhat and strong SPF sunscreen. Wear long-sleeved shirts and full length pants to avoid mosquito bites.

MEDICAL TREATMENT

Peru's health care system is considered quite good. There are several top-notch private clinics as well as public hospitals in Lima. Despite the sometimes-limited facilities in the latter, Peruvian doctors are renowned for their resourcefulness. Smaller cities also have public hospitals and private clinics, however, anyone with a serious medical complaint should travel to Lima, where the facilities are much better. There are many English-speaking doctors and dentists practicing here. Contact the hotel or the tourist information hotline, iPeru (*see p317*), for a list of reliable doctors and related information. If the condition is serious get in touch with your embassy.

PHARMACIES

Peruvian pharmacies, known as *farmacias* or *boticas*, are identified by a red or green cross. Generic medicines and antibiotics are readily available. They can be purchased over the counter without any formal prescription.

ALTITUDE SICKNESS

Altitude sickness pills

Almost all people who visit Arequipa, Cusco, and Puno succumb to some form of altitude sickness. Some of the common symptoms include shortness of breath, fatigue, heart-pounding, headache, appetite loss, insomnia, and nausea. The solution is to take it easy till you get accustomed to the

Coca tea sachets

altitude. Eat lightly, drink lots of water, and avoid intense exercise. Do not consume alcohol, cigarettes or any kind of sedatives. If acute symptoms persist for more than 24 hours, descend to a lower altitude at the earliest opportunity and seek medical advice immediately. The symptoms should not be ignored as severe altitude sickness can sometimes develop into high altitude pulmonary edema – which leads to fluid in the lungs. It can also cause high altitude cerebral edema where the brain starts swelling. Both these situations can become serious, therefore extra care should be taken.

You can resume the hike or the journey after taking complete medication and proper rest. Coca tea and bottled oxygen helps, as does acetazolamide. Locals also recommend Sorojchi pills for altitude sickness. It is wise to stock up on them before you start a trip to the areas located in the higher altitudes.

VACCINATIONS AND INSURANCE

No vaccinations are officially required for a visit to Peru. However, travelers planning a jungle visit should get yellow fever vaccination. Hepatitis A, typhoid, and rabies vaccinations are recommended for people intending to trek to remote areas. Hepatitis B is suggested for visitors who expect to stay more than six months, or who might be exposed to blood, such as doctors, nurses, and health care volunteers. It is always better to ensure that tetanus and diphtheria shots are up to date. Plan your trip to Peru well in advance, since it usually takes about two weeks for vaccinations to take effect. In addition to the vaccinations, malaria pills are strongly recommended if traveling in the jungle.

Travel insurance is very important. Almost all Peruvian hospitals adopt a pay-first policy, and treatment in a

Entrance to one of the Peruvian pharmacy chains

Travelers wearing protective clothes and trekking boots

DIRECTORY

INTERNATIONAL CLINICS

Clínica Anglo Americana
Alfredo Salazar, cdra 3 San Isidro, Lima. **Map** 2 B4.
Tel 01 616 8900.

Clínica El Golf
Av. Aurelio Miro, Quesada San Isidro, Lima. **Map** 2 A3.
Tel 01 631 0000.

Clínica San Borja
Av. Guardia Civil, 337, Lima.
Map 3 F2. **Tel** 01 702 4300.

VACCINATION CENTERS

International Health Department
Jorge Chávez International Airport (Piso 1), Lima. **Tel** 01 575 1845.

International Vaccination Centers
Av. El Ejército 1756, San Isidro, Lima. **Map** 2 A5.
Tel 01 264 6889.

All leading private clinics (see www.cuzco.info/hospitals.htm)

private clinic can be very expensive. Make sure that the insurance policy covers activities that can be dangerous, such as rafting and mountain climbing. It should also have the provision of supporting an ambulance or an emergency flight home.

HEALTH HAZARDS

Mosquito-borne diseases such as malaria, yellow fever, and dengue fever are quite common in Peru. Malaria is most prevalent in the jungles of northern Peru. Mosquitoes are usually at their worst at dawn and dusk. Use heavy-duty insect repellent, mosquito coils known as *espirales*, and a mosquito net at night. Squirt your clothes with a permethrin-based spray even during the day. Wear long pants, long-sleeved shirts, a hat, and shoes to protect yourself. If a bite becomes infected, see a doctor. Malaria pills are advised for travelers visiting the Amazon, however, there is no vaccination for dengue, a viral infection with flu-like symptoms.

Insect repellent

Do not underestimate the power of the sun. Wear a sun hat, 15 or higher SPF sunblock, sunglasses, and avoid the midday sun. Even though it may feel cooler, the sun is more intense at high altitudes. Drink lots of water to guard against dehydration, and take time to acclimatize.

When hiking at very high altitudes, or even taking a long bus trip through the mountains, make sure you are prepared. Have layers of clothing, including fleecy tops, a woolen hat, a rainproof jacket, as keeping dry is crucial, and a lightweight space blanket. Do carry a sufficient supply of food and water. Hypothermia might set in under extreme conditions. The symptoms include skin numbness, shivering, slurred speech, aggressive behaviour, cramps, and dizziness. If afflicted, get the person out of the weather and change their clothes if they are wet. Have high calorie food, such as chocolates, and any hot drinks for immediate nourishment. Rest until the temperature returns back to normal.

Tap water and ice is not safe. Take basic precautions with food (see p282) to avoid traveler's diarrhea. Do not feed or fondle animals, aside from domestic ones. They carry diseases and can react unpredictably. Any animal bite or scratch should be cleaned immediately with soap, water, and antiseptic. Contact the local health authorities in case you need follow-up rabies treatment.

HIV AND AIDS

While official statistics about HIV/AIDS, or SIDA in Spanish, are a little vague in Peru, the UN classifies it as a low level epidemic. Some 75 percent of people affected by HIV/AIDS live in Lima and Callao. Most are men but the fastest-growing incidence of the illness is among women. The risk of infection is small, but take precautions. The concept of safe sex is not common in Peru.

Public toilet signboard in Spanish as well as English

PUBLIC TOILETS

There are public toilets in small towns, as well as petrol stations, bus and train terminals, and markets, but they are not always clean. Facilities in shopping malls, department stores, and large supermarkets are usually better, while toilets at airports and major tourist centers are generally adequate. Carry toilet paper; cubicles rarely have any, though some transport terminals have attendants who charge the visitors for providing a few sheets of toilet paper.

Banking and Local Currency

The unit of currency in Peru is the nuevo sol, although US dollars are widely accepted. Large hotels, shops, and restaurants in bigger towns and cities accept major credit cards. Carry cash in US dollars as other currencies are not always readily available, although the euro is fast gaining acceptance. Carry some coins and smaller notes for taxis, buses, and minor purchases as storekeepers and drivers rarely have sufficient change for larger denominations. There is no limit to the amount of money you may bring in or take out of the country.

A *casa de cambio* **or foreign currency exchange booth**

BANKS AND MONEYCHANGERS

The most well known banks in Peru are **Banco de Credito (BCP)**, **Banco de la Nacion**, **BBVA Banco Continental**, and **Scotiabank** which took over Banco Weisse Sudameris. Banking hours are normally between 9am and 6pm, weekdays, and almost all banks are open on Saturdays until noon.

Banks are the safest places to exchange money but their rates are generally lower than *casas de cambio* (foreign currency exchanges) or street moneychangers. Normal bank commissions can be anything from zero to three percent.

Practice general precautions wherever you exchange money. Count your money in the presence of the cashier, never accept damaged bills, and always check the notes before you leave the counter. *Cambistas* (street moneychangers) usually loiter outside banks and *casas de cambio*. Although a badge and colored vest identify

them as legal, these are not always an indication of their honesty. However, they do offer competitive rates and are open to bargaining but it is best to use them only when exchanging small amounts of cash. Check their calculations and the Peruvian notes before handing over money. Moneychangers are often the only option at border crossings.

CREDIT CARDS AND TRAVELER'S CHECKS

Credit cards are accepted in all major cities of Peru, with VISA being the most popular. Many businesses add a surcharge of up to 12 percent for paying with a credit card, although high-end hotels and restaurants often waive it. Always check the amount you are being charged. In small towns and rural areas, credit cards are less likely to be accepted so always carry cash.

Traveler's checks are exchanged at fewer places these days, and the exchange rate is usually less than for cash. You will be asked for identification so carry your

Logos of the major credit cards accepted in the main cities of Peru

passport. **American Express** is the most recognized brand. Traveler's checks can be difficult to exchange in small towns and villages, and replacing them outside of Lima is almost impossible.

ATMS

ATMs are easily found in major towns and cities. Look for machines with the Global Net sign, as some of the ATMs dispense money only to local account holders. Banks impose a fee each time a card is used at an ATM (check with your bank before departing) and withdrawals are either in soles or US dollars. As a precaution withdraw money at ATMs inside banks or shops in shopping malls.

CASH AND ELECTRONIC TRANSFERS

US dollars are the easiest foreign currency to use in Peru. Most restaurants, hotels, and shops in the main cities accept them as payment. However, if you pay in US dollars, you will receive soles as change. Electronic money transfers can be arranged via Western Union or Moneygram to agents throughout Peru.

Money can be made available quickly but commission is charged. Home bank money transfers to Peru can be difficult, if not impossible.

TIPPING AND TAXES

While not compulsory, tips are appreciated by hotel staff, drivers, porters, and guides. Unofficial parking attendants watch over your car and expect a tip for doing so.

All goods and services attract a 19 percent value added tax (IGV). Hotels and restaurants add a ten percent service fee. As per law, vendors are obliged to show the client the final price, including taxes.

CURRENCY

The Peruvian nuevo sol is divided into 100 céntimos, and is represented by the symbol S/. It was introduced on July 1, 1991, to replace the highly inflated inti, which took over from soles in 1985. Counterfeit currency, in US dollars as well as nuevo soles, is in circulation in the country. Do not accept old, faded, torn, or taped bills as they are difficult to get rid of, although moneychangers may trade them. Shops and supermarkets will routinely check S/100 bills, and these large bills can be hard to change in small towns.

Bank Notes
Peruvian nuevo sol notes are issued in five denominations – S/10, S/20, S/50, S/100, and S/200.

10 nuevo soles

20 nuevo soles

50 nuevo soles

100 nuevo soles

200 nuevo soles

Coins
There are eight coins – 1, 5, 10, 20, and 50 céntimos and S/1, S/2, and S/5. The lower denominations are copper while 50c and S/1 are silver colored. S/2 and S/5 have a copper colored center with silver surround.

S/1   S/2   S/5

1c   5c   10c   20c   50c

Communications

Telefónica's logo

The telephone is the most popular form of communication in Peru. Public telephones, using either coins or pre-paid phone cards, are common in towns and cities. The postal service can be slow and large companies in Lima use a delivery service for more important correspondence. Low cost Internet kiosks are available throughout the country. Peru has several free-to-air television channels, cable TV service, and a number of national and regional radio stations. The leading daily newspaper is *El Comercio*.

One of the colorful Telefónica booths found all over Peru

PUBLIC TELEPHONES

Public telephones are quite widespread in Peru; almost every main square across the country has one. Telefónica is the primary phone company and its mobile phone provider arm is known as Movistar. Claro is another major mobile phone service provider.

Public phones accept coins (both céntimos and nuevo soles) and phone cards sold at kiosks, supermarkets, and pharmacies. Avoid buying cards from street vendors as they are often used cards being recycled. Pre-paid cards with a value of up to S/30 are available and are best used to make local calls. The most commonly used card in Peru is Tarjeta 147.

International calls can also be made from private *cabinas* (cabins) in Telefónica's main offices. Keep in mind that calls made from hotels incur very expensive surcharges and are best avoided. Major international phone cards can be used in Peru but make sure that you have the list of access codes available.

Internet to phone systems are available in a number of Internet kiosks, with cable connections that are usually clearer than telephone lines.

USING A COIN AND CARD TELEPHONE

1 Lift the receiver and wait for the dial tone. The digital display will indicate that you have to insert a coin.

2 At least one nuevo sol is required for calls to a mobile phone; a local call costs a minimum of 50 céntimos.

3 Dial 1-4-7 if using a 147 card. You will be directed in Spanish to dial the 12 digit code provided on your card. You will also be given details about the remaining value.

4 Dial the required number in the following order – country code, followed by area code and then the number. Once you finish the call, your card will automatically emerge.

Pre-paid card

USEFUL DIALLING CODES

- To call Peru from abroad, dial your international access code, the country code, which is 51, followed by the area code minus the first 0, and the number.
- For international calls from Peru dial 00, followed by the country code, the area code, and the number.
- Codes: Australia 61; Canada and USA 1; Ireland 353; New Zealand 64; South Africa 27; UK 44.
- For long-distance calls in Peru, dial the three digit area code, followed by the number. For calls within the same department, omit the code.
- All areas other than Lima have a three digit area code begining with 0 and followed by a six or eight digit number.
- To make reverse-charge or collect calls, dial 108 and ask for *llamada de cobrado revertido* and give the number.
- For directory enquiries, dial 103 and for operator assistance, dial 109 (in Spanish).
- For emergency assistance, dial 105 (in Spanish).
- Numbers beginning with 9 are mobile phone numbers.

MOBILE PHONES

Mobile phone use is widespread in Peru. Almost all carriers work in Lima and other major cities and tourist areas. Travelers with tri-band mobile phones can use them providing their plan has international roaming and their carrier has a partner in the region. It is possible to rent and buy pre-paid mobile phones (called cellulars in Peru). Sale counters are located inside the baggage hall at the airport, as international travelers exit passport control.

Roadside kiosk packed with magazines and tourist information material

INTERNET AND FAX

Cabinas (Internet cabins) are widely available throughout Peru, especially in major cities. Most of them consist of simple cubicles with terminals and sometimes printers. The hourly rates of these booths are quite inexpensive. Only the top hotels in Peru have in-room Internet connections. Wi-Fi is gradually gaining in popularity, particularly in Lima. Hotel business centers usually charge high rates for Internet access.

Fax services are available at many hotels, but they are expensive. Some shops also have facilities for sending and receiving faxes.

PERUVIAN ADDRESSES

Peruvian addresses list the street number after the street name. The *departamento* (apartment) number comes next, followed by the suburb and *código postal* (post code). For business centers, the *piso* (floor) and the number of the *oficina* (office) are included in the address. "Jr" is short for *jirón* (street) and "S/n" signifies *sin numero* meaning without a number.

RADIO AND TELEVISION

There are many radio stations in Peru, however, all of them broadcast in Spanish. There are seven free-to-air television channels. Cable TV is widely available, with Cable Mágico as the most popular provider. More than 100 channels in a variety of languages are

available. Plus TV, which has a range of lifestyle shows, and news channel Canal N are the most famous Peruvian cable channels. High-end hotels offer in-room cable TV.

MAIL SERVICE

The Peruvian mail service is run by a private company, **Serpost**. International letters and postcards usually take a few weeks to reach their destination. A *certificado* (registered mail) service is also available. All major cities have a main post office, open from 8am to 8pm Monday to Saturday; some may open on Sunday morning. The fastest way to send important documents, letters, or packages is via courier. **DHL**, **FedEx**, and **TNT** have offices in Lima.

NEWSPAPERS AND MAGAZINES

The most widely read daily newspaper in Lima is the conservative *El Comercio*, which also has a Friday supplement on arts and

A standard red-and-white mailbox of the mail service, Serpost

entertainment with listings for Lima. *La República* is highly regarded for its investigative news coverage, while *Peru 21* is an easy-reading daily tabloid.

There are no English-language local newspapers in Peru. However, some kiosks in Lima stock international papers such as the *Miami Herald* and the *International Herald Tribune*, although they are usually a few days old. News magazines such as *Time* and *Newsweek* are also available. The most influential magazine in the country is *Caretas*.

DIRECTORY

COURIER SERVICES

DHL International
Tel 01 517 2500.
www.dhl.com.pe

FedEx
Psje. José Olaya 260, Miraflores, Lima. **Map** 4 B1. *Tel* 01 242 2280. **www**.fedex.com.pe

TNT
Av. Benavides, 7th block, Miraflores, Lima.
Map 4 C1. *Tel* 01 444 4509.
www.tnt.com.pe

POST OFFICE

Serpost
Plaza de Armas, Lima.
Map 1 F1. *Tel* 01 427 8531.
www.serpost.com.pe

ONLINE TELEPHONE DIRECTORIES

White Pages
www.paginasblancas.com.pe

Yellow Pages
www.paginasamarillas.com.pe

TRAVEL INFORMATION

Peru is a large country and while the highway system and access to remote areas has improved, internal travel is not always as fast as you might hope. There are airports in the main cities, and flying is by far the most time-efficient way to travel. The air transportation system is well developed. Train travel is almost non-existent. The majority of Peruvians,

and indeed many tourists, rely on buses to get around. Driving can be an alarming experience as road conditions are not good. The reward, on the other hand, is a glimpse of Peru that air travelers will never see. As there is no system of state public transport, a clutter of over-crowded minibuses, dilapidated buses, and battle-scarred taxis ply the streets of Peru's cities.

A vicuña road sign

Domestic and international check-in desks at Lima's airport

ARRIVING BY AIR

The key arrival point for international flights into Peru is Lima's **Aeropuerto Interna-cional Jorge Chávez**, 10 miles (16 km) northwest of the city. Flights from here connect other major cities and towns as well as international destinations.

There are direct flights connecting Peru to various cities of North America such as Miami, the main hub for Latin America, as well as Atlanta, Dallas, Houston, Newark, and New York. The main carriers of this route are **American**, **Delta**, **Continental**, Aero Continente, **LanPeru/LanChile** *(see p329)*. Airlines such as American, Delta, and Continental all fly to Peru from Canada, stopping at their hubs in the USA. **Air Canada** connects with other carriers in the USA, usually via Miami. LanPeru/LanChile stop in Los Angeles, New York, or Miami en route to Lima from Canada.

There are no direct flights to Lima from the UK or Ireland. Travelers must go via Europe or the USA. **Iberia** flies direct from Madrid to Lima, while **Air France/KLM** flies from Amsterdam and Lufthansa flies from Frankfurt. LAN flies direct from Lima to Madrid.

From Australia and New Zealand, travelers can fly via Buenos Aires on **Aerolíneas Argentinas** and then connect to Lima. **Qantas** and LAN have a code share agreement, so travelers can fly via Auckland and Santiago and connect with a flight to Lima, or travel via Los Angeles.

Aeromexico, **Tam**, Gol, Copa Airlines, **Taca** *(see p329)*, and Avianca operate direct flights from Colombia, Brazil, Mexico, and some Central American cities, as well as Cuba.

Airline timetables are subject to change due to unpredictable weather conditions or other unavoidable situations, so reconfirm flight timings.

AIRPORTS

Fourteen Peruvian airports are equipped to handle domestic flights and several are deemed to have inter-national capabilities. In reality, however, Lima's Jorge Chávez airport is the only fully equipped international airport and all international passengers must pass through it. Trujillo, Chiclayo, Piura, Tarapoto, Iquitos, Juliaca, Cusco, Tacna, Arequipa, and Cajamarca *(see p329)* among others, have respectable airport facilities but in more remote towns the runway may be nothing more than an isolated strip.

ARRIVING BY LAND

Visitors can enter Peru overland through Ecuador, Bolivia, or Chile. There are four border crossings for vehicles – from Huaquillas in Ecuador to Aguas Verdes in Peru, from Arica in Chile to

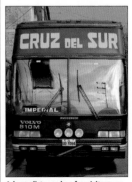

A long-distance bus for visitors on an overland journey

Tacna in Peru, and from Desaguadero in Bolivia to Desaguadero in Peru. Travelers from Quito in Ecuador will pass through the major northern coastal cities en route to Lima. From Bolivia, there is a frequent service from La Paz and Copacabana to Puno, and on to Cusco.

From Chile, most buses travel from Arica to Tacna, connecting with buses to Arequipa or Lima. Since many visitors prefer to enter and leave Peru by bus, companies such as **Transportes Ormeño** and **Caracol** run services linking Peru with neighboring South American countries.

ARRIVING BY BOAT

Peru is an important stop on the itineraries of several international cruise lines. Several cruise boats stop off in the port of Callao, near Lima. Passengers are permitted to disembark for excursions in the surrounding

areas. **Princess Cruises** also stops off in the port of Salaverry in Trujillo for visits to the nearby Mochica temples.

Peru can be accessed from Brazil by boat on the Amazon River via the border crossing from Manaos, on the Brazilian side, to Iquitos in Peru. Smaller ports, such as Santa Rosa, Tabatinga, and Leticia, at the tri-border between Peru, Brazil, and Colombia, are connected by ferries.

ORGANIZED TOURS

Agents in Australia, Europe, and North America offer organized tours to Peru. Nature trips geared towards bird-watching, wildlife-viewing, or jungle treks are popular. Others include visiting archaeological sites,

Tour operator sign board

trekking through the Andes, white-water rafting, mountain climbing and biking, as well as surfing. A range of Peruvian holidays are available via members of the **Latin American Travel Association (UK)**, Australia's **Peregrine Adventures**, and the **South and Central American Travel Association (Nth America)**. Within Peru, **Explorandes** and **Lima Tours** offer a variety of organized tours focusing on special interest (*see pp312–3*). The peak tourist season is from June to August.

DEPARTURE TAX

All travelers leaving Peru are required to pay a mandatory departure tax. It is US$30, and must be paid in cash at the cashiers' counters inside the departure gate area of the airport, prior to passport control (*see p329*).

DIRECTORY

AIRPORTS

Aeropuerto Internacional Jorge Chávez
Callao, Lima. *Tel 01 511 6055 (flight information).*
www.lap.com.pe

AIRLINES

Aerolineas Argentinas
Av. Canaval y Moreyra 370, San Isidro, Lima. **Map** 3 D3. *Tel 01 513 6565.* www.aerolineas.com.ar

Aeromexico
Av. Pardo y Aliaga 699, San Isidro, Lima. **Map** 2 C4. *Tel 01 705 1111.* www.aeromexico.com

Air Canada
Calle Italia 389, Lima. **Map** 4 A1.
Tel 01 626 0900.
www.aircanada.com

Air France/KLM
Alvarez Calderón 185, Oficina 601, San Isidro, Lima. **Map** 2 B4.
Tel 01 213 0200.
www.klm.com/pe_sp

American Airlines
Las Begonias 471, San Isidro, Lima.
Map 3 D2. *Tel 01 211 7000.*
www.aa.com

Continental Airlines
Av. Victor Andrés Belaunde 147, Edifico Real 5, Oficina 101, Lima.
Tel 0 800 70030 / 712 9230.
www.continental.com

Delta
Tel 0 800 50861/ 211 9211.
www.delta.com

Iberia
Av. Camino Real 390, Oficina 902, Lima. **Map** 2 C2.
Tel 01 411 7801. www.iberia.com

Qantas
Av. Conquistadores 256, Oficina 301-B, Lima. **Map** 2 C4.
Tel 01 221 4444. www.qantas.com

Tam
Alcanfores 495, Oficina 507, Miraflores, Lima. **Map** 4 C2.
Tel 01 202 6900.

ARRIVING BY LAND

Caracol
Av. Brasil 487, Lima. **Map** 1 D4.
Tel 01 431 1400.
www.perucaracol.com

Transportes Ormeño
Av. Javier Prado Este 1059, Lima.
Map 3 D2. *Tel 01 472 1710.*
www.grupo-ormeno.com.pe

ARRIVING BY BOAT

Princess Cruises
24844 Av. Rockefeller Santa Clarita, CA 91355.
Tel 1 800 PRINCESS (USA).
www.princess.com

ORGANIZED TOURS

Explorandes
San Fernando 320, Lima.
Map 3 F5.
Tel 01 715 2323.
www.explorandes.com

Latin American Travel Association (UK)
www.lata.org

Lima Tours
Jirón de la Unión 1040, Lima.
Tel 01 619 6900.
www.limatours.com.pe

Peregrine Adventures
380 Lonsdale Street, Melbourne, VIC 3000.
Tel 1300 85 44 44 (within Australia), 61 3 8601 4444.
www.peregrineadventures.com

South and Central American Travel Association (Nth America)
www.sata-usa.org

Domestic Flights

Plane over
Nazca Lines

In a country with a vastly rugged terrain such as Peru, internal flights offer a convenient alternative to long and sometimes grueling bus journeys, especially for travelers with serious time constraints. While air travel is usually more expensive than bus travel, the smaller domestic airline companies such as Star Peru and Peruvian Airlines do offer deals from time to time, although their networks are limited. LanPeru provides a majority of the flights, servicing all the major centers. The flights often make a brief stopover at some of the other Peruvian towns.

Llegadas Arrivals				
Hora Time	Procedencia From	Vuelo Flight	Estimada Expected	Observaciones Remarks
11:00	MALVINAS	06 1650		DELAYED
14:10	PUCALLPA	2I 3234	14:19	LANDED
14:20	CAJAMARCA	06 109	14:25	LANDED
14:40	CUSCO	06 221	14:35	LANDED
14:55	HUANUCO	LCB 1332	14:44	LANDED
15:20	CUSCO	LP 072	15:20	CONFIRMED
16:20	CUSCO	LP 028		LAN
16:45	CUSCO	LP 038		LAN
17:00	AREQUIPA	2I 1234		STAR PERU
17:00	ICA	06 1627		AEROCONDOR

Schedule board at one of the domestic airports

DOMESTIC AIRLINES

International passengers arriving at Jorge Chavéz International Airport in Lima can connect with scheduled domestic flights. Flights leave frequently from the capital to all of Peru's major cities, although flight times can change without warning.

LanPeru, which is part of the Chilean owned LAN airline company, operates an extensive network with regular flights connecting Lima with Tacna, Arequipa, Cusco, Chiclayo, Piura, Iquitos, Pucallpa, Puerto Maldonado, Juliaca, Tarapoto, Trujillo, and Tumbes.

Peruvian Airlines flies from Lima to Arequipa, Cusco, Iquitos, Piura, and Tacna.

Star Peru has flights from Lima to Chiclayo, Talara, and Trujillo in northern Peru, to Arequipa, Cusco, Juliaca, and Puerto Maldonado in the south, to Iquitos, Pucallpa, and Tarapoto in the jungle, and to Andahuaylas, Ayacucho, Huánuco, and Jauja in the Central Andes.

LC Busre currently flies small 19-passenger Fairchilds to Andahuaylas, Ayacucho, Cajamarca, Huaraz, and Huánuco. They also offer charter services.

There are several daily flights to Cusco, however, most flights depart in the morning as weather conditions in the Andes can change in the afternoon. Central America's **Taca** flies to many cities across Latin America and operates three daily flights to Cusco, two flights per day to Tarapoto, and daily flights to Chiclayo, Piura, and Trujillo from Lima.

Distant towns are reached via connecting flights. Flights to Piura, for example, stop in Chiclayo, and Arequipa is often a pitstop on the way to Juliaca. Small towns do not have daily services.

RESERVATIONS AND CHECKING-IN

Tickets can be purchased through travel agents, tour operators, or directly from the airlines on their websites.

Reservations should be made well in advance, especially during peak travel periods, such as June to August, Easter (Semana Santa), Christmas, and the national Fiestas Patrias (July 28 and 29). Fare prices are significantly higher during these times.

Flights are routinely overbooked so it is advisable to confirm all reservations at least 72 hours in advance, and reconfirm the day before flying. Flights are canceled or changed with annoying regularity. Passengers are advised to arrive for check-in at least 2 hours ahead of scheduled take-off, as long queues at the counters and baggage x-ray are routine. Airlines will often reallocate tickets if passengers have

Baggage being loaded on to a LanPeru aircraft

Perú Perú gift shop at Lima airport

LAN offers reduced fares as part of their South American Airpass to travelers with a return international air ticket with LAN or a oneworld alliance airline. The pass is valid for travel within Argentina, Brazil, Bolivia, Chile, Peru, Colombia, and Ecuador, and covers 49 destinations. Travelers must purchase a minimum of three individual one-way coupons, valid on all LanPeru flights. The price depends on the number of coupons purchased and the distance between desired destinations. Travelers cannot be residents of South America.

not checked-in at least 60 minutes before departure time on busy flights, or may refuse check-in.

The economy class baggage allowance for domestic flights is usually 55 lb (25 kg). For international flights, passengers can carry only up to 50 lb (20 kg). Business class flyers are allowed 66 lb (30 kg). Carry-on baggage is limited to one piece, weighing not more than 11 lb (5 kg). All airlines, domestic as well as international, do not allow passengers to smoke on board during the flight.

A small domestic airport departure tax of a liitle more than US$6 is payable for each domestic flight. It must be paid in cash to the cashiers inside the departure gate area.

CONCESSIONARY FARES

Infants under two-years can travel free on domestic flights, provided they do not occupy a seat of their own. Children over two years and under 12 years of age pay 50 percent of the full fare, which buys them a regular seat and standard baggage allowance.

Passengers waiting patiently at the check-in counter

DIRECTORY

AIRLINES

LC Busre
Av. Pablo Carriquiry 857, San Isidro. **Map** 3 E2.
Tel 01 204 1313.
www.lcbusre.com.pe

LanPeru
Av. José Pardo 513, Miraflores, Lima.
Map 4 B1. *Tel 01 213 8200.* www.lan.com

Peruvian Airlines
Av. Santa Cruz 839, Miraflores. **Map** 2 B5.
Tel 01 716 6000.
www.peruvianairlines.com

Star Peru
Av. Jose Pardo 485, Miraflores, Lima.
Map 4 B1.
Tel 01 705 9000.
www.starperu.com

Taca
Av. Comandante Espinar 331, Miraflores.
Map 2 C5.
Tel 01 511 8222 (reservations).
www.taca.com

REGIONAL AIRPORTS

Aeropuerto Alfredo Rodríguez Ballon
Arequipa.
Tel 054 44 3459.

Aeropuerto Mayor General Armando Revoredo Iglesias
Cajamarca.
Tel 076 343 757.

Aeropuerto Alejandro Velasco Astete
Cusco.
Tel 084 22 2601.

Aeropuerto Capitan José Abelardo Quiñones Gonzáles
Chiclayo.
Tel 074 22 9059.

Aeropuerto Inca Manco Cápac
Juliaca.
Tel 054 32 8974.

Aeropuerto Coronel Francisco Secada Vignetta
Iquitos.
Tel 065 260 182.

Aeropuerto Capitán Mondes
Talara.
Tel 073 38 1604.

Aeropuerto Capitán Guillermo Concha Ibérico
Piura.
Tel 073 34 1090.

Aeropuerto Coronel Carlos Ciriani Santa Rosa
Tacna. *Tel 052 314 503.*

Aeropuerto Comandante Guillermo del Castillo Paredes
Tarapoto.
Tel 094 52 3709.

Aeropuerto Capitán Carlos Martínez de Pinillos
Trujillo. *Tel 044 46 4013.*

Corporación Peruana de Aeropuertos y Aviación Comercial (CORPAC) – Information on domestic airports and flights
www.corpac.gob.pe

Traveling by Bus and Train

Symbol for bus station

Buses are the most economical way of traveling around Peru. Deluxe bus services offer comfortable seats, air conditioning, and safe drivers, although you pay more for the pleasure. Avoid the bargain basement operators – their vehicles are usually lacking in the road-worthy stakes and drivers are not safety conscious. Trains in Peru are limited. There is a daily train service between Cusco and Machu Picchu, and a less-frequent service between Cusco and Puno.

A deluxe Cruz del Sur bus, ideal for long-distance travel

BUSES AND TERMINALS

While no one bus company services the entire country, the larger ones, including **Cruz del Sur** and **Movil Tours**, cover almost all the major areas. Each has its own office, either in the main long-haul bus terminal in regional areas or huddled together in one part of town. In Lima, there is no central bus terminal, each company has its own terminal. Do remember to check from which terminal the bus departs or arrives when buying the ticket.

Traditionally, bus terminals are in the poorer districts, particularly in Lima, and bag-snatchers and pickpockets are rampant. It is best to buy your tickets in advance, so that you do not have to worry about keeping an eye on your luggage at the same time.

Small pieces of luggage can be carried on board, larger ones are stowed in the luggage compartment. A baggage ticket will be provided for later retrieval. Make sure all bags are securely locked. Theft of carry-on luggage is common. Place luggage on a rack where you can see it. If traveling alone, try not to fall asleep. If traveling with a friend, take turns to watch the bags. The farther you travel away from the main cities, the worse are the roads, and the

poor conditions of the road can double travel time. Delays are very common during the rainy season in the highlands and the jungle.

Traveling at night is not recommended as some hijacks have occurred on buses along the deserted mountain roads, with passengers being robbed of cash, expensive items, and even passports.

Bus fares double during peak travel times, and tickets can be sold out weeks in advance. Tickets can be bought online from companies, or travel agencies, or directly on the bus.

LUXURY BUSES

For long-distance hauls, Peru's intercity luxury bus services are the way to go.

They are more comfortable, much safer, and more reliable than other services.

The deluxe buses offer fully reclining bed-like seats, direct non-stop travel, all meals, air conditioning, videos, reading lamps, a hostess, and on-board toilets. One bus line even organizes a bingo game for passengers. Companies identify their top services with names such as Imperial, First Class, or Especial.

The next level is the business or *ejecutivo* class, which shares many features of the deluxe service, excluding the bed seats. Both deluxe and business services are much faster as they only make fuel stops, and buses travel with two drivers so that they can drive in 4-hour shifts. The buses have a controlled speed limit.

Economy services run by the large companies include comfortable seats, qualified drivers, and programmed toilet and food stops for long-haul trips. Many travelers, however, bring their own food, rather than rely on eateries in the middle of nowhere.

TRAINS

Perúrail, which is owned by the Orient Express group, runs daily train services from Cusco to Aguas Calientes, the station for Machu Picchu. Three trains depart from Cusco's San Pedro station every morning for the four-hour trip: the mid-range Vistadome 1, Vistadome 2, and the budget Backpacker train. The luxurious Hiram

Backpacker train to Machu Picchu, for those traveling on a budget

Passenger boat ferrying visitors to the islands on Lake Titicaca

Bingham *(see p176)* departs daily from Poroy Station, outside Cusco. Perúrail also operates the upmarket Andean Explorer, and the Backpacker train from Cusco to Puno and back three times a week. They also run a train charter service on the route between Arequipa and Puno.

One of the highest railroads in the world operates intermittently from Lima to the Andean cities of La Oroya and Huancayo *(see p183)*. Information on its services are available from **Ferrovias Central Andina S.A.**

BOATS

Slow-moving passenger boats ferry tourists to various islands on Lake Titicaca, however, there is no service to Bolivia.
Empresa de Transportes Turístico Titicaca S.C.R. Ltda and **Empresa de Transportes Turístico Titicaca Villa del Lago** organize trips to the islands in Lake Titicaca.

Boats carry passengers as well as cargo along the Amazon. Boat names and departure times are displayed at ports. The timetables are flexible as the boats depart only when they have a full load of cargo. Do check with the harbor master, known as the *capitania,* for reliable information. Passengers either rent a cabin or carry a hammock and string it on the upper deck.

The most popular routes are from Yurimaguas or Pucallpa to Iquitos. Travelers can also cross over into Peru

from Brazil via the river, landing in Iquitos.

Companies, such as **Amazon River Expeditions** also operate upmarket river cruises which explore the national reserves of Allpahuauyo-Mishana and Pacaya-Samiria, which is

Taxis are plentiful on Lima streets but not all are licensed

accessible only by boat. Visitors can fish the river or gently cruise the Amazon to the junction of the Marañon and Ucayali rivers. Rivers can swell greatly during the rains and become dangerous for boat travel.

LOCAL TRANSPORT

The cheapest way to get around major Peruvian cities is via public transport. In Lima, that means taxis, buses, or minibuses known as *micros* or *combis* or *colectivos* (see p333). Most of them are aging sedans imported from the US, though Japanese and Korean minibuses are taking over. *Colectivos* usually run on fixed routes throughout Peru, such

Three-wheeled taxi

as between Cusco and Pisac and Huanchco and Trujillo. Taxis can be easily flagged down in the streets but they cannot be trusted. It is safer to call for a radio-taxi.

In provincial towns, *ticos,* which are tiny Korean-made cars and motorcycle rickshaws, known as *mototaxis* or *motokars,* are common. Not the safest means of transport, it is best to avoid them. A more convenient alternative is to contact your hotel or tour agency. Hire a car and driver, or a taxi by the hour or day.

DIRECTORY

BUS COMPANIES

Cruz del Sur
Av. Javier Pardo 1100, San Isidro, Lima. **Tel** *01 311 5050.*
www.cruzdelsur.com.pe

Movil Tours
Av. Paseo de la República 749, Lima. **Map** 1 F4. **Tel** *01 716 8000.* **www**.moviltours.com.pe

TRAIN SERVICES

Perúrail
Av. Pachacutec s/n, Cusco.
Tel *084 581 414/ 084 222 114.*
www.perurail.com

Ferrovias Central Andina S.A.
Av. José Galvez Barrenechea 566 (Piso 5), San Isidro, Lima. **Map** 3 F2. **Tel** *01 226 6363.* **http://** www.ferroviasperu.com.pe

BOAT TRAVEL

Empresa de Transportes Turístico Titicaca S.C.R.Ltda
Puno. **Tel** *051 365 171.*

Empresa de Transportes Turístico Titicaca Villa del Lago
Puno. **Tel** *051 624 772.*

Amazon River Expeditions
Av. Las Camelias 511, Oficina 402, San Isidro, Lima. **Tel** *01 421 9195 / 442 4515.* **www**. amazonriverexpeditions.com

Driving in Peru

"Slow" road sign

DESPACIO

Traveling around at your own pace in a car may seem like the most flexible way to explore Peru, however, you need to keep some general rules in mind. Poor road conditions, expensive fuel, scarcity of fuel stations, and aggressive drivers are just a few of the hazards. Consider renting a car at each destination and using it only in that area rather than traversing the entire country in one car. Driving at night can be dangerous in remote areas and robberies do occur.

Sign showing a speed limit on a highway

RULES OF THE ROAD

Peruvians drive on the right-hand side of the road and distances are measured in kilometers. Wearing of seatbelts is compulsory. Normal speed limits are 25 mph (40 km/h) in streets, 38 mph (60 km/h) in avenues, 50 mph (80 km/h) on expressways, and 19 mph (30 km/h) in school and hospital zones. The speed limit is 38 mph (60 km/h) on rural roads and 62 mph (100 km/h) on highways. Speeds are reduced to 34 mph (55 km/h) in residential areas and 22 mph (35 km/h) in commercial areas when a highway crosses a town. Traffic must come to a stop at all "Stop" (*pare*) signs. Usual international road signs are used.

Bump ahead sign

ROAD NETWORK

Peru has over 48,000 miles (78,000 km) of roads, with 10,380 miles (16,705 km) of *carretas* (national highways). The Carretera Panamericana Norte y Sur, or Panamerican

Highway North, is the most important highway linking the towns along Peru's coast. The Carretera Marginal de la Selva connects towns in the northern jungle with those in the south, near the Bolivian border. The Carretera Central begins in Lima and cuts inland to the central highlands, climbing through the mountain pass of Ticlio, which at 15,810 ft (4,818 m) above sea level, is one of the world's highest railroad pass. Few roads, aside from the highways, have signposts. In towns, street names are rarely signposted. The percentage of unpaved roads increases with distance from main cities.

ROAD MAPS

Pick up a road map prior to arriving as detailed versions can be hard to find. The **Instituto Geográfico Nacional** and the **Touring y Automóvil Club del Perú** sell them. Road maps are included in travel guides such as *Guía Toyota* and *Guía Inca del Perú*.

FUEL STATIONS

Fuel is expensive in Peru, with costs rising according to the grade, diesel being the cheapest. Fuel stations such as Repsol and Primax are plentiful in large cities and towns but less common in rural or jungle areas. Get the tank refilled whenever you get a chance. Stations are not self-service, therefore when the attendant asks *"cuánto"*, either specify an amount or say *"lleno por favor"* (fill it up). Credit cards may not be accepted in remote areas.

CAR AND MOTORCYCLE RENTAL

Car rental companies such as **American**, **Avis**, **Budget**, **Dollar**, **Hertz**, and **National** have offices in Lima and other major cities. All have 24-hour desks at Lima airport. Drivers must be at least 25 years of age and have a driving license from their own country or an International Driving Permit. Optional services, available for an additional charge, include theft and accident insurance, tow truck service, pick-up or drop-off in another city, and airport pick-up.

Make sure you understand the rental agreement and all costs involved before signing. Inspect the vehicle before accepting delivery to make sure it is in good condition. In the event of an accident obtain a copy of the police report. Always carry your driver's license and copies of your passport and the rental contract. Four-wheel drive vehicles are best for remote rural areas and motorcycle rental is usually limited to jungle towns.

ROAD SAFETY

Most roads in Peru have inadequate traffic signs and markings. Speeding buses, minibuses, taxis, and cars are part of the landscape. Driving at night in Peru is not recommended due to the number of obstacles. It is wise to sound the horn and flash your lights to indicate that someone can overtake, or cut in.

Getting Around Lima

The best way to explore Central Lima is on foot, although you need to take some form of transport to reach the suburbs of Miraflores and Barranco. Traffic is chaotic and congested, thanks to myriad taxis and minibuses, and is best avoided during rush hours. If you choose to drive, do so with the doors locked and the windows closed. Use guarded parking lots, rather than unattended on-street parking.

WALKING

Walking is the best way to explore the heart of Lima's historic center, as well as other areas such as Barranco. The main pedestrianized thoroughfare in the center of Lima is Jirón de la Unión, which connects Plaza San Martín with Plaza Mayor.

Footpaths, however, are narrow and crowded, and pedestrians are often forced to step on the roadway, even when they are on an official crossing. This can be dangerous as traffic is heavy and drivers do not automatically stop for pedestrians.

Stop sign, Lima

Pickpockets operate in crowded places. Do not wear jewelry or dangle an expensive camera from your shoulder. Avoid walking across the Río Rimac to Convento de los Descalzos or Plaza de Acho as it is a poor area and robberies have occurred. Even though people congregate in and around Plaza Mayor at night, it is still safest in the daytime. Keep to busy, well-lit streets during night.

TAXIS

Many unlicensed companies operate taxis in Lima and visitors are advised not to flag taxis on the street. Bright yellow taxis, registered with the Metropolitan Lima Taxi Service, hang around the airport, major hotels, and shopping centers, such as Larcomar. As a rule call for taxis from companies such as **Taxi Real**, **Taxinet**, or **Taxi Seguro**. Radio-taxis cost 30 to 50 percent more than street taxis but are more reliable. The fare must be agreed upon in advance as taxis do not have meters. A trip to or from the airport is almost always quoted in American dollars and ranges between US$15 to US$30, depending on the distance covered. Fares increase by 35 to 50 percent after midnight and on holidays.

BUSES, COMBIS, AND COLECTIVOS

Buses are plentiful and cheap but painfully slow. There are buses and *combis*, *micros* or *colectivos*, all minibuses of varying size. Many *combis* charge a flat rate and follow fixed routes. Signs on windscreens indicate their routes. Conductors call out street names as the minibus hurtles along, and hold up fingers to show how many seats are available. They are frequently crowded and theft is common. *Colectivos* run in some Lima areas but are more popular in coastal and mountain towns.

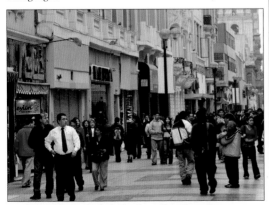

Jirón de la Unión, a pedestrianized pathway, Plaza Mayor, Lima

General Index

Page numbers in **bold type** refer to main entries.

A

Abancay 37
Abra de Warmiwañusca **170–72**
Accommodation 266–9, **270–81**
　booking 266
　budget accommodation 267
　disabled travelers 269
　grading 269
　homestays 151, 268
　hotel chains 266
　jungle and eco lodges 268
　mid-range accommodation 267
　prices 269
　specialist holidays 268
　youth hostels 267
Acllawasi 156
Admiral's Palace see Museo Inka
Adobo 284
Adventurebiketours 307
Agouti 309
Aguas Calientes **173**, 176–7, 269, 274, 294, 330
　Machu Picchu Pueblo Eco Lodge 268, 274, 281
　Michuna Wasi 294
Agüero, Don José de la Riva 60–61
AIDS 321
Air travel
　airports 326
　arriving by air 326
　departure tax 327
　organized tours 327
　domestic travel
　see Domestic flights **328–9**
Airlines
　Aerolineas Argentinas 326–7
　Aeromexico Airlines 326–7
　Air Canada 326–7
　Air France 326–7
　American Airlines 326–7
　Continental Airlines 326–7
　Copa Airlines 326
　Delta 326–7
　Gol 326
　Iberia 326–7
　KLM 326–7
　LanPeru 326, 328–9
　LC Busre 328–9
　Lufthansa 326
　Peruvian Airlines 328–9
　Quantas 326–7
　Star Peru 328–9
　Taca 326, 329
　Tam 326, 327
Airports
　Aeropuerto Alfredo Rodríguez Ballon 329
　Aeropuerto Capitán Carlos Martínez de Pinillos 329
　Aeropuerto Capitán Guillermo Concha Ibérico 326, 329
　Aeropuerto Capitán José Abelardo Quiñones Gonzáles 329
　Aeropuerto Comandante Guillermo del Castillo Paredes 329
　Aeropuerto Coronel Francisco Secada Vignetta 329
　Aeropuerto Inca Manco Cápac 326, 329
　Aeropuerto Internacional Jorge Chávez 326, 329

Airports (cont.)
　Aeropuerto Mayor General Armando Revoredo Iglesias 329
　Anta airport 199
　Arequipa airport 132
　Cajamarca airport 238
　Chiclayo airport 216–7
　CORPAC (Corporación Peruana de Aeropuertos y Aviación Commercial) 329
　Cusco airport 154–5
　Ica airport 119
　Nazca airport 119, 126–7
　Piura airport 216–7
　Tumbes airport 216–7, 232–3
Aji de gallina 287, 303
Albahaca 287
Albergue Churup 277
Albergue Humboldt 281
Albergue Turistico Bottger 281
Albergues 267, 269
Alcohol 283, 288
Alegría, Ciro 31
Alejandro Tello 312
Algarrobo 225
Aliaga, Jerónimo de 62–3
Alianza Francesa 102–3
All Saints' Day 34
All Ways Travel 268–9
Allpahuayo antbird 254
Almagro, Diego de 48
Almuerzo 283
Along the Waterfront 301
Alpaca 32, 111 100–101, 302
Alpaca knits 302
Alpamayo 306
Altitude sickness 320
Alto Mayo 250–51, **256**
Alto, Pueblo 246
Aluvión 200
Alva, Walter 228, 230
Amalia Puga 238
Amantani 268
Amaringo, Pablo 30, 257
Amaru Hostal 274
Amat, Viceroy 94
Amazon Basin 9, 22, 248–63, 280, 300–301, 309
　Chanchamayo region **260**
　Iquitos **252**
　map 250–51
　Moyobamba and Alto Mayo **256**
　Oxapampa **260**
　Parque Nacional Manu **261**
　Pevas **252**
　Pucallpa **257**
　Reserva Nacional Allpahuayo-Mishana **255**
　Reserva Nacional Pacaya-Samiria **255**
　Reserva de la Biosphera de Manu **261**
　River Dolphins **255**
　River Travel **253**
　Ríos Tambopata and Madre de Dios area **262–3**
　Tarapoto **256**
　Ucayali river towns **254**
　Yarinacocha **257**
　Yurimaguas **255**
　Where to eat 300–301
　Where to stay 280–81
Amazon Museum 252
Amazon rainforest 19, 250–51, 308–9
Amazon River Expeditions 331
Amazon Tours & Cruises 309, 311

Amazonas Explorer 306, 311
Ambulances (SAMU) 319
American Express cards 302
American Express Credit Cards 322
American Express Traveler's Checks 322
Amotape Hills National Park
　see Parque Nacional Cerros de Amotape
Amphitheater 76–8, 212
Anapia 268
Ancash 305
Ancient art of healing
　see Curanderismo
Ancient antwren 254
Andahuaylas 37, 328
Andean condors 18
Andean culture 313
Andean harp 29
Andean Kingdom 311
Andean llama wool 32
Andes 306
Andino Club Hotel 277
Angela's Place 298
Anis Najar 303
Anta 199
Antay, Joaquín López 73
Antica Trattoria 290
Anticucherísa 282
Anticuchos 284, 287
Apaec, Ai 228–9
Apurímac 34, 37, 305
Apurímac river 308
Apurímac Tourist Week 37
Aqllawasi 150
Archbishop of Lima 86–7
Archbishop's Palace 60–61
　see Palacio Arzobispal
Archaeological Museum, Cajamarca
　see Cajamarca University Museum
Architecture **26–7**
　Baroque 64, 159, 218, 221, 238, 304
　Colonial architecture **63**, 67, 134–5, 156, 159, 186, 192, 206, 216–18, 235, 238
Arequipa 8, 10, 27, 30, 132, **134–41**, 155, 218, 238, 273, 282, 284, 293–4, 302–3, 308, 321, 328, 331
　Casa del Moral 134–5
　Casa Goyeneche 134–5
　Casa Tristán del Pozo 134–5, 137
　Casona Iriberry 136
　Cathedral 134–6
　Convento de la Recoleta 136
　Iglesia la Merced 137
　Iglesia de la Compañía 135, 137
　Iglesia San Augstín 134–5, 137
　Iglesia San Francisco 137
　Museo Histórico Municipal 136
　Museo Santuarios Andinos de la Universidad Catolica de Santa Maria 137
　Plaza de Armas 134–5
Arequipa airport 132
Arguedas, José Maria 31
Ari's Burger 300
Aribalos 158
Arrieros 306
Arroz con camarones 287
Artesonraju 306
Arts 17, 30–31
Ashaninka 22, 260
Asia Beach 302
Asociación Peruana de Albergues Turísticos Juveniles 267, 269
Asto, Símon de 144

Atahualpa 67, 98, 163 169, 201, 238, 242
ATMs 318, **322–3**
Ausangate 306
Avenidas
Arica 255
España 218
Grau 86–7
La Paz 101
Larco 76–7
Luzuriaga 206
Pedro de Osma 88
Petit Thouars 101
Sáenz Peña 86–7
Aves sin Nido 17, 31
Avis 332
Ayacucho 9, 184–5, 189, **192–3**, 275–6, 295–6, 303–4, 318, 328
Casa Boza y Solis-Prefecture 192–3
Cathedral 184–5, 192
Compañía de Jesús 193
Iglesia de Santo Domingo 192
Iglesia San Francisco de Paula 193
Iglesia y Monasterio de Santa Clara 193
Museo de Arte Popular 192
Plaza de Armas 192
Ayahuasca 24
Ayala, Guaman Poma de 31, 66, 89
Ayllon, Eva 29
Aymara 145, 316
Aymara Love Dance 145

B

Baca, Susana 29
Backpacker 176, 330–31
Backroads 307, 311
Baco 295
Baez, Gasper 137
Bajada de los Baños 86, 89
Bákula, Cecilia 158
Ballestas Islands 8, 120–21
Banks
Banco Central de Reserva del Peru 218
Banco de Credito (BCP) 322
Banco de la Nacion 322
Banco Weise Sudameris 322
banking hours 322
BBVA Banco Continental 322
Scotia Bank 322
Baño de Pescadores *see* Bajada de los Baños
Baños de Barro 233
Baños de Pariacaca 201
Bar Restaurant Romana 297
Barranco 8, 85–92, 100, 270, 290, 333
area map 85
La Ermita 85, **90**
Museo de la Electricidad 85, **88**
Museo Galeria Arte Popular de Ayacucho 85, **89**
Museo Pedro de Osma 85, **90**
Parque Municipal 85, **88**
Puente de los Suspiros 85–7, **89**
Street-by-street map 86–7
Barrio Chino 68
Barrio Santa Ana 9, 189, 303
Bars, Clubs, and Discos **102–3**
Baskets 302, **305**
Batán Grande 216–17, 224, **225**
Battle of Ayacucho 49, 195
Beaches 99, 129, 200, 224, 232, 298
Beads 32
Beer 288
Belén 252

Belén Market 252
Bellido, María Parado 193
Belón, Enrique Torres 144
Bennet, Wendell C. 225
Berrocal, Carmelón 89
BikeHike Adventures 307, 311
Bingham, Hiram 173, 178
Birdingperu 312–13
Bird-watching 312–13
Bisambra Aqueduct 128
Bistro de los Andes 297
Bitti, Bernardo 67, 73, 151
Black Summer *see* Verano Negro
Blood Fiesta 34
Boating 327, 331
Bocapán 233
Bodega Lazo 122
Bodega Tacama 117, 122
Bodyboardperu 308, 311
Bolivar, Símon 96–7
Bosque de Piedras 242
Bosque El Olivar 75, **83**
Botticelli 73
Bromeliads 244–5
Bronze fountain 60–61
Brujos 224
Brüning, Hans Heinrich 224
Budget 332
Budget accommodation 267
Buenavista, Marquis de San Juan de 159
Bujanda, Bishop Baltazar Martínez de Compañón 220
Bullfighting season 37
Bullfighting *see* Feria Taurina del Señor de los Milagros
Burger King 282
Bus travel 326–7, 330
Buses and terminals 326–7, 330, 333
Bustamante, Alicia 73
Butterfly-watching 268, 312–13
Byrne, David 29

C

Cabalgates 310, 311
Caballitos de totora 223
Cabinas 324–5
Cabinzas Islands 94
Cable Mágico 325
Cabo Blanco 232
Cachi river 195
Cadena del fuego 136
Cadena, Josef 138–40
Cafés
Americano 288
Andino 297, 306
Café 282
de Rat 296
del Mar 102–3
el Abuelo 297
la Terraza 296
Cahuachi 8, 118–19, **128**
Cajabamba 236–7
Cajamarca 9–10, 34–5, 67, 73, 95, 100, 187, 236–7, **238–9**, 242–3, 279, 299, 303, 318–19, 326, 328
Cajamarca University 238
Capilla de la Virgen de Dolores 238
Cathedral 238
Cerro Santa Apolonia 239
El Complejo de Belén 239
Iglesia de San Francisco 238
map 239
Museo Arqueológico y Etnográfico 238

Cajamarca (cont.)
Ransom Chamber 238
Cajón 29, 121, 312
Cajones de San Marco 89
Cala 290
Calancha, Antonio de la 223
Calca 154–5, **169**
Caldo de cabeza 287
Callao 93, 94, 321
Callao's Battles **98**
Calles
Capón 68
Córdova 141
de las Pizzas 76–7
Hatunrumiyoc 159
Junín 86–7
Prospero 252
Real 187
Sevilla 138–9
Callejón de Huaylas 197, 198, 200–201, 206, 313
Callua 100–101
Calonge, Bernardino 218
Cambistas 322
Campo Santo, Yungay 198–9, **200–201**
Camusso, Carlo Mario 101
Cancacho 287
Cancha 287
Candelabra geoglyph 116, 121, 123
Candelabro 88
Candelaria, Mamita 144
Candles 303, 305
Cañón del Colca 132–3, **142–3**
Collagua Terraces 143
Iglesia de la Inmaculada Concepción 143
La Calera 143
La Cruz del Condor 142
Reserva Nacional Salinas y Aguada Blanca 143
Yanque 143
Cañón de Cotahuasi 132–3, **144**
Cataratas de Sipia 144
Canopy walkway **252**
Cantayo Spa and Resort 293
Canyon Country 8, 130–51, 273, 293
Arequipa 8, 10, 27, 30, **134–7**, 273, 282, 284, 293–4
Cañón de Cotahuasi **144**
Cañón del Colca **142–3**
Juanita **137**
Juli **151**
Lake Titicaca **146–51**
Lampa **144**
map 132–3
Monasterio de Santa Catalina **138–41**
Puno **144**
Sillustani Burial Towers **151**
Where to eat 293–4
Where to stay 273–4
Cápac, Huayna 169
Cápac, Manco 131, 134, 144, 146–7, 150, 153, 168–9
Cápac, Mayta 131, 134
Cápac, Ñan 47, 170
Capilla de la Virgen de Dolores 238
Capiscara (Manvel Chili) 221
Capitán de Navío Julio J. Elías Murguía 95
Capitania 331
Car of Memories 88
Car rental 332
Caracol 327

Caral, the mother city 42–3, 198–9, **212–13**
  Amphitheater 212–13
  Great Pyramid 212–13
  Pyramid of the Huanca 213
Carapulca 285
Caraz 198–9, **200**, 204, 276, 296–7, 306
Caretas 325
Cargo boats 253, 309
Carhuaz 198–9, **201**, 276, 297
Carnaval 35
Carpentry 197, 206
Carretas 332
Carretera Marginal de la Selva 332
Caretaker's Hut 178
Carved stones 238
Carved toys 304
Casas
  Andina 266–7, 269, 272, 317
  Andina Private Collection 266–7, 269, 273–4
  Arróspide *see* Casona Iriberry
  Boza y Solis-Prefecture 192–3
  Calonge *see* Casa Urqiaga
  de Aliaga 59, 60–61, **62**, 63
  de Arena 272
  de la Emancipación 218, 220
  de la Logia o Montjoy 224
  de Guias 306, 311
  de Orbegoso 219
  de Osambela Oquendo 63
  de Playa Restaurant 298
  de Pizarro
  see Palacio de Gobierno
  del Corregidor 294
  del Moral 134–5
  Goyeneche 134–5
  Grande 274
  Hacienda José 120, 292
  Hacienda Moreyra 292
  Huerta 96–7
  Ricardo Palma 75
  Riva-Agüero 60–61
  Rossel-Urquiaga
  see Casa de la Emancipación
  Tristán del Pozo 134–5, 137
  Urqiaga 218–19
  Victor Delfín 270
  Vieja Hostal 279
  y Ideas 101
Casas de cambio 322
Cascanuez 299
Cash 323
Cashapampa 204
Casinos 103
Casona Iriberry 136
Castañeda, Riña Sebastián de 156–7
Castro, José Gil 73
Catacaos 304
Catacombs 64–5
Cataratas de Quiocta 247
Cataratas de Sipia 144
Cataratas Gocta 236–7, **247**
Catarates del Gera 256
Catholic University, Lima 60–61
Cau-cau 287
Causa 282
Causa de pulpo 286
Causa rellena 286–7
Causa verde 286
Cebiche 282, 284
Cebicherías 282–3
Cedar Choir 162–3
Cedrobamba 173
Ceiba Tops 268
Celendín 236–7, 279, 303
  Hostal Celendín 279
Cely's 300

Cementerio de Chauchilla 118–19, **128**
  mummies **128**
Cena 283
Center for Traditional Textiles of Cusco 305
Central Cultural PUCP 102–3
Central Hall 94
Central Lima
  area map 59
  Casa de Aliaga **62**
  Convento de los Descalzos **68**
  La Catedral **62**
  Las Nazarenas **68**
  Museo de Arte **73**
  Museo de Arte Italiano **62–3**
  Museo Nacional de la Cultura Peruana **73**
  Museo Taurino **68**
  Palacio de Gobierno **62**
  Plaza San Martín **72**
  San Francisco **64–6**
  San Pedro **67**
  Santo Domingo **67**
  Santa Rosa de Lima **67**
  Street-by-street map 60–61
Central Sierra 9, 183–95, 275, 295–6
  Ayacucho **192–3**
  Chavín de Huántar **208–9**
  Huancavelica **189**
  Huancayo **187**
  Huánuco **186**
  Mantaro Valley Tour **188**
  map 184–5
  Pikimachay Caves **195**
  Quinua **195**
  Semana Santa **194**
  Where to eat 295–6
  Where to stay 275–6
Centro Cultural de España 102–3
Centro Cultural de la Pontificia Universidad Católica del Perú 312–13
Centro de Idiomas PUCP 313
Centro Yachaqui Wayi 268–9
Ceramics 33, 80–81, 238, 302–3
Cerro La Raya 225
Cerro Purgatorio 225
Cerro Santa Apolonia 239
Cerro, Sánchez 215
Certificando 325
Cerveza 288
Cerveza negra 288
Chabuca Granda 90, 121
Chacas 197–9, **206**, 276
Chaccu ceremony 36
Chachapoyas 235–7, 243, 246–7, 279–80, 300
Chain of fire *see* Cadena del fuego
Chain restaurants **282**
Chala 129
Chan Chan 26, 114–15, 215–17, **223**
Chancay
  culture 224
  pottery 95
  weavings 95
Chanchamayo 250–51, **260**, 280
Chancos 197, 206
Chapo 288
Charango 28
Charles V, Emperor 66
Charqui 285
Chaufa 284
Chavez de la Rosa
  see Casona Iriberry
Chávez, Gerardo 30, 221
Chavín 32, 276
  ceramics 159
  culture 207, 209
  gold ornaments 219
  stone carvings 95

Chavín de Huantár 9, 114–15, 197–9, **208–9**
  El Castillo 208–9
  Lanzón de Chavín 208
  Sunken Plaza 208–9
  Underground tunnels 208–9
Chelsea Pub Restaurant 299
Chez Maggy 301
Chicha 25, 36, 170–71, 181, 285, 288, 305
Chicha de molle 288
Chicha de siete semillas 288
Chicha morada 288
Chicharrón 283, 287
Chicharrones de pescado 287
Chiclayo 216–17, **224**, 236–7, 277, 297–8, 318, 326, 328
Chifa Ah Chau 298
Chifa Wai Ming 300
Chifas 282
Chifles 287
Chilean Lebels 283
Capiscara, Manuel Chili 221
Chimichurri 287
Chimú 32
  art 221, 224
  ceramics 159
  empire 26, 45, 223
  gold ornaments 219
  mask 98
  textiles 32, 222
Chinatown 68
Chincha Alta 8, 118–19, **120**, 272, 292
Chinchero 123, 154–5, **168–9**, 303
Chinguno 123
Chinkana 150
Chiquián 213
Chirimoya 287
Chivay 34, 131
Choclo 287
Chorrillos 290
Chucuito 151, 273, 305
Chullachaqui Botanical Garden 257
Chullis 305
Chullpas 243
Chulucanas 303
Chuño 285
Chuño lawa 287
Chupe de camarones 287
Chupe de cangrejo 287
Church of Nazarenes
  see Las Nazarenas
Church of San Blas 159
Church of San Francisco 8, 59, **64–6**, 186, 238
Cicciolina 295
Cilantro 287
Chili salsa 303
Cinema and Theater (Lima) 102–3
Circular Houses 244–6
City of Eternal Spring *see* Trujillo
City of Orchids 256
Ciudad de la Eterna Primavera *see* Trujillo
Ciudadela Tschudi 223
Claustro Los Naranjos 138–40
Claustro Mayor 138–9, 141
Clay Licks 262–3
Clemente Church 120
Climate 38–9
Clinica Anglo Americana 321
Clinica El Golf 321
Clinica San Borja 321
Cloud Forest 261
Club Central 220
Club Nacional 72
Coastal Pacific Desert 19
Cochas 188
Cochas Chico 188, 303

Cochas Grande 188, 303
Cocina 138–9
Cock of the Rock 19
Cordillera Huayhuash 198–9, **213**
Colca 8, 131, 142–4, 307
Colca Canyon **142–3**, 273, 312
Colca river 131
Colca Trek 307, 311
Cold drinks **288**
Colectivos 331, 333
Collagua terraces 143
Colonial Art Gallery 73
Colonial House Inn 273
Combayo 24
Combis 318–9, 331, 333
Comida criolla 284
Common District 181
Communications 324–5
    Cable Mégico 325
    Certificando 325
    Courier services 325
Community-based tourism 313
Compañía de Jesús 193
Compañón, Martínez 89
Complejo Arequeologico El Brujo
    216–17, **223**
Concepción 184–5, **186**
Concessionary fares 329
Conchitas a la parmesana 284
Conchitas negras 287
Conquering kingdoms 45
Consulates 317
Contamaná 254
Convent Cloister and Garden 64–6
Convent Library 64–5
Convent of San Francisco 238
Convent of Santa Rosa de Ocopa 186
Convento de la Recoleta 136
Convento de los Descalzos 59, **68**,
    333
Conversación en la Catedral 31
Cordillera Blanca 9, 196–213, 235–7,
    268, 276, 296–7, 306–7, 313
    Campo Santo, Yungay **200–201**
    Caral **212–13**
    Caraz **200**
    Carhuaz **200–201**
    Chacas **206**
    Chavín de Huantár **208–9**
    Climbing in the Cordillera
        Blanca **205**
    Cordillera Huayhuash **213**
    Hot Springs of Monterrey **206**
    Huaraz **206**
    map 198–9
    Parque Nacional Huascarán
        202–4
    Where to eat 296–7
    Where to stay 276–7
Cordillera Huayhuash **213**, 306–7
Coriander *see* Cilantro
Corn beer *see Chicha*
CORPAC (Corporación Peruana de
    Aeropuertos y Aviación
    Commercial) 329
Corpus Christi Festival 36, 156–7
Corso, Andres 68
Costa Azul Hotel & Spa 279
Costumbrista retablos 304
Cotahuasi 140, 307
Coto de Caza El Angolo 232–3
Country Club 271
Country Club Hostal 281
Courier services 325
Craft and textiles 32–3
Crafts 32–3, 303
Credit cards 302, 318, 322
Creole music 37, 102
Creole onions 283

Crêperie Patrick 297
Cruz del Sur 330
Cruz, Fernando Collado de la 221
Cruzpata 246
Culinary tours and courses 313
Culture 24–5
Cumbemayo 236–7, **242**
Cumbemayo petroglyphs 238, 242
Cummerbunds 305
Curanderismo 225
Curanderos 224
Currency 322–3
Cusco airport 154–5
Cusco paintings 82
Cusco School 27, 30, 62, 67–8, 73, 90,
    136–7, 141, 144, 151–2, 158–9, 166,
    167, 187, 196
Cusco 8, 10, 13, 23, 26, 30, 34,
    36–7, 73, 144, 153–5, **156–9**,
    169, 176, 187, 193, 195, 238,
    262, 266–9, 274, 282, 285, 294–5,
    302–8, 328, 330–31
    Calle Hatunrumiyoc 159
    Corpus Christi Festivities 156–7
    Iglesia de la Compañía 156–7
    Iglesia la Merced 156–7
    Koricancha Temple 144, 159, 164
    La Catedral 156–7, **162–3**
    map 156–7
    Museo de Arte Precolombino 158
    Museo de Arte Religioso 156–7, 159
    Museo Inka 156–8
    Plaza de Armas 154, 158
    San Blas District 159
    Santa Catalina 156–7
    Santo Domingo 159
Cusqueña 288
Customs information 316
Cuy 285–7

D

Daughter of Venus 57, 88
Davis, Edward 224
Day of the Dead 34
Day of Saint John the Baptist 36
Decapitator *see* Apaec, Ai
Dédalo 100–101
Delfín, Victor 30, 79
Democracy and dictators 52–3
Departure tax 327
Depiction of St Michael 141
Desamparados 187
Desayuno 283
DHL International 325
Día de la Canción Criolla 37
Diablada 145
Díaz, Alonso 158
Diners Club 322
Disabled Travelers 269, 317
Divine Shepherdess 141
Don Bosco School 206
Dollar 332
Dolls 303
Dolphins 255, 309
Domestic flights **328–9**
Dominos 282
Don José's 301
Don Manuel 293
Donatello 73
Dongo, María del Carmen 312
Dos de Mayo 137
Drake, Sir Francis 98, 224
Driving 332
Drugs 318
Dugout canoes 253
Durand, Jesus Ruiz, 73

E

Earl of Cabrera 158

Earthquakes
    of 1584 137
    of 1650 156–60
    of 1652 68
    of 1655 68
    of 1656 64
    of 1687 62, 68
    of 1746 62, 72
    of 1758 62
    of 1759 218, 221
    of 1940 62, 72, 89
    of 1970 221
    of 1971 200
    of 1990 256
    of 1991 256
    of 2005 256
    of 2007 120–21, 123
Eating hours 283
Echenique, Alfredo Bryce 31
Ecoinka 306, 311
Economy 14
Eco-tourism and Coffee Festival 37
Ecotrek Peru 307, 311
Ecuador 235
Education 16–7
Edward's Inn 277
Eiffel, Gustave 27
El Abuelo 276
El Alamo 301
El Albergue 275
El Angolo Enclosed Hunting Zone
    see Coto de Caza El Angolo
El Batán 299
El Beso 30, 79
El Brassero 301
El Cajamarqués 299
El Califa 301
El Candelabro 116, 121, 123
El Caravedo 122
El Carmen 8, 120–21
El Castillo 208–9
El Catador 122
El Cinematógrafo de Barranco 102–3
El Commercio 102, 325
El Complejo de Belén 239
El Damero de Pizarro 63
El Dragon 102–3
El Ekeko 102–3
El Frontón-Island 94
El Gran Marqués – Hotel & Spa 278
El Mesón 300
El Mirador 272
El Mirador Catalina Recavarren 90
El Mirador de Vichayito 279
El Mochica 299
El Monasterio 295
El Mundo es Ancho y Ajeno 31
El Negrito 162
El Niño 216–17, 223
El Olivar 271
El Otro Peñoncito 292
El Parador del Colca 273
El Partón 293
El Patio de Monterrey 277
El Pizzotón 102–3
El Portal del Marqués 279
El Querubino 299
El Rincón del Pato 298
El Romano Criollo 299
El Señor de los Milagros 37, 68–9
El Señor de los Temblores 162–3
El Silencio 99
El Sol – Escuela de Español 312–3
El Tejado 300
El Trapiche 301
El Triunfo 162–3
El Turko II 293
Electricity 317
Electronic transfers 323

Embassies 317
Emergencies
  Ambulance (SAMU) 319
  Fire Brigade 319
  International clinics 321
  Tourist Police Cusco 319
  Tourist Police Headquarters 319
  Tourist Police Lima 319
  Tourist Protection Hotline 319
  Vaccination centers 321
Empanadas 283
Empresa de Transportes Touristico
  Titicaca S.C.R. Ltda 331
Empresa de Transportes Touristico
  Titicaca Villa del Lago 331
Engraved gourds 33
Equatorial Dry Forest 215, 233
Equatorial saki monkey 254
Equitours 310, 311
Erotic figures 222
Escabeche 287
Espacio Cultural Angelmira 221
Estadio Nacional 103
Estela Raimondi 96–7
Ester Ventura 100–101
Explorama 268–9
Explorandes 306, 311, 327
Exploration and conquest 48

F
Fabrics 100–101
Fardos funerarios 96–7
Farther Afield
  area map 93
  Lima's Beaches **99**
  Museo Arqueologico Rafael Larco
    Herrera **94**
  Museo de la Nacion **95**
  Museo de Oro del Peru **98**
  Museo Nacional de Arqueologia
    94, **96–7**
  Museo del Real Felipe **94**
  Pachacámac **98**
Fax 325
Feast of the Immaculate Conception 34
FedEx 325
Fejos, Paul 173
Felipe V 94
Feria Taurina del Señor de los
  Milagros 68–9, 103
Ferreñafe 224–5
Ferrovias Central Andina S.A. 331
Festivals and celebrations
  All Saints' Day 34
  Apurimac Tourist Week 37
  Blood Fiesta 34
  Bullfighting Season 37
  Carnaval 35
  Chaccu Ceremony 36
  Corpus Christi 36
  Day of the Dead 34
  Day of Saint John the Baptist 36
  Día de la Canción Criolla 37
  Eco-tourism and Coffee
    Festival 37
  El Señor de los Milagros 37
  Feast of the Immaculate
    Conception 34
  Feria Taurina del Señor de los
    Milagros 68–9, 103
  Festival de la Orquidea 34
  Festival de la Vendimia 35
  Festival of San Jerónimo 188
  Festival of the Negritos 34
  Festival of the Virgin of the Candles
    145
  Fiesta de la Cruz 35
  Fiestas Patrias 37, 266
  Founding of Puno 34
Festivals and celebrations (cont.)
  Holy Week Celebrations 192–4
  Homenaje a la Liberated
    Americana 34
  Independence Day 37
  Inti Raymi 24, 36, 158, 266, 269
  Marinera Festival 35
  Pachamama Raymi 37
  Peruvian Paso Horse National
    Show 35
  Qoyllur Rit'i 36
  Ruraltur 37
  Santa Rosa de Lima 37
  Santurantikuy 34
  Semana Santa 35, 194, 266
  Spring Festival 37
  Verano Negro 120
  Virgen de la Candelaria 35, 144–5,
    304
  Virgen de la Merced 201
  Virgen del Carmen 37
  Yaku Raymi 37
Fierroo, Francisco 30
Fiesta Restaurant Gourmet 298
Filigree 32
Fire Brigade 319
Fishermen's Bath
  see Bajada de los Baños
Fitzcarrald, Carlos 262–3
Fitzcarraldo 262–3, 300
Flamingos 123
Flying the lines 126–7
Folklorico 102
Food and drinks 282, 303
Food hygiene 282–83
Fortaleza del Real Felipe 93, **94**
Frailones 242
Fuel stations 332
Fuentes, Carlos 31
Fujimori, Alberto, 31, 53
Funerary chambers *see Chullpas*
Funerary Rock 179
Fusión 292
Fútbol 103

G
Galera Pass 187
Galería de Arte Popular y Artesania
  100–101
Gallo, Miguel Mujica 98
  Museo de Oro del Peru 93, **98**
Gamarra 302
Garbanzos 287
Garland, Luis Miro Quesada 76–7
Garza Hotel 277
Gaston, Acurio 284
Gaudin, Luis 94
Gauguin, Paul 76
General José de San Martín 72, 49
General José Manual Iturregui y
  Aguilarte 220
General stores 302
Giant katydid 261
Giant sculpture 218
Glazed Sevillan Tiles 64–5
Globos de los Andes 310, 311
Gocta Falls 236–7, **247**
Gold Museum
  see Museo de Oro del Peru
Golden funerary mask 230
Gótica 102–3
Gourds 303–4
Grading 269
Gran Hotel Bolivar 270
Gran Hotel El Golf de Trujillo 278
Gran Malocha 300
Gran Peru 312
Gran Vilaya 247
Grand Hostal Caraz Dulzura 276
Grand Hotel Huánuco 276
Grape brandy 303
Grau, Admiral Miguel 95
Great Pyramid 212–13
Green Tracks 309, 311
Green's Organic 294
Grippa, Francisco 252
Gruta de Huagapo 186
Guaguas 34
Guano birds 18
Guerrilla tactics 52–3
Guzmán, Abimael 195
Guzmán, Doña María de 138–9

H
Hacienda San José 120, 283
Hand-painted masks 100
Handwoven textiles 302–3
Hang-gliding and hot-air ballooning
  310–11
  Globos de los Andes 310, 311
  PerúFly 310, 311
  Viento Sur 310, 311
Hats 303
Healers *see Brujos*
Health 320–21
Heath River Wildlife Center 281
Heidi's House 277
Hermit, the Jacob, Dutch pirate 94
Hertz 332
Hervideros 233
Heyerdahl, Thor 225
Hierbabuena 284
High Altar (Maestro) 64–5
High Andean Plain 18
History of Peru 40–53
HIV 321
Hoatzins 261
Home of Agustín Rivas 257
Homenaje a la Liberated Americana
  34
Homestay 151, 268–9
  All Ways Travel 268–9
  Centro Yachaqui Wayi 268–9
  Homestay in Cusco 268–9
  Island Homestays (Lake Titicaca)
    151
Horseback riding 310, 311
Hospedajes 267, 270
Hospedaje La Pascana 280
Hostals
  Ambassador 280
  Bracamonte 277
  Celendín 279
  Corihuasi 274
  de las Artes 270
  El Naranjo 281
  El Patio 271
  Estancia Chillo 280
  Inca 276
  Pilar 276
  Portada del Sol 279
  Rumi Punku 274
  Torreblanca 271
  Tres Máscaras 275
  Loki 271
Hot drinks 288
Hot spring pools 242
Hot Springs of Monterrey 197–9, **206**
Hotel & Spa Laguna Seca 279
Hotels
  Alegria 272
  Antigua 271
  Arizona 273
  Brujo 278
  Caballito de Mar 278
  Cantayo Spa and Resort 272
  Casa Victor Delfín 270
  Comfort 276

Hotels (cont.)
  Costa del Sol 278
  Don Carlos 281
  El Dorado Plaza 280
  El Marqués de Valdelirios 275
  El Refugio 280
  España 270
  Gran Vilaya 279
  Gran Hotel Bilivar 270
  Grand Hotel Huánuco 276
  Huancavelica 276
  Huancayo 276
  La Gruta 267, 273
  Libertador 273, 274
  Marriott 266, 269
  Maury 270, 283
  Monasterio 266, 275
  Mossone 292
  NM Lima 271
  Orient Express Hotels 266, 269
  Paraíso – Trujillo 278
  Parasó – Chiclayo 277
  Posada del Inca 271
  Revash 279
  Río Shilcayo 281
  San Francisco 275
  San Martín 278
  Santa Felicita 276
  Santa Rosa 275
  Sol del Oriente 281
  Sol de Oro Apart 271
  Sheraton 266, 269
  Sonesta Posada del Inca 266–7, 269
  Swissôtel Lima 266, 269, 271
  The Point 270
  Turismo 276
  Victoria Regia 280
House of the Chosen Women *see*
  Acllawasi
House of the High Priest 176–7, 181
Hoyle, Rafael Larco 94
Huaca 1 225
Huaca Arco Iris
  see Huaca El Dragón
Huaca Cao Viejo 223
Huaca del Son y de la Luna 26,
  215–17, 220, **223**
Huaca El Dragón 223
Huaca Esmeralda 223
Huaca Huallamarca 75, 80–81, **83**
Huaca Larga 225
Huaca Pucllana 8, 57, 75, **80–81**
Huaca restaurant 80–81
Huacachina 121, 272, 292, 310
Hualhuas 188, 303, 305
Huallabamba river 235
Huamachuco 235–7, 313
Huamanga 34, 303
Huancavélica 183–5, **189**, 276, 296,
  304
Huancayo 9, 114–15, 183–5, **187**,
  276, 296, 298, 304, 318, 331
Huanchaco 216–17, **223**, 277–8, 298
Huanchaco International 277
Huantanay 153–4
Huánuco 34, 184, **186**, 276, 296, 328
Huaqueros 223, **230**, 243
Huaraz 197–200, **206**, 268, 277, 297,
  305–6, 308, 317, 328
Huariques 282
Huasaí 300
Huáscar 51
Huascarán 18, 306
Huascarán National Park
  see Parque Nacional Huascarán
Huatuscalla 195, 311
Huayllabamba 170–72
Huayllay National Sanctuary 37
Huayna Capac Palace 159

Huayno 28
Huchu'y Qosqo 169
Huerequeque *see* Peruvian thick-knee
Hugo Boss 101, 302
Huiracocha 169
Humboldt Current 18
Humboldt penguins 18, 123
Humitas 284–5
Hummingbirds 19, 126–7

I

Ica 118–19, **121**, 272, 288, 292, 303,
  310, 318, 328
ICPNA (Instituto Cultural Peruano
  Norteamericano) 75, 80, **82**, 103,
  313
Iglesias
  de la Compañía (Arequipa) 137
  de la Compañía (Cusco) 27, 156–7,
    159
  de la Inmaculada Concepción 143
  de la Merced 60–1
  de la Virgin Milagrosa 76–7
  de los Indios *see* Iglesia de San
    Francisco
  de San Agustín 219
  de San Francisco 238
  de San Juan Bautista 144
  de Santa Catalina 138–40
  de Santiago Apóstol 144
  de Santo Domingo 192
  Jesús, María y José 160–61
  La Merced 137, 156–7, 192–3,
    218–19
  San Agustín 134–7
  San Cristóbal 186
  San Francisco 137
  San Francisco de Paula 193
  Santiago Apóstol de Pomata 151
  Santisima Cruz 86
  y Monasterio de Santa Clara 193
  y Monasterio del Carmen 220–21
Iglesias de quinua 303
Ilaria 101
INC (National Institute of Culture)
  98, 239, 316
Inca
  culture **24–5**
  Empire 46–7
  keros 24–5, 100, 158
  mythology 131
  quipu 25, 94
  Trail 8–9, **170–73**
  architecture 26, 178
Inca dishes 285
  Carapulca 285
  Charqui 285
  Chuño 285
  Cuy 285–7
  Humitas 285
  Maíz 285
  Pachamanca 285
Inca Emperors
  Atahualpa 169, 201, 238, 242
  Cápac, Huayna 169
  Cápac, Manco 144, 146–7, 150,
    168–9
  Cápac, Mayta 131, 134
  Huiracocha 169
  Inca Roca 159
  Pachacútec 153, 168–9
  Viracocha 160, 166
  Yupanqui, Tupac 168–9
Inca Explorers 307, 311
Inca Heartland 8, 153–181, 274, 294,
  302–3, 307
  Calca **169**
  Chinchero **168**
  Cusco **156–63**

Inca Heartland (cont.)
  Cusco School **167**
  Inca Trail **170–73**
  Machu Picchu **174–81**
  map 154–5
  Moray and Salinas de Maras **168**
  Ollantaytambo **168**
  Pikillacta and Rumicolca **166**
  Pisac **169**
  Sacsayhuamán **164**
  San Pedro de Andahuaylilas **166**
  Tambomachay Tour **165**
  Tipón **166**
  Where to eat 294–5
  Where to stay 274–5
Inca Kola 288
Inca Tunnel 170–71
Incanto 295
Independence Day
  see Fiestas Patrias
Indian markets 303
Indian's Church *see* Iglesia de San
  Francisco
Indio Feliz 294
Inia geoffrensis 255
Inkanatura Travel 268
Inkaterra 268–9
Institute of Culture (INC) 98, 239,
  316
Instituto Cultural Peruano
  Norteamericano *see* ICPNA
Instituto Geográfico Nacional 332
Insurance 320–21
International clinics 321
International Expeditions 309, 311
International Health Department
  321
International Herald Tribune 325
International PADI certification 308
International Sculpture Encounter
  82
International Vaccination Center 321
Internet 325
Inti Raymi 36, 158, 266, 269
Intihuatana 79
Intihuatana 176–7, 181
Intipunku 170–71
iPerú 316
Iquitos 9–10, 250–51, **252**, 253–5,
  268–9, 280, 300, 303, 309, 318, 328,
  331
Iron House 27
Islas/islands
  Amantaní 146, **150**, 268
  Anapia 151, 268
  Ballestas 120–21
  de la Luna **150**
  del Sol 146–7, **150**
  La Vieja 123
  San Gallán 123
  Soto 146–7
  Suasi **150**, 266–7
  Taquile 146–7, **150, 268**
  Uros 146, **150**

J

Jacks' Café 294
Jaén 235–7
Jakanas 254
Jauja 328
Jeny 297
Jewelry 33, 303
Jirón de la Unión 333
Jockey Plaza 101, 302
José de San Martín 49, 72, 120
José, Hacienda San 120
Juane 287
Juanita 8, 131, **137**
Juli 132–3, **151**

Juliaca 133, 144, 147, 155, 328–9
Jungle and Eco Lodges 268–9
Junín 304–5
Junin y Belén 239
JW Marriott 271

K

Kancha Inca 158
Karajía 236–7, **247**
Keros 24–5, 100, 158
KFC 282
Kin Taro 294
Koky 296
Kolibri Expeditions 312
Kon 126–7
Kon-tiki 225
Koricancha Temple 144, 159, 164
Kotosh 26, 186
Kuélap 9, 114–15, 235–7, **244–6**, 280
  bromeliads 244–5
  circular houses 244–6
  El Tintero 244–6
  Torreón 244–6
Kuskaya 100–101

L

L'Eau Vive 290
La Baguette 282
La Cabaña 296
La Cadelaria 91, 102–3
La Calera 143
La Cantarilla 293
La Caravedo 118
La Casa de Mamayacchi 273
La Casa de Melgar 273
La Casa Nostra 301
La Casa Suiza 277
La Casona 280, 294–5
La Casona de Lampa 273
La Cima Logistics 306, 311
La Ciudad y Los Perros 31
La Compañía 132–5, 159
La Crillonesa 275
La Cruz del Condor 142
La Ciudad Rosada see Lampa
La Donaide 88
La Ermita 85, 86, **89**
La Fonda de Santiago 294
La Gruta Hotel 267, 273
La Iberica 303
La Laguna de los Cóndores 243
La Marina lighthouse 79
La Merced 187, 193, 260, 300–301
La Noche 86–7, 102–3
La Olla de Barro 296, 301
La Oroya 331
La Pietá 144
La Posada de Santa Ines 275
La Punta 93
La Punta Grande 297
La Punta Olímpica 297
La Quinta Eco Hotal 275
La Señora de Cao 223
La Trattorria del Monasterio 282, 293
La Victoria 290
La Vieja island 123
Lagos/Lagunas (Lakes)
  Auquiscocha 201
  Avispa 254
  Carhuacocha 307
  Huacachina 8
  Lagunas 243, 255
  Lagunillas 123
  Llanganuco 9, 198–200, 202–4
  Parón 200
  Rajupaquinan 201
  Sandoval 262–3, 280
  Sauce 256

Lagos/Lagunas (cont.)
  Titicaca 8, 114–15, 131–3, **146–51**, 266–8, 302, 313, 316, 331
  Yarinacocha 280
Lakes Hike 201
Lakshmivan 293
Lamas 23, 256
Lambayeque 224–5, 298
Lampa 132–3, **144**, 273
  La Casona de Lampa 273
Landscape & Wildlife **18–19**
Language 316
Lanzón de Chavín 208
Larco Herrera Museum see Museo Arqueologico Rafael Larco Herrera
Larcomar 27, 75, **79**, 101, 310
Las Arenas de Máncora 278
Las Brisas del Titicaca 102–3
Las Dunas 272
Las Lomas 129
Las Nazarenas 59, **68**
Las Pallas 100–101
Last Supper (Veen) 221
Last Super (Zapata) 57, 64–6, 163
Latin American Travel Association 327
Lavanderia 138–40
Leather 305
Lechón 287
Lemos, Viceroy Conde de 144
Letrán, San Juan Bautista 151
Levanto 236–7, **247**
Ley seca 283
Leymebamba 236–7, **243**, 280, 300
Libertador 266–7, 269
Lighthouse Park see Parque El Faro
Lima 8–10, 13, 27, 29–30, 37, 78–9, 82, 93, 97, 100–103, 155, 158, 187, 199, 216–17, 236–7, 250–52, 257, 266–9, 282, 302–3, 308, 313, 318–21, 325, 328, 333
  Entertainment in Lima 102–3
  map 56–7
  Shopping in Lima 100–101
  Where to eat 290–92
  Where to stay 270–71
Lima School 90
Lima to Huancayo Train 187
Lima Tours 327
Lima Trek 207
Limestone blocks 154–5, 164
Limon 233
Literature 31
Little Cusco see Huchu'y Qosqo
Little Rome see Juli
Liucho 144
Liz's Explorer 307, 311
Llactapata 170–72
Llamerada 145
Llona, Ramiro 30, 90
Llosa, Vargas Mario 31, 90
  La Ciudad y Los Perros 31
Local transport 331, 333
Lomo saltado 285
Lonche 283
Lord of Miracles procession 69
Lord of Sipán's
  tomb 25, 56, 224, 228–31
  burial chamber 228–9, 231
  earring 228–9
Los Aticos Padro 274
Los Baños del Inca 9, 236–7, 242
Los Condes de San Isidro 75, 83
Los Delfines 103, 271
Los Pinos Inn 279
Los Portales 295
Lost and stolen property 318–19
Love Park see Parque del Amor
Lozano, Cristóbal 97
  Manuel de Amat y Juniet 97

Lucanas 36
Lucho del Mar 298
Lucifer Titi monkey 254
Lúcuma 284
Luis José de Orbegoso y Moncada 219
Luis Miro Quesado Garland Art Gallery 76–7
Luminoso, Sendero 52–3, 195, 260
Lunch see *Almuerzo*
Lurin Valley 98
Luxury buses 330
Luya 247

M

Macaws 19
Machacancha 169
Machu Picchu 8, 26, 95, 114–15, 153–5, 170–71, 173, **174–81**, 266, 275, 284, 306, 317, 330
  Caretaker's Hut 178
  Funerary Rock 179
  Intihuatana 176–7, 181
  Pueblo see Aguas Calientes
  Royal Sector 178–9
  Sacred Plaza 176–7, 179, 181
  Sacred Rock 176–7, 181
  Temple of the Sun 176–7
  Temple of the Three Windows 176–7
Madre de Dios 268
Madre Patria 72
Maestro, Presbirero Matías 64–5
Magazines 325
Mail service 325
Maiz 285
Malabar 292
Maldita Ternura 31
Maldonado 328
Maldonado, Admiral Francisco Aldrete 158
Malecón Maldonado 252
Malecón Tarapacá 252
Malls and Departmental Stores 101
Malta 288
Manco Cápac 144, 146–7, 150, 168–9
Máncora 216–17, 232, **233**, 303, 308
Mani 287
Mannequins 80–81
Mantaro Valley Tour 184–5, **188**
Manu Biosphere Reserve 281
Manu Ecological Adventures 309, 311
Manu Expeditions 309, 311–12
Manu Lodge 281
Manu National Park 312
Manu Wildlife Centre 261, 268
Manuel de Amat y Juniet 96–7
Manzanilla 288
MAP Café 295
Maps
  The Amazon Basin 250–51
  Arequipa 134–5
  Ayacucho 193
  Biodiversity 20–21
  Cajamarca 239
  Canyon Country 132–3
  The Cápac Ñan (Royal Road) 47
  Central Sierra 184–5
  Climate 38–9
  Cordillera Blanca 198–9
  Cusco 156–7
  The Inca Heartland 154–5
  The Inca Trail 170–71
  Lake Titicaca 146–7
  Lima 56–7
  Lima: Barranco 85, 86–7
  Lima: Central Lima 59
  Lima: Farther Afield 93
  Lima: Miraflores & San Isidro 75, 76–7
  Lima: Plaza Mayor 60–61

Maps (cont.)
Lima: Street Finder 104–11
Lima's Beaches 99
Mantaro Valley Tour 188
Northern Beaches 232
The Northern Desert 216–17
The Northern Highlands 236–7
Parque Nacional Huascarán 202–3
Peru 10–11, 114–15
Reserva Nacional de Paracas 123
Ríos Tambopata and Madre de
Dios Area 262–3
River Travel 253
Southern Beaches 129
The Southern Coast 118–19
Tambomachay Tour 165
Tour of Pisco Bodegas 122
Trujillo 218–19
Maracuya 287
Marankiari Bajo 260
Marañon river 235, 331
Maras 307
Mari Solari 100–101
Marinera 28, 35, 37, 218
Mariscos 287
Markets 101
Maroti Shobo 257
Márquez, Gabriel García 31
Marquis of Torre Tagle 220
Marquises of Bellavista 220
Martín, General José de San
49, 72, 96–7, 120–21, 123
Mártir, Iglesia de San Pedro 151
Marvelous Spatuletail Lodge 280
MasterCard 322
Matalacha 300
Matanza de Cayaro 89
Mates burilados 188, 303–4
Maté de coca 288
Matés 288
Matrimonial 267
Max Mara 302
Máximo Nivel Executive Language
Center 313
Mayuc 308, 311
Mayupata 295
Mazamorra morada 287
Mazzei, José Cassinelli 'Pepe' 221
McDonald's 282
Medical treatment 320
Meiggs, Henry 187
Menú 282
Mercado Artesanal de San Juan 303
Mercado de Abastos 296
Mercado Indio 101
Mercado Modelo 224
Mercado Surquillo 101, 303
Mero 287
Mesa, Alonso 219
Mesquite 225
Metal burilados 304
Metal jewelry 223
Metal objects 220
Metalworking 32
Metro Cinema 72
Metro supermarket 103
Mia Pizza 296
Miami Herald 325
Michelangelo 144
Michuna Wasi 294
Micros 331, 333
Mid-range accommodation 267
Migración office 316
Military Museum
see Museo del Ejército
Minasmoqo 169
Miniature clay churches 33, 192–3
Miraflores 8, 75–7, 79, 101, 266,
270–71, 282, 290–92, 303, 308

Miraflores & San Isidro
area map 75
Bosque El Olivar **83**
Casa Ricardo Palma **78**
Huaca Pucllana **80–81**
Huaca Huallamarca **83**
Instituto Cultural Peruano
Norteamericano (ICPNA) **82**
Larcomar **79**
Miraflores Clifftops **79**
Museo Amano **82**
Museo Enrico Poli **82**
Parque Kennedy **78**
Street-by-street map 76–7
Victor Delfín **79**
Miraflores Park 266, 271
Municipal Palace 76–7
Museo Amano 75, 82
Museo Enrico Poli 75, 82
Miraflores Clifftops 75, 79
Mishana Tyrannulet 254
Mixto's 293
Mobile phones 324–5
Moche
art 32, 222, 224
ceramics 32–3, 95–7, 144, 219–20
culture 221–4
pottery 222
pyramid 26, 223
Mochica ceramics 159
Mochica gallery 158
Mochica Sachún 296
Moeller, Edmund 218
Molds 222, 252
Molinos 304
Monasterio de la Recoleta 275
Monasterio de Santa Catalina
27, 138–41
Moneygram 323
Moneyhangers 322
Monkeys 309
Montane Cloud Forest 19
Monte Rosa 297
Monteagudo, Sor Ana de los Angeles
141
Monterrey 277
Monterrico 101
Moray & Salinas de Maras 154–5, 168
Moretti, Gaetano 72
Motocarro 252, 256
Motokars 331
Motorcycle rental 332
Mototaxis 331
Mount Alpamayo 200–203
Mount Huascarán 207
Mount Pirámide 200
Mount Veronica 172
Mountain Bike Adventures 307, 311
Mountain-biking 307, 311
Mountain Guide Association 306
MountClimb 306, 311
Movil Tours 330
Movistar 324
Moyobamba 34, 250–51, 256, 281, 301
Muelle de Guerra 94
Mummies 96–7, 128, 238
Mundo Para Julius 31
Municipal Palace 76–7
Municipalidad 60–61, 316
Murillo, Bartolomé 167
Museos (museums)
Amano 75, **82**
Amazon 252
Andrés del Castillo 59, **72**
Antonini 128
Arqueológico 238–9
Arqueológico Rafael Larco Herrera
56, **94**, 158
Arqueológico y Etnográfico 238

Museos (cont.)
Arqueológico Nacional Brüning
224
Carlos Dreyer 144
de Arqueología de la Universidad
de Trujillo 220
de Arte Contemporáneo 85, 90
de Arte Italiano 59, **72–3**
de Arte Popular 192
de Arte Precolombino 158
de Arte Religioso 156–7, 159
de Historia Regional 159
de la Electricidad 85, **88**
de la Nacion 56, 58, 93, **95**, 103, 186
de Oro del Peru 93, **98**
de Sitio Julio C. Tello 123
de Sitio Túcume 225
del Banco Central de la Reserva
60–61
del Ejército 94
del Juguete 221
Enrico Poli 75, **82**
Histórico Municipal 136–7
Huaca Pucllana 80–81
Inka 156–8
José Cassinelli 221
Leymebamba 236–7, 243
Nacional de Arqueología,
Antropología e Historia del Perú
93–4, **96–7**
Nacional de la Cultura Peruana
59, **73**
Nacional del Perú 93, **95**
Nacional de Sicán 224–5
Naval del Perú 93, **98**
Pedro de Osma 85, **90**
Regional Museum 121
Religious Art 60–61
Santuarios Andinos de la
Universidad Católica de Santa
Maria 137
Taurino 59, 68
Tumbas Reales de Sipán 9, 59, 68,
82, 114–15, 215–17, 224, **228–31**
Wari Culture 57
Museum of Archaeology
see Museo de Arqueología de la
Universidad de Trujillo
Museum of Columbian Art
see Museo de Arte Precolombino
Museum of Electricity
see Museo de la Electricidad
Mummies 96–7
Music and dance 28–9, 145, 312
Musica Afro Peruano 29
Música Criolla 28, 91
Muyuna Amazon Lodge 255

N

National 332
National drink 288
National Institute of Culture (INC)
98, 239, 316
National Library 78
National Resources, INRENA 233
Natural disasters 319
Nauta river 253
Naval Museum
see Museo Naval del Perú
Nazca 118–19, 126, **128**, 272, 292–3,
310, 318
Nazca
ceramics 32, 96–7, 126–7, 219
culture 223
mummy 159
pottery 95
textiles 101
Nazca Lines, 126 114–15, 118–19,
126–7, 328
Newspapers 325

Newsweek 325
Nieves, Alonso de Las 219
Nolasco, Peter 219
Northern Beaches **232–3**
Northern Desert 9, 214–33, 277, 297–8, 305
   Batán Grande **225**
   Chan Chan **223**
   Chiclayo **224**
   Complejo Arqueológico El Brujo **223**
   Huaca del Sol y de la Luna **223**
   Huanchaco **223**
   Máncora **233**
   map 216–17
   Museo Tumbas Reales de Sipán **228–31**
   Trujillo **218–21**
   Túcume **225**
   Tumbes **233**
   Where to eat 297–9
   Where to stay 277–9
   Zorritos **233**
Northern Highlands 9, 235–47, 279, 299–300
   Cajamarca **238–9**
   Cataratas Gocta **247**
   Chachapoyas people **246**
   Karajía **247**
   Kuélap **244–6**
   Levanto **247**
   Leymebamba and La Laguna de los Cóndores **243**
   Los Baños del Inca **242**
   map 236–7
   Revash **243**
   Ventanillas de Otuzco and Combayo **242**
   Where to eat 299–300
   Where to stay 279–80
Northwestern Biosphere Reserve 312
Novotel 267
Nuestra Señora de la Asunción 151
Nueva Cronica y Bluen Gobierno 31
Nuevo sol 322

O

Oasis 301
Obelisko Tello 96–7
Ocarina 28
Ocllo, Mama 131, 150, 153
Ocopa 287
Octopus Pectoral 228–30
Ocucaje 122, 288
Odría, Manuel 31
Olas Bravas 295
Ollantaytambo 8, 154–5, 164, **168–9** 275, 295
Olleros to Chavín Trek 198, **207**
O'Murphy's Irish Pub 102–3
Online Telephone Directories 325
Orefici, Guiseppe 128
Organized tours 327
Ortiz, Beto 31
Otuzco 243
Outdoor Activities 306–11
   hang-gliding 310–11
   horseback riding 310–11
   mountain-biking 307, 311
   sand-boarding 310–11
   scuba diving 308, 311
   surfing 308, 311
   rainforest exploration 309, 311
   river-running 308, 311
   trekking and mountaineering 306–7, 311
Oxapampa 37, 250–51, 260, 281, 301
Oxbow lakes 261

P

Pacasmayo 236–7
Pacaya-Samiria Jungle Lodge 255
Pacha Papa 295
Pachacútec, ninth Inca 93, 120, 153, 168–9
Pachamama 297
Pachamama Raymi 37
Pachamanca 187, 284–5
Paddy's Irish Pub 294
Paiche 19
Palacio Arzobispal 61
Palacio de Gobierno 59, 60–62, 159
Palacio de la Exposición 73
Palacio de Las Mamaconas 98
Palacio del Almirante *see* Museo Inka
Palacio Iturregui 220
Palacio Torre Tagle 60–61
Palcamayo 184–7
Palillo 287
Palma, Don Ricardo 17, 78
Palomino Island 94
Palpa 126
Palta 287
Pampa 303
Pampa Galeras National Reserve 36
Pampas de Hospital 233
Pan de Azucar *see* Huaca Huallamarca
Pandisho Ecolodge 280
Pantanos de Villa 98
Pantiacolla Tours 309, 311
Papa 286
Papa a la Huancaína 286
Papa rellena 286
Paracas 95, **123**, 272, 308
Paracas civilization 117
Paracas National Reserve 118–19, **123**
Paracas Necropolis **123**
Paracas textiles 144
Paradise tanger 261
Paribuela de mariscos 287
Parks
   Bosque El Oliver 75, 83
   Parque 7 de Junio 78
   Parque Central 76–7
   Parque de Amor 79
   Parque de la Exposición 73
   Parque El Faro 79
   Parque Grau 79
   Parque Huajsapata 144
   Parque Kennedy 57–8, 78
   Parque Municipal 57, 85, 88
   Parque de la Muralla 59, **67**
   Parque Nacional Cerros de Amotape 232–3
   Parque Nacional Huascarán 197–9, 201–4, 206
   Parque Nacional Manu 9, 261
   Parque Nacional Yanachaga Chemillín 260
Pasaje Paquito 252
Paseo de los Pintores 37, 76–7
Paso horses 218, 221, 310
Paso llano 221
Passion of Christ 57, 66
Passport control 327, 329
Pastor, Celso Prado 228
Patallacta *see* Llactapata
Paucartambo 37
Payments 283, 302
Pearl of Huallaga *see* Yurimaguas
Pedro Ruíz 247
Pelicans 123
Peña del Carajo 102–3
Peñas and Salsodromos 37, 91–2, 102–3
Pensiones 267
People 15–16, 22–3
Peregrine Adventures 327

Perro sin pelo 224
Personal security 318–9
Politics 14–15
Post office 316
PromPerú 317
Peru 21 325
Perú Azul 308, 311
Peru Divers 308, 311
Peru Surf Guides 308, 311
PerúFly 310, 311
Perúrail 330
Peruvian Addresses 325
Peruvian Andes Adventures 311
Peruvian Association of Youth Hostels 267, 269
Peruvian desert fox *see* Sechura fox
Peruvian dishes and specialties 284
Peruvian dolls 33
Peruvian folk art 304–5
Peruvian hairless dog *see Perro sin pelo*
Peruvian Paso Horse National Show 35
Peruvian thick-knee 19
Peruvian Viceroyalty 48–9, 140
Peruvian independence 220
Pesque de quinoa 287
Pevas 250–52
Pharmacies 320
Phuyupatamarca 170–71, 173
Picaflor Research Center 281
Picante de cuy 287
Picanterías 282
Picarones 284
Picasso, Emmanuel 122
Pico Alto 99
Piedra de Huamanga 304
Pikillacta & Rumicolca 154–5, **166**
Pikimachay Caves 184–5, **195**
Pimentel 224
Pinacoteca 138–41
Pinacoteca Carmelita 221
Piqueos 284
Piranhas 309
Pisac 8, 153–5, **169**, 303
Pisco 118–19, **120**, 288–9, 293, 303, 306
Pisco Bodegas 118–19, **122**
Pisco river 120
Piura 10, 34, 79, 98, 216–17, 305, 328–9
Pizarro, Francisco 48, 59, 62–3, 153, 156, 158, 168, 201, 238–9, 242
Pizza Alley 76–7
Pizza Hut 282
Pizza Zocodovar 138–9
Pizzeria Don Sancho 296
Pizzeria Piccolo 297
Pizzeria Ristorante Volentieri 298
Pizzeria Venezia 292
Playa San Pedro beach 99
Plaza 125
Plaza de Acho 68–9, 103, 333
Plaza de Armas 8, 60–61, 134–5, 154, 158, 189, 192, 200–201, 206, 215, 218, 220–21, 238, 252, 274, 333
Plaza Grau 94
Plaza Hotel 276
Plaza San Martín 59, **72**, 333
Plus TV 325
Poblete, Lucas 137
Police 318
Policia de turismo 318
Pollería Joy 282296
Pollo a la braca 287
Pompadour cotinga 254
Ponche 288
Pony's Expeditions 306, 311
Pope John Paul II 141
Porcón 35
Poroy station 331
Portrait vessels 222

Posada del Ángel 102–3
Posada del Puruay 279
Post office 316, 325
Potato dishes 286
Potoyunco 123
Portrait of St Catalina 141
Pottery, ceramics, art and crafts
    100–101, 228–9, 302–3, 305
Pozo, General Domingo Tristán 137
Pozuzo 260
Practical Information
    banking and local currency 322–3
    communications 324–5
    health precautions 320–21
    personal security 318–19
    travel information 326–33
Prado, Ignacio 89
Precautions 318–20
Pre-Columbian textiles 123
Prices 269, 270, 302
Primax 332
Princess Cruises 327
Principle Temple 181
PromPerú 312, 317
Propina 283
Public Telephones 324–5
Puca Pucara 165
Pucallpa 250–51, 253–5, **257**, 281,
    301, 328
Pucará pottery 303
Pucusana 99
Pueblo Libre 93
Puente de los Suspiros 85–7, 89–90
Puente Villena Rey Bridge 79
Puerto 328
Puerto Bermúdez 281, 260
Puerto Callao 257
Puerto Chicama 308
Puerto Inca 129
Puerto Maldonado 250–51, 262, 301
Puerto Maldonado river 253
Pulpo al oliva 287
Puna *see* High Andean Plain
Puno 10, 35, 132–3, **144–5**, 155,
    266–7, 273–4, 294, 302, 305, 318,
    321, 330–31
Punta Arquillo 123
Punta Ballenas Inn 278
Punta Callan Pass 199
Punta Hermosa 99, 308
Punta Olímpica 206
Punta Rocas beach 99
Punta Sal 232, 278, 282
Punta San Fernando 129
Punta San Juan de Marcona 129
Punta Unión Pass 204
Puppets 305
Puya Raimondii, 197, 202–4
Pyramid of the Huanca 213
Pyramids 80–81, 83, 118–9, 128

Q

Q'ente Adventures 307, 311
Qenko 165
Qorihuayrachina 173
Qosqo Ayllu *see* Ollantaytambo
Qoyllur Rit'i 36
Quebrada Huachesca 207
Quebrada Ulta Pass 199, 201
Quechua 145, 164–5, 170, 173, 186
Quena 29
Queñual 18
Quijada de burro 121
Quincha 303
Quinoa 284
Quinua 89, 184–5, 195, 303
Quipu 25, 94
Quito 79
Quito School 144

R

Radio taxi 333, 318–9
Radio 325
Rafael 95
Rafting 268
Railway stations 330–31
Raimondi, Antonio 204
Rainforest exploration 309, 311–2
Rajada, Huaca 228, 230
Ransom Chamber 238
Rancho Rosell 86–7
Real Grill 301
Recuay culture 221
Red Mangrove Forest 215
Reed boats 146–7
Regional development 44–5
Registered mail *see Certificando*
Reinhard, Johan 137
Repsol 332
República 325
Requena 254
Reservas (Preserves)
    Amazonica 262–3, 267
    de Biósfera del Noroeste 215, 233
    de la Biosfera de Manu 250–51, **261**
    de Lomas de Lachay Nacional 19
    Nacional Allpahuayo-Mishana 9,
        250–51, **254**
    Nacional de Paracas 114, 118–19, **123**
    Nacional de Tumbes 232
    Nacional Pacaya-Samiria 114–15,
        250–51, 253, **255**
    Nacional Salinas y Aguada Blanca
        143
    Nacional Tambopata 262–3
Reservations and checking in 328–9
Restaurants **290–301**
    alcohol 283
    chain restaurants 282
    children 283
    eating hours 283
    flavors of peru 284
    food hygiene 282–3
    paying and tipping 283
    Peruvian dishes 284
    Pisco 289
    potato dishes 286
    reading the menu 287
    restaurants and bars 282
    smoking 283
    what to drink 288
    wheelchair access 283
Retablo 73, 91, 100, 192, 303–4
Revash 236–7, **243**
Reynoso, Jorge Vinatea 137
Riaño, Luis de 166
Ribereños 253
Ricardo Palma 13, 78
Riche, Maria 126–7
Ripley 101
Ripley's Departmental store 101,
    302
Riquelme, Bernardo O'Higgins 122
River Dolphins **255**, 257
River-running 308, 311
River Travel **253**
Rivera, Antonio de 83
Rivers/Ríos
    Amazon 34
    Apurímac 308
    Cachi 195
    Chanchmayo 260
    Colca 131
    Guallaga 186
    Huallaga 255–6
    Huallabamba 235
    Huantanay 153–4
    Itaya 252
    Marañón 235

Rivers/Ríos (cont.)
    Madre de Dios 250–51, **262–3**
    Mantaro 187–8, 195
    Manu 261
    Mayo 256
    Napo 252
    Nauta 253
    Pisco 120
    Puerto Maldonado 253
    Rimac 66, 333
    Tambopata 250–51, **262–3**
    Tumbes 233
    Ucayali 250–51, 253, **254**, 255, 257,
        303, 331
    Urubamba 195, 308
Road maps 332
Rock art 131
Rococo paintings 221
Rococo pipe organ 219
Rocoto 287
Rocotos rellenos 284
Rodadero Hill 164
Rojo Bar 270, 283
Rotonda de los Artesanos 78
Royal Commentaries of the Incas 31
Royal Felipe Fort
    see Fortaleza del Real Felipe
Royal Road *see* Cápac Ñan
Rubens, Peter Paul 167
Runkurakay 170–72
Ruraltur 37

S

Sabogal, José, 30
Sacred Plaza 176–7, 179, 181
Sacred Valley 9, 164–9, 168, 266–7,
    284, 303, 307–8, 310
Sacristy 181
Sacsayhuamán 8, 26, 36, 153–5, 160,
    164
SAE Clubhouse 311
Saga Falabella 101, 302
Saint Joseph 30
Salapunco 165
Salas 299
Salsa criolla 286–7
SAMU (Ambulances) 319
San Agustín de Cajas 188
San Antonio 282
San Bartolo 99
San Blas 159, 193, 303
San Carlos de Puno *see* Puno
San de los Diablos
    see The Devil's Dance
San Francisco 57, 59, **64–6**, 73, 257
San Ignacio de Loyola 67
San Isidro 8, 27, 266, 269, 271, 292,
    302
San Jerónimo de Tunán 188, 303
San Martín 256, 305
San Miguel de Miraflores Church
    76–7, 243
San Pedro de Andahuaylillas
    8, 59, 67, 154–5, **166**
San Pedro station 330
San Ramón 76–7, 260
Sanchez Carrion 86–7
Sánchez, Josué, artist 187
Sanctuary Lodge 266, 275, 281
Sand-boarding 310
Sandoval Lake Lodge 280
Sangucherías 282
Sankuay 290
Santa Apolonia Hill 236–7, 239
Santa Barbara 189
Santa Catalina Monastery 8, **138–41**
Santa Catalina 156–7
Santa Clara 257
Santa Clara Monastery 35
Santa Cruz Trek 9, 198, 200, 202–4

Santa Lucía 67
Santa Maria del Mar 99
Santa Rosa de Lima 37, 67
Santo Domingo 59, 63, 67, 159
Santo Tomás 243
Santuario del Señor del Luren 121
Santuario Histórico Bosque de Pomac 225, 232
Santurantikuy 34
Sarhua 304
SAS Travel 307, 311
Satipo 260
Sayacmarka 9, 170–71, 173
Scotia Bank 322
Scuba diving 308, 311
Sea cat *see Chinguno*
Sea raft *see Caballitos de totora*
Seals 18
Sechín 198–9, 213
Sechura Desert 215, 216–17
Sechura fox 19
Seco de cabrito 287
Segundo Muelle 282
Sendero Luminoso (Shining Path) 304
Señor Limon 282
SERNANP 255
Serpost 325
Service charge *see Propina*
Shambari Campa 300
Sheraton 103, 266, 269
Sheraton Lima 270
Shilla 201
Shimada, Izumi 225
Shining Path 89 183, 192, 195, 304
Shipibo People 22–23, 257
Shopping 302–5
Shrine 60–61
Sicán
   art 224
   culture 225
SIDA 321
Silla de Inca 239
Sillustani Burial Towers 8, 133, **151**
Silver 100–101
Silverwork 32, 304
Simpson, Joe 213
Sisa, Quispe 201
Siula Grande 213
Skyline Adventures 306, 311
Sloths 309
Smoking 283
Soccer *see Fútbol*
Social customs 316–7
Sofitel 266
Sol de Mayo 293
Sol de Oro Apart Hotel 271
Sol y Mar Lodging Restaurant 278
Solterito 287
Son y Cueros 102–3
Sonesta 317
Sonesta Posada del Inca 266–7, 269, 273–4
Sonia 290
Sopa a la criolla 287
Sor Ana de los Angeles 140
Sor Ana de los Angeles Monteagudo (Pope) 141
Sotalia fluviatilis 255
Southern Beaches **129**
South American Explorers 306, 311
South and Central American Travel Association (N. America) 327
Southern Coast 8, 117–29, 272, 292
   Cahuachi **128**
   Cementerio de Chauchilla **128**
   Chincha Alta **120**
   El Carmen **121**
   Ica **121**
   Islas Ballestas **121**
   map 118–19

Southern Coast (cont.)
   Nazca **128**
   Nazca Lines **126–7**
   Pisco **120**
   Reserva Nacional de Paracas **123**
   Tambo Colorado **120**
   Tour of Pisco Bodegas **122**
   Where to eat 292–3
   Where to stay 272
Southern Rivers Expeditions 308, 311
Spanish and Quechua classes 313
Specialized Holidays 312–13
   bird-watching 312
   butterfly-watching 312
   community-based tourism 313
   culinary tours 313
   music and dance 312
   Spanish and Quechua classes 313
Spectacled bear 19
Spectator sports 103
Sports 17
Squalo's 299
St Catherine 140
Statues
   Ai Apaec 228–9
   Capilla la Virgen de Dolores 238
   Chabuca Granda 90
   Christ 201
   Daughter of Venus 57, 88
   El Beso 79
   General José de San Martín 72, 49
   Intihuatana 79, 176
   Karajia-style 243
   La Donaide see Daughter of Venus
   La Pietà 144
   Madre Patria 72
   Manco Cápac 144
   Santa Rosa de Lima 67
   St Catherine 140
   Tuturuto 134–5
   Virgin Mary 137, 219
Stone inlay 22, 222
Stonecarvings 239, 304
Street hazards 319
Street moneychangers *see Cambistas*
Sun Temple 26, 180
Sun-dried bricks 80–81
Sunken Plaza 208–9
Sunset Residenza & Ristorante 278
Supermarkets 108–109, 302–3
Surfing 308, 311
Suri Alpaca 100
Suspiro a la limeña 284
Sweet potato 286
Swissôtel 266, 269, 271
Szyszlo, Fernando de 30, 79, 90, 158

T
T'anta 292
Tablas 33, 89, 304
Tablas de sarhua 192
Taca Airlines 326–9
Tacama 288
Tacna 303, 318, 328
Tacu-tacu 285, 287
Tahuantinsuyo 158
Talara 328
Tam 326, 327
Tamale 283
Tambo Colorado 118–19, **120**
Tambo de Mora 120
Tambomachay 165
Tambomachay Tour 154–5, **165**
Tambopata 268
Tambopata Research Center 281
Tanager Tours 312
Taquile 268
Tarapoto 235, 250–51, 255, **256**, 281, 301, 306, 328
Tarjeta 147 324

Taxes 323
Taxi Real 333
Taxi Seguro 333
Taxinet 333
Taxis 319, 333
Taypikala 273
Teach Huaraz Peru 313
Teatro Británico 102–3
Telefónica 324
TeleTicket 103
Television (TV) 325
Tello, J.C. 173, 312
Temples
   Koricancha Temple 159, 164
   Temple of Kotosh 186
   Temple of the Condor 179, 181
   Temple of the Moon 165, 169, 215–17, 223
   Temple of the Sacred Stone 225
   Temple of the Sun 26, 98, 169, 176–7, 180, 215–17, 223
   Temple of the Three Windows 176–7, 179
   Templo de la Luna
      see Temple of the Moon
   Templo de la Piedra Sagrada
      see Temple of the Sacred Stone
   Templo del Sol
      see Temple of the Sun
Textiles 32–3, 220, 238, 303–5
The bronze fountain 60–61
The Devil's Dance 29
The Killing at Cayaro 89
The Kiss 79
The Lady of Cao *see* La Señora de Cao
The Last Supper 66, 160–61
The Lithics Gallery 96–7
The Monkey 126–7
The Mountain Institute 313
The Point 270
The Purple Christ 68
The Red uakari monkey 19
The Soul of Black Peru 29
The Spider 126–7
The Tree 126–7
The Way Inn 277
The Whale 126–7
Threads 32
Tiahuanaco culture 223
Ticket booking
   Metro supermarket 103
   TeleTicket 103
   Wong supermarket103
Ticlio Pass 187
Ticos 331
Timbuche 287
Time zone 317
Times 325
Tintero 244–6
Tipón 154–5, **166**
Tipping 283, 323
Tiradito 284, 287
Tito, Diego Quisp 158
TNT 325
Toilets, Public 321
Torito 305
Torre del Campanaria 141
Torre Torre 187
Torre, Victor Raúl Haya de la 215
Torreón 244–6
Totora 150
Toucans 261
Touching the Void 213
Touring y Automóvil Club de Perú 332
Tourism Protection Bureau 98
Tourist information 317
Tourist Police Cusco 319
Tourist Police Headquarters 319
Tourist Police Lima 319
Tourist police see Policia de turismo

Tourist Protection Hotline 319
Tours 118–19, 122, 154–5, 165, 172–3, 184–5, 188
Tradición Arequipeña 293
Trail 9, 172–3
Trains 330–31
Transportes Ormeño 327
Trapezoids 126
Travel Information
air 326–31, 333
boat 326–7
land 326–7
buses and terminals 326–7, 330
departure tax 327
domestic flights 328–9
driving in Peru
traveling by bus and train 330–31
organized tours 327
trains 330–31
Traveler's checks 322
Treato Marsano 102–3
Treato Segura 102–3
Trekking and mountaineering
Amazonas Explorer 306, 311
Andean Andes Adventures 306
Andean Kingdom 311
Café Andino 306
Cas de Guias 306, 311
Climbing in the Cordillera Blanca **205**
Colca Trek 307, 311
Ecoinka 306, 311
Explorandes 306, 311
High Places 307, 311
Inca Explorers 307, 311
La Cima Logistics 306, 311
Liz's Explorer 307, 311
Mountain Guide Association 306
MountClimb 306, 311
Olleros to Chavín Trek **207**
Parque Nacional Huascarán **202–4**
Peruvian Andes Adventures 311
Pony's Expeditions 306, 311
Q'ente Adventures 307, 311
SAS Travel 307, 311
Skyline Adventures 306, 311
Volcán Misti 307
Wilderness Travel 307, 311
Wildland Adventures 307, 311
Zárate Adventure 307, 311
Tres Esquinas 122
Tres Leches 287
Tristán, Flora 76
Trujillo 9–10, 27, 32, 35, 37, 95, 216–17, 218–21, 236–7, 266, 269, 278, 283, 298–9, 308, 310, 318, 328
Cathedral 218
Casa de Orbegoso 219
Casa de la Emancipación 220
Casa Urquiaga 218
Iglesia la Merced 219
Iglesia y Monasterio del Carmen 220–21
map 218–19
Museo de Arqueología de la Universidad de Trujillo 220
Museo del Juguete 221
Museo José Cassinelli 221
Palacio Iturregui 220
Plaza de Armas 218
Tsunami of 1746 98
Túcume 215–7, **225**
Tumbes 216–7, **232–3**, 278, 299, 328
Tumbes river 233
Tumbo 287
Tuna 287
Tunic 32
Tunky *see* Cock of the Rock
Tunshukaiko 200
Tunupa 295

Túpac Amaru II 49, 158
Turismo Restaurante Espada 298
Turner, Clorinda Matto de 13, 17, 31
Turron de Doña Pepa 287
Tuturuto 134–5

U

Ucayali river 250–51, 253, **254**, 255, 257, 303, 331
Ucumari *see* Andrean spectacled bear
Ulluchu man 222
Ultimate Voyages Birding Ecotours 312
Underground tunnels 208–9
UNESCO World Heritage Sites
Arequipa **134–41**
Chan Chan **223**
Chavín de Huantár **208–9**
Cusco **156–63**
El Damero de Pizarro 63
Machu Picchu **174–81**
Huascarán Biosphere Reserve **202–3**
Nazca Lines **126–7**
Reserva de la Biosfera de Manu **261**
Universities
Cajamarca University 238
Catholic University, Lima 60–61
Universidad de Trujillo 220
Universidad Nacional Mayor de San Marcos 67
University of San Agustin 136
Unku 32
Urpicha 296
Urpu 178
Urubamba 275
Urubamba Cordillera 172, 176
Urubamba river 195
Urubamba Valley 307
Usco Ayar School of Art 30
Usko Ayar 257
Uvachado 256
Uyo 151
Uyo Island 151

V

Vaccination centers 321
Vaccinations 320–21
Vagón del Recuerdo 88
Vallejo, César, iconic poet 220
Valley of the Pyramids 215, 225
Valqui, Thomas, Peruvian ornithologist 312
Value-added tax (IGV) 302, 323
Valverde, Villa de 121
Vasconcellos, Constantino de 64
San Francisco Monastery 64
Veen, Otto van 221
Last Supper 221
Vega, Garcilaso de la 31, 160–61
Royal Commentaries of the Incas 31
Venice of the Amazon 252
Ventanillas de Otuzco 9, 236–7, **242–3**
Ventura, Ester 100
Verano Negro 120
Vichayito 232, 279
Vicos 313
Vicuña 18, 100
Vicus culture 224
Viento Sur 310, 311
Villarreal, Giménez de 160–61
Viracocha 160
Virgen de la Candelaria 35, 137, 144–5, 304
Virgen de la Merced 201
Virgen del Carmen 37
Virgen del Perptuo Socorro 223
Virgen Milagrosa Church 78
Virgin of Mercy 219
VISA Cards 322
Visas and Passports 316, 318

Vista Alegre 122
Vistadome 176–7
Viva Máncora 308
Volcán Misti 307

W

Wa Lok 290
Wakama 272, 292
Walking 333
War of the Pacific **50–51**, 76–7, 137
Wari
ceramics 158
culture 187, 223
Empire 44–5, 189
loom-woven wall-hanging 94
Mummy 80–81
pottery 189
ruins 184–5, 189
textile 80–81, 95
Wasai Lodge 301
Wasai Maldonado Lodge 281
Water Channels 246
Weaving tools 223
Western Union 323
Wheelchair access 283
White alabaster statue 304
White Pages 325
White Range *see* Cordillera Blanca
Wilderness Travel 307, 311
Wildland Adventures 307, 311
Wiñay 100–101
Wiñay Wayna 9, 170–71, 173
Wines 288
Wiracocha 166
Women travelers 317
Women's Hospital 239
Wong supermarket 103
Woodcarvings 186, 197, 206, 303
Wooden idols 95
Wooden masks 33
Wooden plate 33
Wooden utensils 304
Woodwork 33, 100–101, 304
Wollen tapestries 303, 305
Woollen cloths 303
Woven textiles 150

Y

Yaku Raymi 37
Yalape 247
Yamaqna 201
Yanque 143
Yarinacocha 250–51, 253, 257, 301
Yates, Simon 213
The Yavari (Lake Titicaca) 146, 274
Yawar Fiesta *see* Blood Fiesta
Yellow Pages 325
Yellow Rose of Texas 300
Yerupaja 213
Youth hostels 267, 269
Yuca 287
Yungay *see* Campo Santo
Yunza 35
Yupanqui, Doña Inés 201
Yupanqui, Tupac 168–9, 256
Yurimaguas 235, 250–51, 253, **255**, 268, 281, 309, 331

Z

Zampona 28
Zaña 224
Zapallo 287
Zapata, Marcos 64, 66, 141, 160–61
Zárate Adventure 307, 311
Zevallos, Andres 238
Ziemendorff, Stefan 247
Zig Zag 294
Zonate – Escuela de Percusión 312–3
Zorritos 216–7, **232–3**, 279
Zubarán, Francisco de 167

Acknowledgments

Dorling Kindersley would like to thank the many people whose help and assistance contributed to the preparation of this book.

Main Contributor
Australian-born journalist, Maryanne Blacker, moved to Lima in 2005. Prior to relocating to Peru, she lived for nine years in Paris specializing in food and travel writing. Her work has been published in diverse magazines, newspapers, and guidebooks worldwide including *Australian Gourmet Traveller*, *Elle*, *House & Garden*, the *Quantas* magazine, and *Vacations & Travel*. During a career which has taken her from her birthplace in outback Australia to Sydney, Paris, and Peru, she has also worked as a website bureau chief and news editor, newspaper sub-editor, public relations/press officer for a theater company, and as a book editor. She was also the editor of Australia's top-selling cookbook series. She holds a BA in Journalism and an MA in Applied History and is intrigued by Peru's complex and beguiling past, and its present.

Other Contributors
Rob Rachowiecki was born in England and moved to the Americas as a young adult. He has traveled from Alaska to Argentina and is the author of numerous guidebooks to several areas and countries in the Americas, especially about Peru where he works frequently as a leader of adventure travel vacations. Rob has a Masters degree in Ecology and Evolutionary Biology and currently makes his home in Arizona. He dedicates his work to his children: David, Alison, and Julia.

Joby Williams spent much of her childhood in Spain, and her early twenties traveling in Central and South America. She has an undergraduate degree in Hispanic Studies, an MA in Social Anthropology and has just started a PhD. Joby reviews books for the *Sunday Times* and is a regular contributor to guidebooks and other travel publications. She is also a part-time cheesemonger.

Jorge Riveros Cayo was born in Lima, raised in Canada, and lived his university student years in Chile. From being a French horn player, he shifted to journalism while studying in Santiago. On his return to Peru, he worked at a radio station and contributed to local newspapers and magazines. He has traveled extensively all over Peru and has written about travel, tourism, and conservation subjects. In 2003, he won the Biodiversity Reporting Award, granted by Conservation International. He has also contributed to many Latin American regional magazines, as well as to *Americas* and *National Geographic Traveler*. Currently he is in the process of starting his own travel company in Peru, specializing in gastronomic tourism.

Phrase Book
Lexus Ltd.

Fact Checker
Eleanor Griffis

Artwork Reference
Miles Buesst

Proofreader
Andy Kulkarni

Indexer
Ajay Kumar Lal Das

Design and Editorial
Publisher Douglas Amrine
Publishing Managers Jane Ewart, Scarlett O'Hara
Senior Editor Fay Franklin
Project Editor Alastair Laing
Project Art Editor Sonal Bhatt
Editorial Assistance Alexandra Farrell
Senior Cartographic Editor Casper Morris
DTP Designer Natasha Lu
XML Coordinator Bulent Yusuf

Revisions Design and Editorial
Emma Anacootee, Emer FitzGerald, Priya Kukadia, Jude Ledger, Carly Madden, Alison McGill, Susana Smith, Sylvia Tombesi-Walton, Dora Whitaker

Additional Picture Research
Ellen Root, Rachel Barber

DK Picture Library
Romaine Werblow

Production Controller
Linda Dare

Additional Photography
Deni Bown, Peter Bush, Neil Fletcher, Philip Gatward, Nigel Hicks, Dave King, Bob Langrish, Jamie Marshall, Ray Moller, Gary Ombler, Matthew Ward

Cartography
Base mapping for Lima and Peru derived from Netmaps

Special Assistance
Many thanks for the invaluable help of the following individuals and establishments: Lilian Delfín; Fernando I. López Mazzotti at PromPerú; Jonathon Miller W.

Photography Permissions
Dorling Kindersley would like to thank the following for their assistance and kind permission to photograph at their establishments:

Bodega El Catador; Bodega Tacama; Casa de Aliaga; Catedral de Arequipa; Catedral de Huamanga; Cebichería La Mar; Convento de los Descalzos; Don Bosco School; El Caravedo; El Complejo de Belén; Gonzalo Cilloniz at Hacienda San José; Hotel Monasterio; Huascarán National Park; La Candelaria; Miriam Holguin at La Catedral, Cusco; Larcomar; Eliana Romero at Monasterio de Santa Catalina; Hermano Ernesto Chambi Cruz at Monasterio at San Francisco, Lima; Sra Directora Rosa de Amano at Museo Amano; Dr Giuseppe Orefcici and Senorita Indara Chavez at Museo Antonini; Museo Arqueologia, Museo de Arqueología de la Universidad de Trujillo; Dr Giuseppe Orefcici and Senorita Indara Chavez at Museo de Archeológico Antonini; Sonia Moy at Museo de Arte de Lima; Museo de Arte Italiano; Museo de Arte Religioso; Neydo Hidalgo at Museo de la Electricidad; Enrico Poli at Museo Enrico Poli; Museo-Galería Arte Popular de Ayacucho; Museo Jose Cassinelli; Dr Sonia Guillen at Museo Leymebamba; Museo de la Nación; Senora Vitoria Mujica at Museo de Oro del Peru; Bernarda Delgado at Museo de Sitio Túcume; Doctora Carmen Arellano and Maria Elena Mayuri at Museo Nacional de Arqueología, Antropología e Historia del Perú; Mariana Watson at Museo Arqueologico Rafael Larco Herrera and Museo de Arte Precolombino; Pedro Gjurinovic at Museo Pedro de Osma; Museo Taurino; Director Walter Alva at Museo Tumbas Reales de Sipán; Carol Verde Cenas at Museo de Sitio Huaca Pucllana; Parque Municipal, Lima; Pueblo Eco Lodge; Rojo Bar; Santa Domingo; Santa Rosa de Ocopa Convent; Vista Alegre

Picture Credits
a-above; b-below/bottom; c-center; f-far; l-left; r-right; t-top.

Every effort has been made to trace the copyright holders and we apologize in advance for any unintentional omissions. We would be pleased to insert the appropriate acknowledgments in any subsequent edition of this publication.

The Publishers are grateful to the following individuals, companies, and picture libraries for permission to reproduce their photographs:

Works of art have been reproduced with the kind permission of the following copyright holders:

El Beso by Victor Delfin 30cl; Chirapa Callo/ *Lengua de Arco Iris* by Don Pablo Amaringo 30bl; *L'abisso* by Pietro Canonica, Museo de Arte Italiano.

ALAMY IMAGES: AA World Travel Library 170cl, 170bl; Adams Picture Library t/a apl 115ca; Alan King engraving 41c; AM Corporation 91bl; Amazon-Images 253crb; Arco Images 148–49, 188tr; The Art Archive/Gianni Dagli Orti 98bl; Suzy Bennett 187br; John Bentley 18cr; Blickwinkel 263br; Tibor Bognar 37tc; Rachael Bowes 26clb, 253bl; Bruce Coleman Inc. 198bl; Lee Carruthers 22-23c, 253cl; Michelle Chaplow 285tl; China Span/Keren Su 24cl; Gary Cook 65tc, 171cr, TS Corrigan 129cra; Danita Delimont 13c, 19clb, 21crb, 307bl/Andres Morya Hinojosa 116; Eagle Visions Photography/ Craig Lovell 180bl; Emilio Ereza 8cl; Mark Eveleigh 201br; Michele Falzone 147tl; Fabienne Fossez 194cra; Derrick Francis Furlong 252br; Furlong Photography 309br; Mike Goldwater 22bc, 260crb; Jeff Greenberg 50tr; Terry Harris 286cla, 287ca; Hemis 29br; Anthony Ibarra 60clb; Janine Wiedel Photolibrary 147cr; JupiterImages/ Brand X 176tl; Emmanuel Lattes 205cb; Jennie Lewis 156bc; LMR Group 112–113; Melvyn Longhurst 6–7, 8tc, 28crb, 28bl, 64clb, 134bl, 289bl; Emil von Maltitz 204cla; Mary Evans Picture Library 51tl, 288tr; Mediacolor's 20br; Michele Molinari 86cla, 89tr; Magali Moreau 141br, 263tl; North Wind Picture Archives 25bl, 47bl; Chris Pancewicz 310b; Edward Parker 19bc, 260tl; Peter Arnold, Inc. 114cla; Photofrenetic 57tr, 64cl, 66br; Leonide Principe 255br; The Print Collector 61cra; Radius Images 203br; Rainer Raffalski 254c; Robert Harding Picture Library Ltd 143bl, 146tr; Pep Roig 242tl, 254br, 257t; Bert de Ruiter 20clb, 25tl, 205clb; Philip Scalia 124–125, 126cla, 126cl, 127cra; Paul Springett 115br, 232bl; Sue Cunningham Photographic 228bl; Glyn Thomas 262tr; Tribaleye Images/J Marshall 114clb, 287bl; Genevieve Vallee 253cla; Mireille Vautier 24clb, 40, 43bl, 45bl, 49br, 188bc, 284cl; Westend 61 38bl; Wietse Michiels Travel Stock 194br; Peter L. Wilson 145cl; World Religions Photo Library 56cl; Worldwide Picture Library 172c; Konrad Zelazowski 21cr

ALFAGUARA: *La Ciudad y los Perros* by Mario Vargas Llosa 31bc, *Aves Sin Nido* by Clorinda Matto de Turner 31br, *Maldita Ternura* by Beto Ortiz 31fbr
JOSH ARMSTRONG: 165clb

PAUL BECKERS: 192cl
THE BRIDGEMAN ART LIBRARY: War of the
Pacific – Bombardment of the city of Iquique,
Chile, by the Chilean Squadron on the night of
16th July 1879 (engraving), Spanish School, (19th
century)/Private Collection, Index/The Bridgeman
Art Library 50cl, Naval Combat between the
Peruvian Ship 'Huáscar' against the Chilean
'Blanco Encalada' and the 'Cochrane' in 1879,
Monleon y Torres, Rafael (1847–1900)/Private
Collection, Index/The Bridgeman Art Library 50bl,
Ricardo Palma (1833–1919) 1896 (b/w photo),
Spanish Photographer, (19th century)/Index,
Private Collection/The Bridgeman Art Library
78clb, St. Jerome (oil on canvas), Tito, Diego
Quispe (1611–c.1681)/Monasterio de Santa
Catalina, Arequipa, Peru, Paul Maeyaert/The
Bridgeman Art Library 167cl, Atahualpa (c.1502–
33) 14th and last Inca King, mid-18th century (oil
on canvas), Peruvian School (18th century)/,
Brooklyn Museum of Art, New York, USA/The
Bridgeman Art Library 169br, Pottery portrait
vessel, Mochica (earthenware & paint), Peruvian
School/Private Collection, Photo © Boltin Picture
Library/The Bridgeman Art Library 222bl

THE BRITISH MUSEUM: 47tl

MILES BUESST: 60cl, 76cl, 77tl, 77cra

CASA ANDINA: 267tl

ROLLY VALDIVIA CHÁVEZ: 145c, 195br

CHRISTIE'S IMAGES LTD.: 167cr, 167bl

CORBIS: 7c, 49crb, 265c, 315c; Theo Allofs 262tl;
Archivo Iconografico, S.A. 222br; Atlantide
Phototravel 43tr, 220c, 222bc; Yann Arthus-
Bertrand 10cl, 69crb; Nathan Benn 44br, 222clb,
222crb; Bettmann 52tl, 52bc, 55c, 69cla; Bowers
Museum of Cultural Art 44bl; Brooklyn Museum
24–5c, 30tr; Christie's Images 167br; Colita 31c;
Corbis Sygma/Balaguer Alejandro 53tr, 53bl,
/Jean Louis Atlan 262bc, /Julio Donoso 92, /Arici
Graziano 31tl, /Alain Keler 51bl, /Lorpresse/J.C.
Kanny 47tc, /Touhig Sion 23tr; Jay Dickman
250bl; Dpa/Frank Leonhardt 17br; EFE/Paolo
Aguilar 57ca, 80clb; EPA/Paolo Aguilar 25cr, /
Peruvian National Institute 212tr, /Sergio Urday
15tl; Ric Ergenbright 197b; Jack Fields 61br;
Michael & Patricia Fogden 19bl; The Gallery
Collection 47tr; Martin Harvey 19br; Jeremy
Horner 12, 153b; Steve Kaufman 83c; Kelly-
Mooney Photography 157cra; Bob Krist 9tl;
Frans Lanting 261br; Danny Lehman 32–33c;
Charles & Josette Lenars 24cr, 32cl, 45bc; Richard
List 18tr; Kazuyoshi Nomachi 23cr, 194bl;
Gianni Dagli Orti 45c, 61crb, 96clb; Galen Rowell
1c, 196, 207bl; Kevin Schafer 43br, 230bl,
314–315; John Slater 15c; Greg Smith 69bc;
James Sparshatt 14b; Hubert Stadler 63br;
Stapleton Collection 48crb; George Steinmetz
212cra; Francesco Venturi 157crb, 194crb;

Brian A. Vikander 20tl, 262cl; Werner Forman
32c, 44crb; Nik Wheeler 34cr, 34bl; Zefa/Frans
Lemmens 152

DANITA DELIMONT STOCK PHOTOGRAPHY:
Ancient Art & Architecture 234; Jon Arnold 60tr;
Keren Su 36tl

DK IMAGES: Jamie Marshall 200tl

EVA AYLLON'S PRIVATE COLLECTION: Rosa
Rubalcava 29cr

VICTOR DELFÍN: Ana Maria Ortiz 79br

FLPA: David Hosking 261clb; Frans Lanting 19cr,
251cr, 258–59; Minden Pictures/Claus Meyer
261cb, /Mark Moffett 261crb

SALLY FOREMAN: 171tl, 171br, 172tr, 173tc, 173cl,
173br

GEOGRÁFICA EIRL: Heinz Plenge 17tr, 18br,
19tl, 20cl, 21tl, 28cl, 29tl, 29cl, 29bc, 36br, 43c,
63cl, 84, 115tc, 121crb, 137br, 147br, 226–227,
232tr, 232cl, 233tr, 233cl, 235b, 249b, 312cl; Luis
Yupanqui 19tr

GETTY IMAGES: AFP/Robert Atanasovski 29tr, /
Jaime Razuri 42c; _LatinContent/Patricio Realpe
53br; Photographer's Choice/Frans Lemmens 313t;
Stone/Alejandro Balaguer 69clb

GO2PERU.COM: Jorge Mazzotti 183b, 238tr

THE GRANGER COLLECTION, NEW YORK: 24tr,
46cl, 46cb, 46bl, 46br, 46–47c, 47cra, 48tc, 48bc,
48br, 49tc, 49bl, 50–51c, 113c, 179br

INSTITUTO FOTOGRAFICO E. COURRET: 89br

INTERNATIONAL POTATO CENTER: 286c

JOHN WARBURTON-LEE PHOTOGRAPHY: 215b,
216bl

LA GRUTA: 267br

LATIN PHOTO: Claus Possberg 190–191;
Heriberto Rodriguez 107t; Niceforo Ruiz 29bl,
35tr, 91ca, 192tr

LONELY PLANET IMAGES: Mark Daffey 16tr;
Richard I'Anson 74; Anthony Pidgeon 2–3; Corey
Wise 240–241

MAGICAL ANDES PHOTOGRAPHY: James
Brunker 139tl, 172bl, 244br

THOMAS MARENT: 261tc

MARIRI MAGAZINE: Lorna Li 22cl
MASTERFILE: Peter Christopher 58
JORGE LUIS MONTERO: 51cr

MUSEO ARQUEOLÓGICO RAFAEL LARCO HERRERA: 95br

NATIONAL GEOGRAPHIC IMAGE COLLECTION: Gina Martin 170tr

NATUREPL.COM: Hermann Brehm 261bl; Pete Oxford 170tl, 263cr; Staffan Widstrand 19cl

ODYSSEY PRODUCTIONS, INC.: Robert Frerck 3c, 21br, 44tl, 214, 217tr, 217cr

CARLOS OLIVARES: 236bl

PHOTOGRAPHERS DIRECT: Ann Stevens Photography 57cr; ArchivoLatino/Adriana Orozco 23tl, 195tr; Magical Andes Photography/James Brunker 171bl, 212cl, 213cla; Marmotta PhotoArt/ Krys Bailey 132bl, 155t; Spectrum Photofile 17c; Tom Cockrem Photography 246br

PHOTO LIBRARY: Index Stock Imagery/Shirley Vanderbilt 16bl; Jtb Photo Communications Inc 28cr, 54–5; Photographer's Choice/Jon Warburton Lee 174–75; Science Photo Library/Camacho Tony 19tc

PHOTOSHOT: NHPA/Jordi Bas Casas 248, /Bill Coster 261c; World Pictures/Walter Hupiú 145bl

PROMPERÙ: Archivo 37br, 143br, 146cla; 308tl; Mylene D'Auriol 35b; Domingo Giribaldi 194cl; Jorge Martin 63bl; Carlos Sala 34tc; Anibal Solimano 207cr; Michael Tweddle 42t; Renzo Uccelli 205cl

STEVE RAFFO: 142–143c

REUTERS: Mariana Bazo 68bl; Ho New 53clb; Pilar Olivares 24br; STR New 328b; Str Old 52clb
ROBERT HARDING PICTURE LIBRARY:

Derrick Furlong 61tl; Odyssey/David Dudenhoefer 18crb

C.J. SCHEXNAYDER: 76bl

JOHN SERVAYGE: 244clb, 247t
SHERATON LIMA HOTEL & CASINO: 266cl
SOUTH AMERICAN PICTURES: Robert Frances 145crb; Kathy Jarvis 285cb; Tony Morrison 118tr, 126br, 127tl, 127bl, 145br
SUPERSTOCK: Yoshio Tomii 70–71

WIKIPEDIA, THE FREE ENCYCLOPEDIA: 41bc; Jochen Ackermann 18fbr; Asterion 19cb

WWW.PABLOAMARINGO.COM: *Chirapa Callo/ Lengua de Arco Iris*, painting by Don Pablo Amaringo – Escuela de Pintura Usko Ayar – Pucallpa Peru 30bl

WWW.PEROUVOYAGES.COM: Michel Burger 199t, 199cr, 202tl, 203tc, 205tc, 205crb, 210–211, 213tr, 306cl, 307t

Front Endpaper: ALAMY: Danita Delimont br; CORBIS: Sygma/Julio Donoso bl, Galen Rowell bc, Zefa/Frans Lemmens cr; DANITA DALIMONT: Ancient Art & Architecture tl; HEINZ PLENGE: fbl; LONELY PLANET IMAGES: Richard I'Anson cl; MASTERFILE: Peter Christopher fcl; PHOTOSHOT: NHPA/Jordi Bas Casas tr; ODYSSEY PRODUCTIONS, INC: Robert Frerck ftl

Jacket images:
Front: MIMI ROBERTS.
Back: ALAMY IMAGES: Bettina Strenske bl; DORLING KINDERSLEY: Demetrio Carrasco clb, Linda Whitwam tl, cla.
Spine: Mimi Roberts t.

All other images © Dorling Kindersley
For further information see: www.dkimages.com

Phrase Book

In Peru, there are three main different forms of pronunciation of Spanish: variations from the Andes, from the coast (Lima being its center), and a combination of the two which has emerged during the last 50 years due to internal immigration.

In the variation from the Andes, sometimes the **e** and **o** become **i** and **u**; thus, **ayer** would be pronounced 'a-yeer' and **por** is 'poor'. There is often a distinction between **ll** and **y**, where the pronunciation would be like the English **y** for **yes** and **j** for **job** respectively. It is also common that **r** and **rr** are pronounced similarly.

In the variation from the coast, there is a clear distinction between **r** and **rr**. Sometimes the **s** becomes **h** before another consonant as in **pescado** 'pehkado'. In addition, the **ll** and **y** are pronounced the same, such as in the English **j** for job. Finally, the **d** at the end of the word may become **t** or may be omitted; for example, **usted** would be pronounced 'oosteh'.

In the variation which combines Andean and coastal pronunciations, there is also a clear distinction between **r** and **rr**. In this variation, the **ll** and **y** are also pronounced as in the English **j** for **job**. Besides, the sounds **b**, **d**, **g**, and **y** may become nonexistent between vowels; for example, **cansado** would be pronounced 'kansa-o'. Finally, the **s** may become **h** before another consonant as in **fresco** 'frehko'.

Some special Peruvian words

¡A la firme!	*a la feermeh*	Sure!
agua de caño	*agua deh kan-yo*	tap water
bravazo	*brabaso*	wonderful
brevete	*brebeteh*	driving licence
carro	*karro*	car
chamba	*chamba*	job; work
chelear	*cheleh-ar*	to drink beer
chévere	*chebaireh*	cool, great
chibolo	*cheebolo*	young person
chorear	*choreb-ar*	to steal
coco	*koko*	dollar
del carajo	*del karabo*	excellent, very good
estar aguja	*estar agoo-ba*	to be skinny
estar con la bicicleta	*estar kon la beeseekleta*	to have diarrhea
estar hasta la coronilla	*estar asta la koronee-ya*	to be fed up
estar parado	*estar parado*	to be well off
estar piña	*estar peen-ya*	to be unlucky
feria	*fair-ya*	market
hacer cholito a alguien	*asair choleeto a algen*	to deceive someone
los tombos	*los tombos*	the police
pan comido	*pan komeedo*	piece of cake
pata	*pata*	pal, mate
pueblo jóven	*pweblo bobven*	shanty town
rubia	*rroob-ya*	beer
tener caldero	*kaldairo*	to be hung over

Emergencies

Help!	**¡Socorro!**	*sokorro*
Stop!	**¡Pare!**	*pareb*
Call a doctor	**Llamen un médico**	*yamen oon medeeko*
Call an ambulance	**Llamen a una ambulancia**	*yamen a oona amboolans-ya*
Police!	**¡Policía!**	*poleesee-a*
I've been robbed	**Me robaron**	*meb rrobaron*
Call the police!	**Llamen a la policía**	*yamen a la poleesee-a*
Where is the nearest hospital?	**¿Dónde queda el hospital más cercano?**	*dondeh keda el ospeetal mas sairkano?*
Could you help me?	**¿Me puede ayudar?**	*meb pwedeb a-yoodar?*
They stole my…	**Me robaron mi…**	*meb rrobaron mee...*

Communication Essentials

Yes	**Sí**	*see*
No	**No**	*no*
Please	**Por favor**	*por fabor*
Pardon me	**Perdone**	*pairdoneb*
Excuse me	**Disculpe**	*deeskoolpeb*
I'm sorry	**Lo siento**	*lo s-yento*
Thanks	**Gracias**	*gras-yas*
Hello!	**¡Buenas!**	*bwenas*
Good day	**Buenos días**	*bwenos dee-as*
Good afternoon	**Buenos tardes**	*bwenas tardes*
Good evening	**Buenas noches**	*bwenas noches*
Night	**Noche**	*nocheb*
Morning	**Mañana**	*man-yana*
Tomorrow	**Mañana**	*man-yana*
Yesterday	**Ayer**	*a-yair*
Here	**Acá**	*aka*
How?	**¿Cómo?**	*komo*
When?	**¿Cuándo?**	*kwando*
Where?	**¿Dónde?**	*dondeb*
Why?	**¿Por qué?**	*por keb*
How are you?	**¿Qué tal?**	*keb tal*
Very well, thank you	**Muy bien, gracias**	*mwee byen gras-yas*
Pleased to meet you	**Encantado/mucho gusto**	*enkantado/moocho goosto*
It's a pleasure!	**¡Es un placer!**	*Es oon placer*
Goodbye, so long	**Adiós, hasta luego**	*ad-yos, asta lwego*

Useful Phrases

That's fine	**Está bien**	*esta b-yen*
Fine!	**¡Qué bien!**	*keb b-yen*
How long?	**¿Cuánto falta?**	*kwanto falta?*
Do you speak a little English?	**¿Habla un poco de inglés?**	*abla oon pako deb eengles?*
I don't understand	**No entiendo**	*no ent-yendo*
Could you speak more slowly?	**¿Puede hablar más despacio?**	*pwedeb ablar mas despas-yo?*
I agree/OK	**De acuerdo/bueno**	*deb akwairdo/bweno*
Certainly!	**¡Claro que sí!**	*klaro keb see*
Let's go!	**¡Vámonos!**	*bamonos*
How do I get to…?	**¿Cómo se llega a…?**	*komo se yega a…?*
Which way to…?	**¿Por dónde se va a…?**	*por dondeb seb ba a…?*

Useful Words

large	**grande**	*grandeb*
small	**pequeño**	*peken-yo*
hot	**caliente**	*kal-yenteb*
cold	**frío**	*free-o*
good	**bueno**	*bweno*
bad	**malo**	*malo*
so-so	**más o menos**	*mas o menos*
mediocre	**regular**	*regoolar*
sufficient	**suficiente**	*soofees-yenteb*
well/fine	**bien**	*b-yen*
open	**abierto**	*ab-yairto*
closed	**cerrado**	*serrado*
entrance	**entrada**	*entrada*
exit	**salida**	*saleeda*
full	**lleno**	*yeno*
empty	**vacío**	*basee-o*
right	**derecha**	*dairecha*
left	**izquierda**	*eesk-yairda*
straight on	**(todo) recto**	*rrekto*
under	**debajo**	*debabo*
over	**arriba**	*arreeba*
quickly	**pronto**	*pronto*

early	temprano	*temprano*
late	tarde	*tardeh*
now	ahora	*a-ora*
soon	ahorita	*a-oreeta*
more	más	*mas*
less	menos	*menos*
little	poco	*poko*
much	mucho	*moocho*
very	muy	*mwee*
too much	demasiado	*demas-yado*
in front of	delante	*delanteh*
opposite	enfrente	*enfrenteh*
behind	detrás	*detras*
first floor	segundo piso	*segoondo peeso*
ground floor	primer piso	*preemair peeso*
lift	ascensor	*asensor*
bathroom	baño	*ban-yo*
women	mujeres	*moohaires*
men	hombres	*ombres*
toilet paper	papel higiénico	*papel eeb-yeneeko*
camera	cámara	*kamara*
batteries	pilas	*peelas*
passport	pasaporte	*pasaporteh*
visa	visa	*beesa*
tourist card	tarjeta turistica	*tarheta tooreesteeka*

Health

I don't feel well	Me siento mal	*meh s-yento mal*
I have a	Me duele	*meh dweleh*
stomach ache/	el estómago/	*el estomago*
headache	la cabeza	*la kabesa*
He/she is ill	Está enfermo/a	*esta enfairmo/a*
I need to rest	Necesito descansar	*neseseeto deskansar*
drug store	farmacia	*farmas-ya*

Post Office and Bank

bank	banco	*banko*
I'm looking for	Busco una	*boosko oona*
a bureau de	casa de cambio	*kasa deb kamb-yo*
change		
What is the dollar	¿A cómo está	*a komo esta el*
rate?	el dolar?	*dolar?*
I want to send a	Quiero enviar una	*k-yairo emb-yar*
letter	carta	*oona karta*
postcard	postal	*postal*
stamp	estampilla	*estampee-ya*
draw out money	sacar dinero	*sakar deenairo*

Shopping

I would like/	Me gustaría/quiero...	*meh goostaree-a/*
want...		*k-yairo...*
Do you have	¿Tiene...?	*t-yeneb...?*
any...?		
expensive	caro	*karo*
How much is it?	¿Cuánto cuesta?	*kwanto kwesta?*
What time do	¿A qué hora abre/	*a ke ora abreh/*
you open/	cierra?	*s-yairra?*
close?		
May I pay with	¿Puedo pagar con	*pwedo pagar kon*
a credit card?	tarjeta de crédito?	*tarheta deb*
		kredeeto?

Sightseeing

avenue	avenida	*abeneeda*
beach	playa	*pla-ya*
castle, fortress	castillo	*kastee-yo*
cathedral	catedral	*katedral*
church	iglesia	*eegles-ya*
district	barrio	*barr-yo*
garden	jardín	*hardeen*

guide	guía	*gee-a*
house	casa	*kasa*
map	mapa	*mapa*
highway	autopista	*outopeesta*
museum	museo	*mooseh-o*
park	parque	*parkeh*
road	carretera	*karretaira*
square	plaza	*plasa*
street	calle, callejón	*ka-yeb, ka-yebon*
town hall	municipalidad	*mooneeseepaleedad*
tourist bureau	oficina de turismo	*ofeeseena deb*
		tooreesmo

Transport

When does it	¿A qué hora sale?	*a keb ora saleh?*
leave		
When does the	¿A qué hora sale	*a keb ora saleh el*
next train/bus	próximo tren/bus	*prokseemo tren/boos*
leave for...?	a...?	*a...?*
Could you call	¿Me puede llamar	*meb pwedeb yamar*
a taxi for me?	un taxi?	*oon taksee?*
airport	aeropuerto	*a-airopwairto*
railroad station	estación de	*estas-yon deb*
	ferrocarriles	*fairrokarreeles*
bus station	terminal de buses	*tairmeenal deb*
		booses
customs	aduana	*aduana*
port of	puerta de	*pwairta deb*
embarkation	embarque	*embarkeb*
boarding pass	tarjeta de	*tarbeta deb*
	embarque	*embarkeb*
car hire	alquiler de	*alkeelair deb*
	carros	*karros*
bicycle	bicicleta	*beeseekleta*
rate	tarifa	*tareefa*
insurance	seguro	*segooro*
fuel station	estación de	*estas-yon deb*
	gasolina	*gasoleena*
garage	garage	*garabeh*
I have a flat tyre	Se me pinchó una	*seb meb peencho*
	llanta	*oona yanta*

Staying in a Hotel

I have a	Tengo una reserva	*tengo oona rresairba*
reservation		
Are there any	¿Tiene habitaciones	*t-yeneb abeetas-*
rooms	disponibles?	*yones deesponeebles*
available?		
single/double	habitación sencilla/	*abeetas-yon sensee-*
room	doble	*ya/dobleh*
twin room	habitación con	*abeetas-yon kon*
	camas gemelas	*kamas bemelas*
shower	ducha	*doocha*
bath	tina	*teena*
balcony	balcón	*balkon*
I want to be	Necesito que me	*neseseeto keb meb*
woken up at...	despierten a las...	*desp-yairten a las...*
warm/cold water	agua caliente/fría	*agwa kal-yenteb/free-a*
soap	jabón	*babon*
towel	toalla	*to-a-ya*
key	llave	*yabeh*

Eating Out

I am a	Soy vegetariano	*soy begetar-yano*
vegetarian		
Can I see the	¿Me deja ver el	*me deba ber el*
menu, please?	menú, por favor?	*menoo por fabor?*
fixed price	precio fijo	*pres-yo feebo*
What is there to	¿Qué hay para	*keb I para komair?*
eat?	comer?	
The bill, please	la cuenta, por favor	*la kwenta por fabor*

glass	**vaso**	*baso*
cutlery	**cubiertos**	*koob-yairtos*
I would like some water	**Quisiera un poco de agua**	*kees-yaira oon poko deh agwa*
wine	**vino**	*beeno*
The beer is not cold enough	**La cerveza no está bien fría**	*a sairbesa no esta b-lyen free-a*
breakfast	**desayuno**	*desa-yoono*
lunch	**almuerzo**	*almwairso*
dinner	**comida**	*komeeda*
raw	**crudo**	*kroodo*
cooked	**cocido**	*koseedo*

Menu Decoder

aceite	*asayteh*	oil
agua mineral	*agwa meenairal*	mineral water
ajo	*aho*	garlic
anticucho	*anteekoocho*	kebab
arroz	*arros*	rice
asado	*asado*	roasted
atún	*atoon*	tuna
azúcar	*asookar*	sugar
bacalao	*bakala-o*	cod
betarraga	*betarraga*	beetroot
café	*kafeh*	coffee
camarones	*kamarones*	prawns
carne	*karneh*	meat
carne de chancho	*karneh deh chancho*	pork
causa	*kowsa*	potato salad
cerveza	*sairbesa*	beer
chancada	*chankada*	maize cake
chifa	*cheefa*	Chinese food
choro	*choro*	mussel
dulce	*doolseh*	sweet, dessert
ensalada	*ensalada*	salad
fruta	*froota*	fruit
guargüero	*gwargwairo*	sweet fritter filled with fudge
helado	*elado*	ice cream
huevo	*webo*	egg
jugo	*hoogo*	fruit juice
langosta	*langosta*	lobster
leche	*lecheh*	milk
mantequilla	*mantekee-ya*	butter
marisco	*mareesko*	seafood
mazamorra	*masamorra*	pudding made with corn starch, sugar and honey
pachamanca	*pachamanka*	meat barbecued between two hot stones
pallar	*pa-yar*	butter bean
palta	*palta*	avocado
pan	*pan*	bread
papas	*papas*	potatoes
pescado	*peskado*	fish
picante	*peekanteh*	spicy meat stew
pisco	*peesko*	eau-de-vie made from grapes
plátano	*platano*	banana
pollo	*po-yo*	chicken
postre	*postreh*	dessert
potaje	*potaheh*	soup
puerco	*pwairko*	pork
queque	*kekeh*	cake
queso	*keso*	cheese
refresco	*refresko*	drink
sal	*sal*	salt
salsa	*salsa*	sauce
sopa	*sopa*	soup
té	*teh*	tea
té de yuyos	*teh deh yoo-yos*	herbal tea
tuco	*tooko*	tomato sauce
vinagre	*beenagreh*	vinegar
zapallo	*sapa-yo*	pumpkin

Time

minute	**minuto**	*meenooto*
hour	**hora**	*ora*
half an hour	**media hora**	*med-ya ora*
quarter of an hour	**un cuarto**	*oon kwarto*
week	**semana**	*simana*
next week	**na próxima semana**	*na prosima simana*
month	**mes**	*mes*
last month	**no mês passado**	*noo maysh pasadoo*
Monday	**Lunes**	*loones*
Tuesday	**Martes**	*martes*
Wednesday	**Miércoles**	*m-yairkoles*
Thursday	**Jueves**	*hwebes*
Friday	**Viernes**	*b-yairnes*
Saturday	**Sábado**	*sabado*
Sunday	**Domingo**	*domeengo*
January	**Enero**	*enairo*
February	**Febrero**	*febrairo*
March	**Marzo**	*marso*
April	**Abril**	*abreel*
May	**Mayo**	*ma-yo*
June	**Junio**	*hoon-yo*
July	**Julio**	*hool-yo*
August	**Agosto**	*agosto*
September	**Setiembre**	*set-yembreh*
October	**Octubre**	*oktoobreh*
November	**Noviembre**	*nob-yembreh*
December	**Diciembre**	*dees-yembreh*

Numbers

0	**cero**	*sairo*
1	**uno**	*oono*
2	**dos**	*dos*
3	**tres**	*tres*
4	**cuatro**	*kwatro*
5	**cinco**	*seenko*
6	**seis**	*says*
7	**siete**	*s-yeteh*
8	**ocho**	*ocho*
9	**nueve**	*nwebeh*
10	**diez**	*d-yes*
11	**once**	*onseh*
12	**doce**	*doseh*
13	**trece**	*treseh*
14	**catorce**	*katorseh*
15	**quince**	*keenseh*
16	**dieciséis**	*d-yeseesays*
17	**diecisiete**	*d-yesees-yeteh*
18	**dieciocho**	*d-yes-yocho*
19	**diecinueve**	*d-yeseenwebeh*
20	**veinte**	*baynteh*
30	**treinta**	*traynta*
40	**cuarenta**	*kwarenta*
50	**cincuenta**	*seenkwenta*
60	**sesenta**	*sesenta*
70	**setenta**	*setenta*
80	**ochenta**	*ochenta*
90	**noventa**	*nobenta*
100	**cien**	*s-yen*
500	**quinientos**	*keen-yentos*
1000	**mil**	*meel*
first	**primero/a**	*preemairo/a*
second	**segundo/a**	*segoondo/a*
third	**tercero/a**	*tairsairo/a*
fourth	**cuarto/a**	*kwarto/a*
fifth	**quinto/a**	*keento/a*
sixth	**sexto/a**	*seksto/a*
seventh	**sétimo/a**	*seteemo/a*
eight	**octavo/a**	*oktabo/a*
ninth	**noveno/a**	*nobeno/a*
tenth	**décimo/a**	*deseemo/a*

Road Map of Peru